HENCHMAN'S LETTERS

In War Zone C 1967-68

A Vietnam Diary

Todd P. Dexter

Copyright © 2018 Todd P. Dexter
Sedona, AZ

All rights reserved. No part of this book may be reproduced in any form or by any electronic or mechanical means, including information storage and retrieval systems, without permission in writing from the author, except for the inclusion of brief quotations in a review.

Cover and book design:
Naomi C. Rose www.ncrdesigns.com

Text set in Palatino

ISBN: 978-1985855878

All photos courtesy of Todd Dexter.
Jantodd3@yahoo.com

In Memory of John Henchman

LTC. John Marshall Henchman

Dedication

This diary is devoted to veterans of the Vietnam conflict who responded to the clarion call and dedicated themselves to protecting freedom whether the cause was just or not and to my two wonderful sons and my wife Jan who handle well the challenges of growing with a father and husband who is a combat veteran, and to this day a soldier.

Acknowledgment

I would like to thank Naomi C Rose whose unflagging effort, book design and editing breathed life into this work and made it all possible.

I am glad I did it partly because it was well worth it and chiefly because I shall never have to do it again.
— Mark Twain

****

A decade after the United States had ceased combat in Vietnam, almost two-thirds of the Americans who served there, or 1,750,000 soldiers, are officially described as in need of psychiatric counseling.
— Michael McClear, *Vietnam, A Complete Chronicle of the War*

****

In recent testimony before the Senate Committee on Veteran's Affairs, the new director of the Department of Veteran's Affairs, Gen. Eric Shinseki (Ret.), promised to care for wounded veterans "bearing scars of battle, some visible and many others invisible," and to "treat our veterans with dignity and respect."

To date, the Pentagon refused to honor what is widely considered the "signature wound" of the wars in Iraq and Afghanistan because the resulting PTSD is an anxiety disorder caused by experiencing or witniessing a traumatic event, not a wound intentionally caused by the enemy.
— Conn Hallinman, commondreams.org, January 29, 2009

Prologue

What happened to me was unfathomable, left me scratching my head. One day I was in college studying Elizabethan Literature and failing miserably, nights I was working at a meat processing plant pumping brine into a nasty pork product called a picnic, and the day after that I was wearing dark green fatigues with black spit shined boots and running alongside a platoon of young draftees yelling, "I don't know but I've been told Eskimo pussy is mighty cold, hut two, three, four." When I deviated, called my own cadence, yelled, "one, two, three, four this ain't gonna be worth dying for," I found myself toe to toe with my Drill Instructor who crawled down my throat and yelled, "drop and give me 50, Private, and then you get back over there with your platoon and stick with the Eskimo pussy and leave the death to me cuz where I'm sendin' you, young stud, death will come soon enough." Asking the sergeant if he was calling me an Eskimo pussy got me one hundred and fifty more pushups on the bubbling surface of a 105-degree blacktop parking lot. I graduated as the only Private First Class in my training cycle.

Eight weeks later I was in Cu Chi South Vietnam memorizing the serial number of my weapon, when I received a letter from my new wife as well as a copy of the letter which follows:

Henchman's Light Rangers

DEPARTMENT OF THE ARMY
HEADQUARTERS 25 TH INFANTRY DIVISION
APO SANFRANCISCO 96225

12 October 1967

Mrs. Cynthia E Dexter
200 Lafayette St
Grand Rapids, Mich 49503

Dear Mrs. Dexter:

Please be advised that your husband has recently joined the 25th Infantry (Tropic Lightning) Division in Vietnam. As one of us, he will use the best equipment available to any soldier in the world. He will receive thorough orientation training on operations in this part of Vietnam from highly competent and professional leaders prior to participating in operations. We are proud of our heritage and our accomplishments. With hard work and diligence your husband will be able to say with pride that he did his share to contribute to the preservation of Freedom in the world.

Please write your husband often. Mail is by far the prime morale booster for soldiers who must serve so far away from their loved ones. He will be counting on your support in the months ahead.

I assure you that we have the means to take care of every need of our soldiers and provide them ample opportunity to present for solution any problems that may arise. Please feel free to write if you have any questions concerning your husband while he is with the division. We welcome your husband to the division and hope that you, also, will feel as one with us.

Sincerely yours.
F. K. Mearns
Major General, USA
Commanding

August 20, 2016

I found the above letter this morning, tucked in with some other items that my first wife Cindy had kept. Memories of those long-buried events came rushing back and rekindled an interest in the tiny red leather-bound diary that I painstakingly kept, recorded thoughts in every day, until I returned home from Vietnam. According to the diary I had probably been in Cam Rahn Bay, South Vietnam for several days when Cindy received the letter. My journey to that far away country and war began on October 5, 1967, but circumstances that placed me at war were actually set in motion by questionable decisions I'd made many years earlier.

Today as I begin to reconstruct the events from that diary I am a worn-out soldier who is forty-nine years removed from the events themselves and while I do not feel old, the truth is that at seventy-five, my best days are behind me. Combat took its toll. Spinal stenosis and curvature of the spine or scoliosis cause constant and chronic lower back pain and top my personal hit parade of lingering ailments followed by torn rotator cuffs, fallen arches, assorted skin cancers including one melanoma, failing eyesight and tinnitus which necessitates hearing aids, reconstructive oral surgery, a failed sinus operation, out of control blood pressure and an enlarged prostate and nail bed fungus.

These service-connected troubles are all covered by my 100% total and permanent disability for which the Veterans Administration richly rewards me. Hell, the numerous pill canisters and their contents which line my medicine cabinet are all paid for as well, and with my interchangeable replacement parts I am truly on my way to becoming a real six-million-dollar man, a man never thanked for his service to the country but always blamed for the increasing national debt because, in their estimation, my disability benefits amount to welfare. I delight in reminding them that it's because of patriots like me who actually served their country that idiots like them were able to remain at home safely tucked between the folds in their Barcaloungers criticizing targets of their irrational stupidity.

The painful leg and hip wounds and PTSD are a part, as well, of the deteriorating landscape that is my health. In spite of this rather grim scenario I love my life and my family, and regardless of skepticism about my country's chances for the future, and my extreme cynicism concerning politics, I consider myself a patriot and like most of my soldier brothers I would make the same sacrifices again.

As for pride, I have more personal pride in how I served my country than I do in my country's conduct in that war. Communism and domino theories aside the war in Vietnam, like all wars, was being fought more for money than for protecting democracy and freedom. In fact, with each war we lose more of our personal freedoms. I find it ironic that the extremely wealthy make even greater fortunes selling helmet covers, rations, guns, bullets and tanks to the government, while the citizenry of this great country get stuck with the cost of caring for the sick and wounded when we return home.

The Diary

The following diary begins after the completion of eight weeks of Basic Infantry Training at Ft. Knox, Kentucky, USATCA, in the month of September, 1967. I was elected by Drill Instructor SSG Joseph Attaway to be my company's Platoon Guide (asst. Drill instructor). I was a member of the first infantry training cycle ever at Ft. McClellan at Anniston, Alabama. At the time, McClellan was headquarters for WAC (Woman's Army Corp) and CBR School (Chemical Biological and Radiology). Upon completion of the training mission I was promoted to PFC (private first class). There were only two other promotions like mine in the training battalion. Upon returning home to Grand Rapids, Michigan, Cindy and I were married and very soon after that I left to join my division in Vietnam. Leaving was the most difficult thing ever in my life to that point.

Drill instructor Joseph Attaway

October 3, 1967

Tuesday – I ventured out from our Lafayette street apartment and made several stops at old haunts, wandered aimlessly down the streets of my childhood and school days—when will I see them again? Cindy is still engaged with her teaching job. Most of my friends, having successfully avoided the draft, are working at normal occupations so they're not around and that's fine with me. Being alone at this particular time feels right, the sun is shining and a gentle breeze rustles the brightly colored leaves as I drive past my old school, the movie house, the bar. It is a beautiful autumn day in Grand Rapids and I am feeling somber and withdrawn, enjoying the isolation except when I am with Cindy. Why wouldn't I feel this way? I have never gone off to war before so right now, knowing that I will not see my new wife for a year, I am feeling a little confused. Part of me feels like the horny kid in his back seat somewhere trying to get as much of himself stuffed into his girlfriend's pants as possible. Part of me should be praying. Part of me is looking forward to the journey and part of me wants to flee. Everything is picking up speed.

I wandered over to Fulton Heights Market, a favorite family stopping place for meat, and pushed my way through the screen door off the parking lot in back. The door frame snapped shut behind me bouncing the little cotton ball and scaring away several black flies. I purchased some very thick, succulent, stuffed pork chops for dinner. Purchased an Early American towel rack, a gift for Cindy, at the House of Brass and returned to the apartment. I sat alone on the stoop smoking a cigar and watching the traffic move back and forth on Lyon Street.

Mother and Father came for dinner and brought sister in law Linda. Dinner was rather good, enhanced by the succulent chops, tossed salad, string beans with mushroom sauce, rolls and a dessert.

Brother Jed came along later to join our raucous dice game. We talked some and mom and dad left around 11:30. Cindy got bombed which perturbed me. Thoughtless for me because I failed to try and understand the stress our situation has caused her. She got pissed, took a pillow and slept on the bathroom floor with the door closed. I made up the bed and crawled in. Cindy finally managed to join me.

I was proud of Cindy for the effort with cooking her first dinner. We have been together for a year or so and I had no idea if she could cook or not. We've been married less than a month and cooking skills are pretty far down the list of why I love her with everything that is going on.

October 4

Wednesday – Cindy had a monumental hangover this morning. We have always partied heartily so having a hangover wasn't all that unusual for either one of us. Looking at our situation through a slightly different lens I'd have to give her slack because of what was going on, namely me leaving on a journey into uncharted waters. I am Columbus sailing toward the edge of uncertainty. At any rate, Cindy was not at all interested in that one 'thing' that newlyweds do. I understand. She did make it to Grandville to perform her teaching duties though.

I spent the day with Ray Dorrow at his quick stop Trading Post until 3 PM. We watched TV in the back and drank sodas. I've known Ray for about twenty years, can't tell you how many kegs of Pabst I have bought for different parties or how many bets I've placed through Ray on football games. He has been my bookie for years.

Cindy was home from school when I arrived. We made love. Bittersweet because of the leaving. So much on both of our minds. The fear of leaving, doing without Cindy's love for a year, participating in war along with its anxiety and an indescribable sense of loneliness all mixed with the tears that exploded from my eyes. I gazed adoringly at my new wife through prismed eyes, the tears flowed freely and landed on my Cindy's cheeks as she lay looking up at me. Was I feeling the exceptional love I have for my new wife or self-pity because we will soon be separated, something else?

We visited a favorite place for dinner, the Pampas Room inside the Porterhouse Restaurant on South Division. Cindy had gin, lemon and seven and I had gin and tonic. Steak was, of course, the main course. Stopped at friend Vince Belardo's Hilltop for beer and then home to sit like a couple of redneck porch monkeys in the heat of the night watching the traffic move idly up and down Lafayett St.

Hit the sack early. Seems we have spent most of my leave in bed…making up for what I will be doing without for the next year. Leaving tomorrow late afternoon.

Up at seven and drove Cindy to school. Neither of us spoke much and my afternoon alone was a dull blur until I picked her up again at school. She sure looked pretty.

October 5

Thursday - Packed my duffle and talked with Mom and mindlessly polished my uniform brass. Picked Cindy up at her teaching job in Grandville and drove wordlessly back to the apartment. She was wearing a blue outfit and looked really lovely. At home, we drank the sparkling wine given to us by Ray as a going away gift. Drank it in bed and played around.

On toward evening we drove to Mom and Dad's. My brother Jed and his wife Linda were there. Dad knew that I wanted a wrist watch and he presented me with a new Boluva, top of the line. Mother took several pictures of me and Cindy together – to be our last for a whole year. I had a really very weird sort of flash forward image pierce my mind...Cindy is holding one of the pictures of us together when she gets word that I was killed in Vietnam and while looking tearfully at the picture the image of me dissolves in mist.

The sun was fading in the western sky when we drove to the Kent County International Airport. There we met Dave Berg and David Bruning, best buddies since meeting on the Trailways bus to Detroit for our pre-induction physicals. We took all of our training together. Bruning flew down from Tawas City. We had drinks in the lounge until our flight was called then boarded a twin prop plane for the jump over Lake Michigan to Chicago. I kissed everybody goodbye including father who, through much hand wringing, remained strong by doing the typical male thing, remaining stoical and only shaking my hand.

Arrived in Chicago at dusk and having some layover time we made it to a nearby concourse bar and poured down several more drinks. The next leg carried us to the Sea-Tac (Seattle Tacoma) Airport. We retrieved our bags and checked into the biggest luxury suite the airport hotel had. We avoided talking about where we were headed and what might await us in Vietnam. Slept soundly.

October 6

Friday - We arrived at Ft. Lewis, Washington, the debarkation point for long overseas flights to Vietnam. Checked in just before the 11:00 AM deadline. When finally billeted we all sacked out not knowing what to expect next. The uncertainty is enough to give us ulcers. A non-com breezed through the barracks rounding up troops, whom I am sure he thought were malingerers, for a work detail, but we had already bounced out the other end and were in the wind.

I gave a shout out to old high school friends Buck and Kinney Walters who are now residing in Seattle, Bucky works for Boeing. We talked, shared emotions over the phone and I felt like crying. We could not get together. I am feeling really strange, almost like an out of body experience thing. I think I read somewhere about something called environmental shock where subjects don't do well when rapidly extracted from their natural surroundings. That's me, I guess.

Without Cindy, I feel torn apart and I miss her already. I feel hollow! It is fortunate that the two Dave's and I are together…strength in numbers, at least. With just the three of us together I feel like we're the 300 Spartans jammed up against the Greek's at the battle of Thermopile. Strange.

Each morning we are called to a massive reveille formation. The weather is freezing cold even in our Army issue P jackets. The entirety of our circumstance reminds me of how an artist begins a water color painting by soaking the paper before hanging it on an easel. Applying some green, some brown and other warm Earth tones that bleed the paper and mirror my somber mood. The purpose of the formation is to call the names of the soldiers who will

Todd Dexter

Leaving for the airport

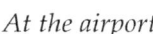

At the airport

Leaving

leave next and the numbers of the flights to which they are assigned. All of the flights are commercial and soldiers are being flown to the war as individual replacements rather than intact units. That can in no way be good for esprit de corps. It's no wonder that we will be called the fucking new guy's (FNG)when we get there.

October 7

Saturday - There are, I'm pretty sure, better ways to spend a Saturday afternoon. The Army has thoughtfully made plans for all of the weekend days in my foreseeable future. Our luck ran out and we finally caught a detail sweeping and giving the G.I. treatment to a barracks for an inspection that never took place. The NCO leader of the work party finally told us to split. We did not have to be told a second time. Wandering the base, we discovered one of the enlisted men's clubs and even though the place was supposedly off limits to troops headed for Southeast Asia we were permitted to stick around consuming burgers and draft beer for most of the afternoon.

The daily formations announcing troop departures seem to be called in order to keep a sense of order to the place…there are several such formations each day. We've been here going on one week. Tomorrow our flight is rumored to be on the call list.

Called Cindy twice. I have a hollow feeling caused by the distance that separates us that I'll not become accustomed to but will have to deal with. Talked as well with mom and dad. The conversations are strained and not much to talk about. How many times can they remind me to stay safe and 'lean forward in my foxhole?' These phone calls whether with Cindy or my parents share a commonality and that is emotion. I had trouble holding it all back.

The two Dave's and I walked for quite some distance to find and watch a very bad movie – *Point Blank* featuring an aging Lee Marvin. Not much enjoyment there...lots on my mind. The weather is cool and sleep comes easily. Weird dreams!

October 8

Sunday - Trailways bus pickup was early. No pushin' and shovin' cuz hey, who in the hell is anxious to get on the road to something that approximates an execution. Through the expansive glass windows inside the Sea Tac waiting area I got a glimpse of our ride to Vietnam...we'd be departing Ft. Lewis, Washington, aboard a Northwest Orient 707 airliner. Guess the military industrial complex wanted to spread around some of the prosperity created by the war. First stop Anchorage, Alaska, for fuel. We were allowed to disembark and being a pretty agile sprinter, I made it to the only phone booth visible on a barren landscape ahead of the other clods. I called Cindy. If tears could create an audible sound, make a racket, then our tear-filled conversation was a winner. We could barely speak to one another. Our conversation would create a poignant movie scene, no matter to whom it was happening. I promised to call again at our next stop but when the plane rolled to a stop on the tarmac in Tokyo we were quarantined, not allowed to deplane. We sat in stifling heat for over an hour. The only personnel allowed on the 707 were health department employees who came on board to clear us through Japan, and food service personnel bringing more food.

The circumstances surrounding our journey amounted to a Kafkaesque nightmare. The sun travelled along to the west with us never diminishing in intensity and even though the side curtains on the starboard side were closed the interior remained in bright electric light. Lifting the curtain, I could see Russia and the Bering Straits to the north as we plodded along. There was no comfort being crammed into the tiny seats and the E-6 staff sergeant, a career soldier, sitting across the aisle gave me cause for concern because he was crying audibly and never ceased blubbering. We were repeatedly served shitty food over and over again by gorgeous stew's wearing white leather knee boots and mini-skirts. Among those seated around me in the cabin were, I presume, at least one or two horn dog's massaging themselves surreptitiously through their class A uniform trousers. We were not given alcohol and the feeling of anxiety was so terrible that my body jumped and vibrated like a stringed marionette. We'd have been more comfortable if the crew would have removed the seats and installed broom sticks for us to shove up our asses.

Thirty minutes before landing in Cam Ranh Bay, after seventeen hours of pure torture the flight attendants moved slowly down the aisle closing all the window curtains. I was, nonetheless, able to glimpse the immense jungle below us as we made the transition from the South China Sea to the land mass. The captain lowered the lights and his voice crackled over the public-address system informing us that we were now over South Vietnam and we would be on the ground (one way or another, I thought) soon. "Gentlemen", he said and I wondered aloud to Bruning to my left and Berg to my right, "what's up with calling us gentlemen? I thought we were highly trained professional killers. Laughs erupted. The captain, a real smart ass, informed us that the local time was 8:30 PM or for unfortunate soldiers that means the big hand is on the eight and the little hand is...and nightfall would soon be upon us. "Ground fire," he continued, "is light to medium with sporadic mortar impacts." "Fuck me," I said, "the captain's really got people skills with his reassuring words and all. Shall we sing him a Hymn?" Everyone responded loudly, "Him, him, fuck him." The sergeant across from me cried harder but I'm pretty sure it was not because he thought our hymn was humorous.

When the ground crew popped the hatch and we prepared to deplane we were immediately closed in upon by suffocating heat and the smell of decaying jungle. Every pore on my body exploded sweat. I could hardly breathe and my only recognizable thought was about my ability to endure this for an entire year. The grumbling was pretty universal but the overwhelming crescendo from all the collected voices was, "what the fuck, my sinuses just collapsed!"

We trudged to an enormous metal Quonset shed with a round, corrugated metal roof. Inside there were many troops slouched on metal folding chairs or laying on the floor using their duffle bags for pillows. Our in-processing was rapid by army standards and we presumed that we'd not be moving on until the pipe line was cleared. For once there was a minimum of harassment because, I guessed, we were near our final destination and going to war. We surrendered our good old US of A currency and were issued in exchange something called MPC which stands for military paper certificates. I was as broke at the moment as I had been for most of my life and had only one dollar which I hid in an inside pocket of my wallet.

We were assigned to a new wooden transient barrack, one of many built on the huge expanse of bone colored sand that was the totality of Cam Ranh Bay. The other feature worthy of mention was the maze of wooden walk-ways that married the barracks and admin buildings to one another. The planks that formed the walkways were uniform in their demeanor, maybe three and a half feet across and were too uniform to have been cut by carpenters, but more likely had, at one time, formed the sides of mortar crates and ammunition boxes. The ground, the walkway, the sky and everything in between was a washed out monochromatic, bleached tan.

I showered under one of many nozzles hanging from an old airplane wing tank, the water still warm from afternoon heat. I shaved using cold water in a rusted steel helmet. Before I jumped into the rack I peered out through the screened opening at the head of my bunk and heard repeated popping noises. The delayed and muffled noise reached me with a metronomic rhythm as though planned with great intentionality.

First, I observed a blinding light and after a delay the popping noises reached my ears. Very eerie! So much new stuff so quickly. Sensory overload, I thought. I watched as the day-bright illumination rounds swung in the still air of the base camp beneath tiny white parachutes that kept the compound bathed in alternating shadow and light. In the distance, the silence was shattered by the faint staccato of artillery and mortar fire interrupted only by bursts from automatic weapons and the buzz of mini-guns being fired from helicopters. In the distance, I could see steady streams of red tracers in the inky void that had appeared to be like staircases I could ascend if I was granted access to them. Before climbing up onto my rack and dozing off I exhaled and exclaimed softly on my escaping breath, "welcome to your new home you stupid sumbitch, you coulda gotten into the National Guard."

October 9

I forgot to mention the International Dateline. We crossed the durned thing somewhere out there over the Pacific on our way in which means we lost a day. I only mention this from the perspective of my journal, otherwise it's insignificant. I believe that the dateline has something to do with time zones so...I designate this as the lost day. And do not ask me about it later because you'll draw blank stares and head scratching then, as well.

Later in the day my little group and I found a place to guzzle some beer and passed the day reclined on a sand dune. If I squinched my eyes tightly shut I could almost believe I was back in Michigan by the Big Lake with my buddies guzzling Strohs and riding around in an antique Century Sea Maid. But I was in the Nam and not, as yet, in the jungles I'd been expecting. Hell no, I'm in a desert. Every step raises a cloud of atomized sand around my ankles that rises upward toward my knees and finally enters my nose and throat to choke me. This was worse than the suffocating heat and humidity I'd experienced when the plane first landed at the airstrip and the huge curved door was pushed back.

Some random thoughts: I am convinced that my father was very disappointed in me because basically I allowed myself to get drafted. I had the opportunity to extend my deferment or join the Guard but I was just so burnt out on studying a curriculum in English that was leading nowhere that I just gave up. I mean, what does one do with an English major? I certainly did not want to become an English teacher nor did I have any interest in law school.

I believe I wanted to get drafted, to take the journey...to see if I was made of the right stuff to soldier. If you must know, I feel that somehow proper training has imbued me with a sense of bravery, shielded me against misfortune and I am comfortable with my vulnerability. How well I realize that I am rolling toward the edge of danger but I am certain that I can and will survive. No one I know would understand how I feel. I have butterflies in my stomach as before the big game but I know the uncertainty serves me well and that I will win. Do not mistake my bravado for stupidity because I am aware of just how quickly my dream of invincibility can be shattered by a single sniper round, a well obscured trip wire or a dung poisoned punji stick.

October 10

Tuesday – Daylight! First chance to look around the base. Mostly sand and dunes for as far as I could see. Met a soldier, a Specialist Fourth Class who is stationed here and he told me that this is one of the most secure bases in Vietnam and that the bay or harbor for which the place is named is one of the largest deep-water harbors in the world and we're here protecting it because the Russians covet the place. And the soldiers next statement was so bizarre I could not wrap my mind around it. He said, "When we get time off, we get to water ski along the shore line."

I coulda shit a brick. "Good for you, Specialist," I said, "cuz I didn't come all this way to ski. I'm gonna kill me some Gooks."

"Good luck with that," he said.

Got some free time and fished my little reel to reel recorder out of the bottom of my duffle bag, climbed into my rack and recorded a tape to send to Cindy later. Cindy is exactly twelve hours away from me, half way 'round the world and in my entire life I have never experienced missing anyone so much. She is probably sleeping when I am awake and vice versa. Strange.

I really thought the weather was hot at Ft. Knox and Ft. McClellan, and speaking of those two spots and the training that took place there, the gang is all here... we're all in this together and the familiarity that this reunion creates is the one security blanket that bolsters us against our rapid withdrawal from our individual realities back in the World. Wayne Johnson caught up with us this morning so it's sorta like the four musketeers. Illumination rounds again punctuated the night along with the muffled sound of rifle fire, I guess, from a firefight not far from the perimeter. Gun batteries fire sporadically through the night at unspecified targets out in the country side or jungle if you prefer. Soon it will be us out there.

Morning formations are called early to avoid the searing heat from the sun while the base cadre announce the names, company and division to which we, the meat for the grinder, will be sent. In this capacity, being replacements, we will fill the holes left by troops who are either rotating back to the states or were killed and will be going home in boxes, bags really, I guess. How macabre is that?

October 11

Wednesday – Lights came on 0200 hours followed by several screaming resident soldiers exhorting us to rise and shine, or else (or else what, you gonna send us to Vietnam). We were instructed to prepare for an immediate departure to Saigon and a place called Camp Alpha which I surmised was yet another processing location carrying us all one step closer to our final destination. In the end, nothing happened. Paul Coombs, a squad leader at Ft. McClellan whom I had clashed with since I was no longer the Platoon Guide, joined our small group as we waited for our departure time. Paul had gone to extra training to become a squad leader. The program was referred to by the rest of us as 'Shake and Bake' because the attendees became instant acting NCO's or noncommissioned officers. We hunkered down in the putrefying heat inside the Cam Ranh Bay air terminal until close to 1000. We had finally been assigned. Dave Berg is going to the First Air Cav and we will not see him again for a while. Bruning, Johnston and I, for now we think, have been assigned to the 25th Division at Cu Chi.

We sagged under the weight of our duffle bags, treated to another dose of tropical heat as we approached the lowered end of a C-130 cargo plane. The jet turbine engines were firing in idle right at us as though they were malevolently alive and bent on burning our fatigues right from our bodies. We all struggled up the ramp, as a member of the flight crew wearing a flak jacket and a helmet with opaque visor and a head set shouted over the roar of the engines, indicating that we were to sit in rows stretching across the flight deck. With feet sticking out and facing the rear, personnel placed a huge strapping belt across our waists. The engines slowly spooled up to a deafening crescendo and we rolled down the runway and lifted into the air at an unbelievable angle of ascent.

We could see dense green jungle below the ship as we made the short hop down to Ton Son Nhut air base, arriving around 1:00 p.m. I am experiencing some very exciting stuff right now made even more so when you mix in the anxiety causing uncertainty of what's to come. Some of us believed we were going up to the Central Highlands, a mountainous strip of real estate populated by the indigenous Montagnard people sometimes called "yards," to Join the 4th Division near Pleiku. Others had heard we were being taken to a place called the 25th Division

Replacement Center. I think that all we can depend on is wherever we happen to be at the next moment in time.

After sitting on a loading platform for over an hour we were picked up by a dark green, olive drab (O.D.) bus with heavy wire grating over all the windows to keep the Cong from pitching live grenades inside, and a snowplow on the front to clear traffic. I don't think we're in Kansas anymore, Dorothy! The bus dropped us at Camp Alpha, a screened and fortified compound near the airport. We learned we will make a short hop to Cu Chi, the home of the 25th Division, tomorrow. Cu Chi is 23 miles to the north west of this huge air base.

Dave Bruning and I got haircuts inside the confinement area by Vietnamese women barbers who we naturally suspected wanted to kill us. Even more so when we did not have anything to pay for the cuts except MPC because, at the time, we had been stripped of our US currency. They wanted Vietnamese currency which is called dong. The rate is 118 dong to a piaster or same same as one dollar American. Anyway, we chilled back at our enclosed screened bunk area. Spent the evening smoking and joking. Bruning told me that he would not be going home with us in a year which I took to mean that Dave thought he would be killed. I jumped up on my assigned cot and just before I fell soundly asleep I said, "Hey, Dave, of course you'll be goin' home with us...we've come too fuckin' far to not be goin' home, ok?"

October 12

Thursday – First call at 0600 hours. Amazing! I slept for almost twelve hours probably because there wasn't any lighting in the Camp Alpha enclosure and there was nowhere to go. No illumination rounds popping overhead and no out-going battery fire but I did have reoccurring and disturbing dreams about roadside thugs snipping the wire over the bus windows and pitching grenades inside to kill us. Ton Son Nhut is a very large and very secure air base close to Saigon and was built by the French during the colonial period in the 1920's.

After chow, we were bussed back to the flight terminal for the short flight to the base camp at Cu Chi. We were once again marched up the ramp of the huge C 130 and strapped to the flight deck for the short hop which took about twenty minutes from the initial engine revving to the final braking process.

We are now at the 25th Infantry Division Replacement center. The base camp, from what I can see, looks like a sizable city that is defended by triple rows of razor wire, called concertina, and monstrous triple thick sand bag fortifications placed about every fifty meters. The roads are a patch work of dry mud. The dust swirls in tornadic clouds falling like brown snow choking the living daylights out of everything.

Bruning and I were finally separated and that's that, the end of our little group. Dave is going to Alpha Company, 1st BN 27th Infantry, 'Wolfhounds', and I will be with Bravo Company, 4th BN 9th Infantry, 25th Infantry. I met a guy named Larry Mitchell on the truck coming in. The unit nickname is Manchu. Dave will be based in Cu Chi but we probably won't see each other after the six days Jungle Warfare refresher school we are to attend before joining our units for field duty.

I have noticed that the hooch's or huts become cruder the closer we get to combat missions.

I'm finally getting all of the last minute personal matters cleared up. Tomorrow I will complete Cindy's class Q allotment which is a life insurance policy on me in the event that I should be killed. The total value of the policy is ten thousand dollars so you can see just how the Army values our lives…or does not. Also, I made provisions for savings (for working around the clock PFC pay equals about .24 cents an hour).

I was assigned to a squad hooch which was a rudimentary structure of cinder blocks on bare earth with wood stringers on which 4x8 pieces of half-inch plywood were nailed. The building, if one could call it that, was approximately sixteen feet wide by thirty feet long and had a galvanized metal roof that holds in the oven like heat of summer and rattles when pelted by monsoon rain. There were rows of empty cots because the company was out on maneuvers. Tomorrow, I've been informed, I will draw all of my basic equipment referred to as "your TA-50" and includes an M-16 rifle.

Rained today. I'm told the monsoons are about over and we are about to enter the dry season which generally runs from November through February. Haven't quite got this or much of anything else figured out yet. Stand by. The company First Sergeant ducked his head into the hooch early after chow and made a waving gesture, fingers curled back on themselves, "follow me," he barked and we walked without a word over to the armorer's shack and ducked in.

There was an E-6 behind the crude counter and several guys smoking and jokin' with the sergeant. After a weird hand shake that appeared to be nothing more than smoke signals using the bumping of fingers the sergeant behind the desk began to pile miscellaneous pieces of equipment on the counter, too much for one man to carry. My back spasmed. There was an entrenching tool, a machete, a claymore mine, poncho and liner, one olive green towel, a web belt and two canteens, helmet with cover and liner, bug repellent, ammo pouches, a ruck sack and boxes of C-rations, mostly ham and motherfuckers and other crap that made me question silently to myself, "holy shit, I'm gonna be carrying this stuff every day," and as a final insult the sergeant threw a metal box, an olive drab colored empty ammo can on top of the pile and said, "the can has a watertight seal and is good fer keepin' yer personal shit dry, it goes under the ruck." I carried the crap back to my hooch and shoved it under my bunk.

October 13

Friday – The thirteenth. Just being here in this jam is unlucky enough without having to endure the stigma of a numerically superstitious date surfacing on my calendar. Breakfast in the early morning dark and then the task of sweeping the barrack. That completed, the Replacement Center stood by for a visit and welcome to the division by the Adjutant General. The 25th Division Band played a round of marches and a bunch of girls from the Red Cross affectionately called doughnut dollies by the troops served juice and what else…doughnuts. The whole event had a sort of embarrassing feel to it so Dave and I gave it the high hat and left to find water and explore a bit. We were razzed by some regulars so we spent the remainder of the afternoon in the only safe place around here…the latrine, where we talked of home and how we missed it so much already. Tomorrow we are to begin the infantry refresher course which takes place somewhere here on Cu Chi base. It is rumored that the graduation exercise is a night ambush patrol outside the wire, which could be an exercise in death for no reason.

Larry Mitchell and I had arrived at Bravo Company with seven other newfers several days ago and we were greeted by the company XO (Executive Officer). Since the company is finishing up an operation in the field things are pretty quiet around here. The population consists of malingerers, walking wounded and operations personnel that take care of things like the mess hall and the orderly shack. I have already heard derogatory terms used describing soldiers who populate the rear area but there is something fucked up about this. The often-used slang is REMF meaning Rear Echelon Motherfucker but this term ignores a most important fact; every army needs supplies and support without which they could not survive or win a battle. The XO whose name is Wilson gave us an orientation talk that was brief and informal and then left us alone for the remainder of the day. Everyone, so far, seems welcoming and friendly.

Rained briefly, again, just before chow and a perfect rainbow appeared out past the perimeter wire. We are near the chopper pad and dust is horrible – which is good for rainbows but bad for drawing breath. We are also close to the edge of the base camps fortified area but as the camp expands we can maybe feel more protected as other outfits form a more complete buffer between us and the enemy. Hotter 'n blazes.

October 14

Saturday – Dodging anyone with a higher rank than mine, and that's just about everyone, has become my highest priority. Being the lowest organism on the food chain means I am surrounded by predators looking to consume me or do me in or...make me work. There are others of similar rank that are in from the field for various reasons and I am picking up bits and pieces of other's experiences and what it is like to be in the jungle. While this is informative it is also, to a degree, frightening.

Intermittent noise reaches fever pitch as various helicopters called choppers (because of the way their rotors smackchop the air) move from the pad to the field or other areas within the base moving soldiers and materials. I found an isolated spot where I could observe comings and goings and along with a guy named Jewett we drank 20 cent Schlitz from metal cans, chilled vapor and foam cascading from the triangular punched holes covering my hand. I have heard that tomorrow I will begin the refresher course, the last obstacle between me and field duty, actually assuming the mantle of soldier.

Wrote letters home until two in the afternoon. Postage costs nothing and is facilitated by printing the words 'duty free' on the upper right corner of the envelope where a stamp would ordinarily be found.

I finally caught a detail. With five others, we were tasked to dig an enormous sump hole behind the mess. The hole became so deep that finally we could only access the bottom by lumbering down a tall ladder whacked together using discarded timber from artillery crates. The heat was murderous at the bottom and yet there was one individual, a tall wiry giant, of mixed blood with dark hair, who was wearing a stateside utility jacket designed for cold climate. He was sweating so profusely I believed he might die. I was told by another soldier during a break from the hole that the guy was avoiding field duty because he was a coward trying to get a section eight discharge.

In the evening our commanding officer, Captain Baker, a good looking tall slender soldier with command presence and sandy blonde brown hair came by chopper from the field and assembled us 'newbies,' called by other longer serving troops FNG for fucking new guys, into his hooch for introductions. There were seven of us standing loosely at attention when the looney in the utility jacket crashed into the Captain's office in the back of the orderly room, picked up a hammer from a corner of the Captain's desk and rushed Capt. Baker. We immediately restrained utility jacket guy until the MP's could be summoned to remove the distraction. Baker informed us that if we ever entertained thoughts of such foolhardiness we would wind up in LBJ (Long Binh Jail) which is a temporary stockade about twenty miles northeast of Saigon. The minimum sentence seems to be about six months which is called bad time that extends your time in country by that amount of time. We got the message.

Four guys from Delta Company were dusted off this afternoon all KIA (killed in action). Several others were also wounded badly in the vicious but brief fire fight. The news for whatever reason had no visible effect on me. I have heard rumors that the Dinks do not usually hit good companies, the ones who have their shit together. They like to hit on the noisy companies who are pretty lax about stayin' alive. This will change when things get more personal so I hope I'm with a good company. I wondered if what I'd heard about guys shitting their knickers during their initial contact with the enemy was true. I heard from a friend whose parents owned a mortuary business say that when corpses are being prepared for cremation or burial they often shit themselves or suddenly sit up on the stainless table and fart real loud but that's more from asphyxiation or gas in the intestines than being an alive soldier who is, as they say, scared shitless.

Several guys from another of our Brigades from up at a place called Dau Tieng were infused into our company and I sat with some of them the first night at the EM club. One said he'd been on the line for three months and seen action but never glimpsed Charlie Cong. Hearing this naturally makes me curious. I mean I'm curious to encounter my first enemy combatant but… these guys were filled with braggadocio. I looked at them blankly and nonchalantly swigged at my beer. Then one of them elbowed one of his buddies and says, "he ain't got a clue, dudes," then continues, inquiring, "you know, like have you faced the elephant…have you been bloodied?" Understanding that they were talking about combat I said, "no. I mean, shit dude (emulating their lingo) I just got here." The conversation stagnated.

October 15

Sunday – The sum total of my day: wrote Cindy, ran a police call of our company area and took three pictures. Walked to the Px, the Post Exchange. The thriving business that has a little bit of everything American is located in a huge aluminum half-round structure with a corrugated metal roof. You name it, it's here: food and snacks, clothes, audio equipment. You want a car waiting for you when you return to the World? Order it here. I purchased an Army issue foot locker to store my possessions while I am in the field. Hell, you can even order tailor made suits from a Chinese tailor that will be waiting for you when (and if) you get back to the World. Somebody told me that the Chinese save on shipping by sending your sports coat, whatever, in a tiny box. The article of clothing literally explodes out of the container when you release the taping. Many of the large ticket items like car's are duty free, so great pricing.

Opted out of going to the EM (Enlisted Men's Bar) for beer and went to a movie instead. We have an outdoor flick that shows dated movies that get shipped over in a Conex container. The projector malfunctions every night and boonierats such as myself throw shit at the screen. You say what's the worst that could happen…I'll tell ya… incoming. Yeah, that's right, and to help protect against this eventuality there are culverts and ditches beside every hooch and along the roads inside the base camp and some are covered with corrugated metal and sand bags all to give you a place to seek refuge when the shit hits the fan.

I should touch on accommodations inside the wire because while rather spartan compared to back home things are still pretty comfortable. The headquarters for the 25th Infantry Division is heavily protected and is here on the base. Our hooch's are wood platforms suspended above the ground. Some of the enclosures are no more than GI issue tents left over from the Second World War. Others are wood sided. Inside we sleep on Army cots surrounded by mosquito netting. There are showers, latrines (that emit a horrible shit stench until diesel fuel is added to burn off the excrement, then the concoction stinks even worse).

The entire base camp is covered by a pall of thick, black diesel smoke, mostly early in the morning on shit burning day. The mess hall is screened and the chow is not all that bad. Soldiers in the field who are participating in combat operations mostly eat C- rats but occasionally get hots. There is an aid station, chapel and a DX (direct exchange) point where once in from field operations you can get fresh boots and fatigues because these items usually rot clean off your body. There is also a motor pool that houses and repairs our vehicles. The camp is currently about two and a half square miles and was hacked out of triple canopy jungle by an advance party from Schofield Barracks, Hawaii, back in 1966.

We are dead center in Indian Country and the camp itself sits atop an enormous tunnel complex which proves to be problematic. The enemy can either infiltrate on any morning along with the huge numbers of Vietnamese that work inside the base and are admitted or they can access the base through hidden tunnels to collect intel or take well placed sniper shots before disappearing back into their spider holes. While inside the base these enemy infiltrators are able to pace distances from buildings to the wire and later calculate and plot mortar fire.

Shit burning detail

October 16

Monday – Word came down early that the company would be coming in this morning. The First Sergeant, who for the most part remains in the rear with the gear, got us rolling right after breakfast with a police call of the entire company area. Cleaning up all hooch's and making them ship shape or STRAC was the goal. When the troops dragged their asses in they were a sorry looking lot: worn and faded fatigues with rips and tears, many sleeveless. Boots were likewise scuffed and unrecognizable from original issue. We had plenty of beer and soda iced down. I did not know anyone and as a complete stranger and an FNG to boot I stayed out of everyone's way and just observed. The high degree of camaraderie was most noticeable as the weary troops dropped their gear, weapons, grenades and all wherever they were standing. I was in awe and impressed. This is why I'm here and I wondered if I would ever be included.

I have been assigned to the second platoon and met my Platoon Sergeant, a huge muscled, strapping negro named Johnson who was carrying a stateside issue M-14. And since I was in my assigned hooch the exhausted soldiers who had recently entered were going to be my squad and platoon mates. They were raucous and pumped to be back in base camp and, for now, out of harm's way. They ignored me as though I'm invisible. Even among them I feel isolated, alone and frightened.

Before I had finished my first beer or been spoken to, a troop who I had seen around the company area came in, pointed directly at me and said, "Dexter, grab your gear, you got bunker guard." A jeep driven by somebody from the orderly room drove me and three others – I knew one of them – to the bunker line and dropped us off while at the same time retrieving those who had had the duty before us. I had no advance knowledge of the SOP (standard operating procedure) so when the officer of the day snuck up on our bunker and caught me reading an Archie comic book I'd found stuffed between a couple of sandbags I was read the riot act and threatened with being put on report. The remainder of our watch passed without incident until our relief came around six in the morning.

The defensive bunkers on the perimeter are wood walled with wooden floors and have sandbagged walls that are a minimum of three feet thick — same for the ceiling and roof. Some of the positions have arc lights on

Bunker guard

top to illuminate the wood line. There are firing ports to the front to protect against enemy advance. Lastly there are metal bunk beds to accommodate the guys who are not on watch so they can get some shut.

Back in the company area I found an old hooch apparently made convenient for holding discarded equipment, mostly tattered fatigues, web belts with canteen pouches and the like. I reclined there to make a tape recording to send home to Cindy. A gentle rain began to fall making a steady rhythm, drops splashing on the tin roof. Soon the shower became a full-blown monsoon rain. I thought I had experienced rainfall until the pouring rain made an insane racket on the roof and just when I believed it couldn't possibly rain any harder...it did. If there had been anyone in the hooch there with me I doubt we'd have been able to hear each other even had we shouted at the top of our lungs. Unbelievable! I understood why there were suspended wooden walkways leading to and from every structure in the area. What happens when rain occurs like this in the jungle? Vision, I expect, would be nearly impossible and the mosquitoes, holy crap the mosquitoes.

October 17

Tuesday - A company deuce and a half (two-and-a-half-ton truck) picked us FNG's up at the orderly shack at 0730 hours after chow. We rode on the rear deck through the swirling dust covered streets and glimpsed for the first time the expansive Cu Chi base camp. The training consisted of more crap like we'd learned at Ft. McClellan. The day's highlight was seeing Bruning and Berg again and also Wayne Johnson. I'd met Wayne in Grand Rapids and we trained together. His wife Anne is living with Cindy. We were given C-rations for lunch and though we'd consumed these marvelous goodies back in Basic they are still surprisingly bad but manageable. Here's a sample: The individual carton contains a miniature box of cigarettes (3), gum, toilet paper and a packet of matches (which work if not wet) and a small P-38 can opener. The main courses are pretty standard. In one you get a small can of pound cake, a small tin of peanut butter, a spoon, in others, pork slices in juice (yuk), or beanies and weenies in juice (pretty good) or lima beans and ham (referred to as beans and motherfuckers by the boonierats) and some other equally pissy stuff.

Meals always proceeded with a kind of ritualistic bartering session that I guessed was taking place with every unit in Vietnam. We kept at it until everybody was satisfied, everyone got close to what he wanted. Once finished someone burped loudly and sarcastically said, "boy, that shit was absolutely delicious…wonder what they're eatin' back in the World?" The only thing missing was male ritualistic nut scratching and perhaps a happy fart or two.

We were supposed to conclude the days training with a mock ambush patrol outside the wire. I believed I should delay being shot at for as long as I could so, leaving my buddies behind, I hitchhiked back to the company area and hid in the latrine and wrote letters until the truck returned to the area for evening chow.

The EM club was closed tonight so Jewett and a guy named Johnston and I travelled on foot down the road to the 65th Engineers club for a couple of beers. My new friends go to the field tomorrow. My turn is rapidly approaching and I admit I am a bit anxious to get on with it. The more or less repetitious routine in the rear area is monotonous and I'm getting tired of ducking work details as well as the possibility of another bunker guard. For now, everything is pretty much known and I've got to get on with it. I have about run through any surprises the rear area could hold for me. What happened today happened yesterday and will happen again tomorrow and so on. After going to the EM club at night for beers, sitting around in some of the hooches listening to but not participating in the gratuitous bull shit sessions about war experiences (real or imagined), I am about spent. Without actually being in combat it actually feels like I know quite a little bit about it. Could this be helpful?

October 18

Wednesday – I was beginning to worry about not receiving any mail from Cindy but today a beautiful letter arrived in which she spoke eloquently about her loneliness. I could barely see through my tears to finish the letter. It turned out to be trouble with the mailing address Cindy used so it took much longer for her letter to reach me. Overseas military personnel and their families use APO numbers which stands for Army Post Office. Using APO numbers assures faster service and there is no charge for me to send a letter to Cindy.

The EM club was closed again tonight so another replacement, a guy named Edwards, who will join the weapons platoon, and I moseyed down the road to the 65th Engineers again for some brews. The dust is less during evening hours because of diminished traffic. I learned that the surface of all the roads here in Cu Chi are composed of laterite which is a rich iron oxide soil material collected from a pit outside the base camp. When dry, the material is extremely hard but turns to mushy shit when wet. Water trucks occasionally spray to keep the dust down.

I stopped into the Orderly Room today to visit the clerk whose name is Stansberry and I swear this is true… there were two guys, whom I didn't recognize, in front of Stansberry's desk. They were playing a kind of mumblety-peg with bayonets seeing who could stick their blade into the floor closest to the others jungle boot. Sure as shit, one throw-down went right through the others boot and nailed his foot to the boards of the Orderly Room floor. Well oh, fuckin-kay! I also heard some scuttlebutt about a rifleman in first platoon that shot himself through the foot to avoid going back to the field. Somebody even pointed the guy out to me, a diminutive guy with blond curly hair. Some called him coward and are shunning him, the silent treatment. I gotta wait on this one, hold my judgement because at this point I am still an outsider.

October 19

I actually had the best intentions, I mean, really, I was going to attend the refresher course but missed the bus and hung out in the schmidt house instead. I fell asleep with my pants down, chin in palms and was awakened when some poor fucker who caught the shit burning detail loudly pulled the barrel out from under the hole on which I was sitting. Guess I can be thankful he didn't light the barrel while I was asleep above.

Light pollution is almost nonexistent here in the Nam and the stars appear more brilliant than I have ever observed them. Identifying different constellations is something that I have not been able to master because I am in a different hemisphere and lack, for now at least, a recognizable reference point.

I had imagined or estimated the size of our base camp incorrectly in an earlier entry. On authority, I have learned that the current size of our approximately one-and-a-half-year-old base camp is an area of almost five square miles. The figure is always an estimate because the camp is growing constantly. The initial battle to secure the area and build Cu Chi base was difficult and many lives were lost. We are on one edge of the Hobo Woods, a mysterious and dangerous Viet Cong redoubt, a vast jungle entanglement with thousands of underground hiding places where the enemy is able to elude us. The woods have been utilized as a jumping off point for attacks on Saigon for the last twenty-five years and is of enormous strategic value to U.S. forces. The Ho Bo's are part of a larger scary place known as the Iron Triangle.

The vast camp gives the impression of impregnability and one feels fairly safe when within. The buildings are all single story, evenly placed city style and have metal roofs that shimmer in the heat. Hawaiian names mark every street corner showing a strong loyalty and proud heritage of unit history which dates back to the Division's founding at Schofield Barracks, Hawaii, shortly after the bombing of Pearl Harbor. We are the Tropic Lightning Division and our shoulder patch resembles a pineapple with a lightning bolt within. Other units have a nick name for us. The Electric Pineapple.

At the conclusion of a class on mines and bobby traps Edwards and I stopped at the PX for some canned goods before returning to the company area. I saw and embraced Dave Bruning who was skipping mines and booby traps. Good to see him. He goes to the field tomorrow for the first time…good luck Dave. He's going to be a machine gunner carrying the M-60 which is actually a crew served weapon meaning he has an ammo bearer at his side.

Over one hundred degrees again today. In spite of sweating profusely I seem to be adding a few pounds.

Saw a friend from Ft. Knox at the EM club but could not remember his name. We left Detroit together by train for St. Louis and then Louisville. Bumping into him conjured a memory of me standing in the opening of the last car on the train. A gate guarded the open door and kept me from contemplating throwing myself on the tracks as I watched the city recede from view.

October 20

Friday – Up at six today, same as every day. I am living a nightmare…the same NCO makes the same rounds through the same hooches every day rousting the same guys in exactly the same manner as he moves through the area. I hear him coming and place my feet squarely on the floor before he enters so I do not have to listen to his shit. Night before last I slept beside the hooch under a water trailer just so I could avoid the morning muster. There are very few mosquitos in the rear and I was very comfortable sleeping on the ground, better get used to it. I heard one beer filled grunt say that he did not give a rat's ass if the ground is cold, wet or hard as long as he could defend it. Sounds rational to me but that's because I have not been to the boonies yet.

Skipped the training again today by hiding out in the latrine until the truck had left. Things are pretty loose in the rear. Seems like all personnel have a job to do and those jobs do not involve keeping an eye on us replacements. The only place to go was the PX so I spent some time looking at cameras. Most of the items for sale are about 40% less expensive than back in the World. I'd have trouble buying most anything because for now I have elected to have most of my pay sent home to Cindy. I could arrange a draw through the company pay officer at the Orderly Room but for now this is not a necessity.

Jewitt's return to the field was once again delayed so he will be available for beers at the EM club tonight. I failed to mention that the company returned to the field exactly one day later after their brief R & R and refitting. It is a mystery to myself and several others just why we did not make the redeployment with them. Rumor says they will return here to Cu Chi on the twenty third which is several days from now.

Johnson got caught sleeping on bunker guard and will probably get busted from corporal back to private first class and you cannot go any lower. He already enjoys a six-month profile which is Army speak for what troops call getting over. He is recuperating from a broken wrist that he picked up on a two-week R & R in Bankok when he fell out a second story window. I'm suspicious. Coupled with sleeping on bunker guard I am getting the picture of an undependable soldier. Call me judgmental but I'd say the guy's a pussy.

I never mentioned…there is not a single tree on this base so the only shade to be found is away from the sun under a building's overhanging roof. One other item I failed to mention is the swimming pool which is a huge rectangular affair constructed of thick canvas draped inside a reinforced wood frame with a huge deck around it. It is over by Division and used primarily by REMF's and maybe the Doughnut Dollies

October 21

Saturday – Today marked the last day of the refresher course and the entire class was crammed into the latrine in the company area. Makes you wonder if the cadre in charge of the informal school gave any more of a crap than we do. The shit stench and the *mama-san's* pulling the barrels out to ignite the diesel finally drove us to making a break over to the recreation area where we could at least write letters and shoot the shit, grab a soda. We all returned to the company area for chow. I should mention that most meals are accompanied with Kool Aid…milk can get rancid pretty quickly in the tropics.

I received a tape-recorded message from Cindy late this afternoon and ducked into the deserted hooch, the one with all of the discarded equipment, to listen. This was the first chance I have had to actually hear her beautiful voice so I was very excited. Then my excitement turned to disappointment as I had to listen to my brother's wife's father…are you following this? Anyway, the clown, who is a very short, very squat alcoholic boor, a lunatic really, was talking about the family's investment in a hunt for gold that is reportedly (rumored) to be at the bottom of a mine shaft within the military reservation at Fort Huachuca, Arizona. Everyone in my family, when asked, invested in one six hundred dollar share to finance the hunt. Cindy and I did pony up the six bills but I was really skeptical until I learned that my sister-in-law's father received the tip about where the gold was buried from a Martian and then I pretty much went ape shit, tuned him out. I am not kidding!

Went to a movie within the company area tonight. The best way to describe it is to say that the whole set up is just like a drive-in movie back in the world except for the frequent mortar attacks. After about ten minutes into the first reel rain pelted us so hard the whole thing was called off. We dee-deed outta there and I hit the sack (my little wooden Army cot) at about 8:30 p.m. which is 2030 hours military and fell asleep immediately. Later, the silence of the diminishing rain awakened me so I trudged over to the shower – a cement slab surrounded by wood walls under an old airplane wing tank. The water was still exceptionally hot after sitting all day in the blistering sun. Dried off and returned to the hooch where I once again got under the mosquito netting and listened to Cindy's tape, recorded one to her and fell asleep once again. Tomorrow I will mail the tape.

October 22

Sunday – False alarm about the company coming back in right away, us newbies or FNG's will be taken to the field to join the company. I spent some time going over my gear to be sure I'm ready. This is weird…I have a new M-16 and more than a dozen magazines filled with live ammo. I also have three live grenades that I have attached to my flak jacket by bending the spoon type handle over so the explosive device cannot fall off. The designation of this goodie is the M-2 fragmentation grenade. It is smooth metal with a coil of steel inside that blows apart when the pin is pulled. You may have heard of an earlier version used in Korea referred to as the pineapple due to the rough segments of iron on the outside.

    I tried on my flak jacket and put on my steel pot and grabbed my M-16 and had Edwards take my picture. Big tough guy. The thought crept in…what if this is the last picture ever taken of me? Really stupid because I believe I mentioned the certainty I have about returning home when this is over. However, that did not stop me from reflecting back to when I told you about Cindy holding a picture of me where I just faded away, turned to mist. By the way, the flak jacket weighs 8.5 lbs. and is O.D. green and constructed of nylon and has twenty-three separate pockets or chambers that hold a form of material designed to deflect enemy fire. It is sleeveless and has a zipper front and a three-quarter collar. Very uncomfortable. The jacket qualifies as body armor and the inventory number is M1952 perhaps because the garment made its initial appearance during the Korean conflict. Some of the guys lighten the flak jacket by emptying some of the pockets.

    The company truck left dust devils trailing along behind as we moved to the chopper pad. The duce and a half pulled close to the lowered ramp of a CH-47 twin rotor Chinook or shit hook as I've heard them referred to. The engines were spooling up and as we ran into the loading bay the heat from the turbo exhaust almost melted us as we strapped in and the ramp ratcheted closed. The resupply was in a cargo net and travelled below us on a long sling along with a water trailer as we headed out into the Hobo Woods.

We arrived at Bravo's night defensive position (NPD) around 2:00 p.m. / 1400 hours. The atmosphere was totally informal and not at all what I had been expecting. The company was laagered in an open circle that had been partially hacked out of sparse jungle, leaving a tree or bush here and there. Two and three-man positions or foxholes lined the perimeter's edge and soldiers moved purposefully around the temporary encampment. Captain Baker was with his command group (CP) near the center of the perimeter under the shade of a small tree and he was washing his feet in his steel pot.

I met my squad and shared space under two shelter halves snapped together to make a small pup tent. The ground was covered with poncho blankets that had a camouflage pattern. There were informal introductions but there was so much goin' on I didn't catch any of the names…maybe the guy named Mitch who was with me on the Chinook and another was Denny. I was sharing the

CH 47 Chinook departing for the Hobo Woods

Ready for my first trip to the Bush to join the Company

little tent with two huge Negro's who had not bathed for about a month and had been field stripping their smokes all day. The stench was unbearable. Welcome to your new home, Hell.

I had the third watch which came in the middle of the night. Everyone went about their business as though there was no enemy within miles which may or may not have been true. I sat on the edge of our hole pretending to be brave but I was scared half shitless. The moon was up full and I coulda read the Stars and Stripes but I didn't have one. I sat there like a dummy, M-16 on the edge of the hole with a round chambered and the safety off.

I didn't pack any necessities along since this was my first time in the field and nobody told me dick. We are still expected to shave every day. Many of the guys are sporting droopy mustaches that hang along the sides of their mouths; a tradition in keeping with our unit designation...Manchu.

October 23

Monday – Just before first light the soldiers around me began to stir, moving from sleep disturbed lethargy to functional alertness. C-rations were traded, a bottle of hot sauce passed around between mouthfuls of the bland food. In silence, I organized my gear and made ready to move out. By word of mouth the order to 'saddle up' passed from soldier to soldier. Promptly at 0830 hours we moved out — notice how I transitioned seamlessly from civilian to military time — the whole battalion trudging in evenly spaced columns; five meters between squad members. The sun had not yet made its appearance and the morning felt cool. To begin with I am not expected to carry much – 55 or 60 pounds and most of that is ammunition for the 60's (crew served machine gun). The experienced men understand the difficulty that FNG's have with acclimating to the extreme heat. Some of them try to help but I'd guess that most feel that baby gotta learn it on his own.

The sun came up hot and the humidity was unbearable, a real robber, nobody ever bothered to explain water discipline to me. I drained off two canteens of water and puked clear fluid at the edge of the trail. Several guys told me to cool it and oh, how I wish I could have...but too late. The hot season is just beginning. The Old Man, commander of the battalion, Ltc. John Henchman, made the hump with us and I found his presence reassuring. He actually stood out like a sore thumb in his freshly starched fatigues. Hell, so did I. It's enough to make me roll around in the dust, get filthy so I'd fit in better.

The battalion commander humping the boonies with us is very big event. His presence is reassuring and sets the tone, assures that the battalion assumes his personality. In the same way, a company becomes the extension of its commander, and members of individual squads and fire teams also assume the personalities of their leaders. In short, the commander's inspirations are felt.

In the evening, I was singled out for listening post (LP). Very mysterious how these choices are made, almost like a modern-day version of rock, scissors, paper. How would I make the assignment equitably without drawing straws or throwing fingers? Hell, I don't know! For sure I would always choose the FNG, the Fucking New Guy, because that way I could save or protect my guys that'd been in the field with me the longest. Anyway, a different assignment was made and, in the end, I was spared. Just so you know, a company usually deploys three, two-man teams to move with stealth out about a hundred meters and remain until near daybreak and report back any activity or movement. These teams serve as early warning if enemy infiltrators are moving toward the perimeter.

Tomorrow we are supposed to sweep back the way we came and eventually move into a place called the Phil Ho Rubber plantation.

Around 1130 hours Charlie Company had a brief hit and run contact with Viet Cong snipers. After breaking the contact Charlie moved to secure our night defensive position and we moved in a circular motion to set in for the night. Funny, I am already beginning to feel like a soldier and several guys have acknowledged me including an older SSG. E-6 name of Boatwright.

Resupply came in as the evening began to cool and the remaining sunlight filtered in through the deep jungle canopy. I was sent to the water trailer with my squad's canteens. The troops waited on line observing the proper tactical distance (one grenade'll get you all). The guy in front of me fell to the ground shaking violently like he was having a fit. He'd swallowed his tongue and was really blue. I turned him over but before I could respond a medic was there and wedged a stick in the guy's mouth between his teeth and retrieved his tongue. I filled the canteens and when I returned to my squad I passed the medics who were cooling the guy down with water.

Received a touching letter from Dad. Touching because my father has never said anything of a personal caring nature. It is great to receive mail but it is emotionally distracting and I feel I really need to pay better attention out here.

Difficult to believe, but I am actually here saving the world from falling dominoes, for freedom and all that absurd shit. More likely I'm going to be fighting to save me and a few buddies but this stinking and still mysterious (to me, anyway) jungle keeps getting in the way.

October 24

Tuesday – I'm beginning to get the hang of this soldiering shit. However, every time someone other than myself gets wounded (WIA), killed (KIA) or is evacuated from the field the chance of me being next just gets better and better. Whether you call it attrition, Russian roulette, a bad deal or losing the lottery I have only one consideration, I must beat the odds no matter what they are.

We began our day again before first light. Ate in silence, buried our refuse, filled our holes and smoothed the loamy soil and then moved out. I walked point. My weapon slung over my shoulder where it would be of little use. My hands were free to swing the machete and break trail. I should have worn gloves or wrapped my hands in adhesive tape to prevent the huge blisters that I now own. The jungle was very dense and progress was slow and the compass man was incessantly prodding me from behind.

I was in a much better mood when we cleared the dense thicket. I thought it was strange that a sizeable rice paddy had been hacked out of the jungle. We rested in place, in our columns. Word filtered back that we were waiting for an air strike…F-4 Phantoms. Out here I am, along with everybody else excepting the headquarters element, an ordinary grunt, a regular GI (government issue) and do exactly as I am told with no questions. No one except maybe the company commander and those very close to him knows where we are going or what the day's objective is.

By noon I was so exhausted I felt as though I could not carry on. I began to pray that something, anything would happen, a sniper, a fire fight so I could lie down and rest. Then it did! My first sampling about what would become almost daily occurrences, endless boredom where nothing happens and one becomes lost in kind of fog; a mindless numbing state of dangerously turning inward to one's own thoughts and fantasies, then all hell breaks loose in a deafening cacophony of rifle fire and explosions. I'd just skirted an enormous hole caused by an earlier B-52 strike and was mesmerized by a bloated deer carcass, half the animals body on each side of the trail, when enemy rounds began snapping all about us.

The amazing thing was that I had no immediate reaction. I actually misinterpreted the small arms fire for hornets or bees buzzing around my head and I must have appeared comically stupid to my squad mates as I stood there in the middle of the trail waving my arms around my head. I actually shouted "what the f***," until one of the guy's shouted for me to get down because we were taking enemy fire. *Fffssst, fffsst, fffsst*, rounds passing very close to my head made sounds like miniature jet planes breaking tiny sound barriers.

My physical perceptions were ultra-alert. Colors were LSD droppin' bright, someone pass the shrooms psychedelic. My reflexes were cat, drop me off a roof and watch me land on my feet, quick. My vision was Visine clear yet the pace of the entire event unfolded in slow motion. There was an audible clapsnap, an unbelievable whizz. Incredible. I finally shielded myself by ducking behind an enormous cement-like ant mound maybe ten feet high. I was immediately swarmed by hundreds of huge red, biting ants, their mandibles piercing the skin of

C-rations

my unprotected arms. I dropped all my gear and my flak vest and some of the grunts around me started slapping at the dark red devils, attempting hopelessly to brush them off my body. The bites left huge welts. The contact kept up and it amused me that we were more concerned about the fire ants than we were about the bullets.

After we reached our NDP and secured our positions we dug in for the night. We again received resupply including another water trailer. I waited in a tactical line, got a helmet full of clear cool water, drank half and cooled my body down with the other half.

I was assigned LP (listening post) with two others in my squad. It was late evening and nightfall was approaching as we moved into the bush out past our perimeter. We found some cover from which we had a good vantage point. Our leader – I still have no names even though a thread of relationship is beginning to form between myself and those I am with – called back with a sit rep or situation report of our coordinates. All quiet in our sector but there was plenty of movement elsewhere. I thought our activity was really mysterious, actually playing hide and seek.

All at once enemy mortars passed over our heads and crashed into the perimeter. One of our ambush patrols made contact and a brief and very loud exchange of small arms fire took place along with loud concussive noises like exclamation points indicating that claymore mines had been detonated. From our hiding place, we observed red tracer rounds (ours) and yellow (enemy) madly zipping everywhere. We later heard and observed as a dust-off helicopter came in and evacuated some Charlie Company personnel. We learned later that one had died of a sucking chest wound.

Around 0430 hours we were radioed to return. We cautiously approached our departure point to avoid being shot for enemy infiltrators. Once inside we hunkered down and waited for a B-52 strike by Operation Arc Light. The mosquitoes were so bad that we had to cover our faces with tee shirts to avoid inhaling the little buzzing, sucking sumbitches. Then the ground began to shake violently as 500-pound bombs detonated all along a path in the jungle just east but almost on top of our position. Detonations lit the landscape like manufactured lightning in a Hollywood production. The ground actually heaved and our helmets bounced uselessly up and down on our heads with each explosion. Truly frightening.

October 25

Wednesday – When the strike wound down we finally settled in for the night and everyone began to relax, the mood lightened and there was plenty of smoking and joking. It seems as though everyone out here has experienced getting acclimated to the heat and functioning with very little water. I would never admit this to my squad mates but sometimes… no, fuck that… each day is torture with me being certain that I will not be able to again place one foot in front of the other…and then I do. I have seen guys actually tussle one another to crowd under a single twig with only a handful of leaves on it to get some shade, avoid the direct sunlight. I have also seen one of our medics holding a troop's head in his lap making the guy breathe into a paper bag to save him from heat prostration. Extreme cases are evacuated to the 12th Med Evacuation Hospital back in Cu Chi. It's brutal out here, every tee shirt and fatigue jacket totally soaked through.

The pace being set by our point element suggested that we were more interested in reaching our destination, a grease pencil mark on the terrain map, than we are in checking the bush around us. Occasionally on longer humps the column halts and everyone collapses in place, some smoke, some take a five-minute blow or nap which on given days is the only uninterrupted sleep we get. Before resuming forward motion, the rear end of the column marches forward passing everyone until the last becomes the first. This is really how I met most of the guys in the company because we pass so closely. Boatwright, the platoon Sergeant always acknowledges me. "Lo, Dexter," he says, "how Ya doin' this fine day?" I always say, "Great Sarge, thanks."

Before too long the column made an oblique turn and began to hack through a thick hedgerow running across our entire front. The company, travelling in three parallel columns, slowed momentarily. I was directly behind the point man, walking slack and when the guy stepped through the hedge a tremendous explosion and concussion rocked us and we fell backward, literally blown down into a dry crater. From that point, I was on auto pilot. A brief fire fight ensued in which my squad and I were the primary target. I climbed to the rim of the crater and returned fire but by then the enemy had broken contact, gone di di mau or made like the wind.

A Red Cross helicopter whirled in for the dust off. One dead and the guy in the crater lost part of his left leg up to the knee. Some pretty weird thoughts were tumbling through my mind. The entire company had come up on line and we were expending ammunition like we were having a 'mad minute' and we had not seen a thing, no Charlie Cong, Dinks, Zipper heads or Sir Charles, what have you. We later found a tunnel complex and I'm thinking what a frightening proposition…I mean what the hell are we doing out here…never seeing the enemy and losing guys every day.

Around 1630 hours my squad leader picked me to join ten others on what he called a 'leave behind ambush patrol.' The squad leader assembled us and checked all of our personal gear like dog tags and sling swivels to eliminate noise. Ditto anything else that would create noise or give away our concealed position or movement. We then watched the remainder of the company depart while creating a noticeable distraction. We quietly and hopefully unnoticed slipped into an abandoned L shaped VC (Viet Cong) slit trench that we'd spotted earlier. The waiting game thus began. At first the heat of the day was unbearable and comfort was not possible because the tiny defensive position in which we had imprisoned ourselves was made by soldiers much smaller than us. Not a word was spoken and after observing for what seemed an eternity and suffering deliriously from the stifling heat I had difficulty believing I was observing light colored

One wounded (WIA) and one killed (KIA) loaded into a dust-off medevac

conical hats of two VC in black pajamas like I'd only seen in training. I nudged the guy next to me and then carefully aimed and squeezed off a couple of rounds. The trench came alive as our 90mm recoilless erupted giving away our position. I cannot believe the level of noise created in these fire fights.

Radioing the company resulted in an order to hang tight which made us feel as though we'd been handed a signed death warrant. Several hours later Charlie hit us again and this time we were instructed to break contact and return to the perimeter. Rained intermittently through the night but I rested well under my poncho half.

October 26

Thursday – Today we had two armored tanks attached to the company, M-48 Patton's. We moved behind the vehicles cautiously and slowly as they pulverized the jungle to their front. Their presence is like the adage about the two-edged sword…the tanks offer a sense of safety and protection with their fire power but also create a huge liability because the racket they create compromises our position. The treads and iron grating on iron creates such an unmistakable noise signature that there can be no deception about what we are up to.

The tanks came up on line at the edge of a densely-wooded area that concealed, what our intelligence platoon informed us was, a Viet Cong base camp. We learned that another of the battalion's elements was to our front so the assault on the wood line was delayed. My squad leader whose name was Lonnigan began checking tunnel openings and pulling punji sticks from the edge of the thicket. Punji sticks, the effective but primitive weapon deployed by the VC, are lengths of sharpened

My squad was following the tanks into the woodline when Sargent triggered a booby trap

bamboo dipped in dung or manure to infect the foot or leg of anyone unfortunate enough to step on them. The sharpened spears point downward forming a Chinese finger trap effect — if you try to pull your foot back out of the hole the punji sticks pierce your feet and legs. Anyway, Sgt. Lonnigan hit a tripwire and detonated a booby trap at the same time I was stooping to retrieve some of the ammunition cans I'd been carrying. A fragment from the explosive device triggered by Sgt. Lonnigan pierced and travelled all the way through my forearm. If I'd not been reaching down I would not have been hit – but I was. The fragment hitting me felt like a slap or an insect bite and being startled I hollered while looking at the thin geyser of blood that spurted into the air. Doc McAdams reached me immediately and applied pressure to stop the bleeding, Doc Lupo was at Lonnigan's side and having a difficult time helping the sergeant who had lost a leg and his genitals.

Within minutes a med evac chopper had us at the hospital back in Cu Chi. After leaving the chopper I never saw Lonnigan again. My wound was not serious. A doctor cut a straight line between the entry and exit holes, debrided the wound and wrapped the approximately three or four-inch gash with a sterile dressing. In three or four days, the wound will be sutured if there isn't any infection.

About ten days and I will be returned to the boonies but for now it feels pretty good to be in the rear; a blooded soldier at last. I guess you could say I'd faced the elephant.

October 27

Friday – Having experienced my baptism of fire or been blooded as that guy was talking about at the EM club has caused me a sort of dilemma, I guess one could say. I am happy to be here in the rear with the gear and to have a few beers again with the company clerk Stansberry and enjoy the weird kind of celebrity that being shot through the arm has given me but…I am feeling guilty about not being in the bush with my new friends. I wonder what they are doing. I wonder if they are in that mysterious place called the Phil Ho Plantation.

And here's another component of the dilemma. The supposed reason and the only reason to be in Vietnam, we were drilled to believe, was to protect freedom, large F, and democracy, large D. However, walking between the pristine and carefully manicured row upon row of rubber trees and risking an ambush makes me question about my country's interest. I mean really, are we here protecting rubber trees and other of this country's resources for selfish monetary concerns back home? Or are we back to that falling Domino shit again and protecting against Communism? Remember the French and also the Japanese tried dominating the Vietnamese during their colonial periods.

To me there is obviously something to these questions that I am probably not supposed to be thinking about, asking. I mean, the plantation is in perfect operational order with a metal bucket hanging carefully on a spigot at the end of a cut spiral down each tree trunk. The buckets are filled with sap ready to be harvested. So why are we really here…profit? What the fuck…am I risking my life for rubber tires? But I digress…

The arm wound limits my duty for now. I walked to the medical facility today to have the bandage changed and for a doctor to make sure there is no infection. So far so good. Kicked back for most of the day and caught bunker guard duty. I believe I did not mention earlier that before actually deploying for the bunker there is an informal guard mount inspection convened by the OD (officer of the day). The guards stand dutifully at attention while the OD inspects weapons, etc. During this inspection, the M-16's charging handle must be pulled back to allow the OD to inspect the weapon's chamber. I could not hold my rifle with a firm grip or pull the charging handle rearward but I believe the officer understood.

Guard duty was boring. Midway through the watch we were surrounded by a very dense ground fog which necessitated the firing of several hand-held illumination rounds. This is accomplished by removing the cap and inserting the tube down into the cap which houses a firing pin. To activate the flare, you bring the tube with force down and into the palm of your hand. A loud whoosh fills the air sending the illuminating element skyward. A loud pop occurs and a small parachute opens and a light ball swings back and forth and lights the area. The fog caused an eerie light that lasted until the flares burned out and darkness returned. The night passed without incident.

October 28

Saturday – Another trip to the med station today to have my bandage changed. You may be wondering why so many bandage/dressing changes. It's the tropics, of course. High humidity and temperatures dictate that cleaned (called debriding) wounds, cuts and injuries are not closed or sutured until fear of infection has passed.

Read a paperback titled *Candy*. A total waste of time made worse due to the last three chapters gone missing. Made a tape recording for Cindy and arranged to have it posted through the orderly room.

Met a Pvt. Mussels at the club tonight. I said his name aloud after reading his fatigue shirt. The guy corrected me saying that you pronounce it moo as you would if addressing a cow. He had really handsome good looks sorta like the Hollywood actor, Jeff Chandler. He just returned to the company area after a six-month stretch in Long Binh Jail for insubordination. He was not specific about his circumstance but he will be returning to the field, the six months in jail added to his time being spent in the Nam. When I sat down Mussles, like the moo cow, was heckling a new kid I'd not seen around before who was petrified about joining the company for combat. I felt pretty bad for the new kid and wondered if moo cow, jail bait had any real experience upon which he was basing his jibes.

There are literally thousands of Vietnamese, mostly women, who are let onto the base every day to work. Some are hooch *mama-san's* and do laundry and straighten up after those who are permanent assignees to the rear like Headquarters personnel, Military Police (MP's) and other staff. They also fill sandbags which is a perpetual thing. They speak little English but are fun to banter with. Some say, as I'd mentioned earlier, that they covertly pace off distances from the wire to targets of opportunity within the base and pass this info to local VC cadre back in their villages. In exchange, they are given a pass by the VC.

October 29

Sunday – Interesting thing about the chow in the rear…every meal is accompanied by goo ga's of Kool Aid. No milk because of the challenge of keeping it from going bad. Hell, we even get ice cream occasionally. The menu is pretty boring – meat, reconstituted mashed potatoes and canned veggies are all staples. Any way you cut it the offering beats the bejesus outta C-rats in the bush, though.

Stopped by the company aid stations to retrieve my medical records and walked to the 25th Med Evac and was on an operating table by 0815 hours and by 0900 the wound was closed with sutures and properly dressed.

A medic in from the field on rotation performed the procedure. I chuckled to myself that I noticed he was wearing white sneakers, not jungle boots. The humorous thing was that I didn't think he was dumb because of this but he'd printed his name, Don, on the tops of his shoes. Why? Maybe he didn't trust anyone in theatre or he didn't want them misplaced. After dropping a couple of stitches, he admitted that he was not much better with buttons.

On the way back to the company area I was rubber neckin' just like I was still a FNG. I'm amazed at the frenetic pace of everything and how fast things seem to get taken care of. There is no apparent wasted motion and it is easy to lose perspective. From all the activity, you lose sight of the fact that if soldiers were not fighting and dying in the jungle around here there would be no reason for the vast Cu Chi base camp to even exist.

Sat on a bunker near the perimeter tonight by myself and watched red tracers pierce the darkness way off in the distance. The silence interrupted once in a while by an artillery battery firing H and I salvos down range into the jungle. H and I is a term for harassing and interdicting fire which is random to keep the enemy back on his heels.

One doesn't often see formations of soldiers while in the rear and though there is strict regimentation in both the rear and the field it would be difficult for a casual observer to understand how an infantry rifle company is organized. If Bravo Company were at full strength (we seldom are) we should be capable of having 121 men plus six attached personnel. A company consists of three platoons and a command post or CP. There is normally a forth platoon, the weapons platoon but we have this group split evenly among the other three platoons. Each platoon has three 12-man squads and a platoon CP. A squad is broken into seven riflemen, a blooper (M-79) man, an M-60 machine gunner and an assistant gunner, an RTO and a squad leader. Our Company CP consists of the captain and his three RTO's. Attached to the CP is a medic, an artillery forward observer who is a lieutenant and his RTO and sometimes a Kit Carson Scout who is a South Vietnamese interpreter. This information is something that the average boonierat understands only on an ethereal, gut level because he's not concerned with organization as much as he is preoccupied with very rudimentary matters like keeping his weapon clean, having plenty of ammunition and C-rats and listening to the steady rhythm of his own labored breathing that drives the cadence of his footfalls through the jungle.

Sgt. Binh, our Kit Carson scout and interpreter

October 30

Monday – The XO (Executive Officer, basically the second in charge) has been letting me skate or get over as it's known in military parlance presumably because of my messed-up arm. Could not have come at a better time because I have been getting a ton of mail. Under the usual circumstance mail is a most welcome event and even more so when the letters are from family and close friends. What's been happening is different though. Many letters and notes are coming from well-wishers, mostly young girls, who are curious about what war is like. My cynicism gets in the way and receiving such missives is akin to strangers slowing down on the highway and causing a bottleneck while observing a car wreck. I like getting the mail but now I feel obligated to answer each one of them. One of the letters contained an accompanying clip from my hometown newspaper, the Grand Rapids Press announcing that they'd published my name and overseas APO address in something called *Vietnam Mail Call*. Boom…floodgates open.

Watched a rain interrupted movie at our company outdoor theatre, the usual bad sci-fi flick titled *The Projected Man* about a guy who was messing with the transmission of matter from one place to another. The experiments went wrong and anybody who touched the test subject went crazy. Attendance was limited to the walking wounded and the rest of the regulars in the rear referred to as REMF's (rear echelon motherfuckers). Several bottles were passed. Alcohol is prevalent…pot is a different animal, haven't seen any or smelled any so if there are 'heads' around they keep to themselves. I actually do not know much about this activity and my personal experience is limited to the few joints passed from hand to hand at the going away party my brother Jed hosted for me.

I had difficulty getting to sleep tonight which is unusual. There was a portable radio tuned to AFVN radio out of Saigon playing rock tunes. I got up and shuffled around the hooch, zeroing in to find the source and when I did I hit the off button. When I reinserted myself under my mosquito netting the noise resumed so I let it go and tossed and turned 'til first light.

Considering the small amount of time I've spent with my company in the field I have decided I would rather be out there.

October 31

Tuesday – Have you ever heard the term SNAFU? Well, it is an often-used rejoinder or, I guess, acronym that means Situation Normal, All Fucked Up! Soldiers invoke these words when something pisses them off and that's everything almost all of the time. Pissing and moaning as my father criticizes me for is the infantryman's lot in life: the food sucks (usually), never getting hot chow in the field sucks, staying out an extra day or two when we thought we'd be coming in sucks…you get the point. Anyway, back to what I was saying. Today is supposed to be pay day; I would not have a care about pay except that I've decided to get myself a camera so I can begin recording my life in Vietnam. The company pay master is reportedly on R & R. You would think that the brass would be certain that arrangements would be made for our pay. Yeah, I understand, we're not going anywhere but really, that is not the point. Pay is one of the very few things beside mail call that we all look forward to so get it done.

The stitches are to come out Friday. I received a message through the Orderly Room. Stansberry came by the hooch to inform me the aid station called and wants me to remove the dressing so the wound gets air and helps the healing process. Even though I decided I would rather be in the field I wondered if leaving the bandage on longer or somehow letting the wound fester would keep me out of the field for a few extra days. Then I remembered the cowardly blond, curly headed guy who shot himself through the foot and I shivered a little. Don't go there.

Here is something that seems a bit odd to me. The company area theatre showed three one hour long episodes of *Combat* staring Vic Morrow, you remember that, do you not? The state side television show is the absolute favorite of these guys here in the rear. I felt like saying, "hey, I know the Company Clerk and could arrange for you to join the company in the Ho Bo Woods." *The Wild Wild West* and *Bonanza* are also popular. Watson, who I forgot to mention got dusted off with me, and I got totally loaded watching the flicks.

November 1

Wednesday – Early morning mail call in the company street by the orderly shack and for the third day I turned and, with slumped shoulders, shuffled dejectedly back through the dusty company street to my cot and the comfort of a partially inflated air mattress. No mail! Big mistake, going back to the air mattress, I mean. I got nailed with KP when the First Shirt came whirling through our tent looking for easy targets. For those of you who may not be familiar with the term KP it stands for Kitchen Police or mess duty. The Army, in this case, uses the word police as a verb as in 'when the Marines were finished with their bivouac they were required to police the area and pick up all of their refuse.'

My duties for the day required me to wipe tables, serve and then clean up or 'police' the mess. Food not qualifying as left overs is placed in large trash bins. Me and two other privates loaded the bins onto the back of a three-quarter ton truck and drove outside the wire, out past the laterite pit to the Cu Chi garbage dump. Approaching the dump at a quarter of a mile we could clearly see a huge black cloud that enveloped everything – flies. Entering the gate, we could see through the scrum of insects, a soldier from the Engineer Battalion pushing the garbage around with a huge blade on the front of a dark green (OD) dozer. His face was covered by a towel. There were children and old Vietnamese with faces similarly covered and with sticks and long poles they were using to sift through our garbage. Sad to say that most of our discarded 'left overs' are better than the stuff locals enjoy in their minimal subsistence. The dump must be the filthiest place in the country and the stench is unbelievable. The population of flies is responsible. Black flies vomit and defecate on the decomposing food matter and when the residue liquefies the flies suck it back up. Pleasant thought, huh? When we exited the dump, we passed through a car wash like set up and the entire vehicle and we were sprayed with disinfectant before we returned to base.

We finally got paid this afternoon but too late for me to look for cameras at the PX (post exchange) and besides, I was still involved with KP. I was again placed on bunker guard and for the guard mount inspection I was finally able to pull back the charging handle on my weapon. I found a mosquito net that will cover my head and I'm planning to be more comfortable in the bunker tonight. The buzzing, I am sure, will nonetheless drive me crazy.

November 2

Thursday – I'm sure I mentioned Watson in an earlier entry. Well, he just re-enlisted. I listened with interest about what he's done. At this point his action holds little relevancy for me or my situation because I am just beginning my twelve months. I had not heard of the course he has chosen for himself. What Watson has done was more of an extension of his current term in the military than it was a re-enlistment. He executed (funny choice of a word due to the implication) or chose to extend his duty or time here by six months in exchange for a permanent reassignment to duty in the rear area, no more combat or line duty. This struck me as unnecessary since he was getting, as they say, short, only had four months remaining before he would rotate back to the States. He told me over beers that he could not take four more months of combat, was afraid that his number was up.

Occupied a little time writing letters home and consumed several cans of Ballentine suds in the process. There is a plethora of beer that, back home, would be considered undrinkable but here in the Nam it's take it or leave it. Troops and officers responsible for unloading the brewski's from Conex containers arriving in Saigon grab the good stuff for themselves and designate what's left for us grunts and line troops in the jungles.

Another movie in the area tonight. This time it was *The Greatest Show On Earth* staring Charlton Heston and Gina Lollobrigida. Supporting cast of millions including David Nelson, brother of Ricky from the *Ozzie and Harriet* show. Cornell Wilde and Jimmy Stewart also appeared in the feature that dealt with circus life and a spectacular train wreck. An element of nostalgia gripped me because, as a youngster, I had viewed this movie with my family on Christmas day as part of our celebration and tradition.

Seeing the film again has led to some thinking and Lord knows, that back here temporarily removed from the threat of combat, there is plenty of time to pursue day dreams or other such musings; not paying attention to business out in the middle of the Ho Bo Woods could have disastrous consequences. At any rate, my thoughts drifted, turned to mom and dad. It occurred to me that my parents must have been terribly disappointed in me abandoning my studies and winding up in the Army. That must have been bad enough for them…but Vietnam. Yikes! Neither one of them ever said that they were proud of me for serving my country even though I was drafted. Growing up I never questioned Mom or Dad, just did as I was told or asked to do. But now…It is hurtful to feel that I do not have their support. Mother always told me she loved me, but Father totally lacked feelings of any kind.

November 3

Friday – I was called for mess duty once again but avoided the tedium of peeling taters when the 25th Evac called the orderly shack wondering why I had not come over to have my stitches removed. The procedure involved snipping each suture and pulling the remnants of the sinewy thread out of the holes with a tweezer. The wound looks well but still some redness.

When I returned to the company area and reported to the Orderly Room I was placed on KP anyway. I was designated outside man which is actually not bad duty. The heavy gas operated ovens had to be lifted and carried outdoors in order to clean them properly. The lifting was difficult and I momentarily believed that the wound might pop open.

It seems to me that a realistic diversion, the only possible way to escape Vietnam or be someplace else is through entering a dreamscape. Heavy slumber is welcomed and today I travelled there. It was not a pleasant journey. I dreamed that my legs had been horribly damaged and the unreal part of the dream was that I witnessed the whole operation as though I was above the operating table looking down. The pain was excruciating. I winced and flinched until I woke up drenched in perspiration. Once in a while your dreams are so wonderful that you wish you could stay awhile or return but not this time. I wondered why I would have such a dream. Foreshadowing perhaps and later in the evening when I went to the movie with a bunch of guys that included Watson and Edwards I was haunted by the dream and do not remember what the movie was. How unusual.

November 4

Saturday – Bunker guard during daylight hours. Brought along my letter writing materials and while keeping a vigilant eye peeled for the Officer of the Day, who makes frequent rounds, I was able to write five letters home.

Believe it or not there was a troop named Matthias who was in the bunker with me. His situation was, to me, misunderstood as was basically the disciple in the Bible whose name he carried. I say believe it or not because there are at least two popular derivatives of this name... Mathis and Matthias.

In the Bible, Matthias was one of the two alternate choices to replace Judas. The Matthias in my story, the soldier in the bunker with me, would probably never be chosen for anything and should be overlooked or discounted due to his behavior. His fatigue shirt had no chevrons meaning he was currently a Private E-1 or that's how he arrived here in Vietnam. That is not unusual as most all new arrivals are private's and unranked. By contrast I was a PFC (one of two from my Advanced Infantry Training outfit) when I arrived in Vietnam and wore a single chevron. If a soldier performs well he would be promoted to the rank of PFC (Private First Class) after twelve months of service. I discern several common threads running through most of those referred to as malingerers in the rear and that is that, number one their language, their banter, is peppered with thoughts and ideas about what they can possibly do to remain in the rear, never be deployed to the field and combat and, number two, they have not attained any rank. When they talk of avoiding duty I remain silent.

I sold my old 35 mm camera, a Minolta, to Matthias and went to the PX and purchased an 11 mm miniature for myself believing that the much smaller camera would be easier to carry with me in the field. At the time, I was unfamiliar with things like format and did not know that 11 mm was about half the size of a 35mm negative and yields images too small to be useful.

Watson and I thumbed our way over to the 125th Engineers because we heard they were showing a Clint Eastwood Spaghetti Western, *Fistfull Of Dollars*. On the way back we stopped at the 25th Med Evac facility because Watson had, and this is no lie, hemorrhoid problems and needed an ass bomb or suppository, I think, to get things moving again.

As we approached the Quonset hut styled building we heard screaming and quite a lot of commotion. Entering we watched as several medics attempted to restrain a young soldier on one of the operating tables. The medical personnel yelled for me and Watson to grab a leg and hold down the guy who was demonstrating impressive Darvon fueled strength. We were told the troop had attempted to kill himself by overdosing on a very strong version of the drug that contains a codeine B.B. inside. The medics already had a tube inserted into the guys' stomach and the contents that began coming out stunk bad enough that Watson and I had to turn our heads and hold our breath. The guy was really small and repeatedly hollered, "let me die, let me die!" When it was all over I could not help myself and I felt compelled to say to him, "if the decision had of been mine to make I would have let you die." Watson and I walked silently back to the company area.

From my limited time here in Vietnam, in Cu Chi, I believe you can understand that I am in a pretty perilous situation. Sure, there is a lot of safety in numbers but who among us is not scared. We continue to do the best we can and for the most part support one another.

November 5

Sunday – A really quiet Sunday almost like back home: go to church, return home to grilled cheese sandwiches and a bowl of tomato soup with a box of saltine crackers and then collapse on the couch to watch the Detroit Lions lose another football game. Talk about being a masochist. I have supported those losers for my entire life and I cannot recall a single season to be proud of.

Received another tape from Cindy. So good to hear her voice that I cried. What would I feel now if I had not married just before shipping over. A difficult proposition to be sure. I suppose the only easier situation would have been to be here in Vietnam with no wife and no relationship to continually put a strain on my heart strings. I have been here for a little over a month now and have not heard from my brother, my sister or mother.

Took a little walk over to the PX by myself to find some kind of an electric adapter so I can tap into the generated electric source in the company area and not drain the batteries in my tape recorder.

Much of my daily behavior, the things I do, the way I dress, what I carry are not known to those back home, the loved ones for whom I am keeping this diary. For instance, everywhere I go either by myself or with others, inside or outside the base camp I carry with me my weapon and ammunition. Different soldiers and soldiers of different rank carry a variety of personal weapons or side arms. Regular grunts like myself carry the weapon which is standard to all infantry and mortar men or guys in the motor pool or for that matter, officers and cooks and that is the M-16 rifle. In addition, some officers carry the Remington Rand Army 45 pistol which is officially designated the M911A1. Some infantry carry the M-79 grenade launcher and also the 45 in case they need it for close in work or their position is over run. Certain soldiers are machine gunners carrying the M-60 which is a crew served weapon but their basic weapon is still the M-16 though they may decline to carry one.

In addition to carrying weapons at all times soldiers must wear the proper head gear, the ubiquitous steel pot which is OD (Olive Drab) in color like everything in the Army. In garrison troops may wear a soft cover, whether a ball cap or a floppy jungle hat. The main difference in clothing is that here in Nam you only have one basic set of fatigues and those are the ones I am currently wearing. Really the only exception to this is a spare pair of socks to help keep your feet dry. This is weird for me because back in civilian life I really liked my clothes although I went shoeless at every opportunity.

Watson has been talking about getting permission to go outside the wire to the actual village of Cu Chi, yes, that is correct, our base camp is named for the village outside the camp. To me the ville is mysterious and scary place that has a reputation of being a VC controlled village – especially after dark. During daylight hours, many soldiers trade and barter there and get boom boom or take a steam bath but right now because I do not know the difference the thought of being there scares the shit outta me.

Bunker guard tonight and after one last trip to have my arm checked out at the aid station I am cleared to return to the field.

November 6

Monday – Returned from bunker guard when my relief came down at first light. Sacked out for three hours, ate lunch and returned to the same bunker for another boring afternoon of watching young kids in front of our position as they rode or walked behind huge water buffalo in the rice paddies.

Following evening chow there was a formation convened in the company street in front of the Orderly Room. This is the first such formation (other than mail call) since I've been here so we buzzed about what could be up. The Company Clerk Dan Stansberry introduced the Company Executive Officer or XO…seems there is, at least, some formality afoot, a degree of decorum in the rear, if you please. Funny to me though…I was thinking that this ranking officer is, nonetheless, a REMF or rear echelon motherfucker as I told you. This is a derogatory term and not at all a term of endearment. Be that as it may, 1st Lieutenant Wilson looks the part, REMF or not. His freshly starched fatigue pants are tucked into or bloused into spit shined jump boots. This in spite of no jump insignia or wings which would entitle him to his bloused boots. His hair was short, militarily so and he had white side walls, the term for being closely shaved at the side of the head, no sideburns.

The LT was all business as he confirmed the rumor which I had not heard that the battalion will be moving up near the Cambodian border to the Province Capital of Tay Ninh City. The area is known as the Parrot's Beak because of how a piece of Cambodia forms a bird-like bulge down into the country. Our new base camp will be near the foot of The Black Virgin Mountain or Nui Ba Den as the range is known. This outstanding topographical feature may be seen from almost anywhere in the 25th Division's AO (area of operation).

Lt Wilson informed us that we will be dismantling our entire sector of the camp here in Cu Chi and transporting everything by convoy to our new home. Structures not currently in use will be carefully taken apart so everything can be reused and an advance party will go first to reestablish us at the new location. The trip by convoy is approximately forty miles up Highway 1 through some dangerous Indian country as they say. There is no way to avoid going directly through Trang Bang which is VC controlled. I have heard the operation could begin as early as the thirteenth of this month.

November 7

Tuesday - Manchu 6, the battalion commander who I mentioned earlier, must have come down hard on Lieutenant Wilson because the Lieutenant or LT as they are referred to, had a bee in his bonnet as he swept through the entire company area around six am turning over cots and rousting everyone for what he hollered was a mandatory breakfast followed by a total police call of the area. My observation is that Wilson seems uncomfortable with his leadership role. He reminds me of Captain Queeg, you remember him from *The Caine Mutiny*, of course. He was the character described as being paranoid, the one who constantly rolled two steel balls in his hand...either hand would do. The psych eval stated that the balls represented repressed childhood masturbation or tiny balls of feces because he'd not been properly potty trained. He, Wilson, just seemed weird to me and maybe that is why he is in the rear instead of in the field leading infantry.

Since my arrival there have been very few regulations that have been consistently enforced with regard to dress, uniform patches and insignia. The LT sent us all to the little Gook shop near the PX to have CIB (combat Infantry badge), electric pineapple patches and our rank sewn onto our shirts. Most of us are broke so I guess we'll have to avoid the lieutenant until pay day or suffer his wrath.

Prayer has always been a part of my life so I feel very comfortable with it. My prayers are not just for myself but are inclusive meaning that my entreaties to the Lord are often about all of us who somehow or another seem predestined to be here in this strange land doing the bidding of our country.

I received a gift package, a box really, from a den of Cub Scouts from my home town in Grand Rapids, Michigan. Of course, by the time I shared the box with my fellow boonierats there wasn't much left but crumbs and part of a home-made popcorn ball hung together with clear Kayo Syrup. Yum! The best part was a note that had been signed by all the little Cub's wishing me a Happy Christmas, and thanks for fighting for our country.

November 8

Wednesday – Morning bunker guard. Wrote notes to Bruning, Berg and a letter to Cindy. In the afternoon, I avoided being called upon for any further work details by finding a shady spot to relax and read part of Sammy Davis Junior's book *Yes I Can*. One of the best parts was when Davis was in Columbia and the local gendarmes were burning several tons of pot. Sammy stood as close as he could to the flames and inhaled deeply. Sorry I missed that one.

LP (listening post) tonight. Our five-man patrol crossed silently from the rally point and as we moved slowly away from the perimeter the moonlight created shadow soldiers' on the dirt, increasing the size of our patrol and giving us a greater sense of strength. Using map coordinates and a compass bearing we marched off exactly seven hundred meters and sat back to back in a small circle. Our exact position gave confidence that out-going small arms fire or H&I fire from the base camp would not endanger us. Our patrol leader, Sgt. Moore, called Hard Core by some because of his prior service in Korea, fired a green star cluster that signaled our touchdown. We began our 100% vigil until first light. Except for a strange, jerky startle response I experienced from being on the verge of falling asleep, the long night passed.

One dud kept slumbering and Sgt. Moore had to repeatedly nudge the guy to keep him awake. When we got ready to unass the area, break off the patrol and return to base camp, the guy was snoring. The Sergeant took the kids M-16 and we silently stole off. About an eighth of a mile removed we all shouted and the embarrassed troop returned to the group scared shitless.

November 9

Thursday – I was intent on getting several hours of sack time when we got in off Listening Post but no such luck, not today anyway. As we approached the Orderly room shack to ditch the radio, Lt. Wilson the XO's raised and concerned voice drowned our chatter. He was relating to battalion that there had been a theft. I thought I heard the lieutenant say that there'd been a death and that he had five suspects right here. Since there were five of us coming in off patrol I mistakenly thought the lieutenant meant us and it scared the pee out of me. As the confusion settled down and the story unfolded it wasn't us at all but five other soldiers in the rear that were suspected of stealing one hundred and seventy-five dollars from a drawer in the Orderly Room.

The company is settled in to what is called a hard spot about a click from Cu Chi. A hard spot is a semi-permanent defensive position maintained for more than a night and a click is jargon for one thousand meters which, coincidentally is the size of the individual grid squares on the maps used for navigation. Elements of the battalion are there in the woods with Bravo and will come in tomorrow. I have been volunteered by Lt. Wilson to be the guidon bearer and march next to the commander at the front of the ranks of soldiers as we approach The Ann Margaret Gate. Different military organizations have different colored guidon's but the size and shape are pretty standard. Our guidon is also festooned with many battle streamers, one each for significant battles or campaigns. So...to have been selected to be the bearer is a considerable honor if one does not conflate the honor with being a target of opportunity for every VC within a two-mile radius as we march toward the gate with me out in front carrying a shiny varnished pole with a flag on it.

Late in the afternoon I was flown by chopper to be with the company for the night. I talked with Captain Baker briefly and shared C-rats while getting reacquainted with my squad buddies. Even though my recent wound, which I considered very minor, gave me a certain celebrity with my fellow soldier's I was still expected to pull my share of watch duty.

November 10

Friday – The perimeter began to stir just before first light. In silence, we ate our C-rations, secured our bed rolls and personal gear and at exactly 0600 hours we organized into a company formation. I pulled the cover off the guidon and stood next to Bravo's officers and Battalion Commander, Ltc. John Henchman. The other companies in the BN (battalion) formed up behind us and sighted in on the guidon. Jeep mounted recoilless rifles exited Cu Chi through The Ann Margaret Gate (so named because the actress always came to our base camp with the Bob Hope Christmas show) and took up our flank to protect us as we mushed along an old two track in the jungle and headed home. I should point out that infantry battalions concluding operations do not re-enter their base camps as we did today. The whole episode or stunt was planned to showcase the 4th of the 9th as we completed Operation Barking Sand and as we entered through the gate the 25th Division Marching Band struck up their rendition of Colonel Bogies March. Off duty personnel came to welcome us home. The whole exercise seemed a bit corny but I admit I felt pride today. For the first time in six months the battalion is at full strength. The typical strength of a light Infantry Battalion in the field is between 300 and 500 infantry fighters. Our strength is recorded at 504 plus the Headquarters Company and other miscellaneous attachments.

  Rain fell for most of the day so the award ceremony was held inside the EM Club. Bronze and Silver Stars were awarded by a Brigadier General who proclaimed with enthusiasm, "This is indeed a great moment in the long and distinguished history of the 25th Division," etc, etc. He droned on about how the Division was formed at Schofield Barracks, Hawaii, and the divisions first battle was on the Big Island when Hawaii was still a territory, blah, blah. And then, "blood and sweat have been shed but not in vain for this is the life of a soldier. We can indeed be proud of our accomplishment of driving the enemy from his stronghold in the Ho Bo Woods, a place they have dominated since 1936. I would like to honor those men specifically who displayed great valor in the line of duty and each man in the battalion."

The reason I was included in the award ceremony was because once again I'd been honored with the distinction of being in charge of the flag. A possible reason I was not razzed by my cronies was that they were overlooking the fact I'd been singled out for a special duty they'd rather not have.

The rain passed in the afternoon and there was another ceremony...a funeral this time for the "not in vain" part the Brigadier had hurried past in his speech. Mimeographed sheets containing the names of those killed during Operation Barking Sand were passed out at the chapel door. Half the company was there to hear Captain Crowley, our Protestant chaplain, say some appropriate words and then we filed outside and stood at attention in front of a line of shined boots with bayonets at weapon's end sticking in the ground, steel pots on top and dog tags draped over the M-16's. Very sad. A little depressing. How many more times am I gonna be doin' this I wondered?

Weapons inspection late in the afternoon followed by Jeeps pulling utility trailers loaded down with free beer, ice and sodas. Steaks were blazing on barbecue grills made by cutting 55 gallon drums in half and the company street was filled with high spirited party animals. The officers made a brief appearance. At night, our Bravo Company EM club was thrown open to the entire battalion and the resulting bacchanalian ruckus was not in honor of Bacchus but to the fact that we had become an effective killing machine and were being rewarded for it. Medals and unlimited booze, what the hell's missing here...fireworks? A rock and roll band of nubile young Vietnamese girls shook everything they didn't have from a makeshift stage at one end of the club. The crowd was so thick that the soldiers who passed out were frozen in place wedged between other revelers. It was complete bedlam. I avoided projectile vomiting by hanging onto four other guys as we balanced tenuously on a bar stool trying to see the show on stage.

Got lots of mail today.

November 11

Saturday – Today is actually Veterans Day but who in our present environment would know that or even care. The day traces its history back to the Treaty Of Versailles or somewhere near that time when Allied Forces signed a treaty With Germany on the eleventh hour of the eleventh day of the eleventh month. Oh, well! I believe that was at the conclusion of the First World War. Germany as a country was humiliated by the loss and violated the treaty within the first week and so did Japan…the beginning of that buildup and other events led to the Second World War.

Company formation and a talk from our commanding officer Captain Baker. He presented some of the guys with Purple Hearts for their wounds received in combat. I did not at this time receive mine.

Lt. Graves will be moved over to the weapons platoon. The platoon is trained with the 81mm mortar and while they carry M-16's these guys are used mainly in support of us infantry doggies when we're in the field. My friend Edwards is in this platoon. Lt. Miller, a first Lieutenant is now in charge of my platoon and that is the second platoon. We have heard that he is a good man.

Our first platoon will be leaving for Tay Ninh tomorrow and my platoon departs on the 16th. Word has it that between the 21st and the 27th we will be deployed on a training mission to tune up for operating in an entirely different type of terrain, atmosphere and weather. Being farther north and closer to Cambodia it is expected that we will have more contact with hard core North Vietnamese Army soldiers. By deduction this infers slightly less contact with VC gorillas but, oh, yeah, they're still there.

We will be discarding our cumbersome flak jackets. They will no longer be required or part of SOP (standard operating procedure) but I am sure that some troops will still feel more comfortable wearing them. The jackets besides being heavy, restrict movement so not wearing one could be an advantage. The Battalion commander also says we can ditch the heavy steel pot helmets and wear floppy soft caps in the field. He, the commander, is reinforcing or building the image that we are a quick response light infantry outfit – different than all the other battalions. Of course, you may continue to wear both flak vests and helmets if you choose.

Had bunker guard again tonight and the H&I fire going down range kept us awake in the bunker for most of the night.

November 12

Sunday - The company area, indeed the entire battalion area, is beginning to look like a ghost town as gradually, piece by piece, the buildings are carefully disassembled and placed on huge flatbed trailers for transportation and reassembly at our new Tay Ninh home.

Rios, Bates and I began tearing down the Orderly Room this morning and then took a break for church services and after lunch we were back at it finally finishing the disassembly job around 1630 hours.

Right now, it is raining so fiercely that you cannot see across the compound but still we are on standby as a reactionary force. This means we must be ready to respond if another element in the battalion gets in a jam and needs a bail out or a get out of jail free card. Unlikely but it does happen. We heard that a company in our sister battalion the Wolfhounds, the 2nd of the 27th is getting messed up over by Trang Bang a couple of clicks from here. Initial reports are that the CO is dead. Hope it isn't Dave Brunings company. Any contact with the VC over that way is cause for concern because our convoys must drive through the town on the way up to Tay Ninh.

We waited and waited and then waited some more but we were not deployed.

November 13

Monday – Another week blacked out on my short timer's calendar. It's easy to fall prey to tedium if I have too much time on my hands. I don't think I have ever said anything about the grunts preoccupation with the amount of time remaining on his time in the Nam. In the back of my diary there is a calendar for the entire year at some time during the evening I ceremoniously totally 'X' out the day I've just completed. Many soldiers use the cloth camouflage cover on their steel pot as a moving billboard. There is no limit to what one might find inked on a helmet cover…anything from one's home town to, oh, say, Jesus is my co-pilot, peace symbols are big along with crosses and of course you'll find some elaborate short timers calendars. When a soldier's full year or 365 days is coming to a close he is referred to as being short. Some guys carry a special short timers stick and jokes abound like, "I'm so short I have to look up through the cracks in the cement in order to see the sidewalk."

Guys also get very superstitious and freaky when they get close to the end of their tour and some company's intentionally place soldiers in the rear because their utility or usefulness to the rest of the company is limited, they become liabilities. Obviously, I do not have to worry about this for quite a while.

Another detail day and the company is all here in camp to work on the move to Tay Ninh. I was on KP again. My squad leader was supposed to relieve me but did not. Ssg. Boatwright came by the wash shed where I was scrubbing pots and joking with three *mama-san's* who are assigned here. He informed me that he suggested my name to battalion to be the Bravo Company PIO or Public Information Officer. I have absolutely no idea how the Sergeant knew I had some background in English and journalism but after a brief interview I was given the position. Besides my expected responsibility as a rifleman I will be responsible for writing company news items and combat scenarios for the Army Times as well as photographs for the 25th Division newspaper, *The Tropic Lightning News* or *Flash*, I believe it is called.

The little job has some benny's like coming in from the field occasionally on the resupply choppers for article turn ins and meetings. The requirement is four articles a week and 36 camera exposures. A Captain Richardson over at battalion heads the program. He appears to be stern and forceful.

Presently I am writing home town news releases for every member of Bravo Company. What a great way to know everyone. This is all very good news.

November 14

Tuesday – Busy again with home town news releases. The task is challenging because I have to track down everyone and get them to share a bit of their bio stuff with me. As the word spreads regarding the knowledge that I can trigger a small article that will appear in their local newspaper back home, they come looking for me.

The effort to move from Cu Chi to Tay Ninh is front and center and preparations are intensifying and there are multiple trips to the dump each day. I was on trash detail with a guy in my squad named Dennis Wagner and a colored guy named Ham. The dump was filthier than the last time I was there, if that's possible. I'm sure there were more kids sifting through our discards for items their families can use or they can sell or trade. There were also many more flies and I will never regard flies or mosquitoes the same again as long as I live. The standard GI mosquito repellant that we are issued comes in little clear plastic 2 oz. bottles and the main chemical is something called Deet. The delivery system is the oil that contains the Deet. The damned stuff coats your skin so thoroughly that it is like a second skin and I swear it's so thick that your sweat forms bubbles under the layer of oil. As I mentioned before the best you can do is cover your face with a tee shirt at night when you're in the boonies. I took a few pictures of the dump and a water 'boo' that was rummaging in the garbage.

I've been feeling a little blue...sort of down in the dump(s) if you'll pardon the word play after the trash detail to the Cu Chi land fill. The reason for feeling bad is that in a letter to Cindy I bawled her out for not writing. How much of a bad actor does that make me for getting angry with my wife who is about nine thousand miles away.

Had some beers with Stansberry and Sgt. Beemer over at Stan's hooch. Beemer is running details for Top (company First Sergeant or First Shirt) since he is getting short. He's one of those guys I told you about; soldier relieved of field duty just before his tour ends and he is ready to go home. I cannot repress feelings of envy for soldiers like Beemer I guess because I'm wishing it was me getting ready to board that big Freedom Bird and book on outa here.

November 15

Wednesday – I volunteered to ride shotgun with a motor pool Specialist 4 on one of the Tay Ninh convoys. This was my first really good chance to see Vietnamese rural life along Highway 1. The road is a worn dirt swath that seems to reach endlessly to the horizon. As soon as we pass through one destitute village we see the next one on the horizon. The convoy assumes a life all its own as the more than one hundred vehicles, with as many different configurations as there are cells in the human body, moves to the same rhythm. A long green line sidewinding its way up north to a new destiny. The average Vietnamese are simple peasants living in tiny one room hovels with foraged wood slabs for walls and C-ration cardboard for insulation and protection from the elements. Some of the roofs consist of scrounged tin cans from landfills pounded into flat sheets. Calling these little shacks homes would be extremely generous and each one has one or more clay cisterns, large earthen jars, for the collection of water to drink and irrigate meager crops like a row or two of corn. Stray chickens here and there create diminutive dust devils as scratchy feet turn up insects or crumbs. If this were America we're talking Appalachia, poverty to the max. Very bleak and also very beautiful at the same time.

All along the convoy route little children as young as five or six are smoking cigarettes thrown from our passing convoy. They all shout, 'Hey, GI, you give me chop chop." Soldiers in the back of our truck are sitting on wall to wall sand bags to protect against bombs planted in the road and they're trying to peg the little kids with cans of ham and motherfuckers, the most hated C-ration. At first, I thought our soldiers were being kind and giving up some of their rations that they did not want but hell no, they were trying to nail the little urchins. Then I became a little distraught when my driver told me that occasionally they "run over one of 'em." I felt ill. Occasionally someone shoots at a peasant way off in a field. Target practice they call it. Could these people possibly love us, regard us as their salvation? I'm beginning to wonder.

Only the *papa-sans* and the kids smoke cigarettes. *Mama-sans* chew beetle nut which is a small bush that has berries that when chewed have a slightly narcotic effect and ease the pain from bad teeth. Their mouths are a nasty red color and you can see a little gob of the beetle nut under their lip. They're always spittin' the shit like it was chewing tobacco. Yuk!

Along the road, I saw evidence of some industry like brick making, rows of peanut plants being harvested and, of course, rice being dried along the road in huge round woven baskets. Convoy drivers often aim at these, too. I wondered if this was the 'winning the hearts and minds' I'd heard about. Also, I saw men making small boats along the Vam Co Dong River which parallels Hwy 1 to Trang Bang. Near Trang Bang the road split to traverse around a tree that is over one hundred feet tall and about eighteen feet in circumference. Just beneath the crown there was a tremendous ARVN (Army of the Republic of Vietnam or South Vietnam soldiers) guard house facility. After Trang Bang the road becomes Hwy 22 all the way to Tay Ninh and patches of the road are crumbling cement.

Portions of the road had to be travelled very slowly and our approximately one hundred and thirty vehicles were not fired upon. Altogether the trip was enjoyable and checking out our new home and base of operations interesting. The base camp of Tay Ninh is larger than I had imagined but only about one quarter the size of Cu Chi. There is an EM club, PX as well as the 45th Surgical unit or MASH. The layout is very similar to Cu Chi only smaller.

ARVN watchtower before Trang Bang

November 16

Thursday – Second platoon was the very last to reach the new home in Tay Ninh. The first Brigade will follow soon.

The convoy was routine except for one sniper incident just before Trang Bang. The trip took much longer than usual not due to the sniping incident but because the dust was unbearable and reduced vision for everyone in most of the vehicles. Except for the diminutive dust dots that were our eyes we were unrecognizable even to one another. Goggles have never been standard issue. In fact, the only goggles or eye protection I have seen here in country was on tank crews and some of the APC drivers. Our duce and a half had zero sand bags on its deck and the metal was so hot you could only sit on the bench seats along the sides which made us perfect targets for snipers. The reflected heat was even worse.

Taking resupply in the Plain of Reeds

Our new company area is very similar to the one we left behind. We are currently billeted in surplus World War II squad tents that are like ovens. Thank God, the sides can be rolled up. There are no wood floors so when it rains the mud turns to mush and everything reeks of mildew. We will construct new barracks as soon as supply scrounges enough lumber off the docks in Saigon. In the meantime, the buildings transported from Cu Chi are rapidly being reconstructed and put back in service again. The orderly shack, the mess hall and the armor buildings are priority then platoon hooch's.

The province capital of Tay Ninh seems to be much more alive and vibrant when compared to the town of Cu Chi. There are many shops, restaurants and small businesses. As soon as you exit the gate and leave the MP's in the rearview mirror you are in the really quaint tree lined streets. Close by is a huge and ornate temple, which is the Temple of Cao Dia, a religious sect that was founded in 1926 and is a mix of many religious beliefs. Our base camp is in a very beautiful place and has a somewhat mystical and secret feel to it. We can see the Black Virgin Mountain or Nui Ba Den from any place on base and we are surrounded by banana trees and tropical palms that seem to go on forever.

I began working on some stories that might be news worthy and I need to borrow a 35-mm camera until I have the opportunity to purchase one for myself. Someone told me I should lose the spy camera because the frames are too small to capture anything noteworthy.

We have been on alert constantly and the tune up or training mission will begin soon. Apparently, this little operation will be conducted in a place called the Plain of Reeds which is back toward Cu Chi and near the Vam Co Dong river I mentioned earlier. Rumor has it that the operation will be air mobile meaning helicopters. The

Plain of Reeds is primarily waist deep water, or at least the real estate that would be used for helicopter extraction.

Fortunate things are happening for me that I consider extremely good luck. From time to time I think about the pride I have in being a soldier. I love it and nothing is more important to me personally than being the best soldier ever.

November 17

Friday – I'm so mad I could eat fried chicken. My brand-new wrist watch that I was really excited about, the one I purchased with money borrowed from Watson, just fell apart. Crazy. Rust sooner or later gets at everything here in Vietnam but this was ridiculous, not really rust. While in the wing tank shower – actually there is another alternative way to shower and it's what is called by the Army a lyster bag, named so by the guy who designed it. Essentially the bag can be supported on a tri pod and filled with water. Some of the bags have a spigot and you could let the water flow into your helmet or splash the water over your body to cool off and clean yourself. But back to the shower…the gold bezel ring on the watch fell off and rolled from the shower into the dirt outside. I tried to tap the bezel back in place and that's when the sweep second hand fell of inside the crystal. My next time piece will be the dependable GI 24 hour Olive Drab with wrist strap… virtually indestructible as well as water proof.

Interesting possibility for one of my story submissions to battalion: I discovered that our buildings are being put back together by some of our NCO (noncommissioned officers) staff using hand tools captured from the enemy during Operation Barking Sand. I was talking with the guys when Captain Baker happened along so we talked a while. I really like him. He snatched up my 11-mm Minolta spy camera, told me it was crap and offered me one of his own 35-mm cameras to use on the PIO job.

Just another rumor at this point but I heard we may be moving out soon to a place farther north so that means very close to Cambodia, a place where reportedly elements of the 2nd of the 27th Wolfhounds tried to penetrate twice but were pushed back. We'll see.

Captain Baker told me that many of our operations will be helicopter operations while we are in Tay Ninh. By that he meant the UH-1 Army Huey Helicopter. We also have at our disposal the CH-47 Chinook which is a twin rotor machine which is like a moving van used for moving anything imaginable including troops for quick insertion and rapid removal.

No mail from home for the past two nights. Could be due to our relocation.

November 18

Saturday – Captain Baker called me to his hooch this morning. He said, "Dex, I'm going to offer you the best deal ever offered."

"Sir?" I questioned, flummoxed by his forthright statement, then respectfully, "Do tell."

"I am going to move you up to the headquarters element with me. You'll travel with us and stick by the radios. You will carry a .45 caliber pistol and a basic load of about one hundred rolls of film. I want beaucoup pictures of this company in action. You will be my historian."

Well, tickle my ass with a feather. You can imagine how excited I was.

Wow! I was in a celebratory mood alright and really not thinking about jeopardizing my good fortune as I got really wasted on grass tonight. After dark, we were sitting around the squad tent pounding brewskis when one of the guys asked if we all wanted to pass the pipe around. Me, Wagner and another guy Mitch wandered out by the wire and dropped trow and sat down on a three-hole latrine and passed the pipe.

I'm not sure it was good fortune or bad but because I was covering the center hole I got to pull on the pipe goin' both ways and therefore got twice as many tokes as Denny or Mitch. The moon was full overhead and appeared to be racing through the clouds rather than, as usual, the clouds passing over the moon. My scalp, I thought, was going to crawl right off my head. Everything was hilarious and, especially the shower stall in the distance that due to its juxtaposition to a nearby duce and a half in our line of vision, seemed to me be on wheels. My proclamation about a shower on wheels and the metaphysical implication was a subtlety completely overlooked by my grunt buddies but I howled in laughter and Mitch and Denny joined in with peels of uproarious laughter that seemingly went on forever. "Shower on wheels," I slurred, "that's rich, har de har," as the two literally dragged me back to the tent.

Later, back at the tent and rolling in my own vomit where Denny and Mitch had dropped me, I was a very, very sick puppy…in fact I puked my guts, got the dry heaves and experienced a total loss of memory that really frightened me. I could really not recall where I was. It felt as though I had one foot in Nam and the other in the World. I was trippin'. I vomited again and crawled through it on my stomach. I could feel individual particles of food crawling like maggots up my throat. When I came to in the morning I was draped over the tongue of a water trailer just outside the tent and still retching violently.

November 19

Sunday – Whew! Having my guts turn inside out is not something I would like to repeat any time soon. The weed was different and actually my only other time that I can compare last night's episode with was brother Jed's going away party which was pretty lame when compared to last night.

No work or details today so a special thank you to our brass. Henchman called a brief formation and he congratulated us for exemplary behavior in the flawless move and transition to our new home.

I walked over to the battalion and found Specialist 4th class Ehrig, introduced myself and handed him three articles and a roll of film for processing. Ehrig is in charge of PIO's like myself from all companies in the BN. He is a small effeminate guy of a soldier who possibly landed where he has because he wouldna made a good soldier. He said so far, the program has been a disappointment to him because I am the only one to take the assignment seriously and hand in any of the assigned stuff.

Sat around most of the remainder of the day checking and double checking my equipment. Early tomorrow we are going to the field again. My first real operation since the incident with my arm.

November 20

Monday – My first air mobile operation and actually my first time in a Huey except for flying out with the Guidon. But I do recall boarding one during advanced individual Training (AIT). We sat on the flight deck, the Huey lifted straight up about one hundred meters and then set us back down…training over. Anyway, we sat at the air strip in groups of eight about 50 meters apart. The first two lifts departed leaving us choking in our towels.

I was on the third lift, chopper number seven. Good luck, huh? I was nervous because nobody bothers to tell you what to expect. Fuck it, don't mean nuthin.' Anyway, the LZ (landing zone) was cold. Our chopper hovered over the top of the grass giving the impression that we were close to the jungle floor. We were not. I was startled at how far I actually dropped through the tall jungle saw grass before I hit the deck on my knees. The abrupt collision with the ground caused my helmet to collide with the top of my nose and leave a bloody gash. Doc McDaniels landed close to me and we immediately spread out to become part of the 360-degree perimeter around the landing zone to protect the final lift coming in after us.

The last lift in we organized and began moving toward our objective. I was with Captain Baker and two of the captain's RTO's (radio telephone operators) and one medic and a First Lieutenant and his RTO from the artillery battery that were our forward observers to spot and call artillery to support our flank. The heat while bad was not as oppressive as the day I got hit back in the Ho Bo's. I only consumed one canteen of the three I am now carrying.

The PIO job and travelling with the headquarters element sure offers a perspective that was, until now, unknown to me. My experience to this point informs me that most of the grunts out here are unaware of objectives, what we are trying to accomplish (other than searching and destroying and killing VC) and where we are headed on a daily basis. The platoon leaders, of course, know these things because of nightly briefings with Baker but everyone needs to do a much better job of communicating this information to their individual squads and fire team leaders. Now I am privy, through the captain, to the day's objective and the reason why the column's stop so frequently. Whenever the point element encounters anything suspicious like a tunnel or abandoned hooch or part of a base camp the captain sends me forward to check it out and take pictures.

Today I recorded the activities of one of our tunnel rats, a smaller soldier who can easily insert himself into an enemy tunnel. The only items the 'rat' carries are a .45 cal pistol and an Army issue flashlight. Later in the day we ransacked an older VC base camp. It was small, containing one command bunker and five smaller shelter areas.

I now spend most of my time inside the perimeter at night unless the entire company pulls a large ambush. I am also in the regular rotation for radio watch. This involves staying alert and taking sit reps (situation reports) from each of the platoons in Bravo and monitoring the battalion push or frequency and knowing how to respond when something occurs.

No mail tonight.

We received two enemy rifle grenades inside the perimeter tonight. I love being out here, feeling useful. In the middle of our NDP or hard spot, what have you, the headquarters element only occasionally digs in. We huddle close and sleep, wrapped up in our poncho liners. It is cool in the evening and if you sleep with your head inside your poncho liner condensation is created and you wake up soaking wet. After first light and before moving out we often make a small fire to dry our clothes.

We had two beautiful German shepherd dogs and their handlers from the 38th Scout Dog Platoon join us. They will be used to sniff out enemy positions and tunnels. They are incredible animals and even travel well on the helicopters. There have occasionally been dogs wounded in the line of duty and I have heard of at least one who received the Purple Heart.

November 21

Tuesday – The choppers returned early to snatch us off the pick-up zone where only minutes before we had assembled in small staggered groups. Even before the rotors had an opportunity to beat the grass into circular patterns we were all aboard and out of the zone.

The day's activity was an Eagle Flight which is Army speak for flying aimlessly around, fourteen choppers in what is referred to as a stagger left or stagger right formation. The 'birds' are so close at times I could see my buddies on the flight deck of the nearest Huey. The idea is to land and surprise the Viet Cong and goad them into a fire fight.

We swooped into an open area and all of the door gunners opened up, spraying the wood line with automatic machine gun fire as the choppers came in low enough for us to dismount. The noise is outrageously loud and results in confusion…is that our weapons firing or is the enemy engaging? I dropped the approximately four feet to the ground, getting the hang of it. My shins sank into the wet, grassy mud. Glancing to my left I recognized the young soldier and his dog, noticed the frightened look on his face. As we fanned out and headed toward the thick jungle I believed that I was beginning to understand what soldiering was about. We do not do the things we do because we want to or what we fear the Army might do if we do not follow orders. No, we do it because to not do it is to admit that we are less than the men we thought we were. I understand that my thinking is at the lowest end of the spectrum and adds no meaning or purpose to the mission.

There I was, standing up and moving through the tall grass, rifle at the ready, trying to show the guy next to me that I wasn't afraid. But I was. I was scared to death. I believed the firing and explosions were the enemy but it was a 105-mm gun battery softening up the landing zone as we approached and, of course, the door gunners doing their thing. The coordination of everything together is impressive.

We humped through the heat of the day in fields and under thick jungle canopy that offered relief from the heat but visibility was, at times, diminished. The jungle possesses an almost hypnotic, mesmerizing and seductive quality created by the sun reaching the jungle through the shimmering leaves and splashing on the jungle floor. Not paying attention, not being alert and not focusing can surely cost you your life especially if you are not keeping an eye out for trip wires and booby traps.

"Sniffer" dog and handler

The afternoon heat engulfed us as we settled into a night defensive position and took resupply. I hitched a ride back to Tay Ninh, cleaned up and headed over to Battalion to find Captain Richardson and hand in some stories I had been putting together. One involved the scout dog sniffing out a tunnel that was about to be entered by the 'rat'. Another showed Bravo troops fording a chest high stream with M-16's and other gear suspended above their shoulders. It is not my job to work on given assignments but submit interesting narrative about life in the field. I thought of my journalism professor back at Hillsdale, a crusty old dude named Applegate, and knew he'd be proud of me but even back then Applegate probably didn't know me from the dirt on Adam's garage floor.

November 22

Wednesday – Captain Richardson reviewed my submissions and said that I was doing a fine job of representing Bravo Company. "Keep up the fire," he said, which is the Manchu slogan.

Returned to the field and found the headquarters element. I forgot to tell you the names of others in the group. The arty Lieutenant's name is Jeff Dossett and his RTO is a Spec. 4 named David Ruggles. Then there's Jacox who handles the battalion push (frequency) and a Negro E-5 Named Snipes who takes care of all radio traffic between us (the captain) and each platoon. There is also a medic or two and right now they are both Specialist 4th class. One is Doc McAdams, the other is a tall drink of water name of Prince.

I am settling into the routine now, have become accepted, just another one of the guys no longer a full Cherry and I'm really liking the grunts way of life. I do not share this with anybody because I'm not at all sure we're supposed to like what we are doing. Supposed to be back at Tay Ninh around the 26th of the month and remain there until the third of October.

I arrived at the chopper pad at 1430 hours but our departure was delayed 'til ten minutes after six. We arrived at the perimeter just at dusk. Ate some chow and threw my poncho over a log to create a little shelter for myself. This trip I brought an air mattress and the additional comfort is like the difference between Ho Jo's and skid row. The extra weight was worth it. Travelling light beats being weighed down by all sorts of personal shit. I carry a waterproof bag for my writing materials, a stainless mirror for shaving, several razor blades and a tooth brush. You'll probably think this is a little insane but I use the one tooth brush to clean both my M-16 and wash my teeth. There are some luxury's that only medics seem to have like cue tips…some time my ears itch like a sombitch and only one of Doc's magic cue tips will get the job done. Another luxury is something called the sundry box which comes in with resupply. Headquarters divides the treasure between platoons and a representative from each platoon comes to pick up their share. The box contains small packs of four cigarettes, matches, gum and toilet paper. Occasionally cheap cigars, pens and pencils and small tablets to write on are also included. Everyone looks forward to the ritual and a good amount of trade and barter always occurs.

Sat around shootin' the shit until it began to lightly rain and then everyone sacked out and the rotation to monitor the radios began. The radios are the heart of the platoon while we're in the field. We again took rifle grenade fire inside the perimeter and had three WIA (wounded in action) that required a dust-off chopper. When there is shelling of any duration at all and we are not dug in, the only thing you can do is lay there on the ground like dogs and wonder if the next round has your name on it. The rest of the night passed uneventfully.

Typical landing zone (LZ)

Captain Baker relaxing in captured V.C. hammock

Spec 4 Dexter monitoring radios

November 23

Thursday – Had a mad minute this morning... everyone on the perimeter firing weapons on full automatic. Not sure of the purpose unless it is to allow everyone to stand and fire from the hip like a bunch of depraved John Wayne's. It is also important to freshen everyone's ammo from time to time. Also, the adrenalin rush is purposeful as well. Assembled on the PZ and waited for our choppers to lift us out. We flew about aimlessly for about twenty minutes until a likely landing zone was spotted. After touching down, we swept west for about nine hundred meters scaring up two rabbits and a stray pig. We again boarded the choppers and they set us down at artillery Fire Support Base (FSB) Betty. The mess hall sent out a hot Thanksgiving meal. The huge aluminum Mermite hot and cold cans were spaced tactically with ten meters between cans and we filed through and picked up our food. The meal consisted of all we could eat turkey (real) with dressing, potatoes and mixed veggies with apples for desert. We also were inoculated by the medics for something new or perhaps it was an update of a prior shot…we were not told. The base is a hard spot like my earlier mention. Arty moves about from time to time but always digs their gun batteries in to have a protected fire control center. I was able to shave and catch a shower.

An altogether good day. I sat among the company officers and listened to some good-natured ribbing. I was on radio watch early then sacked out. Doc McAdams and I put our poncho halves together – they snap – and made a tent. We talked quietly for a while and Doc offered up some weed – why is it that the medics always seem to be holding? I refused, slept like a baby on my half-inflated air mattress and dreamed a sweet dream about Cindy. Usually my dreams are like cake batter that has been blended on high speed in a Cuisinart but there she was, her sweet face and she was reaching out to me. Could it get any better than this? Yes, of course it could. I could be home but…

November 24

Friday – What a relaxed feeling being in an area that offers a sense of security not afforded when pushing through the boonies. Yes, we still maintain radio watch and normal communication with our own company but while in a FSB the artillery group has responsibility for guarding their own perimeter. Slept until almost eight but there was a restless quality to it like shouldn't I be up and about and being more responsible. Eventually I arose, answered some letters, and cleaned my weapon for an inspection that did not materialize. Ordering an inspection for soldiers who understand the important role that properly functioning weapons plays is pointless anyway. I have not made a point of it to the captain but I have never discussed my carrying a .45 cal pistol since Baker first brought it up.

Several families of Vietnamese were brought to us by the artillery guys this morning. They were found near the wire and brought inside the camp. An interpreter was summoned and when questioned the Vietnamese said they had come to sell cold sodas to the G.I.'s. We can be in the middle of nowhere and kids show up to sell, as they call them, Coca's and sometimes young girls accompany the kids wanting to know if GI want boom boom. Anyway, these situations require constant vigilance. Today was in no way different and the effort paid off. The youngest child had an old pineapple grenade concealed in her tunic and you can only look at it one way…that little baby san was not there to sell boom boom to GI's but wanted to go boom with that grenade. Remember, keep your focus.

Hot chow again today and the medics finished the inoculations and once again I was able to get a shower by using one of the lyster bag set ups I'd mentioned several days back. A slight breeze was welcomed and my torso being wet from the water rapidly became chilled. Once in a while depending on location, the water table is so close to the surface that by using an entrenching tool which is a small metal shovel with a wooden handle we can create a tiny pool and dip helmet's full of water to bathe ourselves.

Sitting around with the rest of the headquarters element I related how as a child my parents and I lived next to the old fart who owned the Almond Joy and

Chuckles brand candy. I do not think they believed me or that the old guy actually owned the company. I told them he'd made a fortune when he sold his brand to Hersey's and that he named his boat the Chuckle. Yeah, right. Now they're calling me Chuckle. How long's that shit gonna go on?

Even though security concerns belong to arty we became concerned and sent out a patrol of our own when movement was reported just outside the perimeter. This happened while I was monitoring the net and because of my inexperience Jacox relieved me.

There is no light pollution out here in the jungle and when views of the heavens are unobstructed the stars are brilliant. The Milky Way is a stunning white ribbon racing across the sky. Back in the world there are millions of persons dwelling in cities who have never had an opportunity to marvel at a night sky. I have not seen a sextant or other instrument for navigation purpose but I know that these instruments measure the angle between any two visible objects (stars or planets).

Navigation here in the Nam is generally performed by officers, platoon leaders etc. and is accomplished by using overlay maps of the terrain in which we operate. The maps were 1:50,000 and divided into 1,000-meter squares and each of these squares has numerical designations both north and south so a patrol, whatever, could pinpoint their exact location. This is important for many reasons one of which is knowing your exact location when calling artillery on (near) your position. Captain Backer is constantly showing us where we are on the map. He is an inspiring leader.

Nobody has mentioned that the mission we are on is the training mission mentioned earlier but it does make sense. The mission has been mainly about learning helicopter maneuvering and operations, boarding and proper deployment, etc.

November 25

Saturday – Up early. Hell, we're always up early. Made some cocoa in my canteen cup by heating water using a small, rolled ball of C-4 which is a compound called plastic explosive. Put a blasting cap in it and you can blow the shit out of anything, bunker, hooch, tunnel, you get the picture. It is very stable and you can light a pea sized ball of the stuff, place it in a can with holes punched in the sides and your water, sitting on top, will boil for cocoa in about ten second. However, beware because in spite of the stability I have heard that a tiny piece of the stuff when set on fire could blow your foot off if you stomped down on it.

We have been hanging out on this little hard spot for goin' on three days and I sense a restlessness in the guys like let's get a move on, get the f*** outta here.

We assembled on the PZ and were in the air within twenty minutes. Waiting for a pick up is the most vulnerable time so when it is possible we deploy security on the flanks and these guys rush to jump on the last bird out. Eagle Flight again and third platoon off-loaded first. The landing zone was hot coming in and there was definitely lead coming up at us, yellow-green tracers zinging around.

We moved out and about forty minutes passed and we heard a brief but loud volley of our own small arms fire. If it had been enemy AK-47's we'd have been able to tell the difference because the 47 makes a distinctly different sound than an M-16. Jacox got the report back that 3rd Heard had encountered two Charlies that were sitting on the edge of an old well eating American C-rations. The Platoon Sergeant named Moore, the one called 'hard core' by his grunts because he'd been in Korea and was an old timer compared with the rest of us, and Lt. Graves shot them both and one of them tumbled into the well. Then, as the rest of the company filed past, each guy fired rounds into the remaining VC. who was slumped beside the well. Finally, when our headquarters element past the enemy combatant he was an unrecognizable pulp, expended lead visible all over the ground next to his remains.

I am now totally accustomed to the heat and able to make the longest hump no matter the amount of weight I'm carrying. And speaking of humping, boy did we ever. I'm not certain how many clicks we made but nearing our night defensive position I could not think about anything except getting resupply and a fresh water trailer. I could barely get one foot in front of the other.

We were supposed to set a company sized ambush patrol tonight but apparently, it was called off. I never heard a reasonable explanation about this so I'm guessing here that since there is no moon that may have had something to do with it. One would suspect that moonlight would be beneficial and maybe that is sound reasoning when considering when you would set the ambush. Imagine one hundred plus guys tripping over each other and trying to obey or practice noise discipline. Any benefit gained by having that many soldiers ready to spring an ambush is lost when considering the noise. The enemy would certainly know that clumsy Americans are on the way and fail to engage. No resupply today so no water and that is a first for me. We drank paddy water with Halazone purification tablets added. Terrible taste but safe at least.

We were doing reconnaissance by fire this afternoon. It is a lazy way of doing the work of clearing a path ahead without really having to cut trail through the thick brush. Reminds me of the mad minute we had yesterday morning. We had a troop who was slightly wounded when hit by frags from an M-79 round. The guy's name is Eitner.

He'll be OK, no dust off. Question: will Eitner get a Purple Heart for this? I think not. By the way an M-79 is a handy weapon called the blooper or bloop tube or thump gun by some of the troops. The effective weapon is a breach loading, huge shotgun that fires a giant 40x46mm round filled with double aught buck shot or high explosive rounds or flechettes (small metal darts). The projectiles do not arm themselves until the round travels thirty meters after leaving the barrel and then it is armed and dangerous.

I awoke this morning with a sore throat. I also mishandled some C-4 and burned my fingers. Not a good day.

November 26

Sunday – Our little training mission has been uneventful and I am beginning to think that battalion sent us to places that intelligence indicated we would be relatively safe and not make contact in order to pursue training that will benefit us later in the long haul.

Captain Baker hit the deck this morning in his always happy, always effervescent mood. He was singing and whistling words and the tune for Eric Burden and The Animals, *We've Got To Get Out of This Place, If It's The Last Thing We Ever Do*. After a few moments, the entire group began singing along. I did not tell this to Al but since I have been travelling with him and the headquarters element I truly believe the odds of me and all of us getting out of this place alive are greatly advanced. I have never been around an officer who is so sure of what he is doing, has the confidence to will us through.

We had a time for departing the pick-up zone at 0830 hours. Captain Baker told us that from now on we would ride the first ship in on all of our operations and the last ship out. This won't always work effectively but that's the plan. I like the plan. If exciting things occur, then I will be right there.

We flew about for a while, circled back and landed at hill #15 a place we had travelled through earlier in the operation. Again, there was nothing of note going on. We headed back to the pick-up zone and had to wait for almost forty-five minutes for the lift ships to come in. Report had it that several of the choppers spotted unattended enemy weapons in a clearing and went in to check it out. It could have been a set-up, an ambush but it was not. Unfortunately, the PZ was in the middle of the Plain of Reeds and was waste deep water and we had to stand about and unprotected until the choppers came in.

Back in Tay Ninh there was a huge party over at Battalion mess. Outstanding! Fried chicken and unlimited beer and soda. The officer core circulated freely among the men. Great time.

Got a fruit cake from my Nana and cookies from my mother all of which I shared with my squad mates. Mom and dad also sent a portable transistor radio. I can listen to it when we're in the rear and then I'll have to store it in my foot locker which I can lock.

November 27

Monday – Wrote letters and mailed film home. Had several beers, ate chow and got my gear ready… we're trippin' again…this time into the Bo Loi Woods. We leave tomorrow for this somewhat familiar area. Officially the area is called a wood but actually it is a series of five operational rubber plantations which I explained earlier. The place holds much danger and contains many VC base camps ant tunnel complexes. The 320 VC Battalion and elements of the 271st and 273rd VC Regiments have been reportedly dug in on the northern border of one of the plantations. The Wolfhounds have seen plenty of action there so we need to be prepared.

Very boring day really. I've had a cold catch up to me and it has laid me low. In the rear for a day or so I can relax. If we were out on an operation it would be a different story. I was invited over to Brigade to meet with some of their PIO staff but I decided to flake off. My contact was an RTO from Battalion named Allen. Apologies Allen.

No mail today but six letters yesterday, two from Cindy. Writing letters to my new wife of only two months' is difficult for me. I shouldn't tell her so much about what I am doing. In fact, we are strictly forbidden to mention things like our location or upcoming plans and I feel ridiculous using words like darling and sweetheart or honey. And as to mail, I feel a bit disturbed because I have received so little mail from my family. In fact, not a single letter from my brother or sister.

Three of the first four articles I'd written up and submitted were turned down at the battalion level. I must learn by experience exactly what will be worthy of acceptance. The market for this type of writing is limited due to the repetitious nature of our mission which is seeking out and destroying the enemy. I interviewed a medic on the last operation and this guy had a freaky thing happen. He was tending a wounded grunt when an AK round entered between the lining of his helmet and his head. The round miraculously zinged and rattled around and then exited the other side of his helmet. Something like that depending on my presentation may work.

An interesting note regarding medics is that occasionally you will encounter a Doc who is a conscientious objector. Apparently, some of these guys have achieved a kind of non-combatant status because they possess strongly held beliefs which are rooted in their religion – or so they say – about killing. Our medics all carry M-16's or the .45 cal pistol and I have personally witnessed some unbelievably heroic behavior when our medics rush to the aid of a fallen comrade with complete disregard for their own safety. The rest of us have found cover or are hanging back, not assaulting, and in many cases not returning fire when we observe a medic rushing forward to help a soldier in trouble. These guys are truly hero's.

And while I'm carryin' on allow me to share another thought with you. I do not believe that folks back home have any idea what this war is all about. They only care that because we are here they do not have to be. And I will tell you that I'm pretty sure that most of the civilians back home could not make the grind that we do every day nor would they be able to understand the pride that we possess as soldiers. They would not be capable of understanding the reality of being in the United States one day and then ten thousand miles away the next day and in the middle of an alien landscape, being fired upon. Clean sheets and room service one day and mud holes the next. They would be incapable of making the transition from having everything they ever needed to learning to do without. Without security, without their wives, without showers or personal possessions other than those they could carry on their backs. I do not think that they could learn how to endure mud and snakes and mosquitoes for weeks at a time. The average person from my past would shiver in the cold of the monsoon rain and swelter in the choking humidity and probably not survive slogging through thorn-studded vegetation carrying a 40-pound pack and a radio and a weapon in their hand. And finally, would they be able to learn as I am learning how to maintain their humanity and their dignity while fighting a war against an enemy they cannot see but must try to understand and respect.

November 28

Tuesday – Today was special. Today frightened me and made me tremble and I will never be the same again. Today was my first serious combat experience.

At dusk, the company was on line behind two APC's (armored personnel carriers). APC's are unlike any other armored vehicle in our arsenal. They are huge square boxes with a rear ramp-like door that folds outward and down to allow troops who live and fight from them to have access. They have evolved into huge equipment storage lockers because it can be dangerous to be inside. They are tread driven and many operators ride up top. The usual armament is a 50 caliber and an M-60 machine gun mounted topside. Grunts often refer to their vehicles as tracks.

On line and just behind the tracks and inhaling diesel fumes we proceeded into a dense thicket as the APC's began to flatten the vegetation. A fierce firefight ensued and green tracer rounds from enemy AK's were everywhere like a mess of angry hornets.

The entire company moved forward and into the woods laying down a devastating base of fire, our red tracer rounds mixing it up with the enemy fire. There were extremely loud explosions and detonations. One of the tracks hit a land mine and rolled forward out of its tread. Lt. Miller and his RTO, Allen, had their legs blown apart by a booby trap. The lieutenant had been leader of my platoon for only two weeks. His wounds were much more severe than Allen's. A dust off was called in and Miller had to be carried to the chopper's flight deck because his femur was sticking straight out through the fleshy part of his leg. The fire fight continued through the dust-off activity, my company exchanging volleys with the enemy through the thick brush never knowing for sure if we'd hit any of them or not.

Time was short, darkness was approaching rapidly and we had to withdraw and abandon the track so we formed a makeshift perimeter and hunkered down for the night. The air was humid and thick with the acrid smell of gunpowder and cordite. VC torched the track and stripped the M-60 machine gun. We maintained a 100% alert at every position around the perimeter and our positions were continually probed by the enemy throughout the night. A battery of 105 mm guns was called up from Tay Ninh to fire harassing and interdicting salvos around us for most of the night and steady popping filled the night as illumination rounds arrived overhead. Bright phosphorus fireballs swung beneath the flare's little parachutes and the constantly shifting shadows made seeing the enemy impossible. I prayed for the long interminable night to end. First light was welcome and the enemy withdrew.

Moving cautiously back into the wood line we came upon the personnel carrier we had been forced to abandon the previous night. The M-60 was gone. The woods were trashed and looking down I saw a soldiers' headgear, picked it up and, standing there, I read the words the troop had penned on his helmet cover, *don't shoot me I bleed*. His body was close by. He'd been hit in the head by a single round of AK fire, fallen from the track and been run over and was missing one leg below the knee, one arm at the elbow and an ear. A little later we found some fortified enemy positions but no bodies.

Later in the day forward progress was interrupted when our lead element was ambushed. It was over quickly. Two killed in action (KIA) and one wounded, all by the machine gun the VC had captured. As I rushed forward I encountered two medics working feverishly to save the wounded soldier. One medic held a saline drip. I reached into one of my ammo pouches and retrieved the 35 MM camera and as I peered through the view finder to frame a shot I felt like a completely detached voyeur. I counted thirteen wounds on the soldier whom I did not recognize. He had been shot through and through at extremely close range. One round had plowed from the knee up toward his groin and opened a wound that reminded me of a hot dog cooking on a barbecue grill. One thumb was dangling by a sinewy thread of skin and the soldier moved his hand back and forth transfixed by the movement of his thumb. A medic jammed a Morphine syrette into the guy's leg and he was feeling no pain. He said, oh, look, my thumb's been shot off. He didn't make it. I do not know why I wasn't freaked out.

The dust-off chopper flared just before touching down in the clearing and Captain Baker and I clutched our head gear tightly, turned our backs into the rotor-wash and stooped low. Dust blasted our faces and collected in the creases of our soiled fatigues. When we turned around, the poncho that had been covering the dead troop had blown away on the wind leaving the soldier exposed. Flies were already at the head wound, depositing fat, white larvae… maggots. I stared dully, contemplating the large black fly crawling slowly through the thick viscous fluid oozing from the hole in the soldier's head. This was the first KIA that I'd seen up close and I was a little queasy and said to no one in particular, "why doesn't somebody cover him up?" Silence…and then one of the grunts standing there holding the stock of his M-16 and pressing the flash suppressor into the toe of his jungle boot said, "what fer, he dead, ain't he?"

After another exceptionally long day we formed a night defensive position, one more to our liking and one which could be better defended. We took resupply – hot chow, sent out listening posts and an ambush patrol and got some sleep. Tomorrow we will take up the chase once again.

Dust-off medevac summoned to pick up one KIA and the wounded soldier with the multiple wounds

November 29

Wednesday – Strengthened by a fitful night of rest we prepared to assault the wood line. Three tanks were tasked to the battalion and we hunkered behind the monstrous machines and rested while F-4 Phantom jets came up on station, swooped low over the jungle tree tops, and dropped canisters of napalm on the suspected enemy redoubt. The jungle erupted in black sooty smoke roiled with yellow brown flames. The stench of the burning jelly and foliage reached us and with the guns from the tanks repeatedly firing into the jungle we advanced through the area of yesterday's battle. Once again, the enemy chose not to engage leaving no evidence of his presence except for the blood-stained shirt held in Captain Baker's hand. After an inch by inch search of the area we came away empty handed.

The brass informed us that we had done an outstanding job so why do we, the ones out here on the tip of the spear, feel like we have again had our hats handed to us?

November 30

Thursday – After yesterday's unsuccessful assault behind the tanks we rendezvoused with a company of personnel carriers and rode them into yet another FSB (fire support base), this one named Fire Support Base Wood. Not even choking dust failed to tamp down our good mood caused by hitching a ride on the tracks and the more distance we put between us and the previous assault the better we felt.

Inside the base I joined up with my close buddies from 2nd Platoon, second squad. We lopped coconuts from trees near the perimeter, macheted off the tops to drink the sweet milk and eat the white meat. We then halved the shells and scooped water from the shallow holes to pour over one another and for the moment, at least, life was sweet.

The company First Sergeant, name of Clare, came to the field tonight with the resupply ship and brought us up to speed on how nicely the new company area was coming together. Some units keep their First Shirt with them in the field. Ours has been busy squaring away our new digs while overseeing construction of the new mess hall, the orderly room and the rest of the structures necessary to sustain the company whether in the field or in the rear.

Lots of light hearted joking in small groups and then, with the darkness comes a quieting of all our activities. Headquarters snapped poncho halves together and made small tents and then except for monitoring the radios everyone got some pretty restful sleep. It sprinkled for a while and then rained heavily. I was high and dry on my air mattress but I heard a good deal of cursing from those near me who had chosen to not carry their air mattresses. Flattened C ration boxes did not offer much protection from the soaked ground.

December 1

Friday – A new month...new guys arrive, others leave... more days blacked out on everyone's short-timers calender. Time marches on.

I've not said as much about the inspiring beauty of Vietnam as I should. Since there are very few cities of size in the south of Vietnam, other than Saigon, the best descriptive adjective for the country that I have, to date experienced, is beaucolic. Gentrification is an inappropriate word and does not apply to most of the country. The word provincial seems more apropos. In the north, there is the large capital city of Hanoi, home to Ho Chi Minh.

Also in the north is Haiphong and Hue City which is considered the cultural gem of the country, seat of education and university but that city sits below the DMZ. Obviously, I have not seen any of these. The area in which

I find myself is what would be called country or farmland back home. The country seems backward but a fairer term here would be quaint. If the country were an artist's palette it could not be large enough to hold all the colors one experiences. The vegetation, the jungles and rivers, the clouds and skies, and the blood, oh, yes, the blood, all fill and overpower one's vision. I never imagined that there could be so many different colors of blood. Sometime there is red blood and sometime depending on the volume of it on the ground, blood can appear very black, more onyx, the color of my enemy's eyes. Oxygen content in the blood also makes a difference.

The flag of South Vietnam is also very colorful. I learned something interesting about the flag of the country's people who have always been at war either with the Japanese or the French before us. The history of the flag is much more complex but simply put the flag is a field of yellow which represents the country's people. There are three parallel red stripes that run the length of the flag and represent the unification of the three main regions of Vietnam, north, central and south. The red of the stripes is also representative of blood spilled. But enough of the badly instructed history lesson.

Captain Baker told us in the headquarters element that he has volunteered half of the company to work alongside the mechanized company to make another sweep of the Bo Loi Woods. Did I mention the strategic importance of the Bo Loi, Ho Bo Woods and the Iron Triangle? The Triangle was an area controlled by The Viet Minh during the French Colonial period and still to this day is owned by the VC. It is important for us to destabilize this enemy power base because it is a primary staging area for attacks on Saigon. The rubber plantations and the Ho Bo Woods border the triangle on the west side.

The entire area is part of Bin Duong Province and covers an area of more than eighty square miles.

Anyway, I was pissed at the captain because I thought we would be kickin' back at the fire base but no such luck. The second half of the company got the call to venture out and secure two tanks that, due to their weight, broke through the surface crust and mired down. We established a perimeter for the night on an old no longer serviceable piece of asphalt road and settled in to protect the tanks.

Six enemy mortar rounds preceded by a single rocket propelled grenade walked across our perimeter but we did not take any casualties. The initial explosions gave me a real start and I began to crawl about. I do not have an explanation for why I would feel like anywhere is better than where I find myself at such times, panic maybe. Finally, I ended up in Lt. Dossett's hole. Some time I see behind the Lieutenant's eyes and see his fear but not this night. He was sound asleep.

The other half of the company, the half that was out with Bobcat Charlie, the mechanized outfit, had to dust off five guys that were slightly wounded but still required evacuation to the rear.

December 2

Saturday – The day began with a sweep in the direction that we believed the mortar rounds and the RPG had come from. Along the way we encountered a distinct pattern where the earth had first been disturbed and then replaced suggesting grave sites. With the headquarters group standing by Snipes dug in the loose earth and uncovered three small bundles, obviously, VC bodies. I say obviously because number one there would not be Americans or US personnel buried out here and number two, the bodies were wrapped in light green, transparent poncho liner or maybe it was parachute cloth. The graves were fresh as were the bodies and the stench was overpowering. We unwrapped the first of the bodies, a child. We did this to establish a body count for battalion though the unwrapping seemed unnecessary and rather macabre. On the second body, a slightly older male I observed an ornate gold ring and tried to remove it from the swollen finger but could not. Someone mentioned that cutting the finger off was an option. I did not consider the option nor did I cut off the finger. We had never encountered or participated in war crimes or atrocities nor had we witnessed such behavior in our sister battalions. We reburied the cadavers and moved on.

Later in the day one of the personnel carriers ran over a land mine and shrapnel sprayed up the side of the vehicle slightly wounding several of the soldiers who were riding on top. They complained of deafness and ringing in their ears. One of our Doc's referred to exposure to repetitive concussive events, detonations and explosions as an occupational hazard and something that can cause a malady known as Tinnitus which is a constant ringing in the ears because the ear drum has been traumatized.

Presently I'm feeling pretty low! Two colored soldiers I know from moving past them on the trail were shot and when I went forward I saw them lying in pools of their own blood. Firms was the name of the one who was pretty messed up with multiple gunshot wounds. The other was KIA. Firms told me the first night he came into our squad hooch, alone and frightened, that nothing bad was going to happen to Bravo Company while he was with us because he believed in God and prayed every night and his mamma raised him up Christian.

We captured (found) an AK-47 today. Some of our grunts trade for these highly prized artifacts. Beats me how they'd get 'em back to the States and I have never seen one of our guys using one of them in a combat situation.

Very surprised that we did not get probed or receive any mortar rounds tonight. If the enemy was observing us, and chances are good that they were, they would have noticed that our perimeter was small, undermanned and deployed around the edges of a very small opening with jungled area everywhere. We experienced an extremely heavy as well as lengthy downpour. Rain dripping steadily off the rim of our helmets made observing or seeing almost impossible. We were vulnerable. I had sent my poncho in on an earlier resupply extraction along with everyone else, but I kept my shelter half and though I slept on the mud soaked ground I was still comfortable. The shelter half kept me dry but it was very cold and I was not at all popular. Someone even murmured, "Dexter, yer gonna pay fer this," followed by chuckles.

We received some spotty intel from battalion so we suspected that we may be close to a large VC base area or redoubt. All the more reason to suspect getting hit. 100% alert all through the night.

December 3

Sunday - Today we found the (a) VC base camp. The personnel carriers operating in the area cleared a pick-up zone for us by running several trees to ground and then dragging them aside. Determining the size of the camp was difficult. We started dragging bags of rice, cooking utensils, hospital supplies and articles of clothing to the clearing where a helicopter could extract them. In time, we uncovered a vast tunnel system with fighting positions connected by numerous trenches. I crawled into a small bunker that had already been checked for booby traps and mines but the experience was still a little unsettling.

The complex also contained what appeared to be a mess hall that had a corrugated metal roof. One wonders how all of this 'stuff' gets out here so far away from villages and towns, muleback or bicycle I suppose. There were also sleeping quarters, latrines and showers. Obviously, this place could have accommodated a battalion sized operation or larger. We found no documents or other intelligence of use to us.

We set up for the night and I prepared to return to Tay Ninh to visit the Battalion and the writing staff but missed the flight and will go tomorrow.

December 4

Monday – Caught the early morning Chinook to Tay Ninh after it had picked up our water trailer, Starlight scopes and other miscellaneous gear which would not be carried by the troops today. Something happened that is not all that unusual though. We did not fly straight in to Tay Ninh but diverted to FSB Wood and set down while the pilots and crew checked the ship for newly acquired bullet holes. Occasionally our helicopters pick up sniper rounds. Today I was not aware of any such occurrences but I have been on choppers either heading into a landing-zone (LZ) or out of a pick-up zone (PZ) when rounds have zinged right through the opening of the flight deck without anyone being hit. I'm sure I've not mentioned this but riding on the choppers many troops sit on their helmets because it enhances their chances of not catching a stray bullet in the rear end.

From FSB Wood the Chinook settled down in Dau Tieng which is east of Tay Ninh City, still in our AO (area of operation) and near the Saigon River with yet another rubber plantation, The Michelin. I felt like I was experiencing a Greyhound bus ride back in the World, one that stops at every podunk town along the route before you ever get to the destination you were trying to reach. So, there I sat along with Snipes by two old buildings by the side of the air strip that had a look reminiscent of buildings bombed in the Second World War, a place I have heard referred to as French Fort. Soon a convoy saddled up and was pulling away. I shouted out, "which way? and when the leader yelled back, Tay Ninh we jumped aboard with some grunts from one of our sister brigades and made it back around chow time after suffering another dusty jouncing ride.

Snipes and I stopped by the barber shop next to the PX...first trim I've had since being in Country. Neither of us had bathed is some time and our filthy hair really resisted the brush and comb.

Spent the evening getting squared away, writing to Cindy and listening to her most recent tape. Beers with Stansberry but no shower yet and, I smell as my father would say, as though I'd been living in a goat's nest.

Think I'll begin growing a Manchu moustache tomorrow. No, check that...how 'bout right now. By the way, my weight is dropping and I feel terrific, best shape of my life.

A word about the Starlight scope: Each of our platoons had one of these scopes so four per company, roughly sixteen per infantry battalion. The technology was developed during the 1930's. The scope weighs around seven pounds and can be mounted on a weapon such as an M-16 but we always hand hold them. The scope gathers or depends on ambient light (moonlight) rather than infrared and increases captured light by 20,000 lumens. The image viewed through the scope has an eerie yellow green cast and to see enemy troops advancing on your position is very spooky.

December 5

Tuesday – Cindy's birthday today. Do I get a pass for not sending a card that would not have gotten there on time? I wrote a letter expressing my love. She never writes anything about the frightening side of her thoughts like, "I'm so afraid for you, worry about you." I know she must experience such thoughts though. I did receive a letter, a typed letter, several weeks back that was so touching that I cannot fully explain the letter's effect on me. What melancholy, what longing. Most people have probably never experienced such a wounding of the heart. A similar feeling might be like the feeling of getting 'dumped' by a girl and I have plenty of experience there. How is it possible that love and hurt can sometimes share the same space? The letter was typed on onion skin paper. I keep it tucked safely in the back of my diary. Her words had such a profound effect on me because I have rarely had anybody express such feelings of love for me – ever. Why is it that I find little trouble answering her letters' feelings with my own while we are so removed from one another but when I am next to her I choke up and cannot squeak out a single word.

I turned in some of my writing to Ehrig. He totally tore them apart saying they were short on anything news worthy, long on bull. I could have strangled the little REMF office pogue. Just so you know, pogue is a pejorative term for a non-combatant military jerk-off and that's what he has become in my mind. He is the kind of soldier that rotates back to the States and fills listeners with his tales of daring-do having never seen combat or heard a single shot fired in anger.

I was also shown the results of all of the photographic negatives that I turned in. Battalion is, so far, satisfied. I was not. Here's an interesting note, though. Many of my exposures had so many line streaks in the exposures when printed that I wondered. A guy in the lab over at battalion told me that the streaks were caused by detonations, something to do with electrical discharge, I believe he said. Could that be right? Anyway, he actually suggested that I try to snap the shutter a bit further from the action. I actually stood up in the middle of a fire fight the other day to get a better shot. I was framing a shot of PFC Ruggles calling artillery in on our position when we were in the middle of a hot, landing zone.

Generator broke down tonight so we were completely in the dark in the squad tent drinking beer and doing a sing along to Mitches guitar. A terrible wind came through and almost blew down the squad tent and because we could not hear a thing we all sacked out.

Earlier in the day I'd paid 60 P (piasters, South Vietnam currency under noncommunist control of the country. 100 piastres equal one dong – don't laugh, or roughly a dollar) for a new ball cap and it got completely soaked through. Ruined. Fuck it, don't mean a thing… besides, military ball caps are really bad.

December 6

Wednesday – Today was a complete zero. Safe inside the base camp. No bunker or radio watch, no details, no KP and no convoy duty. Just lazed around all day. I could have explored the base but decided against that too. I get enough humpin' when we're in the jungles and paddies.

This must be almost laughable to folks back home who envision Nam combat roles to be just like the narrative in a dusty old Second World War II book. No way. There are, nonetheless, predictable patterns in base camp and in the boonies, as well; the menu is the same every day, extended periods of boredom for the main course interrupted by horrific side dishes of violence punctuated with copious amounts of blood and then death. It's all ala carte served on a bed of greens. The same can be said about the beauty and serenity of the pastoral scenes we are incorporated into as we roll through the country side on convoy or fly above in green metal machines. It is a never ending, short lived and momentary narrative that can be coopted by death at any time. The Grim Reaper is not a particular task master, I shit you not.

Drank beer with my old mates in Second Platoon plus Doc McAdams and McGuire. Doc and I messed around with an old reel to reel portable tape recorder that he'd found, tried to get it to function and then I flaked out under my mosquito netting. Is it even possible that a simplistic, gauzy material could give me a better sense of security than a Linus Van Pelt blanket? I don't know.

I received a Christmas box from Cindy today. She sent me a Santa Clause candle wrapped in tinfoil which seemed a bit unusual. Maybe she intended for me to light the candle and fashion a hat out of the foil because that's about how crazy being in this place is. In a more serious bent, however, I realized the thoughtfulness of her gesture because I know how she loves candles, always had them around her apartment back on McKee Street in Wyoming, Michigan, when I first met her. Oh, how wonderful it would be to spend this Christmas with her, some kind of Twilight Zone moment, just a fantasy. I think of her constantly. Too many thoughts like that, I'm afraid, leaves a door open to melancholia.

December 7

Thursday – Ehrig called me to one of the hooch/offices over at battalion. He wanted to discuss the first batch of my photos that I'd submitted. I was not satisfied at all. They'd been either poorly washed or the fixer solution was old and tired. The guy working in the lab also took the liberty to crop them. The result was that I felt my art had been stepped on, the photographs had lost the effect that would have pleased me. Ehrig was, for once, kind and tried to offer helpful hints, told me that two had been forwarded to Stars & Stripes newspaper. We will see.

Prepared to move out. We are to convoy over to a small village that sounds like San Dien (I may have that wrong but phonetically that's what the place sounds like … French, maybe?). We're going out there to provide security for battalion doctors and medics while they administer hygiene, shots, dentistry and general care for children and adults, some of whom come in from the countryside. The service is called MEDCAP which stands for Medical Civil Action Program. The program is sometimes called 'Winning the Hearts and Minds' but I wonder how this simple gesture could have a benefit while convoy soldiers take pot shots at farmers and water boo along the roads between villages.

We did experience a light-hearted moment along the way and as soldiers will do while playing or 'smokin' and jokin' as the slang has it, we laughed until we almost peed our pants. McGuire wanted to capture the rest of us riding on the bed of the duce and a half. He backed up a tad too far to get us all in the picture with his Kodak instamatic and fell right on his bum in the middle of the street. The small children lining the convoy route – many of them smoking and begging chop chop laughed uproariously.

McGuire had to sprint to catch up and avoid being struck by the truck behind us.

The afternoon was exceptionally warm and while many of the guys played with the children I tucked up under our truck and read Shakespearian Sonnets. San Dien is at the base of the Black Virgin Mountain and we can see the radio antennae on top where there is a listening post.

Back inside the wire at Tay Ninh for chow. No perimeter guard for me and the radios are down. If the Captain needs me or anyone else in the headquarters element he sends a runner from the orderly room.

Supposed to kick off a new operation tomorrow but no briefing so far.

December 8

Friday – Assembly in the company street in front of the orderly room. Everyone helps the guy next to him shoulder his ruck and check that things are in order and tied down properly. Boarded duce and a half trucks for the ride to the air strip to wait for the choppers to pick us up. There was another unit on deck so we drank Cokes sold to us by Vietnamese kids and waited to get lifted out. We've been told that we will not receive resupply tomorrow night due to the rough terrain and thick jungle we will be operating in. Supposedly we will be out until the 20th and then back for a Christmas break.

The lead chopper dropped a yellow smoke grenade to mark the landing zone for the next flight of choppers to follow and the tall grass immediately caught fire. The rotor wash from our chopper spread the fire so when we landed our immediate concern was swatting flames with the towels that we normally wear around our necks.

We are in an unusual area that we do not recognize. The sparse fields are dotted with extremely tall grass and spindly hardwood trees that have a sort of spotty camouflage look to them. They remind me of Sycamore trees from back in the World. I do not understand just why we could not take resupply in this area but that is another proposition altogether. We have recently taken to making up squad bags containing items we'd rather not carry but like to have with us at night. These bags would normally come out to us on resupply and are a luxury because they contain extra insulated poncho blankets, waterproof ponchos and air mattresses. We should be OK without the extra items tonight because we are in a very dry area. I do not believe I have ever addressed the temperature swing or disparity between daytime and night time. The days (as mentioned) are real barn burners, the nights by comparison can get in the 50's to 60's and make your teeth chatter especially after your fatigues have sweat through and through all day. Winds are normally calm but when they blow it increases the chill.

Captain Baker, while all business, knows how to keep it light. He cautions us to stay alert because we are metaphorically knocking on brother Charlie's back door. According to our nav maps and topo's several objectives will come within a hundred meters of the border with Cambodia in the next week. We are basically acting like bait, dangling ourselves in front of Sir Charles nose trying to entice him into nibbling. We are fully aware of the danger. The area we are operating in daily sits astride the Ho Chi Minh Trail, the major resupply route from North Vietnam all the way down to Saigon. In places, the trail is broad enough and hard enough to support vehicular traffic. Other places the enemy pushes bicycles laden with ordinance. On occasion, we have captured some of these bicycles and, at first, scratched our heads trying to figure what the long pole extensions were coming off one of the handle bars. Then it made sense, one hand on the seat and the other on the extended pole to guide the loaded down bicycle along the trail.

We use Operation Rolling Thunder, Air Force, Navy and Army air corps planes to repeatedly bomb the Trail and disrupt the supply lines. As quickly as we bomb the route the enemy, with help from villagers, reestablishes the trail. I have learned that one Gook pushes his bicycle with its load, maybe a single rocket round, all the way from north of the Demilitarized Zone (DMZ) down inside the Iron Triangle or to the Saigon area and then makes the return trip.

For the first time, we are digging deeper three-man holes and chopping trees for overhead cover. As we work on these new tasks we remind ourselves of danger nearby. We have unsubstantiated rumors that the enemy has larger guns, maybe artillery pieces in this area and perhaps tanks across the border in Cambodia. If that is true we must assume that air bursts in these trees could be very dangerous.

50% sleep and 50% vigilant tonight. We will be hatting up, moving out at 1000 hundred hours tomorrow. Charlie Company will lead and we will follow as flank element.

December 9

Saturday – Up at first light. Ate C-rats and began the process of saddling up and as corny as that refrain sounds it is used with regularity for getting everyone on the move. But first we performed the ritual of smashing cans or any vessel that the enemy could use to fashion a booby trap or explosive device and throw all refuse and trash to the bottom of the holes and then fill them. Snipes performed this duty with flair by smoothing both fox holes with slightly raised mounds. He then cut several branches from nearby bushes and I watched curiously as he fashioned two crude crosses and placed one at the head of each of the holes. The mock graves drew chuckles from the rest of the group and we joked about what the VC might be thinking as they unearthed our garbage.

Humping through the heat of the day caused Charlie Company to request an emergency stop. Apparently, they had nonexistent water management or a lack of discipline because they had guys running out of water and dropping like flies. Choppers had to fly out and drop jugs of water so Charlie Co. could fill canteens. The Battalion Commander who was flying overhead in his OH-23 observation helicopter was pissed. I do not know this for certain and Captain Baker said nothing so this is only supposition. I suspect Tropic 6, the Division commander was livid because Charlie Company running out of water put the days operation seriously behind schedule.

A side note: Commanders are designated by or assigned the number 6. Therefore, the division commander is Tropic 6. The Battalion Commander (in our case) is Manchu 6 and my company commander is Manchu Bravo 6. Captain Baker's RTO's, his radio operators, are referred to as Xray's.

Late in the day after resuming our forward movement we encountered an abandoned VC base camp. Sometime the enemy wants you to believe his base camp is abandoned so they will make their hat, split. And then again, he, Charlie, may stand and fight. The enemy pretty much determines when the battle will be engaged.

Having encountered no resistance and because the camp held nothing of interest we moved into our night defensive position earlier than usual. We again dug in, each hole chest deep to hold three of us. I was impressed because Captain Baker dug much of the hole himself and never complained. He was demonstrating leadership by, in effect, saying I can do this as well. We all sat around panting and sweating profusely.

After dark when all the LP's and ambush patrols were set in place and we, headquarters, sat close together monitoring the radios. Stockman and the Captain were relating the war story to the rest of us about how they received wounds when Baker rushed an entrenched enemy position. I've been told by others, principally my buds from second platoon that Baker is crazy but I say fearless and there is a difference but we may be splitting hairs and no matter what you call it my own keen observation is that every action the captain takes is calculated very carefully.

December 10

Sunday – Today when we moved out we left an element behind on the small perimeter we had established. We have not done this at any previous time. We had been humping for about twenty minutes when we were ordered to take a break in place. We hunkered down to wait further orders from higher. Some genius decided against the move which then necessitated sending a patrol sized group back to police up our bed rolls and other equipment and bring the remainder of the company up to our location.

While waiting on the order to move out Captain Baker accidentally jiggled some vines where we were reclining and immediately we were covered by snapping, biting ants assaulting our position. The ants are vicious, red and about an eighth of an inch long and the particular species bends large leaves in an oblong ball that can be about six or more inches in diameter that forms their nest. The ball or nest contains thousands of the sizeable devils that when disturbed go into some sort of defensive frenzy. Capt. Baker resorted to a frontal assault using mosquito repellant and spraying it like a flame thrower band lighting the repellant stream with his zippo. The rest of us were ordered to take up the assault and attacked with sticks and branches from the flank and continued the bombardment from above with more sticks and branches. The ants were vanquished and the diversion had everyone in stitches.

We are mindful that we have had no enemy contact for some time now. And must stay vigilant.

Our journey today was long and arduous through mostly open dry fields. There just aren't any inhabitants in this area, no green or even the hint of an oasis like condition and absolutely no water that would sustain farming or agrarian behavior. Anyone encountered out here would be considered enemy even if they had not fired upon us. Much later in the day, along toward sun down we entered another seemingly dry area crisscrossed by older rice paddy dikes.

We began to dig in but the water table was so close to the surface of the ground that the shallow depressions of our prone holes immediately filled with water. It was necessary for our protection to place the holes parallel to the raised mound of the dikes. Our perimeter was very close to Cambodia, maybe one hundred meters, some of us closer, some farther depending where the positions were on the perimeter. Headquarters element was set in at an intersection of several of these dikes that formed a geometrically square grid. There was a huge ant mound about ten feet tall and a tree grew out of one side of the mound or nest which afforded us some shade. The mounds when empty – and many are – make good defensive features because enemy small arms cannot penetrate them.

I pulled my stint on the radio bathed in the light of a full moon that rose through black skeletons of leafless trees on the far side of the open field. Alone and watching over the slumbering forms of my fellow infantrymen I had thoughts of home and how I missed it and how much I had to return to, how I needed to survive this shit so that I could go home. I was relieved by Ruggles who plopped down next to the radios, his time to watch and listen, to protect sleeping comrades. I returned to the long running mound that was the dike and stretched my length along it. Jacox snored gently on the ground next to the water filled hole.

I must have fallen asleep immediately because I missed the warning of incoming. With the first impact, I was alert and when I raised my head above the dike I could see the impacts as the mortar rounds walked across the inside of the perimeter toward us. A rocket propelled grenade sizzled overhead, a fiery yellow plume trailing behind. A sudden impact brought a huge tree crashing inside the perimeter. I panicked when I realized the impact rounds were headed straight for me and Jacox. I crawled twenty meters to the protection of the ant mound but as soon as I ducked behind the mound a mortar exploded on the ground so close to me that I lost my hearing immediately. Totally deafened by the concussion I crawled back to find Jacox swimming in our prone hole. I began crawling away and he reached up, grabbed me by the leg and pulled me back into the hole.

We all spent the remainder of the night wet and shivering in our holes. In all, eighty rounds had exploded inside the perimeter. When I looked up there was the tail fin of an enemy mortar embedded in the middle of a burnt spot on the top of the dike not two feet from where I had lain in the hole. Twelve of Bravo guys who were near the headquarters location at the dike intersection had minor shrapnel wounds including me and Snipes. We picked the tiny pieces out with our bayonets. Fuck it, don't mean nuthin'.

Alpha Company had one KIA. Mortar round dropped into his hole, direct hit. How often does that happen?

December 11

Monday – I was amazed today when our path took us from a very dry tundra like landscape into a deep oasis. How can these two such different areas be so closely juxtaposed. There was absolutely no transitional zone…one minute very arid and the next deep green with moisture. There were no pools of emerald water and Arabs eating their dates…did I make a funny? but some of the guys dropped their rucks and hacked coconuts from the fruit trees we were in the midst of. No worry here because we had our flanks protected but this was definitely a place to be wary of, a place to remain alert. The juice was oh, so sweet, and the meat of the coconuts was firm, white and tasty. Most of these guys have never seen a coconut except maybe in a basket in some market and then probably wrapped in cellophane.

Later in the morning, refreshed and rested from the unusual respite, we humped back through the barren expanse of empty fields in the direction we'd come. Heat waves shimmered in front of us causing a mirage like effect. Was I going to see camel caravans? I held the boredom at bay, lost in my thoughts even as I was among other soldiers. My mind, on auto drive, began to wax poetically: each of my tears is a prism through which the war refracts a rainbow of emotion. Corny! Or: The war is a prism through which my soul refracts a rainbow of emotion. Worse! Maybe I should have somehow made it a metaphor or maybe I should pay closer attention or I'll wind up layin' on the ground in a pool of my own blood and Doc McDaniels holding up a saline drip bag, calling in a dust-off an sayin' "million-dollar wound, son. Yer goin' home"

Toward evening we arrived back at the perimeter we had habited two nights before. Snipes grave had not been excavated by the Cong so we carefully dug the original holes even deeper then foraged for logs and made the overhead cover even stronger. At night, I slept in the slit trench we had dug leading away from the hole. Everyone understandably edgy. The last attack put a little fear into all of us. After the mortar barrage the other night I half expected to hear the kind of shrieking tin whistles the Chinese blew at the Chosin Reservoir followed by a massive ground attack.

We were layin' around before dark and someone thought they heard a tube pop and yelled incoming and everyone dived for cover except the Captain who remained sitting on an ammo box. He said, "I'll tell you when, clowns."

I have been handling resupply for the company here in the field since Snipes went to have his wound checked. He had an infection from digging out the shrapnel. Since we have not been resupplied every night the extra duty is a bit much but I can handle it. It involves isolating the sling that is designated for Bravo or if the resupply is smaller and came out on a Huey I just need to line up some of the troops to come and safari the stuff back to our headquarters element where it is divvied up.

It has been very cold in the morning the last several days and when we're up and moving and the mist begins to dissipate the captain has us burn several empty ammo boxes or whatever we can scrounge up to bring heat back to our bodies. This morning we had somebody carelessly discard the heavy cylindrical cardboard container that grenades come in. Problem was the grenade was still in it and it was thrown into a fire pit called a sump and the damned grenade cooked off but no one was injured because the hole was deep enough to stop all the frags. There were a few pissed off boonierats though.

There has also been a near full but waning moon and this means a ground attack is probably unlikely but expect it anyway.

December 12

Tuesday – Infantry soldiers are sometimes referred to as legs and that's because we use them, our legs that is. Another descriptive term is ground pounder and we do plenty of that as well only we call it humping and so today we humped some more. We used our legs to pound some ground, hump back to our original landing zone where this little sojourn began back on the eighth of the month. We originally deployed as a battalion fighting force and our defensive positions at night can be configured in a number of ways. Tonight, rather than digging in as a single battalion sized unit our four company units each formed their own protective defense perimeter and dug in. You can imagine the amount of turf such an operation would encompass and the tactical nightmare such a configuration could present to our enemy should he attempt to infiltrate and attack.

Bravo headquarters dug in next to second platoon and part of a detachment from the 65th Engineer Battalion was with us so I split from the radio operator and dug a hole with Sgt. Blair of the 65th. We were in up to our knees when Blair's entrenching shovel opened up a nest of Scorpions, and two or three of the critters that were as big as a hand scurried about the bottom of the hole. A sting from one of these insects or arachnids, with the identifiable segmented curved tail and stinger at the end, while not lethal, can make one quite sick. We impaled them on our bayonets to show them around before destroying them with our entrenching tools. The Negro troops were petrified.

Captain Baker sent me over to the Battalion CP (command bunker) to copy our objectives from the master overlay map. I accomplished this by placing a clear plastic sheet over the battalion map to redraw the arrows. Returning to Bravo the captain placed the clear plastic over his map and we then knew our objectives by day for the next five days. Later in the evening I sat around with my old squad in second platoon. Attrition has taken a toll. The squad should be ten guys but now numbers only six. How did I get so lucky, I thought, to get up to headquarters?

Ehrig called me tonight on the company push (frequency) to check on my assignments. He must be shitting his nickers having to be out in the field with the rest of us. When he radioed, he wanted to speak with Bravo Six Flash which would be me but I'd never been referred to as such and did not know that I had such a 'handle.' Surprise, surprise. The guys hooted and howled at that one, are now calling me Flash. I call Ehrig rinky dink. Ehrig was pissed because nobody other than yours truly has handed in any copy. We have been rather preoccupied with our primary mission though.

December 13

Wednesday – Air mobile operation today. Different from Eagle Flight. Air Mobile utilizes a pre-selected landing zone or area for the operation whereas the Eagle Flight is random flight to a suspected VC targeted area: the area may be determined by an intelligence gathering effort.

The landing zone was cold and we moved with little effort to our first objective, marked by the numeral 6 at the terminus of a sweeping red arrow on Bakers map. We skirted south to come back up to the objective. Easy going. Delta Company was ambushed and had ten WIA, nobody killed. We cautiously moved to establish what would be an extended patrol base where we could work the area for several days. Resupply dropped bundles of sand bags which we used to build temporary fighting positions. In the early morning before first light we emptied the sand bags and took them with us. We did not use any overhead cover which always makes you feel vulnerable. I'm pretty good now at hearing mortar tube pops and sound the alert while ducking for cover at the same time. I took over the company radio and monitored activity of the platoons until about 0130 hours. Delta took more casualties during the night and a med evacuation chopper was guided in for the pick up using a strobe light. The attack lasted about twenty-five minutes then the dust off came in.

Earlier in the day we blew three claymore mines that one of our columns detected along the trail. All of the paths looked well used and signs like broken twigs and branches were snapped telling us the enemy had been through here earlier. No contact though.

Tomorrow we hump back to where we set up the extended patrol base. We will refortify our positions there and refill the sand bags and add some cover.

December 14

Thursday – We were lead element and moved in the direction that Delta's patrol took casualties last light with the rest of the battalion spread out behind us. Charlie Company will circle around and come in from behind acting as the anvil for us, Bravo Company, the hammer, to hopefully smash the enemy. We were in a dense thicketed area with low visibility when we got into a firefight. We could not acquire any targets and the volley of enemy weapons fire which began slowly built to a deafening crescendo. This was not like the typical fire fight we'd been engaged in over the past month or so. We were in the middle of a mean cross-fire. No casualties to begin with but what there was plenty of was confusion and in that I became separated from the rest of the headquarters element and was somewhere near the rear of the action with an E-5 named Wells.

We did not hit the ground because I think we felt safe in the forested area that the thicket had turned into. Plenty of fire was still coming from our front and when it decreased I could hear Captain Baker hollering for me to get my ass forward. As I moved up I encountered an RTO (radio telephone operator) dead on the ground. I did not recognize him. There was a bizarre contorted look on his face because he'd been strangled by the cord from the radio handset which was wrapped numerous times about his neck. By the time I reached Baker he was shouting that the VC had fled.

Overhead there were several helicopter gunships circling the action while below machetes cut heavy saplings that would be used for makeshift litters to bear the dead away. Charlie had six Kilo's (Killed in Action) including two Lieutenants a medic and the radio operator I had passed which was an indication that some close in hand to hand combat had taken place.

The jungle was so dense that medevac ships could not land and lifting the dead in baskets was out of the question. Instead, we inserted the cut saplings through snapped together ponchos and made crude stretchers. The dead had to be carried single file for over eight hundred meters to an open area where the helicopters could hover down. I along with three others carried one of the Lieutenants. He was wearing a wedding band and his left hand swung with the motion of our struggle to walk. The Lieutenant's mouth was open and a dental bridge was lodged half way down his throat. His open eyes had rolled back in his head looking up at me and his right arm was nearly severed. As we moved through a path cut by the point, the lieutenants head kept bumping against my leg. I briefly looked into his eyes, saw something I would see again and again in the coming months. I reached down and pressed his eyes closed.

After leaving the deceased at the pick-up zone for the choppers I returned to the VC base camp exercising great caution. We had not checked carefully for trip wires and booby traps while carrying our dead. Now, we put out flank security as we moved back. I picked up first one foot and then the other very slowly, deliberately like a Heron scanning the shallows for a morsel to stab at with its beak. I almost chuckled at the thought that I had just served as a pall bearer. Later I noticed that I was covered in blood.

Words alone cannot describe what I saw and experienced on the jungle floor today, my emotions are in high gear, hyperdrive. Shit, I wish I had a six pack or better still a huge splib. The ghostly paleness of the dead soldiers' skin, skin that in the previous hour had been well tanned and pumped full of oxygen, really spooked me. I sat down, shaking all over.

I cannot be alone in thinking that we're not making progress especially when we return to familiar locations, places that we have been before, fought for and then abandoned. This is not something we discuss or shoot the shit about because we all feel strongly about the job we are assigned to do. Winning or losing is something we do not discuss.

When I am alone with my thoughts I sometime think how nobody back home would want to hear anything about my experiences, about this shit. My service to my country is a source of tremendous personal pride and that is aside or different from what I feel about our mission. My father has not said that he is proud of my service. The only thing he said in my last days before leaving was to "get every last one of them Commie bastards and do not come home until you're finished."

And, oh, yes, we did kill two VC today. Shot them out of the trees near their base camp where they had lashed themselves to the trees with rope in order to call directions to their comrades about where to fire. Got their weapons and clothes, too.

P.S. The VC base camp yielded a treasure trove of equipment, rice, clothing with personal identification and letters of encouragement from Ho Chi Minh, documents and a typewriter along with half a dozen bicycles, the ones with the extension poles on one handlebar for pushing huge loads. Progress!? The enemy base camp could have hidden an entire VC regiment.

December 15

Friday – Captain Baker told us this morning that an element of the 9th Infantry Division known as Viking 6 reported that the damage caused yesterday was perpetrated by less than a dozen Viet Cong. This did not seem realistic to me after the size of the base camp we ran into and the equipment we captured and removed. Further, the two snipers shot from the trees would indicate that they were protecting a much larger force. The fortified bunkers could have been abandoned quickly by a large force but something does not feel right about this. I did not say anything.

We moved cautiously for about a click (thousand meters) and hunkered down like a giant ambush patrol... no action...moved back to our perimeter, worked on our defensive positions and hunkered down for the night.

We expected an attack but nothing happened. First platoon had plenty of movement to their front so the enemy was definitely trying to draw the platoon out, get them to fire and reveal their positions but the guys maintained fire discipline and did not open up. After an extended period of silence seven mortar rounds dropped inside the perimeter but no probe resulted. We're trying to win their hearts and minds, they're fucking with ours. Second guessing these jokers is impossible and that is why we are always expecting the worst. Our listening posts and ambush patrols were all away from where the enemy activity was. Coincidence?

December 16

Saturday – Battalion command believes that due to the size of the VC base camp we ran up against yesterday the enemy is not going to abandon the site or leave the area and that we can cordon them off and eliminate them if we are persistent. So today we were up quietly at 0430 hours and began to move out before the grey mistlight of morning. Charlie Company moved away from Alpha, Bravo and Delta making a hell of a racket hoping the deception would be successful in convincing the enemy that we were leaving the area. Our other three companies moved quietly into a horseshoe formation around three sides of their base camp. We waited to engage and force the enemy out of their base at which time they would face a returning Charlie Company for the slaughter. Bravo was dead center on the horseshoe and very near the contact point of yesterday's action. Once in place, a flight of fast movers, F4 Phantom jets, streaked in from behind us and just off the deck and dropped their ordinance of 500 pounders on the base camp. If we had been any closer or standing we surely would have taken casualties. The noise from first the Phantom, then the detonations and the trembling of the ground were indescribable, and I was incredulous that I am actually here in this time and this place and experiencing this insanity.

When the jets had softened the target we all donned our gas masks while choppers came in to rake the area with M-60 machine gun fire and 20mm cannon and then jettison 55-gallon drums of CS gas in the middle of the target. The gas is released in aerosol form and is also called super tear gas and causes your eyes to tear to the point of closing. The gas also has an incapacitating effect and makes normal functioning of lungs almost impossible, you cannot draw breath.

When we moved back into the area we found no enemy but heard small arms fire as the enemy exfiltrated. Impossible to determine how many there had been. The bombs had unearthed the entire base camp and we uncovered so much more than yesterday.

We captured many weapons. Two of them were M-16's, one was a Checz rifle, one a U.S. carbine and the other a Chinese Communist carbine. Also found were forty pounds of VC documents, personal diaries of the enemy soldiers, training manuals, tools, typewriters, tape recorders, opium wrapped in small plastic sheets, propaganda leaflets, other personals, many bicycles and one live pig.

We returned late in the day to our perimeter and at night learned from command that the captured documents revealed that the enemy stronghold was headquarters to eighteen North Vietnamese Army (NVA) companies.

We now have in our possession an evidently top-secret document containing passwords and countersigns for the remainder of the month of December. Whether the intelligence will be valuable is questionable. We believe we are hot on the heels of COSVN, the North Vietnamese headquarters organization inside of South Vietnam. If the organization even exists within our area of operation, the Parrots Beak, we just do not know.

December 17

Sunday – Captain Baker informed me that he was leaving me to watch our sector of the perimeter. The reason was that he wanted me to get caught up on my writing and, this is probably silly but I'm feeling as though he is taking me under his wing, watching out for me, paying special attention to me. Of course, it could be one of those being in the right place at the right time happenstances. No matter, I am appreciative and very dedicated to him. He and I are both the same age, twenty-five but I guess I've said that. Over the past two months we have shared the kind of closeness that a difference in rank, he a captain and me a private, doesn't often permit. He wondered aloud one day, questioned really, if I allowed myself to be drafted. He said I'd be greatly qualified for Officer Candidate School.

I never perused the compliment further but I think it would be possible to leave Vietnam for OCS but of course I'd be right back here again in another six months as a brand-new Butter Bar (Second Lieutenant). There is also the complication of my marriage and how Cindy would respond to being the wife of a career officer because that is what OCS would mean. Then I pondered this a little deeper. I have the greatest respect and admiration for everyone I know in the company and get along with all of the soldiers I have met but my greatest affinity is for our officer corps because of our similar backgrounds. Anyway…I do believe that the Lord has a special plan for each of us from even before our births…and with all of the jerking off I've done in my life I sometime believe that I was born to do this, to be a warrior.

December 18

Monday – We, and by that, I mean Bravo Company, were left behind for a change. I wonder if as a company we are only infrequently left behind, left out of the rotation because we are a stronger company, tougher than the other three and therefore needed up front where the action is. When we are on battalion sized operations one company is sometimes left behind to protect the perimeter or hard spot which contradicts being needed up front.

Rebuilt the overhead cover on the headquarters position using the sand bags we've been toting around forever and fashioned some firing ports. The interesting thing or maybe the weird thing as well as a great comfort to me is the degree of safety I'm accorded by being a member of the headquarters element. In the field, we always travel somewhere close to the middle of the company formation when we are on the move. Oh, sure, we are not on the perimeter where the danger is greater but stray bullets can just as easily find us even in the middle of the formation. There really is no safe place out here, only places that are slightly safer than others.

I had a chance to complete several articles based on the last weeks' actions and wrote letters home as well. The company returned to the perimeter around 1630 hours.

We received resupply so everyone got their ration of two beers or two sodas. Slept well tonight. No mortars.

Bright, moonlit night so while pulling my radio watch I jotted some notes for a story I might concoct and submit to Battalion.

December 19

Tuesday – Well, we are finally leaving this place and from a military perspective the surface has barely been scratched. I usually feel ambivalent about staying or leaving a certain topographical area or place; all places should evoke the same feeling but not this time. Some places instill a sense of foreboding, apprehension and fear unlike any other places we have been. This eerie feeling sometimes reminds me of Dorothy and her friends when they detoured from the Yellow Brick Road into a black forest of spindly trees, and when Dorothy picked an apple and slipped it into her basket the trees suddenly came alive and one grabbed back its apple and slapped the shit out of Dorothy. "Whaddythinkyerdoin," the tree yelped.

The Captain feels that we will be lucky to get out of this area without getting our asses kicked but he only shared that with us in headquarters. So I am no longer ambivalent…let's hat up, make like the wind, leave, get my drift? The bad news is that metaphorically we are headed toward a Dorothy-like dark forest.

Captain Baker briefed our platoon leaders that there has been a sizeable forward base camp named Katum constructed astride a very dangerous portion of the Ho Chi Minh Trail over by Cambodia and we're goin' there sooner or later. The stronghold is large enough to protect an air strip. Bo Tuc which means Lake of Fire is more like a bump on our ass than it is a location on our topo maps and for now our only concern. We are jamming up the enemy and strategically this is the place for us to engage. The enemy must move around Katum and Bo Tuc in order to move deeper into the country and we're gonna stop him.

We are headed for Bo Tuc now. Some good news though, the PZ was cold this morning and then as we approached the LZ and the Hueys flared to drop us off, the exceptional volley of machine gun fire raking the wood line made me so anxious that I bailed early. When I impacted the ground some ten feet below my helmet flew one way, my pack and me another.

Moving toward our objective all was quiet. On the way in we discovered a sizable stack of quality lumber by the trail that measured 2"x 8" by 12'. We also found numerous ARVN styled rucksacks with full gear minus weapons abandoned along the sides of the trail. I felt as though we were detouring into Dorothy's dark forest. Come evening we formed our perimeter near an abandoned Vietnamese well. A worn enemy trail ran past the well and throughout the area that had patches of scrub underbrush and trees here and there. Our sister companies formed perimeters around an FSB (fire support base) and their 105-mm artillery pieces. We learned that the ARVN company whose stuff we found on the way in got messed over pretty badly and they had actually run out of their gear with the VC in hot pursuit. Cowards!?

The ground here is cement-like, making the digging of holes and defensive positions almost impossible. Most of us have bad blisters but the holes must be completed or blisters will not be our worst problem.

I came off radio watch about 0130 hours and crawled back across the trail to the position I was sharing with Jacox and Duffy to get a little sack time. At 0135 hours the enemy launched a combined mortar and ground attack. I peered above our sand bagged position and about a hundred meters down range I could see where the VC had tripped a white phosphorus flare in the wire surrounding Charlie Company's perimeter. The area was filled with white light and through the smoky haze from the phosphorus flare I could clearly see VC throwing themselves at the wire, scrambling over one another to get inside the perimeter.

I watched as five VC sappers ran up to the FSB perimeter, breached it and threw satchel charges into the ammunition dump. Approximately 800 rounds began to cook off (explode) and shrapnel sprayed everywhere and tree limbs came crashing down all about us. Word was soon passed to stay down, keep in your holes. Sporadic fighting and sniping was taking place at each of our perimeters around the artillery emplacement and their guns were levelled at point blank range so they could fire "bee hive" rounds. The enemy became confused as they tried to exfiltrate the area and kept running into our randomly placed perimeters. The exploding ammo dump kept us pretty well pinned in our holes. Many of the enemy were killed trying to escape.

By 0430 hours we had regrouped and driven the enemy back to the wood line. At first light, we collected seventy-six bodies and a huge cache of weapons. Six bodies were found in front of Bravo Company positions, three right in front of our hole. I had been firing from a crouching position but I cannot say with certainty that I shot any of the enemy.

The place where this battle took place is identified on our maps as Bo Tuc and the FSB is named Beauregard. We had six KIA (killed in action) and numerous wounded.

The VC always drag their severely wounded and dead when they withdraw and we counted many blood trails leading back into the jungle indicating that we messed up as many as one hundred more. The bodies we rounded up were dumped into the well and then explosive charges were detonated to cave in the sides of the well.

Dead VC sappers died when their satchel charges blew the ammo dump at Beauregard battlesight

December 20

Wednesday – The artillery FSB had been mauled badly by the sappers and several of their bodies were still in the impact craters. Alpha, Bravo, Charlie and Delta reformed a single perimeter around the arty position to form a more consolidated defensive position. The single position would prevent our companies from firing at one another. Our CP, Bravo, was established on a slight rise with several two-man positions nearby and all now have overhead cover that will withstand anything but direct hits from enemy mortars. Digging was again very difficult and badly blistered hands from yesterday's efforts were traumatized once again.

Just before dark VC mortars came crashing in. The Captain said that he'd never seen a bunch of grunts dig so fast in all his life. We took one WIA. It did not take long to determine that the tremendous tree that must have been twelve feet in circumference and over sixty feet tall was a problem. The enemy could spot this obvious feature from a great distance and they were using it for an aiming stake with deadly accuracy; mortar rounds were landing with precision near our command position. Four rounds, in fact, hit the dead tree. Tomorrow the Engineer personnel will place some charges around the circumference and bring the tree down.

The enemy mortar rounds created a cloud of dust that covered the inside of the perimeter. Diffused sunlight penetrated the cloud casting eerie shadows everywhere. We all remained deep in our holes, watching to the front for a ground attack that did not materialize. Hopefully our pissed off little friends are licking their wounds from last night's battle and harassing us while they make plans for a renewed attack.

Battalion readjusted their after-action report and now estimates from examination of blood trails and equipment left by the enemy as they withdrew that we may have killed or wounded maybe a hundred more. The VC are watching our every move and for now they would prefer to lay in wait and have another crack at us on their terms and that would be in the jungle or out in the open as we move.

December 21

Thursday – The BN moved out early on a S&D (search and Destroy) mission after making sure each position around the artillery gun battery's position was secure. Captain Baker left me behind again this time to write up a citation for 1st Lieutenant Hector Colon and assist the engineers to refortify our command bunker. Denny Wagner from 2nd was around also and we hung out – literally in a VC hammock that someone had captured. We hung it inside the bunker and took pictures of each other posing like tough guys with cigars in our mouths. The Captain got me to smoke one of the cigars from the sundry box and try a chaw of tobacco at the same time. My mouth watered up and I flat out barfed on the ground. I kind of liked the cigar but will pass on the chewing.

In the afternoon, a medic from battalion stopped over to report on an action from the field. While the medic was hanging out we heard a single shot – AK 47 – ring out. No fire fight and no return fire …that was it.

When the company returned to the perimeter everyone was in a grand funk, especially the captain. The single shot had been from a sniper round that had gone through Lt. David Milde's neck and killed him instantly. They were carrying Milde's body. Anytime we lose another guy it is a horrible day but this was the single worst day that I remember to date. Captain Baker is really taking it hard. The Captain told me later at night while we shared a hole that he had tried sending Lt. Milde on an R&R because he was getting' short but the Lieutenant had refused, wanted to stay with his men. Wow!

Earlier in the day and with the company still out and before the medic had stopped by I had crawled inside our bunker and sacked out. Four mortars dropped in but I barely stirred. Radio watch this night was interesting.

There were several severely wounded NVA laying just outside the perimeter that we'd missed while policing up their dead. They moaned loudly throughout the night. Really spooked us.

I almost forgot...the well that we had dumped the bodies into was the source of some new activity. Several sniper rounds were fired from the mouth of the well even after the explosive charges had pretty near collapsed the well. There was apparently a tunnel opening somewhere lower in the well so the engineers went to work again and totally sealed off the well. Problem solved... finally.

Tough guy

December 22

Friday - Captain Baker put me in charge of collecting money for a memorial fund for Lieutenant Milde. I felt honored because I have not experienced such profound feelings of loyalty and love between enlisted men, noncommissioned officers and an officer like David Milde. The first, second and third platoon combined for two hundred dollars. The third platoon has not contributed yet. This does not seem like much for this fine soldier but keep in mind that most of us send our pay home to loved ones in some form of an allotment and rarely have any money in the field with us because currency has little use here. The money we do hold is used for wagering.

Again, today I was left behind. The reason is that as part of a headquarters element soldiers like myself are, in a way, regarded as non-combatants. Anyway, the company got wrapped around the axel in the afternoon. This is another way of saying shit happens or there was a SNAFU and as a result our company along with Delta and the first platoon of Charlie Company will be away from the perimeter over night to pull security for a piece of equipment known as a portable bridge and the two tanks escorting the bridge. Both tanks have blown treads that must be repaired before they can move.

With much of the battalion fighting force away from the perimeter it became necessary to consolidate our defenses so Wagner and myself and others around the perimeter gathered gear from all positions (holes) and reestablished a tighter perimeter which is closer to FSB Beauregard's artillery battery.

Tonight, we hunkered down to wait out the night. If ever there was a situation where I was uncertain about making it through the night this is it because we are spread so thin. The element of the battalion group that has stayed behind has radios and we're in communication with the rest of our elements that are out guarding the portable bridge and the tanks but I have no radio. And, in addition we have three newly arrived FNG's that came to the field yesterday and refused to fight and would not pick up a weapon. Captain Baker was furious and made the trio pull a listening post about a hundred meters out front with no weapons. The Captain finally pulled them back in and threatened them with Article 15's (equivalent of a traffic ticket) and then a fair court martial followed by some time breaking rock over at Long Binh Jail if, as Capt. Baker put it, they kept up the "shit."

Just after we got settled in for the long night we experienced a brief mortar attack. I am not sure that the Dinks have got all of the last several days confusion figured out or the fact that our strength has been cut in half. Maybe they don't know exactly where we are. Christ, I'm scared.

December 23

Saturday – Well, we made it through the night but not without incident. There were many tube pops and incoming mortars all about the perimeter and this kept us up for most of the night but no probes.

While we were cold and hunkered close to the ground amidst the mortars and a few illumination rounds I had the weirdest thoughts enter my mind, one of those mind fuck loop things where I could not shake the reoccurring thoughts or push them away. I kept thinking about the Third Marine Amphibious Force and elements of the First Cav that are in a place called Khe Sanh in Quang Tri Province near the DMZ. I thought here I am in the middle of my own shit storm and I should probably have my head examined for thinking about this but here goes, anyway. I wonder if I could volunteer for duty like that. The Marines have been surrounded there since last summer and it's going to get a whole lot worse before it gets better but could I be part of that somehow? Here's something else, a confession if you will. I have at least two close friends that I can think of who joined the Corps and I regarded them as heroes of mine. If I hadn't been such a pussy and waited to be drafted I coulda joined the Marines but I think the mystique of the Marine Corps and their reputation scared the piss out of me. Anyway...

Around mid-day I wandered over to where the battalion had their communication center set up to see what I could learn. There wasn't any traffic on the net just the audible hiss between transmissions. My company alone has had three kilos (KIA, killed in action) and eight wounded. And I'm thinking that we need to get out of here before there is nothing left of Bravo. Now, it should be noted that is my opinion, the opinion of a grunt. If you talked to the top brass their attitude almost has to be press on, take it to the enemy and never break contact.

Just prior to returning to my position I heard another transmission. The company is on its way back in but had suffered two more casualties, both dead. Interesting to me that I am still new enough that I often do not recognize the names of the dead. A good thing?

It's always darkest just before the dawn. Remember that one? Well, after just writing about getting beat up I hear from the Captain that tomorrow we are to be picked up by CH-47 which you may recall from an earlier comment is a Chinook helicopter sometimes referred to by grunts as a Shithook or just plain Hook. We will make the short hop over to the new forward base at Katum with all our gear and work out of there, spend Christmas there. I had forgotten all about Christmas until the Cap mentioned it and I looked a couple pages ahead in my diary. If I were home I'd probably have all of my Christmas shopping done and be up to my ass in snow and jingle bells.

Haven't received any mail for a long time.

December 24

Sunday – The 2nd Battalion 14th Infantry Golden Dragons arrived in a Chinook amidst a couple of mortar rounds. We were ready to board and the exchange took less than five minutes and we were on our way to Katum. I do not care if we ever see this dismal, dangerous place again and for the first time since I have been with the Manchus I can see the fatigue in the faces of the guys around me. For now, this is one group of exhausted soldiers. We have been driving hard since we left Cu Chi and it is beginning to show.

The time in the air over to Katum was only ten minutes. An advance party led the troop trucks from the air strip to our new home. There is one huge command bunker with fifteen to twenty inch logs for overhead cover. The timbers are covered with three layers of sand bags and around this fortified position there are three smaller holes that represent a good start. We will add cover as we go. I have not seen the perimeter defensive positions but have heard that they are substantial as well. I'd say that our position is about an eighth of a mile from the landing strip which consists of PSP (pierced steel planks) and can be disassembled and moved very quickly. It has not been established yet if our duty here will include manning the perimeter bunkers. For now, we are inside and away from the bunker line. For the time being our orderly room and logistical support and resupply remain in Tay Ninh. There is a very tall tree with a wood ladder leading to an antenna at the top which facilitates communication back to Tay Ninh.

We all got new issue fatigue shirts, pants and boots and are able to take baths with soap in a huge B 52 bomb crater that filled with water. The darned thing is more than sixty feet in diameter and ten or fifteen feet deep. What a friggin luxury. When we got back to our position mail had been delivered and since this is Christmas eve, which is weird, we all opened gifts. I did not discuss with anyone but receiving gifts has depressed me terribly but I kept my happy face on. The feelings are reasonable, explainable, because this is the first Christmas in my life that I have been away from family and loved ones. It is very difficult for me to imagine what, if anything, my family thinks or discusses about me and my absence.

Everyone is relaxed, how great to be temporarily off the line. The gun battery next to us shared their full Christmas dinner with us including turkey with stuffing and veggies. We played scrabble in the afternoon and filled our bellies with candy and other goodies from home. Also, played poker but not much money changed hands and nobody cared. We all slept very well and no worries about guarding our front. No incoming. Sleeping through the gun battery and their fire missions is problematic as it interrupts sleep. Because most of us are, of necessity, light sleepers and accustomed to frequent disruptions we sometimes can hear the gun crews softly speaking as they ready the big guns. If one were to look in the direction of the gun emplacements one would see figures illuminated by flashlight as they chart and prepare to fire. The noise is horrendous and the gun's concussion when firing actually knocks leaves from all the surrounding trees.

Soaping up in a bomb crater

December 25

Monday – Christmas day, nineteen hundred and sixty-seven. Lethargy personified! We laid around all day, dogs lickin' our nuts because we could, still much better than humping the boonies. Played board games that some of us were sent from family back in the World…checkers, chess and Scrabble mostly. Once again, the artillery must have felt sorry for us boonierats and asked if we'd join them for a second time, leftovers we'd call this back home, Heaven on Earth is what you call it at forward base Katum. Again, we unabashedly strapped on the old feed bag and once again had turkey, stuffing, sides and for dessert this time, mince pie. I ate so much that when the time came for our own Bravo Company celebration I could not partake of a single bite.

All the contact we have experienced with the VC in the last several weeks has made the process of writing or submitting film and articles nonexistent for now and Ehrig from battalion has not even tried contacting me. The break from that grind is welcomed.

Later in the day a bunch of us wrapped in towels and wearing only jungle boots with shouldered weapons, sauntered over to take a dip in the bomb crater and clean up. The day passed. Captain Baker and Lt. Dossett were around most of the day and participated in games. The Lieutenant received a box of El Producto cigars and generously passed them around. Someone scrounged up a small tree that we decorated. I received a goodie box from mom and dad that included mostly nonsense stuff but a small stainless shaving mirror was greatly appreciated. Turned in early, said a prayer and fell asleep as our Coleman lantern fizzed out and darkness filled the bunker. The last group to inhabit the bunker were kind enough to build double decker sleeping racks from discarded ammunition boxes so we are actually comfortable.

December 26

Tuesday – Captain Baker awoke very early and shook each of us and announced that Christmas was over and now the work would begin. Item number one on the Captain's agenda was the construction of a latrine. First a suitable hole was dug and filled with gravel and then a brass shell casing from a 175 mm round with the end removed was sunk into the gravel and a screen was placed over the end of the opening. Dirt was packed on top of the boards that totally covered the hole so the shell casing sat about a foot to two feet above ground level. The shell casing is what is called a piss tube. We do not want to cover the ground with piss where we live, the Captain informed us. The crapper was going to be slightly more difficult. First, we all pitched in and dug a slightly deeper hole that was approximately three-foot square. Two by fours traversed the hole and an opened ended ammo box was set in place on the two by's. The remainder of the hole was covered with boards and a layer of sand bags covered with more dirt. The Rube Goldbergian contraption worked like a charm, a very crude stool by anyone's estimation but it gets the job done. It would not be advisable to sit on the box for too long or the sitter on the shitter would get square ass cheeks and perhaps hemorrhoids from lingering too long on the square opening,

Next task assigned, and all of our officers pitched in to help, was to enlarge the existing holes. We are going to do it right and make it a three-day project. One of the holes needing the biggest makeover is approximately seven' by 5' by 4' deep. The hole will be doubled in size and have timbers added and then covered over with sand bags so that the position could withstand a direct hit.

I have little feel for the size of our base or how many soldiers are here at this time. I do know that there are plans to push the bunker lines out farther and there are Rome Plows (named for the city in Georgia where they are manufactured) here to clear the jungle and establish fields of fire to make ground attacks more difficult. The distinctive feature of the plows is that their blades are set at a severe enough angle to the body of the treaded machine so that when the engineer operating the plow drives straight at a tree the blade slices through the tree and it falls. There are some trees and scrub features inside the base but basically the place was carved out or triple canopy jungle. Reportedly, Katum sits squarely on an intersection of the Ho Chi Minh Trail and was purposefully situated here to monitor and interrupt enemy activity.

There is also a CIDG (Civilian Irregular Defense Group) compound being constructed near hear and that is another purpose for us being here. Our engineers are doing the construction. The compound houses the AFVN soldiers and their families in a mounded, star shaped fortress that is easily protected against enemy attack.

An issue of the Tropic Lightning News came out today. There were none of my articles but there was one of my photographs printed. The picture is of our second platoon fording a small river. Cool! I got my byline under my photograph.

December 27

Wednesday – Are you wondering how I resolve the 5 W's, or do you wonder what they are – the 5 W's that is. So, to begin the 5 W's are: what, where, when, who, and why and they are thought to be the basics, the foundation of good journalism, getting the facts and details of a good story and getting them correct. Maybe you're not so much wondering what they are or how I resolve them as you are how do I collect them and get them into written form while I am chasing bad guys in the jungle. The answer may surprise you. I keep my diary securely locked in my foot locker in whatever or wherever our base camp is. Currently that is Tay Ninh and the locked chest made the trip with me from Cu Chi to Tay Ninh.

While on operations I write at night if that is my only opportunity and I do this under my poncho by flash light. I write and scribble important details on any scrap of paper that I can scrounge. Cardboard from C ration boxes works and some of the time, if I can keep it dry, I carry a small lined notebook and when I return to base camp I retrieve the diary from my foot locker and record all from the scraps of paper. I have even written on my hands and Arms with a ball point that I carry at all times. The plan is to make a formal document from my experiences once I am safely back In the USA. Then all of my buddies that made it through and will, at that point, be sick with dementia and arguing and insisting that such and such or so and so happened like this and when their experience in Vietnam is all they have left I can pull out the diary and say conclusively, "no, no, my compadres, this is how that went down," case closed.

Most of us are still suffering some sort of lethargy probably from all the food and sugar we've ingested for the past days. It would be something like feeding your dog very rich table scraps when all the mutt should be getting is the dry stuff…the sudden change in diet causes your loving dog to barf all over your new carpet. Anyway, we were spared or saved today when the Battalion except for us, Bravo, had to pull clover leaf patrols away from Katum to keep the enemy at bay.

Clover leaf patrols are exactly what they sound like. A patrolling element, could be a company, leaves the perimeter and loops out about two hundred meters and then back to the perimeter and reenters… If the Dinks are watching and expect you to make these short patrols they will more than likely leave you alone, not engage.

We finished the additional improvements to our positions in the afternoon and relaxed, played poker again with only slightly improved results. I am so amazed at the rejuvenating power of a couple of days rest. No briefings but I am guessing our time of sitting around on our keister's is to abruptly end. I mean, really, how long can the battalion carry on in the field without Big Bad Bravo, huh?

Pretty good hot chow followed by a quick waddle over to the bomb crater for a good douche. Returned to our refortified position and took a turn at monitoring the radios.

We hear now that Katum will be our residence for an unspecified time. Our first Brigade is also here for now. Could we move here permanently from Tango November (military phonetic alphabet used in transmitting radio messages) Tay Ninh.

I told Specialist 4th class Stockman, the Captain's radio operator (RTO) to take a hike this afternoon and he asked me why and I told him because all he does is lay around and kiss up to Baker and do absolutely no work. He's pissed. I was off base but the feelings I have are real. I am a little envious because Stockman enjoys an obviously tight relationship with Capt. Baker. Whatever Stockman is doing works because he is being promoted to E-5, Buck Sergeant. My time will come, too, I am confident. Also, Stockman is getting short which means some rearranging, maybe promotions.

December 28

Thursday – Up before first light. The mess sergeant served a hot breakfast on the road, our rally point before moving over to the air strip. Captain Baker himself remained behind this morning to be decorated for an action that he took part in before I joined the company. He is too modest to speak of these things but I have surmised that the action was the one where he charged an enemy bunker and was wounded in the melee. He will be awarded the Silver Star for valor and the Purple Heart. Another troop name of McCarthy and known to me only as 'Mac' will also receive the Silver.

Second Lieutenant Darrell Jobman who had been acting XO (executive officer or second in command) will take charge of the company until the Captain returns. The mission we were tasked for the day was road security and we at once became lost. Maybe it is unfair to use the term lost; slightly out of position would be more suitable since there is only one road to secure and that dust trail led to a place called Soui Cut and a relatively new FSB named Burt. The road as such is just wide enough to allow military vehicles to pass in only one direction at a time.

The Captain returned from the award ceremony and due to our close location to Katum, Baker joined us. The road was clear and waiting for the convoy gave us plenty of time to shoot the shit as we reclined in a small swale beside the road. There was some speculation about the mechanized unit that would be passing through on their way to reinforce and continue establishing FSB Burt. Actually, we are only several clicks from Beauregard where we had the skirmish with the Zipperheads.

Delta was patrolling four or five clicks from here which places them back over Beauregard way and they found one dead Gook who was tucked up next to the trunk of a gigantic eucalyptus tree in the weird flanges of the trunk that ran out in all directions from the tree's base.

Baker talked about his love of politics and how he'd been involved with campaigning at a time in his early life. We talked about our lives back home, schooling and missing families. Pulling road security is a bore after a time the same way that laying around inside the base camp is a bore. I'll bet you never thought you would hear me admit to that. I'm lying in this ditch with the rest of the guys under some low hanging brush and using one of the radios for a back rest.

The APC's – remember I told you they're called tracks because of how they are propelled down the road – finally came roaring by, troops perched on top, hiding behind huge smoked glass goggles and faces covered with either towels of kerchiefs to keep from inhaling the dust.

We waved at each other. The convoy took almost a half an hour to get totally past us and included jeeps, flatbed trucks carrying several huge metal Conex containers. I believe the tracks were part of the 3rd of the 22nd Infantry.

Back inside Katum for late chow and then some relaxing bunker time. It is so dark here, no light whatsoever, viewing the stars is glorious.

3rd of the 22nd convoy moving past on the way to FSB Burt

December 29

Friday – Saddle up! Operation by Huey, so over to the air strip by 1230 hours. We were gifted with the presence of a French correspondent because Bravo is considered by top brass to be the best in the battalion, so the guy rides with us.

Side bar: Companies within the battalion earn their reputations on a daily basis and occasionally the luck of the draw results in one company or another becoming known as the bad luck company. This can occur, as an example, when like ingredients coming together to make a great cake one of the ingredients is added in the wrong sequence and a disaster occurs. Lately Charlie Company seems to have repeatedly drawn the proverbial short straw…guys have died. We've all got it coming and sooner or later it will be Bravo's turn in the barrel but still, we're really cocky.

But back to business. Last minute change and as we lifted up into cooler air and joined the formation, a stagger left, I saw below me, as the ships lifted and fell on the buffeting air, the little French guy looking pretty much out of place, wearing a cute French beret while sitting on the flight deck perched atop a steel pot helmet. The jungle tapestry stretched out below us all as we moved toward our objective.

No Sweat. We landed in an open field of dry, dusty grass with the door gunners spraying the wood line as we touched down. No contact. The choppers disappeared over the trees at the end of the LZ and we were engulfed by a suffocating, hot stillness. Organizing rapidly, we humped into an area of low brush where another element had deployed CS gas against the enemy and we had to rapidly place our gas masks over our heads to keep our eyes from tearing so we could breathe freely. A Lieutenant who joined our ranks recently and who is regarded by almost everybody as being really nerdy, out of it actually, did not get his gas mask on quickly enough and he vomited violently, inside his gas mask. He bent double at the knees. His name is Lt. Smith. He came to us from the National Guard and as he continued to stand while bent double he expectorated mucus and slimy shit from his nose. We stood and waited for "Smitty" to regain his vision so we did not have to lead him by the hand through the jungle paths. I could see Jacox and Snipes laughing eyes through the huge lenses of their gas masks. CS gas can lie dormant in the grass and become reactivated by scuffling feet. The gas totally dissipated later as we passed through a shallow marsh.

Ssg. Otis Boatwright who is the negro platoon sergeant of second platoon told me as I passed him on the trail today that he was putting me in for a promotion to Specialist 4th class. I was grateful and also excited having received this good news. I believe that I am still carried on the roster as a member of the second platoon even though I am travelling with the headquarters element of Bravo Company. I wondered if something like this could slow future promotions that would come my way. I mean, I wonder who exactly would notice my work and put me in for the promotion. We humped all the way back into Katum. Felt like a million miles. Cleaned up in the bomb crater once again. Refreshing.

December 30

Saturday – Everything seems to have slowed down considerably, either that or we are in the middle of a blessed period. Short operations and back to the relative safety of Katum. What makes my statement about relative ease and about these small movements in force sound almost absurd was the arrival of a letter from Cindy that was sent here to our forward base from Tay Ninh. The article was clipped from the Grand Rapids Press, my hometown newspaper, and announced that elements of the 25th Infantry Division are currently operating in a new forward base camp that sits astride a major intersection of the Ho Chi Minh Trail and, I am quoting from the paper now, *the men of the 25th Division are surrounded by an estimated 16,000 Viet Cong and NVA soldiers.* Well, that's grand news coming from a newspaper in the United States about ten thousand miles away. One has to wonder where does this shit originate since we are told repeatedly, for security purposes, not to tell our loved ones exactly where we are. We're lucky I suppose because the news article could have included map coordinates so the enemy could draw a direct bead on us with their mortar tubes.

  We made a short sweep out from the perimeter, no more than a hundred meters, and then back in again. The jungle is so thick that we actually lost sight of the bunker line. Charlie Company…hard luck Charlie? Overburdened Charlie? had one of their listening posts (LP) get lost or more precisely out of position by thirty meters and that was the beginning of their troubles. The bunker line detected movement to their front and before opening fire called the LP which as it turns out was the movement that they had detected. The bunker line asked the LP had they seen anything and at that point the LP reported seeing a light which had somehow originated on the bunker line. After the smoke had cleared from the two elements firing on each other the LP had two dead. There will be an investigation, of course. You'd be surprised how often this happens. They are referred to as 'friendly fire incidents' and are often just forgotten. Usually there is a Huey gunship involved that has been working too close to troops in a wooded area or along a wood line between rice paddies.

Just got the poop for tomorrow. The battalion will sweep and we will remain to secure most of the perimeter which spreads us thin but no sweat, we can handle it. We also received with resupply yesterday evening three anti-intrusion devices which would be useful if one of us actually knew how to set them up. They either operate on some kind of pulse emitting radar or have a probe which when inserted in the ground detects movement. The darned thing could replace LP's and maybe save troops from shooting at one another.

December 31

Sunday – Well, well, last day of the year. Can't really say that I'm sad to see it go or happy for that matter. However, the year of our Lord, 1967 has, when I reflect, been rather tumultuous. I completed training for the US Army and I am very proud of that achievement but let us be real about the circumstances for just a minute. The reality is that I jerked around and finally lost my student deferment with predictable results, Uncle Sam and his damned draft Nazis came after me and here I am, up to my arm pits in mosquitos, lousy food – compared to back in the World – sleeping on the ground without a blanket and some little Zipper headed Gook, motherfucking Dinks trying to kill me in any one of, oh, say, a hundred or more ingenious ways. Hell, under different circumstances I might even like these slant eyed little shits.

But worse than that is the fact that I'm doing the dirty work of some capitalist, free enterprising, false flag waving patriots who are lining their pockets with blood money from the sale of bullets and the like. I wonder which came first, the chicken or the egg, the war or war profiteering? In the end, the answer is relatively inconsequential. There is no escaping the fact that as soldiers we are at the end of the world's longest conveyor belt, a gigantic supply line that begins in the factories of the United States and ends with me, on the other end, chambering a round in my M-16. You cannot supply me and my boonierat brothers with enough bullets, weapons, tanks, helmets, etc. in order to win this thing but, oh, yes, we can fill the pockets of the friends of government with boo coup bucks. Cynical enough for you? Anyhow, succeeding so far as a soldier is not the grandest achievement of 1967 for me. No, the really big gold star on the refrigerator of my life is my marriage to Cindy. The most notable thing about the marriage is that Cindy came along at a time in my life when I figured I'd never find the 'one' if you know what I mean. Before Cindy, I had more relational failures than the collapsing Tacoma Narrows bridge had engineering problems. But again, I digress.

Didn't do a single notable thing except lay in our captured Gook hammock in front of the command bunker reading a paperback titled *Men and Women* by one of my favorite authors from my childhood, Erskine Caldwell. I also filled out some home town news releases for FNG's and wrote up a citation for Captain Bakers Silver Star. Also, wrote up some stuff for Ssg. Moore alias 'hardcore' Moore because he is one of our old timers with a service record dating back to the Korean War (conflict really…just like what we're in now is not a war but a police action).

Finished out the day playing Scrabble by the light of a Coleman lantern deep underground in our bunker. The light-hearted participants were Snipes, me, Doc McAdams and, of course, Captain Baker. Baker, no surprise, is a wordsmith.

We had five cases of beer for the entire company to celebrate the New Year. That is actually less than a full beer per troop. The Christmas Truce that we are under has been extended for forty-eight hours. Charlie will never be able to hold his fire for that long, the itchy little bastard. Happy New Year! Only two hundred and seventy more days left on my tour. Shit, my short timers calendar is beginning to take shape.

Side bar: I should mention that the Vietnamese like other East Asian countries honor the Chinese Zodiac calendar. Their New Year or Tet does not coincide with ours. There are twelve signs or symbols (animals) that are assigned to a twelve-year repeating cycle that make up the Chinese Zodiac. Thus, 1967, Nham Than, is the year of the Monkey. The other animals are rat, ox, tiger, rabbit, dragon, horse, snake, goat, rooster and pig. All Vietnamese celebrate their birthday's together on Tet and not on the actual days that they were born. Culturally, Tet is the most important day in the lives of the Vietnamese people.

January 1, 1968

Monday – Charlie and Delta moved out first securing the small trail by deploying protection on the flanks as they moved. We, Bravo, then moved approximately two clicks (two thousand meters) along the protected trail while following behind the most massive bulldozer I have ever seen. The tractor drive mechanism and the blunt blade were what one might expect of a large earthmover of this type but it was the way the equipment was fortified that set it apart. The driver could not be seen behind the controls because he was obscured by armor plate that was not jury rigged but was an integral part of the rig from the period of its fabrication. The entire machine was OD

(Olive Drab – the Army's favorite color) except for an assortment of bright red handles strategically placed. The cab had many slit windows that I assumed were made of bullet proof glass. In fact, the contraption was an equilateral metal box that only the Department of the Army would build or own. However, the most impressive feature of the dozer was a menacing 50 cal. Machine gun mounted on top which was only accessible through a port hole in the roof. You cannot blame the operator for wanting to be safe and the ballsy SeaBees, and this guy is one of them whom we do not see in this part of Vietnam, would usually be sitting out in the open daring the Gooks to shoot at 'em. They are really part of the United States Naval Construction Forces so in a sense I guess they are really Marines. Doesn't matter, we're all on the same side.

The mission for the day was to bag and remove approximately seventy-five tons of what is called super rice. The dozer was to be used to clear a landing zone big enough for a CH 47 twin rotor helicopter to land and then extract the rice. The huge quantity of rice is a fair indicator that the enemy had done the stock piling. In theory if we deny the enemy the rice his fighting capabilities are diminished. The only bags we had to sack the rice were the same sand bags that we use to fortify our defensive positions so the process is long and tedious work. Hot too. By days end we had only bagged and removed about fourteen tons.

Back at the perimeter the big guns are silent, no fire missions because the truce is still in effect.

Tonight McAdams, an engineer named Garlado and myself slept out in the open on top of the bunker because the rats inside the bunker were becoming a huge problem…they run right over your legs as if they own the joint. They were also swarming in the bamboo thicket which is close to the bunker and over hang it.

Rather sudden but Captain Baker left tonight with very little ceremony, not even a goodbye. This is normal SOP (standard operating procedure). Line officers serve six months on line with an infantry oufit then rotate to the rear and are replaced by a newbie...dare I say FNG again because regardless of the new officers' time in grade we will still have to show him the ropes. This is just the way it is. Officers and especially career officers need time in the combat roll. It is called getting your ticket punched. If an officer is in a combat theatre but does not lead in combat it could be a career killer.

Our newly assigned CO, also a captain like Baker, is a huge, strapping guy named Captain Fritz Weiss. He seems aloof, cannot fault him for that since he just arrived. He has a monster of a handlebar moustache and I right away nicknamed him Cap'n Crunch. Weiss was our acting XO for a while but I was unaware of this because I have been in the rear so little. He is due to, as they say, DEROS pretty soon meaning rotation back to the World so he is understandably anxious to get some command time with us legs. We will have the new Captain with us for a while before he rotates back to the World and then we will have one more before my time is up.

Side bar: So you know, DEROS stands for Date of Return from Over Seas (sic) and is the one date that every one of us has committed to memory.

January 2

Tuesday – I was awakened at 0330 hours. The big guns next to our position were booming once again, called up on a fire mission, shaking loose the few leaves that remained on the trees. I heard Captain Weiss briefing the platoon leaders right outside the bunker. The whole scene was surreal and I believed for a moment that I was dreaming because the New Year's Truce wasn't supposed to expire until late today.

    I figured something big was going down and sure enough it was. FSB Burt was in the middle of a human wave attack. Between the spent shell casings from the 175 mm howitzers clanking to the ground I heard small arms fire and 50 cal and 105's that began slowly and then reached a sustained pitch…a very real crescendo that showed no sign of slowing or tapering off. This could be bad and we were being rallied to get up there by chopper to reinforce. The unit(s) that were engaged belonged to the 2nd of the 22nd Mechanized and the 3rd of the 22nd Infantry and the 2nd of the 77 Artillery who had made up the convoy of guys that we waved at when we were lollygagging in the ditch the other day while pulling road security. Correction: The artillery had been air dropped earlier into what then became Burt.

    By the time we got saddled up and over to the airstrip it was about 0430 hours and it was a huge cluster fuck just getting there. I mentioned at an earlier time how dark it is here in the Nam on nights when the moon is some other fuckin' place doin' whatever it does. We had to hold onto the guys ruck that was in front of us and hope the lead guy knew where we were headed. Once at the air field we sat by the edge in formation and waited. It was then that it occurred to me how dangerous it was going be to move all of these guys by chopper in the dark and then join an already raging battle. I did not share these thoughts with anyone else but merely sat and waited, hunkered down feeling insignificant among my fellow boonierats. I could feel the gravity of our situation and a sense of impending doom began to creep in. I pushed back…the only goal of a combat grunt is survival and that's it, pure and simple.

Then I thought that if we could get close and move toward the embattled position anyone we could identify would be enemy personnel that were exfiltrating the area so we could shoot on sight. But would we not encounter firing from inside the perimeter that would also be coming in our direction. Then everything changed, got really fucking scary. The helicopters began to arrive and two Hueys collided over the air strip and a huge yellow orange fire ball of immense proportion consumed men and ships and the wreckage fell to the ground. I shuddered. Silence prevailed except for the mummering sound of flames consuming what remained of the wreckage.

Side bar: The original helicopters, over 7,000 in the first consignment of the war were designated HU-1 and because of the designation became known to troops, pilots and personnel as Huey's. Later there were many variations including one known as the stretch. This night the helicopters were all from the 187th AHC (Assault Helicopter Company) and the 188th AHC. We had been carried by them many times and they had always flown in support of us when we were in the jungle.

Cookie, our mess sergeant and his crew, brought hot breakfast to the edge of the field that we tried our best to stomach while the engineer battalion cleared the detritus of what had been serviceable helicopters. We sat silently in small groups and waited. No one spoke and feeling the gravity of the situation most of the grunts around me turned to the single most repetitive action known to the infantry...they cleaned their weapons. Laying their OD towels flat on the ground the boonierats disassembled their rilfes and cleaned them, polished them, applied a light coat of LSA oil and reassembled them. Finally, at 1130 hours we were on our way up to Burt to see what help, if any, we could offer. There was still the occasional report of sporadic AK fire but the battle, I assumed, had concluded probably with the NVA dragging their dead and wounded back into the jungle at first light.

It was difficult to determine the direction of our approach because by now the sun was directly overhead. The Huey slicks dropped us at some distance from the action and we approached cautiously sweeping on line. The closer we got to what was left of the perimeter the grimmer the picture became. The artillery had fired intensely at point blank range and every tree in sight was cut off waist high or lower forming a perfect circle out to over one hundred meters from the perimeter. Many of the dead VC and NVA were tangled, sometime two or more together so that individual bodies were unrecognizable. Many were nailed to tree limbs by flechettes which are tiny metal darts fired from artillery Bee Hive rounds at point blank range. With the barrel of my M-16 I lifted a face off one pile – a single face, no skull and then let it fall back to the ground.

When we got inside the perimeter the sight was unimaginable, something from deep inside Dante Alighieri's Inferno. 50 caliber gun barrels on many of the mechanized tracks were melted and sagging toward the ground. Piles of shell casings and the links that join the shells together were in piles everywhere and still smoldering. The remains of enemy combatants were all about, some missing arms and legs. Venturing further I came across a GI jungle boot with the shin bone and sock still inside. Many of the vehicles had been hit by armor piercing rockets and were burned and gutted almost beyond recognition. Burnt diesel was everywhere and the stench of hot gun lube filled the air.

There was activity all about the perimeter now, men moving to the task of getting organized again. It was obvious that a last-ditch effort had taken place and the heroism of the participating soldiers, while difficult to grasp at the moment, was awesome.

We pulled a short clover leaf patrol away from the perimeter and back in again policing up bodies of the dead as we returned. Later we learned that twenty-three American lives were lost and eventually four hundred enemy were brought to two collection points where the numbers of bodies on the piles mushroomed. Bodies were searched for intelligence and personal effects gathered and after photographing ourselves with the cadavers John Garlado and I joined a detail that grabbed individual bodies by the arms and legs and pitched them down into the huge slit trench that had been carved out by a dozer. Framing the bodies in my camera was a macabre experience and unnerved me.

Later toward sundown we moved to occupy the positions that the infantry had occupied the night of the human wave attack. We now are rebuilding the structures and have chain saws that were dropped in for us. Compared to the way we dig in at night I have several observations and I need to be fair, remain objective. First, the infantry that was here to protect the mech and the arty did not have time to prepare holes with overhead cover before the attack commenced. This seems unlikely because they passed us on the road two days ago and had time or, second, they lacked discipline or leadership. It's not my call really but the positions we are now expected to take over are really inadequate and need squaring away. The infantry withdrew rapidly when we came to replace them and they left personal gear and items like web gear and harnesses…totally unmilitary.

NVA dead at Fire Supoort Base (FSB) Burt

NVA dead at Fire Supoort Base (FSB) Burt

January 3

Wednesday – This place is totally scary and I believe that the brevity of our days patrolling activity bears this out. Each of the Battalion's companies pulled clover leaf patrol's, moving out through the concertina or razor wire that has now been strung around the perimeter. Once through the wire we move forward and out and my patrol was so short that the patrol leader was back inside the camp before the last soldier exited the perimeter. This could be an indication that at this time we are more interested in defending what we've got than we are in engaging the enemy. We did police up several more dead NVA soldiers and a boy of about fifteen or sixteen who had part of his left foot blown off. The overripe stump was already maggot infested. He cried chieu hoi which means, I've been told, open arms and signals that he was turning himself in. Sometime these enemy that surrender are trained in the Kit Carson program which basically means they are used as scout interpreters. The program was U.S. initiated and has shown positive results because the surrendering enemy brings his weapon or weapons with him.

Found time in the afternoon to go over to the battalion command post and visit with one of their medics, a guy named Lupold. I wanted to give him some film I shot around here to forward to Ehrig – remember him? We shot the breeze for a while. All of our positions are being fortified as though we'll be staying a while but no briefing and I've yet to see much of Captain Crunch. Some baptism of fire he's getting. There is a double row of coiled razor wire on the bottom with another coil on top. There is det (detonation) cord stretched forever with packets of C-4 explosive tied in with blasting caps. The cord is basically a fuse that burns at sixteen hundred feet per second which means that a piece of the plastic explosive at the front end of the cord explodes simultaneously with the packet all the way on the other end. There are claymore mines in the wire facing the enemy's approach each containing over 200 ball bearings packed tightly in a curved piece of high explosive. These are hand triggered devices so when an enemy makes the slightest noise when approaching the device is triggered and explodes. To top it all off there is a 50 cal machine gun mounted on every fifth bunker with excellent overlapping fields of fire. If the Slopes come calling again we are ready.

Battalion intelligence warns there could be another ground attack so all of the watches will be doubled along the bunker line. Just after dark an Ox cart was spotted moving down one of the two tracks just outside the wire. Our second platoon's ambush patrol was set just after dark and are totally surrounded. Sgt. Merriweather could barely be heard when he called in his situation reports. He then communicated with us by using a radio hand set click or double click. They made it through the night and came back in at first light.

When you sit on watch in the bunker while others sleep things occasionally get pretty creepy. In the pitch dark, you'd swear on that proverbial stack of bibles that you see movement and the longer you sit and stare the more convinced you become that the movement is real. If you utilize a little trick known as off center vision which involves turning your head to the side while you try to stare straight ahead you stand a better chance of seeing the movement if it is real. The creepy part is that after staring at some stationery object to your front you swear that it is moving. Next comes the decision to fire or hold fire. We were probed several times, detected noise to the front but nothing happened.

January 4

Thursday – Bravo staying in today to protect the battalion's portion of the perimeter. I had my radio watch and since the company is inside the wire here at FSB Burt there isn't much traffic other than the battalion calling infrequently to maintain proper protocol. We had a police call of the area, the inside of the perimeter is once again standing tall compared to the chaos and aftermath of the recent battle and truce violation. New fatigue shirts and pants were flown out from supply back in Tay Ninh rear but not so we could feel and be clean since our last bomb crater douche back at Katum which was several life time's ago. No, not for that, not at all. The shirts and pants were choppered out because word has come down that the valor and tenacity of the fighting during the human wave attack on the second of the month will be rewarded by a visit from four-star General Westmorland. He will be here personally to review the troops and hand out a medal or two. The kill ratio from the attack was impressive: final count was 23 American dead, 153 wounded and 401 VC and NVA dead and undetermined number of wounded.

Westy never made it in but, really, who cares. The important thing was the fresh clothing we received and who knows, if the body count had of been higher we might have gotten new boots, too. Actually, the irony of the whole thing is the fact that the guys that did all the fighting should be the recipients of the new clothing and the Westmorland visit. They may even be due a much needed in country R&R over to the resort and coastal town of Vung tau, but this did not happen.

We were assigned a South Vietnamese interpreter named Sgt. Binh today. He roughly translated some of the papers from the enemy dead that I did not turn over for collection to intel services. Strange to get that close or be that close to our enemy even though they are dead. Searching the enemy cadavers was kind of spooky. They were just normal young men like us, carrying as much of their personal lives with them as their pockets would permit. There were letters from their home provinces as well as from friends and families. There were notes of encouragement from leader Ho Chi Minh, pictures and keep sakes. A truly remarkable development. A few of our guys have NVA belt buckles with a red communist star. There was a certificate of medical appointment for the soldier who was a medic with the 731 NVA Battalion. The same soldier also had a list containing serial numbers of the weapons his comrades carried. He also had a note from a politician in Hanoi who was wishing the medic a Happy New Year and encouraged him to push hard for victory.

I know I have never mentioned this but Cindy and I have planned from the start that my major R&R (rest and relaxation) would be in Hawaii and that date is now one hundred and fifty-seven days away.

I have my moments. I have a difficult time believing that I am here where I am and making it through. I am experiencing some seriously scary shit. At the beginning of each day you devote little thought that this could be your last day. It's really almost humorous, strange maybe that you can hate this war shit but almost love it all in the same split second, the same freeze frame.

January 5

Friday – When I review my daily journal efforts and I always do this sooner than later, I notice a certain lackadaisicalness and it is entirely on me, created by me and it always centers on the appearance that this outfit does not conduct regular briefings between the commander and his platoon leaders. Bullcrap! The process is normally triggered by my visiting Battalion TOC (tactical operation center) and retrieving the order of march for the next day's activities. And very frequently it is the captain, Captain Wiess, performing this duty himself. It is vital and it is always getting done either the previous evening or on the morning prior to moving out. I am sometime not privy to the dissemination of the information but there still is the exchange for platoon leaders given by the company commander. Sometimes the captain calls the platoon leaders to our CP just after dark. The captain and his lieutenants sit in a small circle, always Indian style, with legs crossed and knees touching. The platoon sergeants hunker down just behind the platoon leaders and the CP personnel just behind that. Plans are presented, dissected and discussed in voices whispering low so the enemy could not hear anything in the deathly still of the night. The objectives must be clearly understood. Captain Weiss and Baker before him emphasized more than anything our continued courage under fire and how we must continue to close with the enemy and kill them. Tomorrow we will be on the move again and participating in an Eagle Flight out of here at about 0900 hours.

January 6

Saturday - The Huey's picked us up on the road coming in ten ships at a time single file. When the first lift is in the air it will circle back around allowing the second lift to join in and then we move toward our first objective or insertion into the landing zone.

The directness of our flight led me to believe that rather than a random flying and searching we were instead headed for a pre-designated LZ (landing zone). The LZ was hot but the hostility did not begin at once. Our lift was on the ground and the second lift was in bound... it would require three separate lifts to get Bravo on the ground. The soldiers from my chopper were moving away from me and into the wood line. I took out my camera and was recording the landing when 51 caliber machine guns opened up and began raking the landing zone from one end to the other. I looked up and saw the third ship in the lift take a bunch of hits. Flames erupted under the belly of the ship and rapidly engulfed the tail boom. The ship faltered and began to drop from the sky and at the last possible moment lifted up and scraped the tree tops and then dropped into the adjacent field at the end of the landing field and crashed. The volume of small arms fire was impressive and most of it was aimed at us. Shit was flying everywhere and well-spaced tracer rounds impacted the jungle trees that we were trying to reach for cover. I ducked into the wood line, camera dangling from the strap around my neck and raised my weapon to the ready. I saw Hardcore Moore with a severely wounded guy across his shoulders moving as rapidly as he was able considering the burden. They reached the safety of the wood line's edge.

We finally got the ships down and the remainder of Bravo Company into the woodline away from the heavy 51 caliber fire and small arms fire. Bravo was digging in, furiously. An air strike was imediately upon us and began to stem some of the machine gun fire but I could not determine if the close in air strike was responsible for the exploding tree branches along the wood line or was it the withering machine gun fire raking the landing zone. A small patrol sized element began working its way to the wreckage of the downed chopper. There was no way that I was going to miss the opportunity to photograph a burnt-out chopper so I tagged along, following the patrol to the end of the landing zone. The crew chief was killed and trapped inside the rapidly burning air frame and soon a chopper came to the scene from graves registration and sifted the wreckage and located the remaining door gunner. We were drawing concentrated enemy fire so worked quickly and close to the ground. Major Roush was there with his RTO and everyone was following his lead. Even though the door gunner's face had been protected from the flames by his helmet and face shield his face was a contorted rictus. His skin was burnt so badly that when one of the soldiers from graves registration touched the gunner's skin with an entrenching tool it just disintegrated. We guided the co-pilot and the remaining door gunner back to where our headquarters element had hunkered down and listened as they debriefed us on what had happened.

Patrols were sent across the open field to check the wood line on the opposite side from where we had received the fire. Trenches were found but a thorough search turned up only discarded and bloody clothing belonging to enemy combatants.

Later we sat in small groups on the (now) PZ – pick up zone and waited for the 187th to come on in and get us out but they had been diverted to assist Delta's extraction. Delta had also made contact. The ships finally made it in under heavy fire and I along with headquarters got on the last Huey and as it lifted us up and over the trees at the end of the pick-up zone the enemy had reset his tubes and began a heavy mortar barrage. The Huey's dropped us back at Burt and we immediately humped on over to the company area and began to monitor the radio net of Lieutenant Hector Colon's platoon. The situation was dire. The platoon was being overrun and was engaging the enemy in hand to hand combat. The Viet Cong had

Burned Huey at the Hour Glass
pilot, co-pilot and one door gunner survived the crash

Major Roush and RTO check out downed chopper at the Hour Glass

Ssg. Moore carrying wounded off landing zone at the Hour Glass

Staff sergeant Devore arriving at the Hour Glass
Ssg. was trapped on the ground and died that day

been watching and waited until most of the company had lifted out before they rushed across the open field and engaged Colon and his men. Shells blasted the clearing and machine guns ripped at the overhanging branches as the embattled platoon clung to the slight depressions in the jungle floor. When it was over and choppers were able to get back in just before dark, Colon came out with only nine men standing, seven dead and fifteen wounded.

The sad and tragic thing was that we had all been together only moments before. Then, with darkness approaching we were separated and could not go back, only listen as our friends were cut to ribbons. Heroic chopper pilots of the 187th volunteered and finally went back in for the extraction.

January 7

Sunday – At any given moment there are, in our area of operation, a pre-determined number of air ships (Huey's) available for scheduled operations. In addition to normal circumstances like Huey's being out of commission for repairs or reoutfitting there are happenings like yesterday when Delta Company observed weapons in the open and diverted to check the situation out. This allowed the enemy to prepare and launch their surprise attack on us when we landed at the Hourglass.

Sidebar: The location where we landed yesterday was shaped very much like an hourglass and Ltc. John Henchman moved quickly to name the distinctive topographical feature.

I am becoming acquainted with our interpreter Sgt. Binh. The rest of the guys call him Sergeant Bill, probably because Bill is so close to his actual name. Compared to American soldiers one could say, however, that Sgt. Binh is very lithe and this would be correct and in no way an intentional slight. In fact, you could fairly say that sergeant Bill is very much like a China doll, dusted porcelain face and all. But, there, all comparisons must be suspended. I forgot to mention that when first platoon was being overrun yesterday Sgt. Binh's weapon, he carries an M-16, jammed and he pulled his bayonet and literally slashed his way off the PZ, killing two enemy combatants to save his own and the lives of those around him in the first platoon. The entire first platoon will be decorated and that includes Binh. We are so proud of him.

Binh lives in Saigon, is 21 years old and is dating an English girl whom he hopes to marry. He shares living quarters with an American Military Policeman. He has friends in New York and hopes to study biology at the University in Saigon when the war is concluded. Binh like other South Vietnamese has three years of service to complete but his service is, I believe, voluntary. Each month he gets three paid days to travel to Saigon from wherever we are to collect his pay.

I was devastated yesterday when we got back to base camp. I went to visit with an older soldier, a father figure really, named SSG Devore to see if he was OK. The last time I saw him was on the pick-up zone at the Hour Glass. The Sergeant was waiting for the choppers that were inbound and I said, Hello, as I always did, as I moved with the Captain to board our chopper. We pulled up and out, mortars came crashing in and everyone scattered. Devore did not make it. I learned that he had crawled into one of the shallow depressions we'd dug when we first landed. SSG Devore took a grenade and died there on the Hour Glass. Some of the guys from First Platoon told me that he spoke highly of me and I will always treasure that. We'd spoken of visiting after the war. He was from Indiana.

Our company has taken a bunch of hits lately and we are down around half strength or eighty men. There are hardships that we are enduring currently like jamming too many guys in a single hole because we cannot dig fast enough. There is some grumbling about Captain Crunch but not from me...I am one of his greatest supporters. It is very difficult out here for new guys and especially a new commander. Now, I gotta tell you a weird thing. Right in the middle of the hot LZ yesterday I was watching Crunch and he picked a huge bugger and rolled it between his thumb and second finger...swear to God...but what the fuck I still dig the guy.

We are reportedly (rumored) to be going into Katum pretty soon to refit and get our shit back together.

January 8

Monday – Bravo now holds the smallest portion of the Battalion perimeter here at Katum. Today's activity amounts to a two-hundred-meter patrol away from and back to the wire. Nothing more and only our second platoon made the hump.

Stockman cleaned up a little and flew back to Katum to depart for his seven-day R&R. Crunch filled the slot with who else, me. Nobody has mentioned a thing to me about this change being permanent but it makes good sense and causes the least amount of disruption to the rosters for each of the platoons within the company. And, figuratively at least, I have already taken the position, carried the radio once or twice in the past two weeks. Stockman has proven himself valuable in the post and he is actually getting so short that he may not come back to his old job but travel with headquarters like I did as a sort of jack of all trades. And, speaking of the jack of all trades scenario I have no idea what's to become of my PIO liaison position between the company and the battalion. I suppose there are several considerations with all of them depending on the Captain's preferences. Actually, I have handed in very little copy but I have submitted scads of photographic negatives during the recent chaotic times

John G, Doc McAdams and I wasted a good deal of water this evening by carrying jerry cans back and forth between the water trailer and the headquarters bunker. With all of our activity lately and especially the air mobile stuff nobody has expended time or energy to construct any shower points within our sector. There is a small stream running close by and the water could easily be diverted through a heating element and bingo, hot showers. But for now, the water feels just great splashed liberally over one another's hot, tired bodies.

Had difficulty falling into sleep tonight but is this really a problem? We are enjoying the relative safety of being inside the wire, not in contact with the enemy or in imminent danger and well fed, what's the problem. Even when we are afforded an opportunity to kick back and just reflect on the natural beauty of the place, we're never truly relaxed.

I lay sleeping on my side with my arm sticking straight up…hey, maybe that's the problem…I couldn't sleep because I was too clean, not dirty enough. Naw! A bat had somehow entered the bunker and smacked into my stationary arm – wait a minute now, I know what you're going to say about the uncanny ability of bats to avoid objects by using sonar, etc. but I swear this much is true, the critter hit me. I shrieked out loudly because I had been startled. Murray O'Donnell (we call him OD or Oscar Delta as in the military phonetic alphabet) mumbled in his sleep, "who, what". Murray was asleep and must have thought we were under attack. Everyone settled back into troubled slumber including Crunch.

January 9

Tuesday – This was the first day that I humped the AN/PRC-25 radio all day and the 23.5 lbs. of weight entitles the wearer to refer to it with impunity, as a motherfucker. The radio was, however, because of the designation PRC being part of its nomenclature, more often called the 'Prick 25" or simply the 'Prick' for short. The rig is mounted on a flat board and worn on your back like a rucksack. Basically, it's a large, sixteen tube transistor radio and wearing one especially with the auxiliary antennae in position means that your life expectancy puts you in the same category with 2nd Lieutenant's and ordinary houseflies and that's about fifteen days, give or take. The straps exert an unbelievable amount of pressure on your back and shoulders and means that along with the other lifesaving shit that you carry with you like food, ammunition and your weapon just to mention a few, you are carrying between forty to sixty-five pounds.

But cheer up because there's good news. I think I look very cool and all the guys wanted one too or thought I was crazier than a shithouse rat and wanted nothing to do with me or… they thought I was crazier than a shithouse rat and wanted to talk to 'that' dude anyway. Another piece of good news seemed to be that the "Prick" might stop a round from severing my spinal cord and turning me into a complete vegetable. Oh, and one more thing… the "Prick" makes an excellent back rest for when you stop along the trail about a million times a day. Because of the radio I figured I knew just about everybody in the company. Guys were always sayin' shit like, "oh, yeah, he's the Old Man's RTO, Bravo Six Xray. And no matter how you looked at it, I knew almost everybody and I figured at the very least that with all of those guys around me my life expectancy soared and that was a positive.

The channel I monitored was the Battalion 'push' or frequency which meant I was either talking to the Old Man, Manchu 6 or his Xray and for being savvy and having an inside track on what the relevant skinny was, it didn't get much better 'n that.

Parting the wire in the morning I could have sworn I smelled death and it bugged me all day. Once you get that unmistakable smell in your nostrils it does not abate. Returning at 1430 hours in the afternoon my suspicion was confirmed. Two bodies that actually smelled more like two thousand were located in very shallow graves at trail's edge. Someone with a bizarre sense of humor had positioned the arm of one dead VC so that it protruded just above ground with the now stiffened fingers holding a can of Ballentine Ale. A small stick placed beside the hand held a note that stated, I could kill for one of these! The arm holding the can was such a provocative image that everyone in the Battalion had to have a photo. One of our lieutenants came rushing forward hollering, spread out, one grenade'll get you all", and "it could be booby trapped." Before moving on we all pulled our dicks out and urinated all over the putrefying arm.

Side Bar: Ballentines is the kind of shitty swill beer the Army dock workers send us up here in the boonies... and we did refer to the horrible stuff as piss water. The good stuff like Bud and Coors and maybe Pabst they'd keep for themselves and use for bartering.

Negative contact all day. Major Bill Roush walked point all day with his RTO. They were both wearing soft caps. Roush had a 12-gauge pump slung across his shoulders like he'd ever need it and the RTO was carrying

Dexter takes over radios after Stockman leaves for R&R

a holstered 45 caliber Army issue that you'd be lucky to hit the side of a barn with. What a casual attitude I thought at the time, acting as though there weren't any enemy within a dozen clicks. I guess maybe for some of the newer soldiers such a thing could almost act as inspiration but I thought it'd get you killed. This is the Majors second, I think, tour and he's getting short once again.

Mortar attack after dark. Only nine rounds incoming but that was enough. Charlie called a dust off for three guys.

Captain Crunch (Fritz Weiss) is beginning to grow on me and I feel pretty comfortable with him in spite of the sudden nature of his appearance and Bakers leaving. The Captain was a police officer near Detroit before he joined and attended Officer Candidate School. He is more uncomfortable with us grunts than we are with him. It shows in some small ways. Here's one. It is very obvious that even as a captain of infantry he has not yet been in any situations where the troops he is commanding treat him with trust or familiarity. This is what made Captain Baker so effective. He knew exactly where the 'line' was between him, the Captain, and the rest of us Regular Army or Draftee soldiers and he could live with it. It is what made us all so great together. And do not think for one minute that we – the grunts – didn't know where that line was. Baker did not have to remind us. Hard to explain but the whole thing worked not in spite of respect but because of respect. I can see Captain Wiess's wheels turning. He's getting it!

January 10

Wednesday – Today like many others lately was spent safely tucked inside the wire. Our numbers having been severely whittled away has got to have something to do with this. This is not the kind of information contained in a company level briefing but something that transpires at the top between Manchu 6 and his operations officer.

Our positions are all inside the perimeter line and have been fortified and refortified over and over again so things can get pretty boring around here. Wrote a letter to Cindy and read – and I mean I read – a Playboy cover to cover, screw the centerfold.

A rumor that we will cycle back to Tay Ninh for several days continues to circulate. The recent briefing has guys commenting about the unlikely chance that we will be immediately redeployed because our numbers are so low. We badly need an infusion of new meat for the grinder before again entering the fray.

And speaking of boredom…I put myself through the same cigar and chaw thing that I did with Captain

Baker a while back with the same predictable result...I got sick. Ugh!

January 11

Thursday – Once again we are the leave behind company. I hung around the company bunker reading and napping, lack of curiosity kept me from roaming about the Katum base camp. Additionally, the facility is pretty limited, bare bones with no PX, barber etc. I do better personally when we are in the boonies and doing what we do with no spare time. That way I am exhausted at days' end and sleep comes more naturally.

You may recall me mentioning some time ago where I had submerged the camera that Captain Baker gave me to use for the PIO job. He has never asked for the camera back but that's not my point. Having most of my pay sent home to Cindy every month means I have very little if a need arises. A rusty camera certainly qualifies as an emergency 'need' but my only way to address this is through the written word to Cindy. I have asked for a hundred bucks and all I have received so far is a hundred bucks worth of grief. She says, by letter to me – which is about as expeditious and efficient as the kid thing with two tomato soup cans and a piece of string – that she does not trust the mail and that the money might get lost. What am I to do? Well, getting angry or being disagreeable through long distance mail is rather difficult but I sent her a nasty response anyway. We have said to each other that we would not let money become a source of anger in our marriage but...

I have completely changed my mind about the new Captain or is it possible he is that good and in effect, changed my mind for me. Our conversations are good ones and involved if we happen to be alone somewhere.

Easier to get along with than Baker who had me tag along everywhere. Of course, I always had the Prick on my back and he was walking out ahead of me and he never had to remind me a second time to keep up. I did notice once during an air strike where Weiss had Lieutenant Dossett call for the shot that he, Weiss, visibly displayed his angst, was really frightened. I could read it in his eyes. Captain Baker displayed unbelievable cool under fire.

January 12

Friday – Charlie Company out-posted and flanked the trail coming back in this afternoon and Alpha and we, Bravo, high-balled it through the safe zone created by Charlie Company and when we passed Charlie's last out-posted position we veered off into the jungle and reconnoitered three pre-determined objectives. Later we established a two-company perimeter and hunkered down while our patrolling elements searched the thick jungle area more thoroughly. Everything was going well until Alpha's patrol sitting astride a high-speed trail panicked when a company of VC sauntered down along the trail. The patrol engaged the enemy with small arms fire and did it too quickly – before the enemy company had fully entered the kill zone – and as a result several enemy were killed but Charlie also had several wounded in the brief fire fight that ensued before the majority of the VC had fled.

Most of us, myself included, have been involved in too many skirmishes with the enemy, exchanges of small arms fire where we do not actually see the enemy nor does the enemy see us. We rarely see faces. I am curious about these situations beyond the sterile mechanics of two groups of soldiers engaging each other or observing each other in one another's midst. I mean, what was going on beyond an enemy patrol emerging out of the dimness of late evening. Did one of our guys carefully aim down the barrel of his M-16 rifle, did our American infantryman sight on the first Viet Cong, the leader of the patrol or did he shift his rifle a few inches right or left to look at the next soldier. Did he see the enemy's eyes or wonder how old he was or did he have a family? girl friend or father? Did he go to church? Did he laugh or cry and what did he think of having his country invaded since before his grandfather was born? If any of these things happened in my country, in my neighborhood, to my family, I wouldn't stop until I'd killed every last one of the fuckers. If I didn't have a weapon I'd wrestle the invaders to the ground and tear their ears off with my teeth.

Later in the day we came upon and uncovered seven very fresh enemy graves. We claimed each for our battalion as body count. Bravo now has more compiled body count than the rest of the Battalion combined but who's counting. Get real, these statistics are at best imaginary and highly inaccurate and only exist to prove that we are winning or making progress. Some of the things that are daily required of us cannot possibly capture the feelings of disorder and confusion, the utter meaninglessness of what we are doing. Our body count since the beginning of this operation known as Operation Yellowstone is 93. Today's action marks the first time that we, Bravo, had a contact but not had a KIA. Wounded yes. But no deaths.

January 13

Saturday – We are still operating out of Katum. Today we swept east of Burt. Burt is one of those places that I mentioned earlier that highlights the absolute futility of what we are doing here in Vietnam. The original battle for this place (as told in this diary) was fierce and we return here frequently but our only success, our only progress is a burnt-out hole, scared earth and twisted metal and shell casings that the enemy turns into their home-made mines and booby traps to use against us.

Heard for sure that our rotating back to Tay Ninh has been delayed until further notice, or as Crunch succinctly put it, "always seems like the only thing coming our way is the day after tomorrow, doesn't it?"

Tomorrow we will return here, sweep away from Burt and accomplish this with Alpha Company,

With all of our movement I have misplaced my tape recorder and on it my last tape to Cindy that I was working on.

Heard from Ehrig over at Battalion that six of my recent photos have been forwarded to the Tropic Lightning News, the division newspaper, one will be published with my by line.

January 14

Sunday – We must have humped a zillion miles today. Blast oven hot! With each new, exhausted step that I was able to pull from an almost exhausted reserve my numb mind repeated one more, just one more and… maybe somehow my empty canteens will magically refill themselves. Marching like this is very dangerous and such a loss of focus means that a misstep could occur, I could be wounded (again) or worse, killed. Crossed a creek and past an old abandoned VC base camp. Was that the smell of cook fires or just my mind fucking with me. Passed another village or was it the same one? Concentrate, for God sake concentrate. Are we following a map or lost?

Finally, we stopped. A chance to lay back against the radio while our platoons set out small ambush sites. Crack some c-rats. Bum some water. Relax and close my eyes.

I must not be the only one who is exhausted. We somehow became separated from Alpha. Hearing single shots fired in rapid succession Crunch fired off a green star cluster hoping Alpha would zone in, find us. The captain thought it was the Cong trying to coyly suck us into a fire fight but nothing happened.

On the way back to our point of origin and having rested for an overly extended period of time to hopefully satisfy battalion that we weren't screwing the pooch, we stumbled through a mesmerizingly clear stream. Thoughts of submerging Baker's camera reminded me about the importance of somehow procuring a new camera. Except for a splinter thought about ruining the Prick 25, I badly wanted to recline in the stream, close my eyes and drift away. The whole camera thing caused me to obsess on earlier thoughts about not being disagreeable with Cindy about money. But I did receive a most prickly letter from her trying lamely to explain that her only concern that money sent me would become lost. Really, Cindy. I had replied with a one sentence letter…just send the damned money…Love, Todd. I probably will live to regret this. Again, I do not need the distraction while I'm out here and the real down side of stuff like this is that it gets filed away in that little black folder of the mind that is forever there and not completely erasable.

A really unusual and irrational thing about being in the jungle, being a killing machine, and developing the closeness I develop with all kinds of fellows that I am travelling this road with is the immensity of the isolation that I experience. Like seeing Staff Sergeant Otis Boatright every day and knowing not one thing about him except for the fact that he needs a fresh pair of socks or Doc McAdams has cue tips if my ears really get itchy or that Stansberry is from Des Moines but I don't know how he got here or if he has a family. These are weird relationships. I wonder if we'd be good friends under other circumstances?

January 15

Monday – Unless the Battalion's mission is clearly stated operations seem pointless. It could also be said that a boonierat's job is to not question why but to do or die…all that bullshit but that does not change the fact that I'd personally be able to do my job better if I understood what the goal is, our mission or do as my father instructed me to go over there and "don't come home 'til the job is finished, you've killed all of those slant eyed commie pinko bastards."

Anyway, today's exercise in futility serves as example. We humped over four clicks (remember that a click represents one kilometer as viewed on topographical maps used to navigate). Once at the terminus of the march we were to establish a base and then send out clover leaf patrols. However, the armor unit we encountered named Fullback was already operating in the area. This is what is called a SNAFU…situation normal all fucked up. Fullback was engaged in fire missions so to avoid interference we just sat in place for most of the afternoon. In the end, we humped out and back, a total of over eight kilometers for what seems to be nothing. We rested in place occasionally so the hump, in spite of the extreme heat, was not a total ball breaker.

The activity for the entire day yielded several long abandoned and dilapidated gun pits. We could see that the perfectly circular holes that were approximately two and a half feet deep and had solid pillars of earth in the center were used to place guns that could be swiveled 360 degrees to bring down aircraft. Also found were several fighting positions and spider holes and a long dead and decaying body. Parts of the body were strewn along the trail, a leg here, part of the torso a little further on and next to the head we found a back pack with a deck of cards. The Ace of Spades had been left in the mouth of the cadaver, a calling card used by some American units to mess with Charlie's mind because Vietnamese have superstitions about this funky shit.

We also found one other corpse that was dressed in the brown kaki of a North Vietnamese soldier. He had crawled between the huge roots of a gigantic Banyan tree to avoid outgoing fire during the Battle for Burt. There wasn't much left of this character and the calcium white of exposed bone and teeth was beginning to show.

It seems that we are going in tomorrow and will be passing through Katum and then down to Tay Ninh. Hector's platoon is to be decorated for their brave stand at the Hourglass on the 5th of the month. Did I mention that Ltc. Henchman named the feature in the jungle the Hourglass due to its shape? None of us will ever forget what happened there, I can tell you that. Rumors have been floated that we may return to The Glass but there is not much enthusiasm for a return engagement in spite of the fact that as previously mentioned, we are always anxious to engage the enemy. When an incident (ambush or enemy attack) takes us by surprise it has a tendency to be a bit unnerving. If a contact like that is something that is planned or covered in a mission statement then we have time to get ourselves amped up with the anticipation.

I received a letter this week from my Little Brother in my ATO fraternity from college. He was telling me to check out another frat member, a guy named Brent

Motheral who is at the 45th Surgical MASH in Tay Ninh. The guy was behind me at school so I don't know him but will look him up.

January 16

Tuesday – Saddled up just after sunrise. Route step, unorganized march, from close to Burt where lift Huey's were ready to drop us back to Katum where without delay we boarded a C-130 for a quick ride back to Tay Ninh. Shit, when was the last time we were even near this place. Duce and a halfs were waiting and brought us to our company area. The first thing I saw was Stansberry's smiling face greeting us from the stoop of the orderly room. The best news of all was that Dan handed me my tiny reel to reel tape recorder and the two reels with a full tape were still on it. Right after Christmas at Katum before all the chaos descended upon us Snipes had convoyed back to Tay Ninh and taken my recorder with him. I had totally forgotten. On that convoy he, Snipes, took some shrapnel in one of his eyes…still haven't heard how he made out from that episode. I think he was evacuated to Japan.

After cleaning up and sloppin' down some chow the second squad of the second platoon – which is the bunch I began with – all walked to the PX a couple of city blocks distance and purchased twenty-two cases of beer which we planned to consume on our brief stand down. Each member of the squad carried a case on each shoulder and calling cadence as we marched back into the company area to ice down the brewskis. If anyone can put down this much beer it's gonna be second squad, second platoon.

Sgt. Boatwright had put me in for Specialist 4th Class a while back and the paper was completed by the time we got in. It will be official very soon and the pay hike beside the pride of wearing the new patch will be a forty-nine-dollar adjustment to my pay voucher.

Watched a movie tonight with my old squad mates but was too sloshed to really see *Barefoot in The Park* featuring Robert Redford and Jane Fonda. Could not tell you if it sucked or not.

January 17

Wednesday – A wooden platform that was to become the base for another company storage building became a great place for rowdy poker games on or around each pay day when we were all in base camp. The games of chance, mostly draw poker and seven card stud always, as today, drew huge boisterous crowds. Since the number of cards in a deck limits the number of actual player's, side betting on who will win the pot as the hand progresses with each new turn of a card is also popular. And though I've played my share of cards with good results I have mostly been an observer at these events. I limit my participation to an occasional pull at the bottle when one circulates through the crowd. Gambling with such a reckless crowd, guys who may get greased the next time out scares the shit outta me. Officers refrain due to the perceived conflict of interest.

Yet another memorial service in the chapel across from the company area. There was a rifle salute as we all entered the chapel and while these services for fallen comrades are not mandatory almost everyone attends. The twenty-seven men who gave their lives since we last met here in this chapel were put to rest with proper ceremony. Their names were all printed properly in the program passed out as we entered the chapel but I did not accept one. There were many somber countenances and some tears as each soldiers' name was read. In a weird sense, these services somehow galvanize the resolve of the rest of us to carry on, stop our shrinking numbers though we know that such thoughts are unrealistic. Revenge killing gains momentum each time we lose another brother.

Later in the afternoon there was a service of an altogether different nature and purpose. Chests were thrust forward and some smiles returned as Brigadier General Wm. K Mearns, with the entire battalion as witnesses watched as the general pinned medals on the remainder of the men in the first platoon, a Silver Star for 1st Lieutenant Hector Colon, Bronze for the rest for gallantry in action against a hostile ground force.

And, of course, I had a bizarre thought go shooting through my mind. The soldiers of the first platoon, many my good friends, were fighting for their lives that day the same as we all do each day we go outside the wire. How come we do not get the same medals. Then my own answer: we do get medals if they are actually that important. They are called Purple Hearts and Combat Infantry Badges (CIB's). Also, to not give the special recognition to higher medals would diminish their importance. I'm not sure I can say this correctly. I do not believe that anyone questions the commendation medals awarded to individual soldiers for heroic behavior under combat conditions but don't we all qualify each time we leave the wire. Perhaps the answer lies in the unit citations that result in a banner or streamer to be added to our division guidon.

Battalion party cancelled for now…maybe tomorrow after we Eagle Flight back up north and west around Nui Ba Den.

January 18

Tuesday – Up with the light, 0500 hours. Choppered up to Katum and then out in the direction of The Black Virgin Mountain, Nui Ba Den. This is the closest I have been and I had no idea of its immensity. The mountain is a cone shaped mountain of solid granite covered with trees. Near the summit sits a two-acre American base that communicates with U.S. units in the area. The Mountain is eighteen miles from Cambodia and was taken from the enemy during a helicopter assault in May in 1964.

The landing zone was not prepped with air strikes and we landed cold. The remainder of the battalion also landed with no difficulty. Alpha led and their movement away from the LZ was restricted by the very dense bamboo. They hacked their way for over an hour only making about one hundred meters so we sat near the landing zone.

When the sun reached its zenith the still air and the heat was so intense I believed I'd pass out. We sat in the open, spread out around the zone and then were lifted back into Tay Ninh around 1630 hours. We popped smoke so the lead choppers would know where to set down and the brush immediately caught fire. We needed all hands to stomp the fire out. Captain Crunch pitched in, later wishing he had not. The flames licked up and burnt off one entire side of the captain's beautiful Manchu handlebar moustache. What a laugh.

Back in the company area we enjoyed the huge barbecue with steak, chicken, veal and all the beer and soda we could consume. There was a large volleyball game but it was hot and I was too full and lazy to participate so I just watched.

January 19

Friday – First call of the day scheduled for 0500 but due to a generator malfunction everybody kept on marking time in the sack, no one was up and about until around 0700 a.m. The reasoning was that the CQ or charge of quarters was unable to see sufficiently to perform wake up duties. So, I wondered, all flashlights malfunctioned as well?

Finally, we were trucked to the air strip for C-130 to Katum. Alpha was off first but forced to return because Katum was under mortar barrage. As we sat by the air strip I overheard someone who was reading from what was apparently a hometown news clip. The ensuing discussion was, at first, pretty calm by GI standards – we can be rowdy and opinionated but when the flames of our discussions receive a new source of oxygen, stand back. When provoked we sometimes shout and holler as well as we do when we're fighting. There is a lot going on back in the World, subjects that due to their volatility or because they are controversial are off limits as far as *The Army Times, The Stars and Stripes* and division publications are concerned. The discussion I overheard, which became heated, centered on guys, dissenters I guess you'd call them, seeking asylum in Canada rather than allowing themselves to be drafted. Another hot button topic back home, one that divides Americans, is whether or not our war is a war at all or merely a police action. Regardless of what one would call this mess it is something that has the potential to divide us as soldiers or military personnel and interfere with how we do our job and therefore the brass does not want us discussing it and usually we do not. Another subject, aside from whether the conflict is called a war or a police action, is the legitimacy of the entire proposition. Some believe that the Gulf of Tonkin

Resolution legitimizes our country's escalated attacks on North Vietnam because the resolution is predicated on North Vietnamese gun boats attacking an American destroyer the Turner Joy and the gunboat Maddox in the South China Sea. Some argue there was no such attack. And while I really know nothing about the alleged attack I do have a strong opinion about some of our young countrymen fleeing to Canada but for once I'll reserve that opinion for myself. My deeply held convictions and Patriotism demand of me that I serve but at the same time I reserve the right to defend the right of those who would choose not to serve. This, I am afraid, if discussed openly, would make me unpopular with my fellow soldiers. And another thing, I wonder quietly how is it that so many Negros find themselves in the service to their country, whether drafted or enlisted. I greatly admire them for serving a country that treats them so harshly. After all, it has only been three years since LBJ managed to get Civil Rights legislation passed. There are so many places in their own country where they are not allowed to vote, are treated poorly, and yet here they are fighting to protect freedoms that in many cases they do not themselves share. Questionable! Also, admirable.

 Before long the operation, cancelled because of the mortar attack, was back on. When we received word to return to the air strip, this time to the chopper pad, we were already back in the company area and enjoying beer and sodas. We were placed on thirty-minute standby and finally got under way this time. Hurry up and wait…go Army!

 Bodies bent low to avoid the tremendous heat of the backwash from the engines of the CH-47 that were spooling up in anticipation of departure, we marched up the gang plank and sat on pipe rack and canvas seats that lined the hull of the ship.

Back in Katum after the short hop we moved into an area that was being vacated by Delta. For once we did not get screwed over in the exchange. Our CP bunker is huge and spacious with three descending steps chiseled from the rock-solid ground that lead down into a cavernous hole. There are sleeping racks and tremendous overhead cover – logs about a foot and a half in diameter and covered with three layers of sand bags. We are close to the perimeter and the CP itself borders on a bamboo thicket probably populated by dozens of rats and fuck you lizards. The perimeter defensive positions are impressive as well. Delta did a fine job.

Our status will be static for the next several days or at least that is my hope. Then I expect we will begin patrolling – many areas previously visited – in an attempt to knock out some of the mortar sites that have been shelling this perimeter. As we were moving in to replace Delta there were several incoming mortar rounds and at once there were two companies crammed into the defensive positions usually occupied by just one company.

Coming in I glimpsed the star shaped fortifications of the CIDG camp and from appearances I'd venture a guess that they are close to up and running and totally capable of defending themselves, the point of each star houses a heavy gun emplacement. Now that this symbiotic relationship seems to have been consummated, if you will, and our resources could be better served somewhere else and Katum could be closing soon.

Hot chow tonight but no mail.

January 20

Saturday – Sleeping inside the bunker is safe and comfortable but the confined space retains heat due to inadequate ventilation. The poncho at the head of the stairs can be pulled back allowing more air but the mosquitoes gained makes for a poor exchange. Also, the poncho serves as a light block when the Coleman lanterns are running after dark. With as many as eight guys sleeping on the racks and the lantern in operation we're all borderline oxygen deprived but the well-lighted bunker enables us to read which is a real luxury. The light also allows the captain to call his platoon leaders for briefings for the next day's activities.

Last night I barely slept at all due to the above-mentioned problem with ventilation and Doc McAdams informed me that about halfway through his turn at radio watch a big fat rat climbed down from the ledge above my head and perched on the side of my air mattress.

Long hump up the road toward Beauregard. The small road has been cleared back about fifty meters on each side by the engineers and their Rome plows. Since the trees that were cut remained where they fell walking off the road on either side is challenging. Our point man on the right side of the road, where I was walking in column, spotted some movement ahead and shortly after that observation there was a tremendous detonation and a column of dirt and debris shot skyward a hundred feet or more. A good guess was that the explosion was caused by a command detonated (an enemy was observing and triggered the explosion) mine, probably a buried 105-mm howitzer round. The incident killed one of our new replacements, a FNG. The soldiers' possessions including shredded uniform pieces, wallet and money fluttered in the breeze as the equipment cascaded back to the jungle floor. Several guys rushed forward and policed up what remained of the dead boonierat, threw the remains in a poncho and when a LOCH (light observation helicopter) arrived on station the poncho was chucked onto the flight

Prince and McAdams both medics deep in our heavily fortified Bravo command bunker

deck and away they went. The day's sweep continued on as if nothing had happened…all of us alone with our thoughts.

Later we engaged in a small fire fight. Could it have been with the same Gooks we saw crossing the road just before the command detonation. I do not know. We had been pinned down by one or two VC. I only detected fire from one AK-47.

One of the Mechanized outfits helping to protect our perimeter had a mad minute tonight at dusk. Many soldiers along the bunker line probably did not receive word because everyone on the west side of the perimeter opened fire or they just joined in to burn up ammo and replace with fresh. I've got to tell you it really feels good to stand up, hit the selector to full auto and scream over the racket at the top of your lungs.

January 21

Sunday – We swept both sides of the same road again today but further back into the part of the jungle that had not been cleared and probably won't be. Very monotonous work. We established a small perimeter and each platoon sent out a small clover leaf patrol. Third platoon got lost for a time which only means the platoon leader misinterpreted his map. Back on track they returned to the perimeter. The highlight of first platoons stumbling was that they encountered a small falling down hooch or shelter. No contact with the enemy.

Bravo has been assigned three Chieu Hoi's that surrendered to another of our battalion elements over

Sweeping the road

in the Ho Bo woods. They will be part of what is being called the Kit Carson program and each of them is actually referred to as a Kit Carson. I met them personally while they temporarily travelled with us in the headquarters element. They are useful because they can interpret VC radio traffic that jams our net every once in a while. They are also good at detecting booby traps and trip, wires. The one I got to know was about four feet seven inches and his M-16 looked enormous in his hands. I was unable to understand the proper spelling of his name but it sounded like Coo. He is married and has a wife and children in Saigon and a mistress in Cu Chi, or so he told me. His family wanted nothing to do with the VC which is understandable so he surrendered to us. Coo's surrender to us creates a delicate balancing act for his family. Whether or not the family sympathizes with the VC determines if the VC will leave them alone or murder them.

The three Chieu Hoi's appear to be effective fighters and good under pressure but the possibility that they could lead us away from enemy strongholds or intentionally into an enemy ambush is anyone's guess. They enjoy firing the M-16 rifle and say they like it much better than the Viet Cong's basic weapon, the AK-47. This seems a little weird because the GI's I know that have handled both prefer the AK. They speak very little English and instead shake hands incessantly as if to reassure us of their loyalty and they smile constantly.

January 22

Monday – Our operations officer, Bill Roush, a major, chooses the rotation that determines whether a company in the battalion rests in the rear or participates in the day's field operations. Today Bravo was inside the wire. This is a cherished time when troops rest, relax, clean weapons, write letters and refit. I do all of this, of course, but I also get in a nap or two and cannot escape the feeling that in Army parlance, I am getting over. Due to me being senior in our headquarters element means I have a say in who has radio monitoring during what time period in the day. I have rearranged the rotation so I am able to sleep most of the night, getting an uninterrupted stretch. Then again, sleeping during daylight hours causes a problem because of the number of fuck you lizards in the bamboo stand next to the bunker. Very annoying.

Today I was trying to catch a few z's and woke from a bad dream in which I was thrashing back and forth and dreaming that I was being electrocuted. When I came around I discovered that I had fallen asleep on my arm and the tingling sensation was, I guess, kind of like being jolted with electricity. Sometime I think that once I am back home and this is all over that the things I have seen and participated in will cause bad dreams of their own. Also, in a way, it seems as though I've been away from home for so long now that this is my home…I no longer have a home the way I once did. Could I become a career soldier thoughts creep in occasionally? Only time can resolve these thoughts, indicate to me whether or not a full career in the Army would suit me.

January 23

Tuesday – Everything is going great the past several weeks and my spirit is in fine shape and even though I did not need to walk I wandered over to the TOC (tactical command bunker) and picked up Bravo's evening patrol order.

We literally crawled three thousand meters today and because of the bamboo did not find a single place we could stand and stretch our legs. I am not all that familiar how bamboo grows as an organism or propagates itself but I'll take a stab at it. I believe that due to the bending over or draping tendency of the plant that when the shoots grow to sufficient length gravity brings them back in contact with the jungle floor and these shoots attach and begin new growth. The jungle is a tangle of small tunnel like openings we must crawl through. The progress forward is very, very slow.

My knees are killing me. We left Alpha Company behind to set up an ambush and we began crawling back in the direction we came. Looking skyward I could just make out the CH-47 that makes an evening run up to Katum. I am positive that the bamboo partially obscured us from the choppers vision and because they were not monitoring our frequency they had no idea that we were friendlies and they opened fire. Considering the volume of fire striking the ground all about us it was miraculous no one was hit. No place to duck for cover so we lay motionless so we'd not be mistaken for more enemy movement. We learned later that the Chinook had reported taking fire from our general location and that was the reason the CH-47 returned fire.

Last night the rat that is cohabiting our bunker with us got brave. In the silence inside the bunker I listened intently, could hear his squeaking on the ledge above my head where the dirt ends and the overhead logs begin. The critter bailed off the ledge and landed on a corner of my air mattress displacing enough air to bounce me upwards a bit…big rat. Tomorrow I will concoct a little gift of C-rat peanut butter, rat poison and cheese and see if that will take care of the problem. I jumped rapidly myself and aimed the beam of my flashlight and there the bastard was, a huge rat almost seven inches long not including the tail. He squeaked twice, jumped to the floor, scurried up the steps and out into the night.

January 24

Wednesday – Air mobile today. Lt. Jeff Dossett our Arty Forward Observer has been breaking in his new replacement these past few days. The replacement's name is Lieutenant Smith and he is a ROTC by-product or Rotsy and I mean that in the most unflattering way imaginable. Spec 4 David Ruggles who is Dossett's RTO would make a much better and more qualified replacement except the slot is a lieutenant's position. I got a bad vibe about Smitty right off when he emphatically reminded me that he was Lieutenant Smith and not Smitty. I said, "I'll keep that in mind…Smitty," and immediately followed that with a gratuitous…SIR. The whole thing was disrespectful but tacking on a sir usually ends such folderol.

Smitty is from Cincinnati, smokes a pipe that he is constantly fiddling with and cannot seem to keep afire. His eyeglasses are Coke bottle thick. To sum it up in the jargon of the troops, Smitty is a dud. He actually walked at the beginning of the day's sweep way up on his tippy-toes. Considering we slogged almost six clicks Smitty was one worn out dude at the end of the day.

Smitty or I guess I should really refer to him as Lieutenant Smith or the Lieutenant makes you wish you'd have attended OCS, and become a lieutenant as well just so you could hassle him on his own level. I suppose the other way to regard the situation is to be thankful you weren't a lieutenant because that way you'd not have to share in the embarrassment of having to say that you were a fellow officer. He keeps giving me bad looks as if he's thinking I am too friendly with officers. Well, Smitty, you and I are on a rough road together until I get you broken in, teach you that out here in the jungle the rigid chain of command, officer vs enlisted crap is a more relaxed proposition and everything works just fine.

January 25

Thursday – Another uneventful day is expected. The 28th of the month which is three days from now is, we've been told, Tet. There is some confusion regarding this holiday in my own mind. Several weeks back, Christmas week to be exact, I may have referred to the period as Tet which, if I did, was an error. I was probably confusing Christmas and the truce we were supposed to be enjoying with the enemy as Tet. So, forgive me that. However, having said that and not to confuse things even more – I think of shit I have trouble explaining as one of my personal International Dateline incidents - do you recall my mention of that cluster fuck? Anyway, Tet begins on the first day of the first month of what is known as the Lunar calendar. This is different than the calendar we Americans go by and, I promise as God is my witness, that someday I will figure this all out. Adding to the difficulty is leap year and also the fact that the Tet Holiday usually runs for seven consecutive days. To be sure and not relevant to my rant is that Tet is upon us and there will no doubt be truce violations or at the least a violation of the time for ending the truce.

Slept in until nine. Ah, the luxury of being a radio operator and not part of the line squad. No ambush patrol, no listening post and being deeper inside the base camp when we are home or inside the perimeter or hard spot means there is some buffer between me and the Dinks.

Took a shower, rinsed and dried my underwear. Shot the shit with Captain Crunch. His badly burned Manchu mustache is slowly returning to its original, face diminishing size. I actually laughed at the sight and he asked me what the sam hill was I laughing about and I told him, "sorry, Capt'n, but I cannot help myself, it's your stash." He, or I should say we had a hell of a good laugh about that one. He asked me if I'd liked Captain Baker and I said that indeed I did. Captain Baker is going to be one of the all-time great soldiers, I added. "I know you got that right," Crunch chimed in and we sat in silence until one of the lizards in the bamboo thicket interrupted the silence with a perfect, "fuck you!" and we laughed even harder.

"Mind if I ask you a question Captain Wiess, sir?"

"No, not at all."

"Well, I know you enlisted and volunteered for Officer Candidate School knowing that as an infantry officer you'd be headed for the Nam and probably a combat leadership role."

"Correct, so what's the question?"

"The question is why? You might not know this but I was drafted when my student deferment expired. The decision about me being here was made for me. In training, I was pretty well brainwashed with all the yelling from the Drill Instructor that the spirit of bayonet was Kill, Kill, Kill. It was drummed into me but still…"

"You're not sure if you could pull the trigger."

"Even though my job description means killing and I have participated in many skirmishes without actually seeing the enemy I am not sure what's gonna happen when I look in some Gook's eyes…if that ever happens."

"Well", the captain began, paused before picking up the thread, "I guess nobody can be certain when it gets down to the big you or me question. I believe God knows and that he will be guiding you and me…His hand on the tiller and that sort of thing." The Lizard did not stir and silence closed about us.

Spent time trying to distract myself by looking through some audio magazines to determine which make of reel to reel tape deck I might like some day when the time is right.

January 26

Friday – Hotter than hell in the bunker made worse by a mistake on my part. Instead of using Kerosene I filled the Coleman with diesel fuel. The smell was horrendous and everyone slept on top of the command bunker until the odor and sooty smoke had cleared. "Shoulda blamed it on Smitty," McAdams giggled.

While monitoring the radio on my watch one of our elements, the 1- 5, checked in to alert the bunker line that their AP (ambush patrol) was approaching the perimeter and coming in so be careful not to fire on them. I called each platoon to make sure everyone was alert but could not raise the second platoon…tried again with same negative result, still nothing so I threaded my way carefully along the established path that led away from the command bunker toward the line and then ran along behind each one of our positions. I did not bring my torch or flashlight with red filter and by the time I stumbled up to the second platoon's position I was rather pissed. I shook SSG. Greer awake and asked him where his radioman was. "Right over there on the ground, ain't he"? "No, he ain't,' I said rather sarcastically using his form of butchered English language. Greer is Canadian, not that that has anything to do with it…some people with an educational equivalence of a fourth grader do rather well but not Greer. The sergeant is not well regarded by the rest of the troops and usually can be found around the fringe of a group observing but not yukkin' it up with the rest of the guys, not participating.

I said rather too sternly, "someone is supposed to monitor that radio at all times are they not?" I sounded more like a line officer chewing out one of his men than a specialist 4th class addressing a platoon sergeant. Before Greer could respond a muffled voice from under a nearby poncho close to the squad radio timidly asked, what time is it?" "When I answered 0505 hours," the voice responded that it was his watch. I was furious and shouted that they'd better get their shit together because we have a patrol that has been trying to reenter the perimeter for the past quarter hour.

By now sergeant Greer, crimson enough to make my flashlight unnecessary, yelled at me, "Watch your mouth specialist, you are talking to a platoon sergeant E-6. Greer, in my estimation, was deflecting because he then accused my own headquarters group of sleeping through our own radio watches.

In the morning, Lt. Jobman and E-6 Greer pulled me aside and tried to deal with me privately and even threatened me with an Article 15 for insubordination in the incident. I was confident that this would never happen and I'm certain they knew that the captain would be severely pissed if the incident came to his attention. Emboldened by this I pressed the issue. "I suggest that we figure out how to settle this here and now," I said. "I understand that the sergeant feels his toes were stepped on but the negligence involved with a sleeping radio operator endangering the lives of every soldier in this base camp far outweighs Sergeant Greer getting his feelings hurt. I suggest that we forget about this so we needn't proceed up the chain of command beginning with Captain Wiess," I concluded by adding the little intimidation. Greer and

Jobman remained silent, then conferred with one another, readdressed me by telling me they'd get back to me.

Another six-thousand-meter sweep today. At one-point Greer passed me on the trail without looking directly at me or speaking a word to me. I did not share the circumstances with anyone but I stewed for most of the day over the incident. At one point, I entertained the thought that perhaps I've become increasingly bold but then dismissed such thinking as being an outgrowth of being good at what I do.

During the afternoon Charlie Company called on the horn and told us to pick up the pace. That was a little pissy I thought, that's something we would do.

January 27

Saturday – I received a letter from my brother expressing his concern for my safety and asking that I take care of myself, keep my head down. His letter contained a copy of the same article that Cindy sent me a while back about all of the enemy activity around the new forward base camp established by the 25th Division. There was one particular sentence that I did not record any thoughts about before but is worthy of mention. The article reported that the new base is certain to meet with a great deal more violence than was required to establish the fortress initially. Looking back now I believed that these words were meant to suggest that the new base camp itself was in extraordinary danger of being overrun or enduring some sort of ongoing siege. The kind of engagements with the enemy that took place at Beauregard, FSB Burt and then the Hourglass and the loss of lives on both sides was, I think, more reminiscent of WWII engagements than the jungle warfare that we've been experiencing up until now.

Things are escalating. The establishment of Katum was, in a way, responsible for all of the actions in the area but in the end the enemy fought us on his terms, in the jungle rather than attacking our well-fortified position at Katum itself.

All of the previous speculation about Katum encountering a great deal of violence as the newspaper article suggested is, so far, perhaps just speculation because we have now been back at Katum for seven days with only sporadic mortar and rocket fire incidents. However, G-2 (intelligence) insists that Charlie could be biding time and preparing for an all-out attack that seems eminent and most likely would occur during Tet which is just around the bend. We have heard already that we will honor a thirty-six-hour truce agreement but it beats me why after the VC violated both the Christmas and New Year's truces. I guess the enemy honoring our traditional holidays has little meaning for them.

We had a small company sized sweep down the rugged little road to the east and set an ambush that yielded nothing. We were hoping to drive any VC in the area into Charlie Company as they lay in wait further down the trail.

Returned to base, relaxed and wrote several letters. Occurred to me later that I had missed mother's birthday. I think given my circumstance she may find it in her heart to forgive me. Hard to remember stuff like that being so far away from home.

January 28

Sunday – Beginning of Tet, short for Tet Nguyen Dan which stands for First Morning of the First Day, also signifies the arrival of Spring in accordance with the Vietnamese calendar. According to the appropriate symbol (different one for each of twelve years) this is the year of the Monkey. And...I believe I mentioned that all Vietnamese celebrate their birthday's during this time of year. Just wondering...do many Vietnamese know as much about American traditions as I just displayed here? Doubtful! Know your enemy.

We were prepared to move to action at 0730 hours and then our time at the PZ was moved back to 0900. As we finally marched in loose formation (route step) we began to receive mortar fire in the Second Platoon's area. An FNG named Harry Andrus, who I knew slightly, was hit in the head by mortar frags as he dove for cover. At first, he did not show any signs of distress but soon retched and began to vomit which is standard for head injuries. He thrashed violently as he was carried ahead of us, placed on the front of a jeep and moved to the air strip for dust off to Tay Ninh and the 45th Surgical Battalion. Goodbye Harry.

The day's objective was altered due to the mortar attack and we were flown in the direction where the rounds originated to establish a blocking force. Alpha was then inserted and began moving toward us to trap the enemy. As is often the case the result was a zero. We humped back into Katum which was a considerable distance. I know it probably sounds simple when I mention that we humped here or marched there but the reality is generally far different and involves a large portion of that day's activity.

At one point the battalion commander's C&C (command and control) observation helicopter took several rounds from the ground as it circled behind us. We suspected then that the VC may have allowed us to pass by and were closing in behind us and giving chase. John Hernchman called for gunships to flank our column and strafe the jungle about us. The sudden eruption of machine gun and 20 mm cannon fire startled Captain Weiss and

Smitty and they practically came out of their skins right then and there.

My imagination was in over drive this afternoon. We had stopped our forward motion, resting in place. I had pulled one of the three canteens I carry from its pouch on my belt and tipped it straight up to allow the last trickle of water to run down my throat. I imagined being surrounded like the Calvary in some John Wayne movie when I tipped my canteen an enemy bullet passed through the aluminum can without injuring me. I laughed out loud. Captain Weiss gave me a weird look like maybe I was losing it. As I related my thoughts a warm grin filled his countenance but still he must have thought me nuts.

January 29

Monday – Briefings never really cover the rationale for going to a given map location or why we would return again to the location of a previous skirmish. That responsibility belongs solely to upper echelon and who knows, maybe Tropic 6, the division commander receives direction totally unknown to us. Today we returned to Bo Tuc, the battlefield of FSB Beauregard. Our LZ was just outside the intersection of the jungle paths that were familiar to me and the site of the well from which some of the enemy emerged and that we latter collapsed with explosive charges. The position of the artillery battery that was partially destroyed by Viet Cong sappers had been further reinforced then abandoned, the guns pulled back to Katum. The location now resembled a roadside park in America with trash everywhere. Someone had spray painted an old WW II slogan, Kilroy Was Here, on a half full sand bag.

When we first landed OD (Murray O'Donnell) a fellow RTO tried to help me get oriented to the location but I failed to recognize anything until it was almost PZ time and the slicks were inbound to make the pick-up. I discovered our old CP positions and the hole I'd occupied the night we killed three Cong right in front of the hole as the enemy tried to leave the area.

The day was routine with us, Bravo marching through endless open fields trying to draw the enemy in for an easy kill. Later while attempting to extract everybody I believed that we would get mortared. Delta was totally disorganized and the helicopters sat on the pick-up zone for almost ten minutes.

We are staying back again tomorrow so I'll be able to get a shower and clean the command bunker. The cheese and rat poison combination did not phase the rats who seem to be increasing in numbers and the stench is overpowering. Whew!

January 30

Tuesday – If I were to search back through the pages of this diary I feel confident I would discover that whoever figures the rotation - which company actively participates in the days' operations, and which company tends to business inside the base camp – I'd discover that we, Bravo, have been richly blessed in the numbers of days that we have remained inside the wire.

We are being held in reserve once again today. The VC hit the perimeter with rocket fire early this morning but I continued to mark time safely on my sleeping rack deep underground in the command bunker. When I did get myself going I wrote several letters and walked down to the shower point. The luxury of a hot shower belongs to the stay behind company. The primitive structure is basically a tent with a suspended wooden slat floor to allow for good drainage. Water pumped from a nearby stream is heated and delivered to each of three shower heads attached to overhead pipes. Totally rejuvenating and the one time we are not constantly nagged about water conservation.

Back at the bunker I waited patiently for Cap'n Crunch to finish reading the Playboy so I could get my hands on it.

Midafternoon a guy named Lucido came in from Tay Ninh by chopper. The guy is our company armorer, takes care of the company's weapons, recording serial numbers, putting individual weapons back under lock and key when someone is killed or wounded or medically evacuated and no longer needs them, etc. Anyway, Lucido informed me when Captain Weiss was away from the bunker that we were getting another commanding officer. Why do we always hear this stuff through the grapevine? Lucido told me to check it out cuz the new guy has been around the rear area and seems a rather empty shirt. Great, a new CO that we'll have to show the ropes as if we didn't have our hands full enough with Smitty who is still stumbling about. I decided right there that I'll be cautious about new personnel since I was rather harsh regarding Captain Weiss and I really liked him the longer he was out here with us.

Tomorrow is payday and then I'll be broke again for another thirty days. I am, however, expecting to receive a little residual pay left over from my PFC rank.

Another rumor. We're headed up around Cambodia again and maybe into that country. We were so close last time, who knows, we may have miscalculated our map coordinates and actually been inside Cambodia…illegally. That place is mortarsville for sure. Ugh!

January 31

Wednesday – 0330 wake up for an action involving a lot of humping – over fourteen thousand meters (clicks) all together – if we hadn't got a lift back to base at the end of the day. I could have used a good night's rest but due to a slow leak in my air mattress my chest made contact with the slat boards on my sleeping rack every three quarters of an hour or so.

We exited the wire at about 0350 and had not proceeded more than 500 meters through thick under growth and in complete darkness when the Slopes began their daily mortar and rocket barrage. An element from Katum, the Golden Dragons kept firing illumination rounds which necessitated us hitting the dirt to avoid detection. There was no artillery in support of our movement so it didn't take long to surmise that the mortars and rockets that began to crash in the jungle around us were harassing fire belonging to the enemy.

We made it to our first objective about sun up and it was only five hundred meters from Cambodia. The terrain was sparse with trees scattered here and there. Delta took several casualties and their assailants evaporated into a Cambodian sanctuary.

Continuing on we discovered many hooches and protective, camouflaged positions that we destroyed as we moved, leaving burning wreckage in our wake. We found one hospital containing bandages and supplies, another mess facility with cooking equipment and a class room with a standing chalk board. On the chalk board was a diagram of one of our ArmoredPersonnel Carriers (APC's) with arrows pointing to the most vulnerable points on the Track (yet another name for an APC) to disable the machine with RPG (rocket propelled grenades or shoulder fired weapons).

We moved back toward base by traversing a previously used trail whose terminus is Katum. Like most trails we encounter in the jungle when we are miles from villages and villagers, this one due to the obvious traffic upon it, is most likely a Ho Chi Minh trail artery. Movement along these artery's causes us to be very cautious, more so than the monotony induced when we are passing through open fields. When on trails that show wear, one expects to encounter an ambush.

Later in the day we received a radio contact from battalion that radar had picked up a sizable force about eight hundred meters to our front that was moving to intercept. We double timed for almost forty-five minutes. Nothing happened.

After the incident of mortars hitting all about us in the jungle, the enemy shifted his focus and began raining mortar and rocket fire on the base itself. At that same time, Tan Son Nhut Air Base and Saigon had reports of VC hit and run movement in many streets of the city and surround. Machine gun fire in Cholon as well. Cholon is on the West Bank of the Saigon River and is where most of the city's market activity takes place. The area is known to be the largest Chinatown in the world. Meanwhile, in Saigon, infiltrating VC seized the American Embassy. Elements of the 101st Airborne were brought into the city and soldiers of the 173rd landed on the embassy roof and fought their way down and out into the streets killing 21 VC. Beginning of Tet Offensive for the enemy?

February 1

Thursday – Captain Weiss, the Crunch, left unceremoniously today. I feel privileged to have personally observed the transformation of a young officer as he moved from shiny new fatigues and polished jungle boots to just another one of the grunts diving for a spot in an overcrowded bunker as mortars came crashing through the low tree limbs. And through everything we… the company…experienced, he was an exemplary leader and a text book example of how a new line officer should conduct himself. How, you question, would a lowly specialist like myself make that call? Well, I'm qualified because I can compare Captain Weiss to my former commander Captain Alfred W Baker, the soldier you will recall I opined would be one of the Army greats of all time.

I had a moment with Captain Weiss, my second commander, and we shook hands heartily and I wished him luck on his new assignment which is with the Old Guard in Washington D.C. Not many people know this but an assignation to the Old Guard is highly prized and so well respected. The Guard protects the Tomb of The Unknown Soldier and is involved in all burials of the military's highest-ranking officers at Arlington Cemetery. The Old Guard is known for its spit and polish. A very prestigious outfit. Ordinary soldiers do not make it into the 'Old Guard.'

As with Baker, I felt there was a sharing of mutual respect between my latest captain and myself. I respected him way outside his rank…I respected Captain Weiss the soldier, the man. He was less than a year my senior in age and this kind of makes me think once more about my missed opportunity with OCS and way, way back in the dust bin of my mind – my lack of courage in not enlisting but waiting for the draft to claim me does haunt me.

Lieutenant Jobman, who I greatly admire in spite of the Sergeant Greer and the sleeping radioman incident, again took command of the company for the day. Seems the new CO is under the weather. The day's activity was a sweep toward Bo Tuc, where else? The routine was becoming ingrained. We set up a base and sent out small patrols. Charlie Company was approximately eight hundred meters away doing the same. I know all of you movie goers out there anticipate that this combat thing is as glorious as depicted in your movies so let me put you on alert. There is a sameness, a monotony to what we do... patrol here, set an ambush there...hours and of hours of boredom punctuated by very brief periods of tortuous anxiety, deafening noise and explosive killing with lots of blood. Not at all glamorous, believe me.

Returning to Katum we heard the report of impacting mortar rounds and when we radioed ahead the battalion informed us that they were taking quite a few rounds inside the perimeter and along the air strip. As on previous operations we could hear the signature pop of mortar rounds being dropped down the tubes followed by a faint swooshing sound as those same rounds passed overhead from the direction of Bo Tuc where we'd been operating for most of the day. Katum had taken so many rocket and mortar hits since our being there that the base was nicknamed Kaboom by the troops. As we neared the wire a number of short rounds began falling all about us. Charlie Company took casualties, three ambulatories meaning they could walk OK but two of the WIA's were serious enough to necessitate an evacuation chopper to come out. The task was difficult because there wasn't an open area of sufficient size for the medevac ship to land and even less time to hack out an LZ in the jungle. The chopper pilot was damned good and hovered long and low enough to allow Charlie's guys to load the wounded.

There is so much frenetic activity following incidents such as these that one scarcely has time to catch one's breath let alone think about what happened. Describing the feeling of helplessness experienced while laying out in the open with mortar rounds impacting around you and your fellow soldiers is sobering. Looking through the splayed fingers that were uselessly attempting to protect my head I could see the faces of Jobman and the rest of headquarters guys curled up around me in the fetal position and trying desperately to wriggle closer to the ground. There was actually some nervous laughter mixed in with the, Holy shit's and other invectives hurled skyward at God who, we felt, was probably not listening.

Lt. Smith has a rotten cold and, you guessed it, now I've got the sniffles as well. First time I have actually felt off my game since I have been in the bush... for the first time since I've been in the Army, actually.

February 2

Friday – Another glorious day in the rear for Bravo. As my watch concluded and the sky was turning rosy pink, I woke the company so they could get some chow. I remained in the rack until almost nine, I hate breakfast. Voices talking up top and just outside the bunker entrance aroused my curiosity and when I finally surfaced the first thing I heard was someone saying, "and haircuts for every swingin' dick in the outfit." I assumed that the directive was coming from the new CO since I'd never seen the speaker before. Just what we need, I thought, another ROTC guy going by the book, never seen combat or a shot fired in anger, blah, blah. Turns out it was not the new CO but someone from over battalion just preparing us, he thought, for the new CO coming aboard. Captain Weiss I learned is still being carried on the morning report and Lt. Jobman is still at the helm until all the red tape passes through channels, etc. This will be my third commanding officer (CO) since I have been with Bravo and do not believe that our efficiency has suffered with these changes in our command structure.

Wrote letters home, did some reading. Slept on top of the bunker at night. Cooler up there with good air circulating about. Has not rained for a very long time. Since I have been carrying the radio I traded my M-16 for the M-79 grenade launcher. I know I mentioned this weapon before. In essence, the M-79 turns the troops who carry it into grenadiers or mortarmen. I carry some high explosive rounds that look like gigantic shotgun shells and also some rounds that are packed with buckshot for close in stuff. Since my main responsibility is the radio, and due to being with the headquarters element and near the middle of the formation as we move through the jungle, I rarely fire any rounds and seldom need to clean the weapon. Others (squad members) clean their weapons every chance they get because weapons are finickier and jam more frequently.

February 3

Saturday – Heard during our briefing today, Jobman still acting CO, that the 2nd of the 14th, Golden Dragons will be pulling out and returning to Tay Ninh. This will mean a shrinking and rearranging of the entire bunker line and we (4th of the 9th) will defend the entire base. Part of the briefing informs that we will be returning to Tay Ninh sometime after the thirteenth with a stop just down the road from here at a place called French Fort. I am familiar with this location and mentioned earlier that we sat in the shade of these old bombed out French looking structures, probably dating to the 1800's and the French Indochina period. We were at the air strip there waiting for a convoy. We are also supposed to spend time at another place known as Sien Dan. Also sounds French but I may have the spelling incorrect.

Word around the base is that Katum will be closing and when I heard this I reflected back to my observation that the base could close down due to the CIDG camp being almost completed. The Battalion will be last to leave and the artillery will pull out before we do, leaving us a little vulnerable. Plans for what happens after Kaboom falling to the Rome plows is as uncertain as ever.

Bravo Company marched one side of the trail toward Bo Tuc today and Charlie was on the other. No flank security since the trees and all brush have been cleared back on both sides of the trail for more than fifty meters. We did veer off into the jungle several times on our side to send out patrolling elements. Charlie ditto on the other side. Alpha came down the middle once we and Charlie were fully off the trail. Alpha finally set an overnight ambush patrol. Before the ambush was fully settled in they had engaged and killed seven VC who came barreling down a side trail on bicycles. Weapons including two sub-machines, clothes and some documents outlining plans for several hamlets in the area were captured.

Alpha returned to Katum with us because their position had been compromised. Charlie Company out posted the trail ahead and we highballed it back to the barn. Alpha Company brought along the captured booty and passed us riding the bicycles and were having a good time celebrating their success.

Earlier in the day our first platoon found a dead and badly shriveled VC body in the jungle. Could have been death by air strike but Bravo claimed and called in a body count of 1. How irrational is that?

February 4

Sunday – Staying back again today. The First Platoon, however, will patrol close to home. Nothing too strenuous and close in enough so weapons platoon can back up with small mortars if necessary.

Best scenario for us staying in today was that Lieutenant Jobman was required over at the BN command center to discuss and plan for the relocation of the bunker line. The engineers will begin blowing holes in which the new bunkers will be constructed. Sand bags will be emptied along the existing bunker line and moved to and then refilled for the new positions. The engineers will then plow the abandoned bunkers and level the jungle even further out. Open fields of fire benefit us in the event of a ground attack and also discourage the enemy from attempting to overrun us.

The first platoons' movement today was once again along the trail toward Bo Tuck which is an actual place on the map and also the location of FSB Beauregard. Late afternoon Delta Company moved in next to us. The consolidation of the bunker line will be accomplished.

While patrolling yesterday…well, actually we were low crawling, through an expansive bamboo thicket, the gold cross and chain that Cindy gave me just before I boarded the plane for Fort Lewis Washington was torn from around my neck. I discovered this later in the day and was pretty torn up about it. The weird thing about the incident was that that was the first day I made the hump without wearing a shirt.

Lieutenant Smith, Smitty, is becoming a bigger dick with each passing day if that can even be possible. I should send you a picture so we can laugh together. He, as I mentioned earlier, is a byproduct of an ROTC program at some college. Consider that I did not and would not have joined something that about ninety per cent of any student body would consider beneath them to join and you get an idea of what we're dealing with here. Smitty really does not belong in uniform. We recently trekked past an old 55-gallon drum of CS gas and all of our scuffling stirred the gas which can remain active if left undisturbed. This material which, I believe, is often called riot or nerve gas can disable breathing to quite an extent and then some interesting things happen like not being able to draw breath, loss of control of bowels and snotty puking. OK, so, now you've got the picture. Oh, yeah, it also makes your eyes tear and impairs your vision. Most of us were somewhat affected by the gas as we rustled by but the lieutenant went crazy. Snot came flying out of his nose as he panicked and, just as rapidly, put on his gas mask. The rest of headquarters just stood by and watched the wretched display and…he wore his gas mask for the remainder of the day.

When we set up our NDP (night defensive position) Lieutenant Jobman requested that Lt. Smith call in his pre-plotted air strikes to fire direction control. As we waited, I pulled a couple of warm beers from the auxiliary sleeve that houses an extra-long antenna for my Prick 25, and handed one to Lt. Jobman who was perched on a rock. Meanwhile the company was digging in for the night and we were ready to call the resupply ship in with ammo and the usual. Just an ordinary day in the jungle. Smitty got off the radio and threw himself on the ground and pulled his flak vest over his head. When Lt. Jobman asked Smitty what in the hell was he doing Smitty yells out, "ya better get on the ground, too, cuz I've got no idea where this stuff's going to land." We all cast glances at one another because the FO is supposed to know exactly where we are on the map and that tells where the ordinance is going to come in. We were all chuckling until the salvo came in one, two and three right square in the middle of the perimeter. Fortunately, nobody was injured or killed. Smitty's days could be numbered with Bravo Company.

February 5

Monday – In again today, how unusual is that. I believe this the first time we have been the stay behind company two days in a row. I awoke to a card and a letter from Cindy. Being up here forward of Tay Ninh the mail service has been poor to lousy but we have been so busy that there is not much time to dwell on lousy mail service. When we set up at night in order to receive a resupply the mail catches up to us.

I hate to continually harp about Lt. Smith but this cat has really got my goat. The saga continues. Somehow, he senses or understands that he does not fit in, that he is the anomaly, a square peg in the round hole. Maybe it's a complex of sorts or the result of being so unsure of himself. One of the other RTO's commented to me that it would somehow make more of a man outa the guy if he had never been a lieutenant but just an ordinary grunt like the rest of us. Hard to believe that he did not somehow get washed out of OCS before he got into the pipeline. But when I got drafted there was no escaping it, you were goin' and that was that, you coulda deep tongue kissed the guy in the line next to you at the physical…no matter, queer or not you were going. However, once in Basic Training there were several extreme cases where guys were washed out, sent home. One guy had glasses thick as Coke bottles and when we were summarily marched from the reception center to the first aid building for a blood draw the same guy, Cook was his name, passed out right after he was given a glass of juice and was sent home at once. Then there was Ebaugh, so overweight and fat he could not keep up with the rest of the platoon and he was sent home. He received huge 'care packages' from home containing nothing but cookies, cakes and pies. Now that I think about this it was probably mommy's way of washing her precious baby out of the military. There were these two monolithic landmark hills at Ft. Knox named the Agony and the Ecstasy and there was no way the company could make the summit because Ebaugh kept falling farther and farther behind. The DI would make the whole platoon execute a reverse march to go back down the hill and retrieve Ebaugh. The asshole just could not make it and the entire platoon was punished for it.

Any way you slice it, Smitty bugs me. Last night he pestered me for over forty-five minutes to go out and scrounge some ice for our cooler. I was reading a magazine by the light of the Coleman and rather comfy and had no intention of leaving the bunker to stumble about and try to find ice. Frustrated and beginning to get angry I just said to the lieutenant, "why don't you get the ice," and then pausing I added, "Sir." Funny thing was that until the rest of the enlisted guys in the bunker started to laugh Smitty had begun to climb out of the bunker to go for ice. The lieutenant then waged a finger in my face and threatened me with an Article 15.

Do not get me wrong. I am not obsessed by thoughts of death but we know that death is all around us here and, yes, I do occasionally think about death and especially the random nature of it. One thing for sure that has happened to each one of us here in the Nam, wounded or not is a certain preoccupation with thoughts regarding our demise. I have observed the most dedicated among us, the hardest fighters be killed and I have also observed soldiers who are going through the motions, do as little as possible and are truly petrified and I've seen these same guys get their tickets punched, get on that big Freedom Bird and headed for home. Makes no sense. Does not seem to matter if you are spiritual or not, a great combatant or a coward, I think that when your number comes up that's it, the end, lights out. The Grim Reaper moves among the ranks randomly pointing his finger and that's it.

February 6

Tuesday – A word about Lieutenant Jobman: In addition to being this company's Executive Officer, XO or second in command, he has, during the three changes in Commanding Officer, been acting CO for almost as long a period as either Captain's Baker and Weiss served as commanding officer. Considering some of the difficult times this lieutenant has marshalled us through, he deserves much more credit than he receives.

Today he assembled our platoon leaders and platoon sergeants and delivered a 'poop talk' or situation report about developments in our area of operation and things appear to be disintegrating rapidly. The highway from our original base camp at Cu Chi all the way to Saigon, about twenty-six miles, is under VC control. Not too long ago a single jeep or a convoy could move freely and unmolested either way on the road but no more. Sniping, firing and explosive devices and land mines planted in the road inhibit travel in either direction. B-52 strikes, limited to this point, have been employed along the route in an effort to drive the enemy back and away. Cu Chi is having a difficult time as well. The town itself which is located just outside the wire of the base camp and for which the camp itself is named has been ransacked by Charlie and those villagers lucky enough to escape are now in bunkers within the base camp or just outside.

The citizens of Tay Ninh City are having a big religious ceremony and intelligence predicts that the two battalions of VC that are reportedly infiltrating the area will employ their usual tactics of beheading village chiefs and general harassment to gain support.

We are on a twenty-minute standby alert. Choppers are on call and we are ready. If we go it will likely be to the inner city (Tay Ninh). The 2nd of the 14th Golden Dragons will go first followed by us as needed.

In the meantime, the efforts to make Katum defendable goes on. The bunker line is consolidated and almost completed. The command bunkers for each of our companies are already constructed so basically, we are sitting on our hands until ordered to move. Tomorrow I will carry the radio and stick close to Lt. Jobman in case we get the order to move out.

With all that is happening closer to Saigon and on down the highway there probably is little concern that we would be deployed in that direction unless things get really messed up. The primary responsibility for this sector of our area of operation is handled by the Big Red one and sometime elements of the 1st Air Cav. We will wait and see what develops.

February 7

Wednesday – Based on Lieutenant Jobman's briefing yesterday you'da thought our world was about to come crashing down. It did not! I think the lesson here, one we should have learned from some of our past experiences, is to be more circumspect about the information we receive from higher up the chain of command. The convoy out of Saigon headed for Tay Ninh was ambushed after passing Cu Chi. Very few casualties and the 2nd of the 14th Golden Dragons responded as they were so much closer.

The company spent the afternoon working on the fortification of our new sector of the perimeter by adding more sandbags, can never have too many and beefing up the overhead cover always pays dividends. The engineer battalion is still levelling the old bunker line and pushing all of the brush and trees felled by the gigantic Rome plows even further out. There is now more than a hundred meters from the consolidated bunker line to where the jungle begins. There is a level of comfort given by these improvements.

Our new digs (bunker) is more spacious and the walls are totally sided with boards from ammo and mortar crates and again we have wooden racks to sleep on. There is plenty of room between the wood sides and the dirt walls of the hole. There is sufficient head room to allow standing. For now, we have Coleman lanterns for light but soon we will have a generator. I confiscated a real mattress from the former tenants and if I am able to stave off someone with higher rank from taking it I am going to be in for some decent slumber.

February 8

Thursday – My monitoring of the company radio and battalion net ended at 0600 so I sacked out until nine. O.D. actually woke me so I could assist the rest of headquarters move over to our new command bunker. Took us to about 1300 hours to get all squared away. One of the South Vietnamese soldiers, a Chieu Hoi, swept out the bunker for us and in the process, someone's transistor radio went missing. I do not really call this stealing because of the difference in the way we look at things compared to the way the Vietnamese look at them. In their minds, they are simply using the darned radio and I do not think that the soldier thought that removing something from the bunker constituted stealing. I would not have even been aware of the incident if one of the troops who moved out of the bunker hadn't returned looking for it. I did know where the Chu Hoi had gone, down to second platoon with my buddie's so I tracked him down and returned with the radio, gave it back and nothing more was said. The Chu Hoi did, by the way, try to deflect by telling me as best he could that a *mama-san* had given the radio to him.

    I may have mentioned that occasionally our weapons platoon is taken to the field as another rifle platoon and because our numbers have not been built back to full strength their numbers are welcomed and needed. In base camp, the mortar guys work with 82 mm (or is it 81mm) which were too large to hump through the jungles and because the primary weapon of every infantryman is the M-16 that is what they carried. I have occasionally seen our weapons platoon carry a 60mm mortar on missions and would sometimes place the tube in a steel pot for firing because humping the base plate and other auxiliary equipment was far too burdensome. When we were to be in one location long enough the mortars were brought in and pear pits, so named because of the relative shape, were dug. The platoon finished digging the pits and placing their aiming stakes and the tubes, which are always inside the perimeter rather than on it, are belching out rounds again and it sounds good, reassuring.

    No mail today. Have not heard from Cindy for over a week now and it's no fun not receiving mail. I write whenever I can and often accomplish the task while we are in the field and send stuff back to Tay Ninh to be posted to the States. We built ourselves a shower right next to the CP bunker, a 55-gallon drum with a crude spigot in the bottom which is nothing more than a short length of copper tubing pinched shut at the end. Very adequate and while not luxuriously warm like at the shower point it saves the walk. Also, we have to haul our own water in five-gallon jerry cans.

My legs are covered by a rash that itches far worse than Poison Ivy and I haven't a clue what it is, maybe chiggers.

We are spread pretty thin here at Katum so we're trying to create the impression that there are actually more of us here than there actually are. We are not employing scarecrows or placing dressed up soldier dummies on the bunker line and we are not worried. We have the tremendous buffer zone between the camp and the jungle as well as excellent over-lapping fields of fire and many claymore mines just inside the razor wire that rings the base camp. The engineer battalion did a most excellent job in slicing the Katum base camp almost in half and confidence is extremely high that we could turn back any attack.

February 9

Friday – The only real chore around the new and improved Kaboom involves policing up the new area. Read most of John Steinbeck's *Cannery Row*. Some day when this is all over I plan to visit the places he writes about and will have already been introduced.

Supposed to have an air mobile operation from here on the thirteenth coupled with a long hump the day after. Between the thirteenth and the twentieth things are rather uncertain due in part because we still do not have our new CO yet. Cannot imagine what could be holding it up. Heard in the afternoon from Lt. Jobman that Major Roush, the Battalion Operations Officer that we will be pulling back to Tay Ninh again and prepare for another foray into the Hobo Woods and the Bo Loi area. Not sure whether I'd like to stay here or move back.

Chow in the evening was served from a line of strategically spaced gigantic thermos cans capable of maintaining either hot or cold food stuffs. Our mess sergeant and mess hall are still maintained in Tay Ninh and hot meals are sent out from there by helicopter. We had the tastiest Mulligan stew that I've had in some time. It contained broad flat noodles, tomato and ground beef or lean hamburger. The line was set just away from our command bunker so we, the headquarters element, could relax in the shade of our poncho roof in the captured VC hammocks that travel everywhere with us. Many of the guys sat in the shade with us after they had filled their plates. Because I know one of the mess sergeants, a pleasant guy, a specialist who happens to be from Muskegon, Michigan, confided that we were actually eating dog meat. "I'll be damned," I replied with great surprise, "that's the best shit I've eaten since arriving in country." He then told me that "we Apache eat it all the time on the res." "Who'd care," I said. His name is, believe it or not, Alvarez but we all call him Chief because he claims to be a full-blooded Apache. He told me something I'd not heard and that was that supplies at the docks in Saigon and the convoy routes from Saigon all the way up to Tay Ninh have been so badly disrupted and that supplying base camps like Cu Chi and Tay Ninh has been very difficult in recent weeks and that he had to engage in some creative cooking. Chief then shrugged his shoulders and gave me the old wink and a nod saying, "but the troops gotta eat, don't they?" I laughed. He told me to keep it under my hat and just before getting the mess kit disassembled he asked one of the guys in my VC hammock, "Hey, you guys seen any dogs around?"

February 10

Saturday – Off radio watch at six. When we are relatively safe and tucked inside the base camp/hard spot, monitoring the radio is a necessary but boring proposition. One guy is required to sit next to the radios, two are of primary importance. The radio I carry in the field is tuned to the battalion frequency. My main contact is the battalion commanders radio operator. In one scenario, he and I relay messages to one another that are then passed on to our respective Sixes or commanders. In other words, I give messages from the battalion commander to my company commander and he responds through me back the battalion's RTO who passes the message to the Battalion Commander who is Manchu 6, John Henchman. A different scenario would be my captain taking the horn from me and speaking directly to the battalion commander. This happens when things really get dicey. On occasion, I speak directly to the battalion commander. If my CO were seriously wounded or killed I would be capable of running things for a short period.

The other radio of importance that needs to be monitored twenty-four hours a day communicates directly with our platoons. When we are deployed beyond the wire the communication is constant. There is one other radio in the headquarters and that rig belongs to a Lieutenant who is our artillery forward observer. He has his own RTO who takes a turn monitoring the radios at night whether in base camp or the field.

The mattress which I have been able to hold onto is, what I imagine heaven is like, sublime. Slept until 0830 after completion of my watch. Then wrote some letters and later we all laid in and around the hammocks like a bunch of lazy dogs licking their balls. Reminds me. There are two guys who stop and look over a picket fence and observe a really nasty dog licking his balls. One guy says, "boy, I sure wish I could do that," and the other guy says dryly, "I think you'd better pet him first." Get it!? Har, de Har.

Helped another one of our medics named Prince work on the overhead shelter for the hammock area. The area is perfect for Jobman to use when he briefs the platoon leaders.

Rations are running low and tomorrow we will begin a strict regimen of C-rats. Oh, how I am longing for some of Chief's Mulligan stew. Ruff, ruff.

There is an almost unnatural quietness lately. Not a single mortar round or rocket propelled grenade to interrupt the silence. When are we going to move out again? The most fun I have is messing with Lieutenant Smith. The more I jerk him around the more he believes we are close friends. It's as though the difference in our rank has disappeared altogether. He brought up in discussion that back in the World he worked for Ford Motor Company in Dearborn, Michigan. Apparently, he was a member of the computer applications division and he invited me to stop by for a visit some day in the future. I said, "you mean if you live." "Very funny", he says. I told him I was just joking him and that I probably would stop in and Smitty says, "you mean if you live." Touché, Smitty. The little exchange took place under our new and spruced up poncho and hammock shelter.

February 11

Sunday – Reclined in my hammock all day reading, AFVN radio blasting from the small transistor radio that always hangs from the engineering stake that supports one of our three hammocks. Music has always been the single most recognizable and constant backdrop for my time in country followed by exploding ordinance and rifle fire. The same can be said for all of my buddies. The daily broadcast always begins with the long dragged out greeting of Go-o-o-o-o-d- Mo-o-r-ning Vietnam followed by unusual chimes. This morning when I lowered myself into the hammock next to Smitty I heard the haunting refrain of *White Rabbit* by Jefferson Airplane followed by *The End* by Jim Morrison and the Doors. I lay the opened book I'm reading on my chest and with my fingers laced behind my head, I let the morning dreamily envelope me hoping that Smitty wouldn't interrupt my reverie. I travelled back to my time at Ft. Knox Kentucky when each morning began with the Rascals and *Groovin*. I was Platoon Guide and occupied the top floor room in my barrack right next to the mess hall where the mess staff began preparing breakfast around 0430 hours and played the Rascals hit tune over and over and over again…the sound track for my time in the military.

  I remember the day we made a brief on line sweep in a sparse jungle forest before we marched into a small hard spot to enjoy a real Thanksgiving meal and get our inoculations updated. And, I promise this actually happened. We have this guy from the Dominican Republic, I don't know his name, and he was at the end of the column as we swept slowly into the clearing, and he was smoking a K Woody pipe stuffed with ganga and on his TA-50 Web gear hung a small radio and it was Armed Forces radio playing *Happy Together* by the Turtles. Well, alright! Just before we entered the small perimeter we scared up a wild hog with tremendous tusks and with grunting noises the huge pig sprinted back into the jungle.

    Two guys from the weapons platoon, Bess and Edwards and myself climbed what we called the radio tower to scope out the surrounding jungle area. The tower

Ladder leading to radio antenna

is a huge, thick tree that erupts out of the base camp jungle and rises twenty or thirty feet above the rest of the trees. Mounted on top was a two niner two antenna that would boost our transmissions back to Tay Ninh. Short pieces of two by fours nailed into the tree allow climbers access to the top. I snapped some pretty impressive pictures from the top. When I returned to the ground I thought to myself, that was pretty stupid, what a great sitting duck for some well-trained sniper.

    I loosened the threaded stopper on Lt. Smith's air mattress tonight after everybody had retired to get some shut. The very slowly escaping air did not make any noise, no audible hiss and would probably work itself out on its own and then Smitty's mattress would deflate. As it worked out, I left the bunker to take a wiz at just the right time. The mattress was flat on the lieutenant's rack when I reentered. The Coleman lantern had been lit and there was quite a bit of grumbling and complaining. Because I was absent when the event occurred and because I had to pass the head of the lieutenants rack I was the accused. Lt. Jobman and Smitty convened a Kangaroo court and with enthusiastic chuckles from the rest of the group the two lieutenants did Perry Mason bits for about thirty minutes and threatened to ban me from the bunker or string me up. The case was finally thrown out of court for lack of proof. Smitty laughed about the whole thing, once again wagged a finger in my direction and everyone retired happy with the tension broken. The darkened bunker was quiet except for the wheezing sounds coming from Smitty in the corner as he blew into his air mattress.

The pull back to Tay Ninh has been delayed again.

February 12

Tuesday – Air mobile operation, so we are finally on the move again. We rode Hueys of the 187th to a landing zone at the road intersection nearest Bo Tuc. No trouble landing and once on the ground we began to sweep the North side of the road back toward Katum. Our mission was to protect Alpha Company's rear. They were pinned down by two Cong snipers and took two casualties both WIA that required a dust off to Tay Ninh. These little contacts always carry with them a degree of suspicion. What are just two VC doing out here in a relatively desolate landscape, no village or settlement nearby? Did we interrupt several travelers on their way to a meet? Were they part of a larger element that chose not to engage? Later we, Bravo, killed such a loner and at first believed we had killed one of our own because the corpse was fully dressed in US issue utilities and a full complement of TA-50 including newer jungle boots.

We took a turn at outposting the road ahead of Alpha and they high balled past us and on to Katum.

Full moon tonight and that means the guys along our sector of the bunker line had an easy time of it. If the enemy were bold enough to approach our perimeter across the flat open area between the jungle and our wire they'd be spotted immediately and eliminated. Headquarters lazed around outside the command bunker and shot the shit and listened to the transistor on low volume while monitoring the company radios. The time passes quickly.

Jobman called the platoon leaders to our position and he gave what he billed as a top-secret briefing. I thought how silly something like this is…what's with all the drama? Who would we share sensitive information with? And none of us has a security clearance. Anyway, the lieutenant told us about a relatively new 105 round containing thousands of metal darts that slaughter the enemy at close range. Another type of ordinance, yet another 105 round, contains small bomblets that are spread outward upon initial detonation of the main 105 mm round and cover a radius of about six hundred yards, inflicting a much higher casualty rate.

Our new commanding officer is finally here and gave a more or less "getting to know you" briefing to all platoon leaders and platoon sergeants and the headquarters element. Seems OK and we will all have to wait and see but I have questions. Jobman pulled me aside before he departed and told me that the new CO whose name is Graves, a captain, was some kind of Armored tank commander originally out of USATCA which stands for United States Army Training Center Armor which is situated at Ft. Knox, Kentucky. Word has it that Graves wanted to be assigned to an infantry Company so he could earn a Combat Infantry Badge (CIB). By itself this seems almost insane because the implication is that an Armored Captain wouldn't know diddly shit about the infantry and how we operate. This scares me but like having the nose of the camel under the tent we will be able to take the new guy under our wing, and without being obvious about it, teach him what he needs to know.

Side Bar: The CIB is a queen of Battle blue rectangle with a silver border and a wreath and running the length of the rectangle is a long rifle. Only infantrymen who have been in battle are authorized to wear the decoration. Even our Forward Observer does not qualify because he is an artillery officer. Tankers definitely do not qualify but as I understand it, Graves, by being assigned to the infantry, will qualify and we heard he really wants the CIB.

February 13

Tuesday – Yet another air mobile operation. Someone mentioned that if we keep riding the Huey's we will qualify for an Air Medal. The medal has been around for an eternity and most soldiers believe it is awarded to pilots involved in air combat for destroying enemy aircraft, and while that is true, it is also awarded to participants in operational flights where exposure to enemy fire is expected. According to that criteria everyone in Bravo qualifies sooner or later.

Our mission was to be dropped at a pre-selected landing zone that is north and west of Katum toward the Cambodian border and check old VC bunkers at a base camp we'd once moved through on an earlier mission. As we moved off the LZ and began to rendezvous at our rally point our radios were jammed and our frequencies scrambled. This tactic, we have been told, is often employed by the enemy even though we'd never encountered it. I may not have mentioned this but while we were engaging the enemy at the Hour Glass the day we lost the chopper and many soldiers from First Platoon, many of our radios while not jammed, were slammed by transmissions that sounded an awful lot like Australians. This was weird because there aren't any Aussie's operating in this area. True, they're here just not in our area of operation. What was that radio traffic about… probably just the enemy messing with us.

Anyway, Manchu 6, Ltc. Henchman, who was above us in his OH-23, set down and picked up an interpreter and returned. The intercept was talking about four VC battalions who were planning an eminent attack on Katum so we returned to base camp immediately to make ready. The radio intercepts could have been a diversionary enemy tactic to get us to return to Katum to prepare for an assault when the real target could have been Tay Ninh. We cannot be both places at once so we hunkered down at Kaboom and waited. On the way from the air strip to our positions a little puppy dog, a light brown bitch, followed me. We have her now. Best to hang on to her so she doesn't end up on the menu.

Got a huge care package from Cindy with a Valentine Day card, her fourth. Lots of cookies, candies and a fifth of Jim Beam that disappeared in a hurry.

50% alert all over the camp in anticipation of an attack. Just being aware of the possibility has everyone on edge. Rearranged my weapon and ammo so I could grab it quickly in the darkened bunker after we extinguish the Coleman lantern.

Things are getting crazy. The entire battalion is to be involved in a gigantic mission tonight. Rather than waiting for an attack, part of the battalion will be moving out at 0330 hours on an ambush patrol? …are you shitting me...we are actually going out to greet Sir Charles. Tie down anything that jingles or makes noise like dog tags, rifle swivels and use lots of duct tape. If there are four battalions of VC out there who do you think is going to be ambushed? We have listening posts outside the perimeter and they have already heard movement.

February 14

Wednesday, 0300 hours – Happy Valentine Day! Association with the color red. Hope we don't get any of that tonight or is it day...gets confusing. (sounds like another one a them international dateline thingies). 50% alert due to possible attack based on yesterday's rumor. That means for the six of us that monitor the radios at night we each only get about three hours of sleep. Bummer!

We were up and prepared to move at 0245 hours and finally departed the perimeter at 0310. The waning moon was at ten o'clock and still bright as hell, too bright to be attempting an ambush type maneuver involving over three hundred men trying desperately to conceal their movement. We tried to hump the wood lines to keep us in shadow but much of the time we were in open areas and exposed. Smitty called in artillery to parallel our march and did a fine job. Soon we outstripped and left the carefully placed artillery explosions behind and marched in silence except for frequent missteps in gullies that resulted in muttered obscenities. Finally, we reached our destination, an old dilapidated Buddhist temple where we set our ambush. We were stretched out all over the place but I felt relatively safe up against the remains on an ancient brick wall. Time 0445 and actually setting and getting everyone placed took way too long. The fact that we did not take any fire probably meant there weren't any enemy in the area. If there had been we'd been cut to pieces.

This was Captain Graves first field exercise as our leader and all bull shit aside he performed admirably except for flinching noticeably every time an artillery shell exploded anywhere close by. We maintained our positions and observed silence protocol.

Attacks on Katum, Tay Ninh or Cu Chi or even the hamlets between never developed.

When we returned to the bunker I dropped my gear and retired to the bunker, exhausted with red puffy eyes. I blew my nose and bled all over the place. Exhausted.

Since every major city south of the DMZ sustained attacks and heavy damage including Saigon and Tan Son Nhut air base I have not heard from Mike Hondorp. Mike is a friend from our time at Ft. McClellan and our advanced individual training cycle. Last time I saw him was at Cam Ranh Bay before we were all split up by individual assignments. Mike was assigned to an MP Company in Saigon.

February 15

Thursday – Held in reserve today. It'll be great to have time to recuperate after being out all night. Got another care package from Cindy. Included was a note written by longtime friends Russ and Sue Hook from long ago school days. Russ wrote how all of my friends and especially those who know me well are praying for my safe return and said that if mentally concentrating on a thing could make it come true I'd be sure to make it home.

We were supposed to air mobile in the afternoon back to the Cambodia area but there was so much incoming mortar and rocket fire all about the perimeter that the Huey's were cancelled so we will do some clover leaf sweeps instead.

The new CO, Graves, was at the battalion command post for much of the day. Late in the afternoon, and I do not know any circumstantial facts but for some reason the CO warned Kenny Baus to watch his mouth when conversing with officers. Made me reflect on my own behavior with Lieutenant Smith and that I should cool it from now on. However, and I think this is probably disrespectful, but when talking with the rest of headquarters I simply refer to Captain Graves as the CO and this is because I have not fitted a nickname to him.

I am trying to write this entry and listen to the CO give his evening poop talk to the platoon leaders. CO is playing the role of serious commanding officer and I caught a few eye rolls between several off the Lieutenants and their platoon sergeants. I think this is because he, the CO, is still too green to have much of a grasp for the procedural junk he is spouting off about. That's OK, he'll get it eventually. Remember that armored command is vastly different than infantry and when it comes to maneuvering and cover and fire the differences are even greater. He is bound to make mistakes during his learning process. I just hope he does not get anyone killed while he's smartin' up. A medic I know named Prince cruised over from his squad area to shoot the shit this evening. He is from Alaska and before getting drafted Prince was a trucker all over that state. He asked me if I was familiar with the Alcan Highway that was built by the, I believe he said, Army Core of Engineers around the time of the Second World War. Huge project. Said I wasn't familiar with it. Kenny said, "doesn't matter much, really. My main job back home was as a commercial crab fisherman." Most dangerous job ever, he said. I told him that I thought we now have the most dangerous job ever. How could he not agree?

Incoming down by one of the arty batteries after chow tonight. Several WIA and one of them died making it a KIA.

February 16

Friday – Captain Graves presented me with my Purple Heart today. I was given the medal, paper work will be mailed to Cindy. The captain also let me know that my promotion to Specialist Fourth Class was now official even though I'd considered this a done deal when Ssg. Boatwright told me that he had put me in for the promotion.

Call today National Boner Day or the day Spec 4 Todd Dexter totally misread Captain Graves. I'm afraid I will have to retract my compliments about the captain's exemplary behavior on that large ambush maneuver. Nothing went right for any of us today. First, Alpha Company ran out of demo stuff (C-4 plastic explosive) and could not complete the blowing of the enemy bunkers they encountered. I guess this is why we usually have members of the engineering battalion with us…because that is their job to have enough explosive, blasting caps and det cord. Often we do this ourselves and Alpha was not prepared. Then we, Bravo, under the direction of our new commander, got lost, not once but three times. Now this is not unusual. We often veer off course and sometimes when reading the map is difficult we have the forward arty officer, Jeff Dossett, call for a one round air burst of willy pete which is an explosion of fluffy white phosphorus. The noise of the burst and the cloud allows us to pin point where we are on the map. The stupid thing about our getting lost was that we were only fifteen hundred meters from base camp. Graves seems to know less than zero about radio procedure and asks other junior officers rather than the one carrying the radio what he should do.

A more exciting part of the day by far was when we were mortared by the base camp. Later it was explained to us that Katum had received incoming and an outfit at Kaboom, Bobcat Charlie fired counter mortar and the rounds came in our direction. At first, we thought the enemy was firing at us because we heard a tremendous whooshing as rounds flew overhead. The first salvo came in and should have been an immediate clue because the enemy fires random patterns and not groups of three.

Sacred Temple of the Cao Dia sect

Anyway, we squirmed on the ground as the rounds came in extremely close, geysers of dirt and cascading debris all over us. A frightening sensation, laying out in the open, no cover but hands over helmet. We could hear the tubes pop when the first salvo was on the way followed by two more salvos of three each. When the tubes popped a second time someone shouted, "oh, fuck, here we go again." Since we did not know who was firing on us out of Katum there could be no call of cease fire. Just wait it out. No casualties and we were relieved to get back in and get a cold beer. Heard someone wise crack as he passed us in column, "if we'd a got hit ya spose we'da got a Heart?

February 17

Saturday – 105 days until I meet Cindy in Hawaii for my R&R.

We drew another insignificant assignment today, a short Search and Destroy to the north, near the Cao Dai Temple, a religious sect with strongly nationalistic ties. The temple is a huge, multi-colored, rectangular structure with a spire on each of its four corners'. The sect and the temple itself, it seems to me, could become a point of contentiousness between the South Vietnamese and our northern enemy, the enemy who is infiltrating from the north and whose ultimate goal is to overturn democracy in the south and replace it with Ho Chi Minh's brand of communism. That is why I am here with my fellow soldiers, to not let this happen. Because of that and that alone allow me to alter my opening statement: when it comes to what we are doing here there is no such thing as an insignificant mission and even passing by the Cao Dai Temple could be very dangerous and perhaps have consequences of which we are unaware.

I have had feelings or call them suspicions that these little excursions of ours are not at all as pointless as they seem on the surface. Moreover, they are tune up exercises to get our new commander, Captain Graves, up to speed, broken in. Having a "green" commander adds to our vulnerability and lately I have been reflecting on how this effects our existence, could lead to our demise. There is an aspect of soldiering here in Vietnam that we newer discuss among ourselves and I mean never because discussing this thing, this "aspect," may jinx us or put us in harm's way or endanger our lives. Every time we move through the jungle there is a probability that we could be attacked with disastrous results so talking about how this has happened to other units could become a self-fulfilling prophecy.

Oh, sure, we do talk more locally how Charlie or Delta lost a couple of guys or there was a dust off required but I've never heard anyone talk about how 40,000 Viet Minh soldiers surrounded the French on the Plain at Dien Bien Phu back in 1954 and wiped them out ending the French Indochina War. 1600 French were killed and 4,800 wounded but we don't talk about it. Nor do we talk about the more recent battle at the Ia Drang Valley in 1965 that was the first encounter between elements of the 1st Air Cavalry and North Vietnamese regiments that lasted days with 155 Americans killed. The battle began when the Air Cav's chosen Landing Zone was smack dab in the midst of a monstrous enemy base camp. American casualties were approximately 250 dead. Over 1000 NVA bodies were counted. We do not talk about that. Then there's the Battle of Dak To in November of this year where 361 Americans were killed and 15 were missing. We cannot afford the distraction and, concentrating on what we are doing is more important.

Back inside the perimeter I relaxed by reading the rest of a book titled *Second Ending* by an author named Hunter. The book was about a drug addicted horn player and, in a certain way, reminded me of the 1956 movie *Man With The Golden Arm* staring Frank Sinatra.

We were visited late in the afternoon by an intelligence officer from battalion who was handing out new copies of something called the *SOI extract*. Since I am the senior radioman for Bravo the SOI belongs to me. The acronym SOI stands for Signal Operating Instruction and contains all of the call signs for the battalion as well as all of our radio frequencies. The small, semi-top-secret document does not require a security clearance and contains a code letter or number for combinations of six-digit numbers that make up map coordinates. The letters change daily and the book is good for the entire month. The procedure eliminates the possibility of the enemy intercepting the locations of our LP's and AP's. When I know the location of our LP (listening Posts) and AP (Ambush Patrols) I take the map coordinates and codify them by substituting letters for the numbers and radio this to battalion. The other companies do the same each night so battalion knows where every element is outside the wire. There are several reasons for this: number (1) we will not fire on each other and (2) any movement detected that is not one of these locations is, by deduction, the enemy.

Presently we are in the middle of the dry season so temperatures are soaring and often in the one hundred to one ten range and worse in low areas where there is exceptionally tall saw grass and no air movement.

Seventeenth of the month already and I just spent my first dollar – bought a roll of 35 mm film from Denny Wagner. It'd be great if I could show that kind of restrain back in the world but unfortunately there are retail outlets everywhere.

February 18

Sunday – Pretty laid-back day pulling road security for the Engineer Battalion and their Caterpillar tractors outfitted with Rome plows. All we had to do is maintain a vigil on the side of the road away from the plows and watch as the huge dozers felled the jungle trees. At one point a large flying squirrel bailed from the tree his nest was in and glided to another tree out ahead of the plows. Then as that tree was pushed over the squirrel glided away again. Guys were soon placing side bets on how many times the squirrel would repeat this process of climbing and gliding to avoid the falling tree and then gliding once again.

We were loaded onto deuce and a half's and delivered to the starting point where we would protect the plows. Bob Cat Alpha ran their APC's down the road ahead of us firing 50 cal. machine guns into the woods to discourage the VC from approaching the road. I should point out that the road had previously been partially cleared but three recent ambushes made it seem like a prudent idea to clear both sides back about two hundred meters more.

We spent a long day baking in the sun. The dust from passing convoys was suffocating and got worse each time a string of vehicles passed us by. The troops, most of whom were mounted on top, looked like cowboy banditos with their neckerchiefs tied snugly to their noses. The dust clung to sweat soaked fatigue jackets and the dust caking around their eyes made them all look like racoons, either that or ghost-like apparitions. Now and then we'd spy one or two with tears streaking down their cheeks…probably thinking I'd rather be home or anyplace else for that matter but I got a job to do.

The highlight of the afternoon was a huge tree that fell the wrong way and crushed the metal roof of the dozer that was obviously idling in the wrong area. The driver executed a painful exit. Back in by 1:00 hours.

February 19

Monday – Security for the road clearing operation again today. I got 'hot under the collar' at The Old Man, Captain Graves. Every time we would settle down and I would remove the radio and situate my gear the Captain would make up his mind to change our location and for no reason that I could determine. This may have had something to do with being where he could observe everything, play Mother Hen to us chicks and for that I cannot fault him. Our job out here really is two-fold, maybe three: (1) watch the road (2) protect the engineer battalion and (3) keep our eyes peeled in all directions to protect us all from the enemy infiltrating our positions as we are strung out along the road. Graves is like a kid in a movie matinee crawling under theatre chairs and changing seats every time he restlessly gets the notion.

I do not know how but an old comrade of Captain Graves found him out here. While they were reminiscing, the Captain's buddy, a Warrant Officer set his piece down on a tree stump. The dust cover to the ejection port was open and when I stooped down to shut it I pulled the charging handle to the rear and what I observed surprised me. First, I should not be concerning myself with an officer's firearm but when I exposed the firing port, I guess I may have been curious to see if the WO had a round in the chamber, I observed that there was an excessive amount of lubricant (LS-8) gumming up the works. Maybe one could expect a non-infantry type to treat his Car 15 this way but any grunt knows that you oil your weapon well and then rag it dry because too much lube attracts dirt and dust especially around choppers and, excessive dirt invites jamming.

The same flying squirrel was back at it again today climbing high to escape the plow. Amazing to observe the animal jump. The wings, folds actually along his body between front and back legs would billow as they filled with air and the squirrel would glide out in front of the crashing trees. The little guy covered an amazing distance to live another day.

February 20

Tuesday – The little white, mesh bag or mantle as it is known, that had brought such bright light to the interior of our bunker, continued to make a barely audible, muffled p-f-f-f-t sound that informed the educated ear that the lantern had not completely extinguished itself and still had fumes inside the glass. Unaware of an impending disaster I began to pour fuel into the small hole at the base of the lantern and was horrified when my hand was engulfed by a giant ball of bright lighted fuel. Startled, I pitched the can up into the night and away from me and the flame jumped from my hand and followed the huge arc of fuel cascading from the can and for an instant, as night turned to day, I witnessed the abject horror on Kenny's face as the conflagration engulfed his legs. Fire was everywhere. I chased Kenny, wrestled him to the ground and covered his body with mine. After a few moments, I was able to extinguish the flames. Doc McAdams, our medic, scurried from the bunker, cut off Kenny's smoldering pants and quickly stabbed a morphine syrette into the upper thigh and administered an unctuous salve to the wounds but the damage caused by my reckless behavior had been done.

The third degree burns to Kenny's lower extremities were severe enough to require a dust off to the 45th Surg at Tay Ninh. I felt sick to my stomach.

Only moments before Ken had been kneeling beside me and bubbling enthusiastically about the guitar ballad he was composing and now he was host to debilitating pain as he rode a chopper to the field hospital. Captain Graves had cautioned me to be certain the flames had been totally extinguished before filling the lantern. I'd really screwed up and as I wallowed in self-pity an image of Buddhist monks dousing themselves with gasoline in the Saigon's central marketplace in 1963 or maybe it was 1965, filled my eyes with tears. The many incidents of self-immolation were protests against the repressive policies of Ngo Dinh Diem toward Buddhist's.

February 21

Wednesday – Over to the chopper pad at first light and rode up north and west for a meet and greet with an American Special Forces A Team that needed help with security while they established a small, temporary base for their operations. The CH-47 dropped us off on a road that appeared to have been abandoned long ago and once on the ground we put out security on both sides and hunkered down to wait. We received a brief radio transmission on the BN net from someone who identified himself as Milce Force saying they were approaching. OD grabbed the horn and alerted the platoons that we were expecting company so hold fire. Soon a very ragged American wearing Tiger fatigues and wearing a US issue boonie hat broke out of the jungle. He had a beard and was carrying his own radio and behind him, in single file, followed twelve equally rugged looking Cambodies carrying an assortment of weapons.

We didn't learn if their call sign was significant, only that they were mercenaries from across the border deep inside Cambodia. We assumed their mission probably involved movement along the Ho Chi Minh trail before it crossed into Vietnam. They did not say and we did not ask but they did want as many American cigarettes as we could give them. The leader told me he'd been with his rag tag outfit for over three years and he was married to a Vietnamese woman who lived in Vung tau where there is an American Rest and Relaxation facility on one the South China Sea's most stunningly beautiful beaches. He was an E-7 but wore no insignia.

We followed the nameless sergeant who had three other US noncoms to help handle his platoon sized group to a small cleared area that was carefully hidden and camouflaged. We established a perimeter and secured the area for Milce Force until late afternoon while they filled sandbags and fortified several crude fighting holes. We returned to Katum in late evening before sun set.

We were met by a battalion officer, a first Lieutenant named Paris. His call sign is Manchu 4 3 and for lack of additional information I will call him our flight officer. I had spoken with him every time we were operating by helicopter. He shook my hand and says, "there's that Bravo X-Ray that I'm always givin' the raspberries." I let him know that I'd always thought he was being tough on me and he said he was but it was because I was doing a fantastic job. Hell, he even asked me if I'd be interested in joining up with him and being his personal RTO. "No thanks," I said, "I'm pretty happy where I am, LT." He said, "Think about it, softer bed, safer too." That was about it.

Big poop talk this evening and that is why Lt. Paris came out to be with us. His main concern is coordinating all of the helicopters necessary to get us all back to Tay

Ninh. We knew this day was coming but the short notice – the way the Army always does these things – left little room for emotion.

February 22

Thursday – Leaving Kaboom for good! Up at 0530 we set about destroying the command bunker that had served us so well. Sand bags were emptied into the hole and the roof timbers crashed in. I let the rest of the guys handle the flammables as we fired the timbers.

Destroying our command bunker

All about the base camp one could witness flames licking the sky. The 65th Engineer Battalion drove their Rome plows over the holes, filling them in. Vietnamese *mama- sans*, children in tow, swarmed over the interior of the base camp scavenging anything we were leaving behind. Before pulling out I snapped a rather melancholy picture of an ancient Viet woman standing in front of the flaming bunker and pointing to a Playboy centerfold that she held in her hand, huge smile on her face.

Mama-san *and local civilians move in when we move out*

We saddled up for one last time and, carrying everything we could, route-stepped over to the air strip where several CH-47 "Shithooks" were waiting to ferry us back to Tay Ninh. We'd had a bittersweet time at Katum and I, for one, was anxious to get back to Tay Ninh and move back into our old digs. As the helicopters circled one last time I glimpsed the finished CIDG camp out one of the port holes and wondered how long they'd last before being overrun by enemy coming across from Cambodia, possibly with Russian tanks.

Twenty minutes later we were back in Tay Ninh where we boarded the trucks that Stansberry and Top sent to fetch us. Enjoyed hot chow, beer and soda rations immediately and then spent considerable time locating my trunk and all my personal stuff. God, it has been so

View of completed CIDG camp

long since we have been in. Had a couple more beers and jaw-jacked with Stansberry.

Got a tape from Cindy and family, mom and Dad, Jed and wife Linda that contained all the latest Top 40 tunes. Went to sleep on my old cot with music blasting through new headphones. Slept like a baby.

February 23

Friday – Awoke at 0730 in the midst of featherbrained, nightmarish dreams. Took a few moments for my gray matter to catch up with actually being back in Tay Ninh. Coffee at the mess hall rather than a canteen of water boiled over a piece of C-4. Painted my radio, cleaned up and walked over to the PX. I then sauntered down the laterite surfaced road and over to the 45th Surgical MASH unit. Checked in and walked on cement pathway to a corrugated Quonset building and found my way to Specialist Fourth Class Kenny Bauses rack. He was smiling a Cheshire cat kinda smile when I sat beside him. "Kenny, I am so sorry about what happened. How will I ever make it up to you?" "Are you shitting me," Kenny grinned. "Because of you, I am being shipped outta here day after tomorrow for Japan, and then I'm goin' stateside. Shit, man, I'm goin' home," he said. "Yeah, but are you going to be OK," I questioned. "Oh, sure," he said having difficulty containing his excitement. "When I get to Camp Zama they'll do some skin grafts but the whole thing'll take too long to keep me here in the Nam…million dollar wound and I may be able to figure a way to make the Army to pay for it someday." I was relieved and stuck around just to get Kenny caught up on what Bravo was up to but I could tell he didn't give a shit so I trucked on outta there. After stopping several medical personnel dressed in scrubs, and inquiring about where I might find Brint Motheral, the friend my fraternity brother had written about, I was directed to an area at the edge of the facility that was populated by rows of very neat hooches. Each of the buildings were adorned with metal roofs that extended close enough to the ground to keep out driving rain but still permit air circulation. The bamboo matting that hung away from the screens provided privacy. Each building had a patch of grass and a free-standing barbecue grill. The area was obsessively clean and well maintained, probably by hooch *mama-sans* that came onto the base each day to perform menial tasks.

Brint's quarters were strac (an anacronym for being really squared away), everything standing tall as if there would be an inspection any moment. By contrast our infantry squad quarters always had the appearance of an adolescent child's bedroom or a dust explosion in a grain silo, shit everywhere…weapons clean and at the ready but everything else in disarray.

Having just come off duty as a nurse's aide, Motheral was still in powder blues. He opened a tiny fridge and offered me a beer. The small cooler was packed with steaks which caused me to do a slow burn because grunts like me never saw such luxury. There were two rather exceptional looking round eyed blonde American nurses in civvies perched on the neatly made cots that occupied the space below a row of screened windows. Carpeted floors and funky Vietnamese art adorned the walls. Sneakers, apparently the foot ware of choice for hospital personnel, were neatly spaced beneath the bunks. The women moved to two overstuffed chairs – *where does this shit come from* – and were drinking beer and smoking cigarettes. I was totally blown away, these guys really had it dicked, I'd never seen such excess, didn't know that there were scenes like this playing out all over the country.

And Brint was pretty much what I'd expected, stocky, well-built all-American type, well bred, good looking cookie cutter guy like my fraternity brothers back in Michigan. We all shot the shit 'til evening, smoked several joints and when Motheral's roommate Long Tall showed up we smoked another splib and cooked up some steaks. I asked why he was called Long Tall and he shrugged and replied "cuz my last name is Sally." I got it. Good enough for me.

    I need to back up here for a moment. I called the American girls, both great looking by the way, Round Eyes. I must apologize for this and also referring to the Vietnamese people as Dinks, Slopes, Gook motherfuckers, Zips or Zipperheads. All of these terms dehumanize our adversaries and, I suppose, makes killing them easier but to me it is highly distasteful. If I brought this concern to my buddies they would more than likely say, "fuck it, don't mean a thing."

    Anyway, after the booze and the weed, the steaks and the exceptionally good time away from my usual grind, I needed to get back to the company area. Long Tall procured or should I say borrowed (stole) a jeep from the commanding officer of the Mash unit and drove me back to my company area. On the way, Long Tall handed me a small pipe and a lighter saying, "toke on this," which I did even though the pipe appeared empty. "Opium," he chirped, "the residue will burn just fine, you'll see." By the time I reached home I was out of my mind and thought the brightly burning light emanating from the orderly room, the humming generator and the gaggle of men gathered around the desk with the captain were a hallucination or a dream that I was becoming a part of. I walked into the middle of the Captains briefing. He looked up and said, "glad you could make it, make sure your crew all have fresh battery packs by morning," and he returned to the maps spread out on the orderly room desk and resumed the briefing. I had trouble concentrating because I was blasted but the gist of the whole thing was pretty simple, really, and awfully scary. We would be moving down inside the Saigon City limits which will be a real departure from the jungle fighting we have been engaged in since October. Fighting could be door to door and involve traversing a labyrinth of canals that are very difficult to cross due to extreme tides. Small bridges are choke points probably controlled by the enemy or neighborhood militia. The greatest part of this territory, at least on our maps, is covered by waist deep water and new, growing, rice plants. Intel believes that somewhere in this area we will uncover the sights from which 120 mm rockets are being fired on Tan Son Nhut Airbase causing great damage.

February 24

Saturday – Preparations to move out began early, company formation in front of the orderly room with everyone's gear in place at their feet. The call to saddle up is something to behold, a symphony of movement where we help one another get our gear, ruck sacks and miscellaneous equipment, ammo belts and cans, weapons, radios plus anything else appropriate to getting an infantry company under way on our shoulders and squared away. At noon, we route stepped to the air strip to board the slicks – helicopters without armament – belonging to The Blackhawk AHC (Assault Helicopter Company) to be ferried down to our new AO (area of operation). We landed inside the base camp at Cu Chi and then trucked into our old company area to await further instruction. Finally received word from higher that there was difficulty with the arty prep of the landing area close to Saigon so the operation was scrubbed until tomorrow.

Being in Cu Chi for the first time in months was strange enough but throwing our rucks and equipment down in two or three structures that remained from our last presence here was just weird. Some of us went over to the PX to load up on goodies including one of our staples, when we can get it, tins of Vienna Sausage. The sausages themselves are like short, miniature hot dogs in a slimy, salty sauce. Preferred method of eating is to jam your index finger down inside the can and dislodge the first sausage, pop it in your mouth and take a suck on a bottle of hot sauce if you're lucky enough to find one, and then repeat the process…damn, that's good!

Back in our old Bravo Company area we noticed a huge group of soldiers jammed in around two jeeps and cheering wildly. Murry O'Donnell and I shoved our way to the front to become part of a nightmarish tableau. Two monkeys on long tethers attached to the jeeps steering wheels were screaming wildly, jumping into the air and bounding from jeep to jeep, fornicating with their little, bright red wangers and picking the bugs off each other's asses to the wild cheers of the soldiers. Opened bottles of hooch and Vietnamese beer called "33" or Baum e Bau that tasted like shit because it contains formaldehyde circulated through the crowd. There wasn't an officer within a mile of the scene.

We bedded down for the night in an old abandoned hooch that I'd mistaken for our old sector of the perimeter but I was wrong. Someone said the 101st had been in here recently.

No radio watch/monitoring tonight as we are all here inside the perimeter, no responsibility. I am not sure where Graves flaked out and a rest from the captain is welcomed. Slept well except for sporadic incoming mortar fire. A siren sounded the all clear and I quickly resumed my slumber.

February 25

Sunday – We loaded onto the Huey's of the 187th for the flight down to within several miles of Tan Son Nhut airbase. This was a very different ride. For the first time, we are flying into a densely populated area at approximately eleven hundred feet and one hundred knots speed. No more jungle. What we are seeing is lush and green. It appears to be one vast village composed of a grid like arrangement of canals and homes surrounded by a vast expanse of rice fields. Most of the fields are filled with water and contain young rice plantings. The air is warm and humid and our ship rises and falls gently on the buffeting air.

We off loaded on a roughly paved surface of road where the Vietnamese people responded as though what they were witnessing happens every day. They simply moved to the side of the road as the choppers landed and we got out.

Our mission as I previously mentioned is to pinpoint and then eliminate the rocket sites that are pummeling the air base and Pentagon East, General Westmorland's headquarters. The immediate area is congested with homes, shacks and some ornately decorated temples. We had not been on the road for more than fifteen or twenty minutes when we began to take sniper fire. We dived to the opposite side of the road from where we received the initial fire and became mired up to our waists in a drainage ditch filled with feces. The only thing worse than the overpowering stench was the realization that the enemy intentionally drove us into the stinking ditch. The sniper fire continued. The longer we remained in place the lower we sank. We had two killed in the brief encounter and one of our squads got pinned down inside a small home. The sniper who was in a palm tree was finally eliminated. We learned quickly to scan the palms for a leaf bent down in an unusual way because it could be hiding a sniper. Lessons need to be learned rapidly here. We are no longer in the jungle where anyone you encounter is the enemy. Here they are all the enemy. Large earthen jars utilized for collection or rain water can hide a Viet Cong as second platoon learned firsthand.

Most of the day was spent searching house to house with very little result, I mean, what the fuck are we looking for? I will say this though: the beauty is so visually stunning that it practically takes your breath away. Very lush and very beautiful. So much activity. Air strikes and gunships strafing all about us and Eagle Flights landing as civilians stand idly by and watch as their community is invaded and decimated. The timid have fled their homes and left the area.

Freedom Birds, so called because they carry soldiers home to the World and the safety of their loved ones, can be viewed just over the tree tops as they land and exit Ton Son Nhut. Seeing that really stirs emotions. How come I can't be on the next one out and I do not mean in a bag with a long zipper.

A little dog followed us all day. Someone named him Sniper. Wonder why?

Our NDP was battalion sized and our defensive positions were shallow holes that immediately filled with water. We were able to fashion some overhead cover by chopping palm logs further endearing us to the locals. Tin roofs and boards were stripped from nearby homes to be used as well. Homes were burned or destroyed to level the perimeter. Sad really. These people cherish what little they have and we're burning and looting like crusading Visigoths run amok.

Relatively quiet night. The reassuring pop of illumination rounds overhead lighted the area and the muffled sound of artillery was reassuring simply because they were not on top of our positions. Radio watch again and I loved the solitariness of my alone time watching the occasional tracer rounds arc into the dark void. Routine reestablished once again.

Arriving in heavily populated area near Siagon. We were ambushed immediately. House to house fighting commenced at once.

February 26

Monday – Morning of the second day. I do not know what the rest of my fellow soldiers are feeling about the hostile environment that is now our area of operation but I am filled with apprehension and dread. We are now surrounded by the Vietnamese people and must suspect that any one of them could cause us harm – so different from being isolated and in the vast jungles of Tay Ninh province.

We filled in our holes and began to move out. Our lead element was moving forward but the captain and the headquarters element had not even left the area that had been our night position when we were pinned down by a fusillade of AK fire coming from every direction. Writhing on the ground I felt like a bug in an entomology display case with a big pin fixing me to the waxed surface. The fear in the eyes of those around me was palpable.

The entire area while not covered in the waist deep water we had anticipated is crisscrossed by a vast system of rice paddies and dikes that are fed water from a series of canals. Rice is, along with fishing and rubber, the backbone of the Vietnamese way of life. Rice is called white gold. The paddies which are dry beds at certain times of the year are flooded and then planted with new shoots brought from a section of the paddy that serves as a nursery. The flooded quadrants are what we must cope with.

Our first element was approaching what has been designated as Canal 9 Bravo on our maps when we first began taking more enemy fire. We had one killed (KIA) and eleven wounded (WIA) in a constant fire fight to cross 9 Bravo that took the entire day. Fresh troops were constantly brought forward to attack the choke point. In all we moved two hundred and fifty meters today.

Two snipers had done most of the damage. Both were eventually eliminated.

Once across the canal we had planned to take a pagoda and occupy the structure as our command post for the night. Again, we were pinned down by a vicious cross fire.

At the moment, I am feeling empathy for Captain Graves because I am beginning to like him. However, I can daily see the indecision in his face as he tries to do the proper thing during this most difficult time. Major Roush basically relieved Graves from command today and took over Bravo. Graves was still with us but as more of an observer than commander. The company was relegated to a reserve role and Charlie company moved up to fill the gap. We were getting our asses kicked all day and while I'd not like to witness Graves being permanently relieved of his duties this might be best for the company. He really is not cutting it.

We had eleven wounded today and just as we were preparing to set in for the night and form a defensive perimeter, Delta got wrapped around the axel. Gunships were working the wood line when four Delta soldiers were killed in the friendly fire incident, one a lieutenant.

The entire area was under water as we set up for the night. We received resupply by CH-47. The slings, wrapped in tarpaulins, were dropped in the water filled rice paddy. We placed our radios on the paddy dike to keep them dry and spent the night with our heads resting against the incline the dike offered. Morning came and the first hour was spent burning leeches off our legs and torsos with lighted cigarettes. The leeches gain access by coming in through the two brass eyelets near the soles of our combat boots.

February 27

Tuesday – Held in reserve again today and I am convinced that the decision is to protect Bravo for a time while Major Roush guides us through this period of uncertainty before returning the reins to Captain Graves. Graves has not revealed to us his feelings at this time so everything is a little uncomfortable.

Alpha brought one of Delta Company's KIA's from yesterday evening's friendly fire episode to our location and after we secured the required space for a dust off, a Red Cross evacuation helicopter swooped in and made the pick-up. Every time I see an evacuation chopper with the huge Red Cross emblazoned across the front I wish I could be on it even though I do not wish to be wounded severely enough to require a lift to a MASH unit.

While we were busy with the dust off the rest of the BN moved through sporadic sniper fire as they exited the area. Around 1400 hours in the afternoon Charlie Company found an enemy pear pit. Tubes, ammo and firing devices were all there and we destroyed them before moving down a dry creek bed to help Charlie who was taking sniper fire. When we joined the engagement, we were all pinned down for almost six hours. The artillery battery that was on station fired an estimated fifteen hundred rounds of 105 mm during the lengthy encounter. I was with the rest of the headquarters element. It was unbelievably hot and I rested my face on a bandana that I frequently tie around my neck. During the long ordeal, we had one killed and seven wounded including Spec 4 David Ruggles the Artillery Forward Observers RTO and Denny Wagner one of the machine gunners from my old squad who was shot through both forearms.

The fire fight stalled out and turned into a stalemate. Major Roush and his RTO both walked past me, Roush carrying a Car 15 and wearing a soft utility cap which was his style. Roush, from Detroit, Michigan is on his third tour and very close to going home. He's so short. The next thing I recall was Roush being carried back past me. Dead. There was a single dot of bright crimson blood square in the middle of the major's forehead. We later learned that he hadn't even chambered a round. The air went out of all of us today.

Gunships of the 187th Blackhawk AHC reported that they could see a huge enemy force, perhaps battalion

Villagers informed us that a reinforced squad of NVA soldiers inhabited this structure the previous night

size of larger moving in. Alpha and Charlie moved to block and assist us and were immediately pinned down. Just before dark we were able to pull back and regroup and finally set up for the night in a little farmstead. The out building must have belonged to a family with resources. The floor was straw which made comfortable bedding and if there were animals they're gone now. The construction was modern by Vietnamese standards, the blocks held together with mortar were yellowish, the equivalent of American cinder block. Our perimeter is as secure as possible and the structure offers good protection. The many canals in the area make movement very slow for us but makes it just as difficult for the enemy to get at us...we hope.

The major will be so missed. He was an inspiration just being with us on operations. He only had twenty days remaining until he went home, rotated back to the States. In a way, though, Major Roush is home.

February 28

Wednesday – The telltale hiss from the monitor was intrusive as I sat and listened to the radios expecting something to break loose at any moment. I felt like the parent wondering when his young children asleep in the next room would erupt and require me to do something. Finally, off watch my sleep was fitful imagining all those little Gook (oops, sorry,) bastards running around out there planning something big for us. We received a briefing from battalion tonight that we are dealing with the 88th NVA Battalion. This was startling news because it is the first time this particular battalion has been spotted this far south.

We left our perimeter precisely at 0830 hours making our way back to the area we spent our first night and had contact. No enemy activity on the way. The experience to this point has been completely weird, weird enough to make me wonder if our current reality, operating among the indigenous peoples, is more common to the American experience than I had previously thought. I find the beauty and tranquility one moment and then the eruption of violence, blood and shattered lives, ours and theirs, almost incomprehensible.

We are held in reserve again today and by that, I mean we are not actually the tip of the spear or leading the way.

Many villagers have returned to their homes either believing the VC have been driven off or because the disruptions have become so much a part of their lives that they do not care. Some are returning to undamaged homes while others stand on burned out plots and weep. Either way, they smile and bow as we pass. We feel that we have liberated their homes from VC control but I doubt they view the circumstances the same way. At best, we have disrupted a condition where the villagers are completely dominated by the VC. The villagers, nonetheless, continue to supply the enemy with rice or be killed or tortured.

Upon returning to the area we talked with the ARVN troops that are manning the outpost, a bombed-out tower at one end of a bridge that was detonated and now lies at the bottom of the river. They informed us that when we left an oversized squad of thirty-five NVA troopers inhabited the barn-like structure we had used just the night before. They were carrying many wounded so our persistence is definitely making a difference.

Manchu 6, LTC John Henchman, spotted from his observation helicopter, a truck dropping off personnel along the hard surface road we used on our original foray into the area. The truck had a motorcycle escort. We will be moving back in that general direction hoping that Charlie Company, out in front of us, will locate a suitable laager position so we can set up for the night. Could we be expected to have another scrimmage with Sir Charles?

We used the same holes from an earlier night and it was relatively quiet causing me to believe the enemy was reluctant to approach because of the mushy ground and the paddy dikes. There was a single shell, that could only have been one of ours, that impacted inside the perimeter. The concussion awoke me and my first conscious thought on being roused from sleep was…what the fuck. I was on my hands and knees in two feet of rice paddy water.

Ltc. Henchman's observation helicopter

February 29

Thursday – Alpha swept out of here just before first light in search of a suitable location for a new battalion perimeter. I believe to this point that my recorded thoughts have been ego centered. Let me explain. Most of the time I write about Bravo Company and that is the ego centered part. You need to understand that we seldom act as a stand-alone element meaning Bravo all by it's lonesome. We usually operate like a single organism and that is to say Alpha, Bravo, Charlie and Delta together and that requires that battalion operation center to be close by…not back in Tay Ninh or Chu Chi or Katum, but physically close to us although the radio suffices. We are moving back in the direction from which we came. If Alpha does not find a suitable place we will remain close to where we are now.

Henchman gave us a revised figure on how many rounds the artillery battery fired in support yesterday. It was not fifteen hundred rounds but eleven hundred, enough to require arty to call for an emergency resupply. The important detail that I forgot to mention in all the confusion is that Denny Wagoner and Ruggles, while still alive, have been evacuated and in probability I will not see them again. Tremendous loss, Roush just as bad because I had spoken with him on so many occasions. The major was fond of short track race car stuff in civilian life.

Charlie and Delta completed a sweep of the area as follow up to yesterday's action and came upon an entire NVA squad all dead. Recovered were 38 cal. Pistols and many RPG's.

Got the word…we are staying here for the night. The corner of our perimeter is on the opposite side of the river from night's past but we can still see the river and the blown bridge with the tower at either end. One of our ambush patrols just popped their claymore mines – one dead enemy soldier. Everything settling down. I walked to the edge of the river naked except for my combat boots and my M-79, waded out several meters and ducked down into the slowly moving current. I am not positive and have not been told but believe we are either on the Saigon River on a tributary. Murky, dense water, not at all pretty.

Radioman PFC David Ruggles being removed from canal

March 1

Friday – This was a difficult day, a bad way to begin a new month. Let me see if I can get all of the details sorted out. Our AO (Area of Operation) for the day began in a routine way. We were checking hooches, buildings that could be called small rice farms. Very idyllic, pastoral scenes, vast rice paddies with a few buildings at strategic intersections of canal and paddy. I occasionally blooped an M-79 grenade out into one of the fields just to keep in practice. The concussive explosion would send a geyser of mud, water and rice plants skyward. The final objective of the day was a plot that contained some dry ground and a variety of trees including banana palms, Tamarinds, Mango, Dragon fruit and Aralia. The only avenue of approach for us was a single dike elevated about a foot and a half above the water in the paddy on either side and about two to two and a half feet wide. The worn path entered the oasis about seventy-five meters to our front.

We are always aware that we are being observed by the locals and the VC and in this case the NVA and though we are weary, we do not let this inhibit our movement. Patience is a particular virtue of the Vietnamese. Our advance on the oasis had been slowed while artillery prepped the entire area with 105 mm howitzer fire. When the bombardment ceased the woodline was further saturated by Second Platoon who laid down a heavy base of fire on each side of the trail as a squad from First Platoon advanced down the trail on the top of the dike. The enemy waited until precisely the right moment and then opened fired instantly killing the squad leader as well as the third and fifth member of the patrol. The second soldier was wounded but lay still and the fifth member of the squad was friend Burt Haugen and he was wounded but alive. He took one in the leg and a round spun miraculously around between his helmet liner and head before exiting. The situation was critical and to make things worse a new second lieutenant panicked and crawled back to where the rest of us were laying in the water of a busted dike that was rapidly filling with water from an adjacent paddy that was full.

The CO, Captain Graves who had resumed control of the platoon the day Major Roush was killed, sent part of the Third Platoon forward to continue firing on the wood line and try to extract the dead and wounded. It went badly. We had young soldiers all over the dike and they had expended their ammo. The only shots being fired were well calculated rounds originating from the numerous spider holes along the edges of the oasis. I was becoming angry…nobody was responding, just lying on the ground, not returning fire afraid to hit our guys. The Captain froze. Somebody had to do something. I shrugged out of my radio pack, gave the hand set to Captain Graves and told him to call for Tac Air and have 'em on our frequency when I get back. Next, I gathered all of the ammunition bandoliers I could muster and then low crawled out the dike to throw the ammo to whoever could reach it. I then stood and threw smoke grenades as far out on each side of the dike as I could before returning to Graves and the headquarters group. Enemy fire was snapping everywhere. Time stood still! My mind was tripping and I found myself thinking the weirdest thing. I was born to do this. Everything was going freeze frame on me, I was emboldened and thinking, fuck everything, this is what I'm supposed to be doing.

Gunships of the 187th Blackhawks were on station and executed several close to the deck screaming passes to get the lay of the battlefield. I grabbed the handset from Graves and said, "this is Bravo Six X-ray, how do you read, over?" "Ah, I hear you Lima Charlie (loud and clear), 6 X-ray, what's your situation, over." "I've got Victor Charlie's in the wood line and WIA and KIA on the dike. Smoke out, can you identify, over." "Ah, roger, X-ray, Identify yellow, over." "Ah, yellow, that's a rog," I yelled too loud into the mouth piece and added, "spider holes along the grass line near the trail head are hot." "Ah, 6 Xray I can see your personnel on the dike and will place beaucoup fire across the front. Get em down." "Roger that Blackhawk, out."

On the second pass, the gunship laced the grass line with 20 mm cannon fire and the second ship in strafed everything in front of our guys with machine gun fire. Immediately some of third platoon moved forward and began to pull everyone off the dike and back to a safe area. The tide was coming in and water was rapidly spilling through the hole in the dike. Quickly inflated air mattresses were used to float the wounded back and out of the area. Discipline totally broke down as we beat a hasty retreat. Captain Baker used to laugh like hell in situations like this and say that we never retreat, we just attack in the opposite direction. I've got a feeling that Captain Graves is going to suffer for the events of the day.

Alpha out posted the road that ran through a rural area. The road was lined with civilian noncombatants that just stood and watched us pass rapidly by them. We were moving fast, night was approaching. Strange. And if the events of the day to that point hadn't been bizarre enough Lieutenant Smith did not let me down. I watched as he approached a corpse in the middle of the road that was so bloated that fluid was actually bubbling just beneath the totally transparent skin all over the body. Smitty bent over at the knees and blew lunch all over the stiffened corpse and when he stood, long strands of puke hung from his mouth and nose. The rest of us just walked away.

Later in the evening Capt. Graves gave a briefing, the highlight being that higher was very pissed that we did not continue on and press the enemy, take the fight to him. The fact that daylight was going rapidly may have given us all something to be so pissed about that many of us were willing to Give Graves a pass on his performance.

Aftermath of the Charlie company ambush

March 2

Saturday – Forget the rapid withdrawal, the air mattresses and the top brass being pissed that we withdrew, today was a very tough day for every Manchu and one that will someday, no doubt, be written about by Manchu historians. Someone will share the details with an associate beginning with, "Oh, yeah, that was the situation involving bridges, canals and loss of the better part of a platoon in a very short period of time." And is that not the way we learn of such situations? Hell, had we known, any of us, we could have altered the reality so that the damned situation never occurred in the first place. But it did.

There were certain elements of the day's battle plan that were so subtly changed or missed or perhaps even overlooked that the combination yielded disastrous results. Some of these things only came to light after it was all over, rumors maybe. For instance, our battalion commander, Ltc. John Henchman was distracted by higher for what in my opinion was a series of pointless harassments over the day's battle plan which we heard about later. Our commander had gone airborne to examined the terrain, the battlefield before we moved out. There was disagreement about arty prep of the flank areas parallel to the line of march. There was an ARVN outpost less than a click away that believe it or not refused, yes, I said refused to reinforce and lend a hand. All of these things required the attention of Henchman and in the meantime, Charlie Company hit the line of departure at a bridge to far up the road. The bridge behind them was cleared and was the point from which they should have departed. Missed detail!

Bravo Company was held in reserve again due to the mauling we had experienced for the last two days. We were supposed to lead today but just after first light when we began to move we were pinned down by enemy fire. So was Delta. We were hamstrung by a vicious, unrelenting crossfire and I watched as the rounds ploughed through the wood siding in the place our headquarters element had holed up for the night. Early morning sunlight danced along the dusty shafts of light when each new round tore through the crude wood sided building opening more holes. The look on Captain Graves face was priceless. His torso shook reflexively with each shot. Splinters of wood flew through the air but it didn't feel like we were in immediate danger, at least not then, because most of the rounds were high. My thoughts raced back to Advanced Infantry Training at Ft. McClellan, Alabama and how cadre preached endlessly for us to *bring it down, bring it down, your aiming too high.*

    My radio was crackling with traffic. I handled most of the messaging myself because the captain was incapacitated with what was going on and to his credit he was working all of the transmissions coming in on the company net, a radio hand set in each hand. We could hear a volley of small arms fire being exchanged and then the intensity picked up, and after ten minutes, that felt like an eternity, an unbelievable climax was reached followed by nothing, a complete void. Charlie had apparently outstripped their flank security and route stepped (slow march) their way up the blacktop and into an ambush almost one hundred and fifty meters long before the enemy opened fire. A perfect killing zone. Pedestrian traffic (the same as seen fleeing earlier) on the road turned and moved rapidly out of the area and could (should) have been a tip off.

    48 members of Charlie Company were killed and 29 wounded as well as two members of the 65th Engineer Battalion and numerous grunts from Delta that were able to move to reinforce. The battle (soon after) was referred

to as the largest single loss battle in the history of the Vietnam War.

All communication was lost between Charlie Company and the BN RTO (known to us as Cricket) for a shockingly long period. We at first feared that the command element had been wiped out but later found Captain Willie Gore, alive but wounded critically when he called artillery on top of the company's position. Later he said that Gooks were everywhere on the road grabbing weapons and killing those still alive after the initial ambush.

The direction of the fire eventually shifted and we were able to move forward and get up on the road to assist Delta in collecting the dead. Some were laying on doors from nearby homes, and combat boots could be seen under the ponchos that had been used to cover them. After five hours, the area was secured. Huey gunships continually laid down smoke screens on both sides of the road giving an eerie appearance to the scene. The 2nd of the 14th Golden Dragons flew in to assist along with a three-quarter ton truck to remove all the bodies. The truck was picked up and removed by a CH-47 helicopter.

The fact that Ltc. Henchman was having disagreements with his boss and also Tropic 6, the Division Commander, over how he, Henchman, was running the battalion tipped the scales. Tropic 6, who overflew the operation in the late stages, landed his personal chopper in the middle of HWY 248 late in the afternoon and after some time together Henchman was relieved of his duties. He will be missed, never forgotten. The Commander loved this outfit and as hard as it is to believe Ltc. Henchman knew almost every short timer in the battalion by name and given how many soldiers cycle through a combat battalion in a single year that is a commendable attribute.

Henchman's immediate replacement was another Lieutenant Colonel whose name is Simpson. The new commanders first utterance was, "we will never break contact with the enemy," and while on the surface this seems rather harsh it really is not when you consider what our mission is.

Before setting in for the night we, Bravo, made an on-line sweep away from the highway for almost a half a mile through mostly open paddies, some drained and some full. The entire length of the ambush site was honeycombed with trenches and well-hidden fighting positions that were stocked with food, ammunition and medical supplies. Hard to say how long the enemy had waited for us to slip up and use the well-travelled road again. As we moved on our sweep away from the road everything seemed normal. Families' were hunkering outside their dwellings and tending to cooking and other chores. We returned and placed our headquarters close to the center of the company and settled in for an uncertain night. After dark, I was leaning against the outside wall of a hovel, listening to the radio's. All's quiet. A low flying aircraft came across our position and a tremendous light filled the area for a split second…aerial recon plane taking photographs. When I turned in I simply lay on the ground, exhausted and tucked myself in to a fetal position. The stiffness of my sweat soaked fatigues and the stink from my own body kept me awake for some time. Weariness, uncertainty and the insanity of the past few days had taken their toll but then…finally…I slept.

March 3

Sunday – The remnants of yesterday's ambush were cleaned up this morning after first light and the 18 survivors were air lifted back to Tay Ninh where they will begin the painful process of rebuilding. No one knows for sure but it is possible that grunts from each of the battalion's other companies will infuse numbers into Charlie Company even though this would weaken all of the sister companies.

We are in reserve once again but, nonetheless, pulled a sweep into an area that we had covered previously and then returned close to the 248 highway and set up a perimeter. While setting up we heard small arms fire – Delta made contact with snipers but made it back just before dark.

1st Lieutenant Jobman has resumed his duties as the XO and came in tonight on resupply with everyone's pay. This is the first resupply we've had in several days and we had a mail call and also hot chow. This is the first night in quite a while that we did not set up our headquarters element in a house. We were comfortable because resupply brought in our overnight kits.

The Captain let me read the letter that was from Henchman upon his being relieved. I cried.

Side bar: night kits were an element of Lieutenant Colonel Henchman's plan to lighten the load of each grunt in the battalion. Other elements of the commander's plan were losing the heavy flak vests and wearing soft caps rather than steel pots in combat field situations. Important to note that if individual soldiers chose to wear these items or carry everything that was fine. We earned the name of Henchman's Light Rangers at the division level. Morale soared as a result of Henchman's personal touch.

March 4

Monday – Back to the grind, business as usual, marching down 248 away from the ambush site and maintaining the proper interval between the troop ahead of me (so one grenade won't get us all), I am alone and isolated. I did not know anyone in Charlie Company but my heart is broken, is still breaking. The eighteen survivors back at base camp today, what must they be thinking? What trauma, what a horror.

Strung out along the road there was, on the left, the high wall of the ARVN Compound and, yes, it is the same place that houses the chicken-hearted motherfuckers who refused to reinforce us the day of the ambush. On our right is a Viet compound consisting of two rows of bare cinder block buildings with many portals but no doors. They are empty, the inhabitants fled. The compound has a sizeable dirt yard and an iron mesh fence enclosing it. It is bleak.

Graves and I entered the ARVN compound while the rest of the company stood down while the captain and I met with the American soldier/advisor. His call sign, his handle is Duffle Canvas and we met to see if there's any useful intel we could glean from talking with him. Not much with the exception of a mention that approximately one hundred NVA are operating in the area. Same ones that ambushed us? Probably! He requested that we return in a day or so to give him some time and see if he could learn anything helpful.

We continued in the afternoon with a sweep of a lush green area which contained several canals with active rice paddies. I have noticed two ways that the farmers fill the paddies with canal water. (1) they employ long poles at the end of a fulcrum or tipping point to lift woven buckets of water from the canal and then dump it into the paddy or (2) they pedal a crude bicycle gizmo that turns a water wheel that transfers water from the canal into the paddy. Both effective as well as time consuming. These are a patient people. Some rice farmers dry their rice on huge round woven mats on the side of the road. Convoy drivers enjoy driving over the drying rice scattering it to the wind. This is called winning the hearts and minds.

Moving through a burnt-out cane field near a canal we were sniped at with the brunt of the action taking place in Alpha Company's area. After cane fields are harvested the stalk remnants are burned to prepare for the next planting and the stink is unbelievable. Alpha had five wounded, two litter that eventually were dusted off, and three ambulatories that could make the rest of the day's hump with us. We pulled back to the far side of the canal and waited for resupply. We were low on ammo and C-rats. Before the resupply came in the area was strafed by F-4 Phantoms firing 20-mm cannon. We spent an uncomfortable night in mud near the walls of the dikes for protection. The mosquitos and sand fleas made sleep next to impossible. Air strikes and artillery bombardment continued through the night, illumination rounds as well. I along with almost everyone else had sent our night kit stuff in after yesterday's resupply so we damn near froze but Staff Sergeant Allen saved me by sharing a corner of his poncho.

I should mention that all of my company PIO (information officer) duties became suspended with all of the fighting that has been going on. No telling when or if this will resume.

It has completely slipped my mind how guys are wounded and leave the field or are killed or their year is up and they leave for home and I never see them again. Case in point is both David Ruggles and Dennis Wagner who were both badly wounded and airlifted to the 12th Surg and I never saw them again. The last look I recall of Ruggles is his being pulled from a canal by Prince, an agonizing look of terror on his face.

We also just lost Lt. Dossett but under slightly different circumstances. The LT had recently returned from an R&R and when he came back to his duties with headquarters as our forward observer he wasn't worth a shit...to put it mildly. The R&R, in my estimation, got the lieutenant so close to freedom that he lost his perspective or his courage to be blunt and thinking about coming back made it difficult for Jeff to cope. I think this is why some grunts go AWOL. Anyway, we were on a sweep and the jungle grass was so tall and so dry and closed in so tightly about us that we were crawling on our hands and knees in single file. As we moved we could hear a rustling noise moving parallel to us. We all knew that we did not have flank security out so it was an unnerving situation. Lt. Dossett had a very real panic attack to the point we almost had to restrain him. Several days later he was gone, reassigned. This was not a dark machiavellian thing. No, it was a case of what was best. Lt. Dossett was a great forward observer and being taken off the line should be regarded as a natural part of his tour like other officers who rotate to the rear or other duty to make room for another lieutenant to get his shot on the line.

March 5

Tuesday – Jesus H C*****, that was one of the coldest nights in my memory. How on Earth can it be one hundred and sumpthin' during the day and get so cold at night. A fifty-degree swing is reasonable but at fifty degrees at night I am positively chilled to the bone especially with no protective cover at all. There is one other condition that's just as bad and that involves sleeping with your multi-colored green cammy blanket laced inside your rain poncho. The combo provides some cushion from the ground but if you roll yourself completely inside to avoid mosquitos and other creepy crawlers, like the eight-inch orange centipede, your breath forms condensation and upon waking you are soaked through and through and shivering like a bitch. So, let's hear it for sunny days and warm nights.

Moving about a little and getting a cup of metal canteen coffee with a packet of hot chocolate mixed in we finally got some circulation going. For added warmth we burnt some of our C-rat boxes and anything we could find without tearing down somebody's home.

After being in this area for a while I have many new impressions about how this place differs from the jungle. Here are three. (1) after clearing several homes or searching them I noticed that at least locally the indigenous peoples do not have beds. They sleep on pallets, mostly wood and there is no such thing as a pillow. They rest their heads on long wooden rolls or logs, some ornately carved. (2) The distinctive smell of a wood fire carried on the wind usually means trouble and the farther we are from a hamlet or a village when we smell smoke the bigger the trouble. In the boonies and jungles, for instance, if you do smell a fire you can bet you have moved with stealth and are about to interrupt Charlie's repast.

Last night we got a chance to view some F-4 Phantom's as they strafed and dropped their ordinance very close to our positions. I heard someone jokingly question how could a huge chunk of metal whose wings tip up and tail points down even fly. But they do and they are beautiful to watch up close. There are several versions of the supersonic jet interceptor which is capable of speeds of mach 2.2 and has the ability to carry almost 18,000 pounds of armament some of which is fired using rotary cannon. Several paint schemes or patterns are in use. One is a stunning green and jungle brown camouflage paint job and the other is solid gray. Both are built by Mc Donald Douglas. Once in a while after a run the pilot of the two seat tandem inverts so the pilot in the second seat can take photographs. Many soldiers yell "get some" as the jets leave the area.

After observing what these machines can do it is difficult to believe that our enemy has not been vanquished. But when you begin to move out again as we did this morning and once again encounter stiff resistance it blows your mind. How can they be dug in so deep that heavy bombs do not dislodge or kill them? That kind of tenacity must be given a modicum of respect.

We entered the cane fields once again with Alpha moving out in front of us about five hundred meters. The sun was almost at its apex and walking in and around the stalks, some reaching ten feet, the heat was unbearable. High above the clouds were dover white, fluffy and frequently dulled the sun. We were approaching the Saigon River and our line of march was parallel to (our maps indicated) canal 15 when we were pinned down by small arms fire and called gunships to free us. By the time we closed the gap with Alpha Company they came upon ten dead NVA soldiers including a Captain and a Lieutenant. The gunships, it was suspected, drove off the enemy participants in the firefight. The dead were laid low by the Phantoms last night. Found were two RPG (rocket propelled grenade) launchers, two AK-47's and a 19-mm pistol.

Pulled into a NDP (night defensive position) around 1400 hours. The area is bordered on three sides by beautiful clear water creeks and is a vast open area, very easy to defend. We are back near the ARVN compound and the wire mesh surrounding the cinder block compound.

Our listening posts could spot the enemy before they got in mortar range.

Everyone in the company took turns visiting a tiny slice of paradise, an oasis of unimaginable beauty where one of the streams spilled over a tiny dam comprised of boards that could be either added or removed to raise or lower the water level. We walked approximately fifty meters wearing only our jungle boots and carrying our individual weapons for protection to dip down into the cool clear water. We kept one guard alert and the rest of us squatted or sat in the water hidden from view by the lush tufted grass. This is as close to Heaven as we're going to get for the time being unless...

Cleaned weapons, read, had hot chow and mail call. Everyone's mood is elevated for the first time in days as we prepared for ambush patrols, more listening posts, radio watch and sack time.

March 6

Wednesday – Captain Graves, myself and Smitty, another of our radio operators and not Smitty the lieutenant, returned to the ARVN compound and met again with the American advisor. With an assist from special police on loan from the compound we cordoned three Viet hamlets near the perimeter we'd established last night. The hamlets yielded nothing of value, no weapons, no ammo, no rice cache's and no materials for constructing booby traps. We even searched the bunkers that can frequently be found beneath the dirt floors of peasant dwellings. There were few people and most of the hamlets were practically deserted so there were few people to flee. The second platoon found one American grenade. An exceptionally beautiful and also very young

Viet girl child approached me and asked if I wanted some pussy. The phrase almost made me laugh. First time I ever heard that...usually it's "Hey, GI, you want boom boom?"

As we marched back up the road toward the second hamlet the special police filled the ranks between our properly spaced guys giving the appearance (from the air) that we'd created a disorderly cluster fuck. The brigade commander whose call sign is Warrior, and who must really have a case of the ass after the ambush on the second, and also because the division commander is crawling up his ass, landed his chopper right on the black top and gave Captain Graves the ass chewing of a lifetime right in front of all of us. I mean, Graves was so at attention a bronze statue could not have done it better. Graves hands were straight down along the seam in his fatigues and his heels were locked. Later when he and I were alone he confessed that he felt so low that he was contemplating asking to be relieved. Bad career move. He also informed me that he liked the job (read that help) I've been doing and that he was promoting me to Sgt. E-5 to officially fill the company commo chief slot. This I did not expect as I have only been a Spec 4 for twenty days or thereabouts.

Company sized patrol back to the area where Alpha found the NVA officers. Took as long as usual to set up. We detected movement but nothing developed as the night wore on. I actually think I can save Captain Graves from himself.

March 7

Thursday – Returned to the battalion perimeter just after first light and made an immediate about turn and went right back out again, this time to secure both sides of a canal that was too wide and too deep to ford so Delta was going to make a second attempt to cross in rubber boats. The crossing would have enabled Delta to sweep new areas but unfortunately the first attempted crossing failed when VC shot holes in several of the rafts and lobbed grenades in a third. Delta's grunts bailed out as the grenades came sailing in.

Side Bar: I've just got to say this. Talking about the canals in our new area of operation and the extreme tide pull, sometimes as much as ten or twelve feet and the very thick muck at the canal bottoms, has reminded me about a topic that so grosses me out that I'd rather forego it all together. I tasted this shit only once since I've been in country and I swear to God, I'm tellin' the truth, I blew chunks, tossed my cookies, called for Sgt. York, drove the porcelain bus. It was awful. I am, of course, talking about Nuoc Mam or Vietnamese fish sauce. Holy shit, this stuff is disgusting and the reason I even go there is because a *mama-san* told me that it is actually a seasonal sauce only available because one of the ingredients is a worm that is about two feet long, like a tremendously long earthworm that attaches itself to the mud at the bottom of the canals and waves back and forth in the current. These li'l fuckers are harvested and after fermentation has taken place they are made into this sauce that I promise you if you just barely get a whiff from the bottle your gut will churn and fight to empty itself. Enough, whether it's true or not, who cares, rotting cadavers are easier to stomach.

Graves set our CP in a burnt-out hooch. I did not say a word but I know that Captain Baker, who I really miss, would have been roving up front where he expected the action to be. I am trying to subtly suggest things to Graves that will help in his learning. For instance, I did suggest to him the day before yesterday that upon completion of his briefings to company personnel he could excuse the platoon sergeants and then ask the platoon leaders for suggestions and or comments. I am not sure how the captain received this, we'll see. I do not believe he would be showing weakness if he did this and would actually add to his base of knowledge.

We were supposed to get in around noon for a little siesta or break, what have you, since we were out all night but as I've shared with you before, things have a habit on hardly ever working out the way you expected. Flexibility is, indeed, a virtue. We took resupply, to include ammo and chow, and prepared to move out.

Our objective was a bridge that crossed a canal. We moved to secure and move across but our lead element, a recon team detected noise, laughter actually, from the area around the base of the bridge on the other side and reported back. Captain Graves decided to pull back, call in the arty and make the crossing at first light.

Lieutenant Smith, Smitty, who I have not mentioned for some time, is still on my nerves. During the night he called for a pre-plot or an artillery salvo which usually comes in two sets of three. He did this without calling for an adjusting round and all six rounds again landed inside the perimeter and could have had devastating consequences. This, as mentioned before, happened one other time and the captain basically told Smitty that when we got in from this operation he, Smitty, was through, kaput, fini, gone.

Overnight kits did not come in on the resupply bringing the ammo and chow so again, I slept wet, on the ground, in the fetal position with my legs tucked up close and my arms down and in between. The mosquitos sucked on me like they were beatin' on a Grand Canyon mule. I retreated further inside my poncho liner fully realizing I'd wake up wet.

March 8

Friday – We moved across the bridge with no resistance and proceeded to sweep one whole quadrant. Intelligence believes that one of the enemy units operating in this area is the Go Man Battalion, an always combat ready and potent fighting force. It is difficult to determine the strength and numbers for the Go Mon but it is probably safe to say that their numbers were not diminished by the ambush. Believing that we have their battalion bottled up in this area (as intelligence seems to be indicating) would be a mistake. More than likely it would be like having a tiger by the tail. We have heard rumors that their training is extensive, making them somewhat like American Green Berets.

Everyone was beginning to loosen up, to function well together when an M-60 machine gun opened up. After several minutes, we figured that the gun was being fired directly at us and not with us as first suspected. Turns out to be one of the weapons Charlie Company lost during the ambush. Later in the day we thought we had an MIA (missing in action) but further searching turned him up, dead. Throughout the afternoon we received small arms and rocket fire all hit and run stuff. The enemy was playing his game, not engaging. We spent a good part of the afternoon behind a high berm, exchanging fire with the enemy in a tree line across the open field from our position. At one point Captain Graves decided to move back toward me where I had the radio next to me on the ground. When I told him that as he ran toward me sniper rounds trailed just behind him kicking up little geysers of dirt atop the berm, Graves' face turned white.

We called air strikes and artillery on the woodline before attempting to move again. We were carrying the dead troop, who I did not recognize and we were leading another soldier who had been partially blinded by blow back from the exhaust port on one of our crew served weapons, an M-60. Forward progress became difficult. Back at the bridge and losing light we called in a dust off for the dead and blinded soldier and then headed back to the perimeter. The past several days have been exhausting, the heat terrible and some attitude is beginning to show so the stand down is really welcomed by all.

Feels great to be able to have a normal conversation at night before dark and not have to whisper. Had my air mattress but I am so used to curling up on the ground I had difficulty falling asleep.

March 9

Saturday – Does our presence in this area of operation (AO) have any benefit, reap any reward at all? What are we accomplishing here? We sweep through the same place time and again, a tiny ville with a few elderly women whose mouths perpetually drip beetlenut juice while proffering wide grins, small children in their arms and close by a canal with swamped dug outs. The large earthen jars catching rain water under the corners of the roofs are always full, no contraband, no weapons and no Gooks.

Came back to our sector of the perimeter early today. The old man told me that the battalion sergeant major requested me to be Ltc. Simpsons RTO and driver. I told Captain Graves that I was flattered but my loyalty at this point remains with him and with the company and I'm not interested in making a change. Also, I do not want my old friends in second platoon to think that I'm "getting over." The Cap said good because he did not want to lose me.

At 2030 when it was pitch black, no moon, we moved out under a blanket of brilliant stars, pin pricks in the curved roof of the sky above us, and moved to set a company sized ambush. The First Shirt, Clare is his name, is going along and also the battalion Chaplain Captain Crowley. The first sergeant is usually in the rear which is customary. Crowley is a different story. I mean, what's the reason for him to tag along unless he would earn a CIB if we came under fire. Hope Top Clare does not get hurt because he will be putting me in for my promotion for Buck Sergeant tomorrow.

We were on schedule and would have set the ambush nicely until I lost my balance and toppled off a narrow foot bridge and plunged into knee deep water submerging the hand set for my radio. The tide was on the way in and two of our squads had to squat in water to hold up their end of the ambush. We'd only been in position for about two hours, two hours of slapping mosquitos and hiding under our towels when two Gooks carrying a litter with a wounded comrade slowly walked into our kill zone. Everyone opened up with small arms and popped a couple of claymores. The hellacious racket compromised our position and when we combed the trail where the Gooks had been there was no trace of them, just a battered AK-47 with a splintered stock that had taken several rounds. Amazing that they escaped. There were blood pools and trails leading in to the denser jungle at trails edge but that was it. We moved to a different site and hunkered down for the remainder of the night.

At first light while the tide was slacking we moved back into the area for a thorough search which paid off. We uncovered scattered body parts that roughly made two corpses that had sunk into the muck. We continued to search and finally located the third member who was cowering under the foot bridge.

March 10

Sunday – The captured VC was blinded in the ambush and could not have escaped. We had him dusted off, taken back to Cu Chi to the 12th Medical Evacuation facility for questioning and first aid treatment. We heard around chow time when the resupply chopper brought in food, mail and other essentials that questioning the captured VC revealed that we have disbursed or killed about half of the Go Man Battalion…if you can believe the result of hard questioning (read that torture).

Made our way back to the perimeter. Slept for part of the day. Alpha and Delta stayed out and, sure enough, made contact with the enemy and the extended fire fight had us on standby but finally the two companies broke contact and we did not need to respond. Tomorrow we are to chopper into Hoc Mon which is a fly speck on our maps and we will then convoy our way back through Cu Chi and home to Tay Ninh.

Since the ambush on March 2, I have been plagued by troubling images of HWY 248, the bridge, the site of the ambush and the doors torn from nearby homes lining the west side of the road. Each door holds the body of a fallen soldier, a friend, resting upon it and totally covered by an olive-green poncho except for the jungle boots which are exposed and reveal the toes of the boots pointing skyward. When I took pictures, I felt sick. I was invading their privacy.

During waking hours I have been consumed by thoughts of the senseless and at once paradoxical difference between the low points I (we) experience visa vie the ambush and the tremendous loss of lives, the absolute blackness, end of it all, the bottomless pit, the finality and grief on one hand and the absolute high, the exhilaration, the chest pounding adrenaline rush of having survived another firefight, another contact with the enemy and the back slapping camaraderie of hugging my buddies that also made it through such a dark experience. And, then, I wonder how will I cope with such emotional swings when, after it all, after I reach home? I think as well about Lieutenant Colon. How does he cope now with the death and wounding of most of his platoon at the Hour Glass? He is still here, still with us and performing his duties although I'm not really sure the LT is really here. It is as though he has climbed inside himself, retreated. What will he be like when he returns home? Will any of us be the same, ever? Perhaps the only thing we will ever be good for is soldering.

And then there's this one more troubling thing. Back slapping camaraderie aside, the boonierat spends most of his time in the jungle alone even though he's in the midst of his company. Grunts condition their minds to be the perfect place in which to spend most of their time. Picture yourself as part of a serpentine column snaking its way through a dense jungle, an impenetrable bamboo thicket or a barren copse of stand-alone trees. The heat presses down on your forehead until you see nothing but the shimmering, miragelike silhouette of the soldier six to ten feet in front of you. You do not speak to each other for hours and the only thing you can do is crawl inside your head where your mind replays one of the innumerable fantasies you have created there. After being a closed off, bottled up introvert for a year how can you be expected to return home and be the life of the party?

March 11

Monday – As we rode the slicks heading for Hoc Mon to join the convoy our positions were swarmed over by local Vietnamese *baby-sans* and *mama-sans* who ravaged the perimeter and dug in our garbage sumps for anything that would suit a useful purpose. We are careful to punch holes in all of our discarded C-ration cans so they cannot be given to the enemy or used by VC sympathizers to make crude booby traps. It felt terrific to leave this place of seductive beauty, a place of such exotic splendor that it is easy to be hypnotized and then, without warning, boom or should I say Kaboom?

Including our time in the Katum area this has been one of the worst combat stretches to date for the 4/9 Manchu's and that is, for sure, the perspective of us lowly grunt's and NCO's. To the brass it's probably referred to as just a bad stretch, it's what we do, etc.

We landed at the Hoc Mon hard spot, the area where our resupply has been staged, around 1230 hours, and sat in small groups shootin' the shit in the shade. Finally, on board the duce and a half's we pulled out and headed to Cu Chi and on to Tay Ninh through a landscape of pastoral beauty. Some of the guys purchased Cokes from children along the route and some wise acre got a load of boom boom girlie pictures that got passed around to some good-hearted chortles. The ride was a pot hole jarring, dusty, kerchief in the face, bump along. The heat was searing with not a cloud in the sky and the only thing that tamped down some of the heat was the double thick layer of sand bags covering the bare metal deck of the trucks.

Prince and I got ourselves cleaned up and walked down to the 45th Surgical Mash Unit to see if we could hook up with Motheral and throw back some cold ones. The Surg guys do not see what we do and we do not really understand what they do so Motherall and Long Tall were begging for some of our war stories. Later, and stumbling back to our company area after too many beers Prince had himself a case of the ass, that is to say, that he was mildly to somewhat pissed that Brint and Long Tall had their very own fully stocked fridge with access to American girl type nurses. The perpetual supply of steaks and booze and the possibility of pussy along with no tracer rounds, booby traps or short artillery rounds interrupting their fitful slumber caused Prince to blow a fuse. I probably should not have taken him with me.

When we returned to our safe area it was apparent that most of the battalion was having a grand old time. It seems as though the top brass had adopted a lenient posture on our first stand down after a tough combat period. However, this, to me, seems rather inconsistent with the extremely hard assed posture the new BN Commander, LTC. Simpson put forth. Remember his we will never break contact with the enemy directive? For the most part, we did not break contact and our pride grew and our morale is very high currently. It is amazing to me, however, that no one rolled a frag grenade under Simpson's tent flap.

Packy, Wenberg and Mitch were trying to be funny but all they were was drunk when they stood outside our field tent and sang "we love you Toddy" when Prince and I returned. How the hell is a body supposed to get any rest? I got up and we had some more beers then crashed.

March 12

Tuesday – All radios were turned in to yours truly to be cleaned and then painted. This responsibility fell to me and me alone because as stated by the captain, you are the new commo chief to be for the company. The refitting and refurbishing of the radios and all communication gear is labor intensive due to the pounding this stuff takes while in the field.

Listened to some tape recordings. Not much happening tonight until Motheral showed up and wondered why I was late for his steak fry. I tried to beg off, told him I'd forgotten due to getting so drunk over at his place last night but Brint wasn't buying, so I went on down. Had some great chow, eased off on the booze and was back to get some good rest.

Brint leaves tomorrow for one of his two allotted R&R's. He's going to Thailand to get some of that slant pussy and try some of that great Thai stick marijuana.

I forgot to mention this. Going through the chow line this morning I ran into one of my acquaintances, a smallish troop from Puerto Rico. He was leaning way forward on the stool he occupied while taking head count at mess. I asked him why and he said he'd rather not talk about it. I pressed him until Smitty gave me the cut off sign by passing the fingers of one hand across his throat. When I asked Smitty later he said the story was that the Rican whose name is Rivarez was asleep in his cot when his service 45 discharged and a round went through and through on one of his ass cheeks – and that's why Rivarez was leaning almost off the stool. Rumor says he might have shot himself to avoid the field. Another weird thing about this cat is that, and I've seen this in the bush with my own eyes, Rivarez always covers the flash suppressor at the end of his 16 with a condom to keep the dirt out of the barrel. Do not ask me where he gets the damned things, but he does. Actually, Rivarez looks too young to buy rubbers.

March 13

Wednesday – Sat on a cot for most of the day with all of the bits and scraps of paper on which I'd previously jotted notes while in the field. Quite a task to reassemble them now in proper order and create entries for the diary which I keep under lock and key in my foot-locker in Cu Chi base camp. Thank God I put a specific date on each slip of paper.

In the afternoon, we were mobilized and flown from the air strip to Fire Support Base Wayneright to pull security on their perimeter. They had a huge gap in their perimeter they could not cover due to a part of one of their elements having to stay in the boonies overnight. I slept very well. When Prince woke me for radio watch he mentioned I was mumbling something about the red and gray wires.

Back in Tay Ninh the next day, a CQ (Charge of Quarters) runner was dispatched to bring me to the orderly room and when I asked the runner what was up he responded that he did not have the foggiest idea. I found out soon enough. My closest buddy, David Bruning's name had shown up on the morning report. He was killed in action on the fourth of this month. David was a machine gunner with the 2nd of the 27th Wolfhounds which is a sister outfit to us Manchus. He was killed over by Ton Son Nhut air base about the time of the Charlie Company ambush. You will, no doubt, recall my mention of being close to the air base and having a sick feeling in the pit of my stomach watching the Freedom Birds leaving Tan Son Nhut for the World and me not being on one of them. Dave was hit by one of the very rockets that was the reason he was there with the Wolfhounds in that area. I first met Dave on a Trailways bus taking us to Detroit for our pre-induction physical. I next encountered him the day we were sworn in and subsequently shipped to fort Knox for basic training. We were finally separated at Cu Chi when we reported to our units. We were as close as two guys thrown together by a war ever could be. I will miss him every day for as long as I live. There is something truly disturbing about this incident. You will also recall that when Dave Bruning and I were at Cam Rahn Bay with Berg and Johnson that Bruning was having confidence challenges, remember? Dave told me that he would not be going home with us. I said, "Oh. Yes, you will, Dave. We have all come too far and trained too well to not be going home." My heart aches as I write this and now I have too many questions about things like spirit and confidence and human will and I am wondering what a psychiatrist would tell me about one's chances of survival in a situation based on whether the individual in question says, "I ain't goin' home," or, like me, "I know for damn sure that I'm gonna be goin' home." What would that doctor say?

I have been receiving news clippings from both family and friends about the increasing number of protests in almost every major city in the United States and the growing unpopularity of the war. I am bitter and confused. Did David K Bruning die for nothing? for capitalism? do I respect guys for burning their draft cards? avoiding the draft? fleeing to Canada? I am so proud of me as a soldier but increasingly ashamed of my country whose only goal seems to be to keep this war going for as long as possible. We have heard rumors surrounding fact and fiction about the so-called Gulf of Tonkin incident upon which escalated attacks on North Vietnam were based. Were our ships fired upon or not? Was that information based on government lies that were promoted and passed on by a pliant media? Can you comprehend my frustration? Likely not. Fuck it, don't mean nuthin! Push on through soldier.

March 14

Thursday – We air mobiled around burning fuel (jet fuel or JP4 is a mixture of 50 % galsoline and 50% kerosene) while doing a glorified Eagle Flight. When we arrived at the air strip and were waiting for the choppers to land for the pick-up, Lt. Paris showed up in his Jeep. He had a driver but no RTO. He sauntered over to where I was leaning on my radio and doing the shuck and jive with Graves and the rest of the headquarters guys. Paris heard about me turning down the radio and driver job with the new battalion commander and said, "I don't guess I'd stand a chance of getting you to work for me if you turned down LTC. Simpson...is there? Pretty sure he was pulling my leg so I Cheshire grinned him.

We were in a huge open field of dried out rice paddies and waiting for the birds to come in and pick us up. Dozens of water buffalo were grazing idly about the field up until the choppers were inbound. The closer the slap slap of the Huey rotor blades got the more agitated the water boo's got and when the choppers settled into the field the buffalo headed for the jungle. Most of them have huge rings through their nostrils and it is not uncommon to see them yoked and pulling a cart or wagon on the way to market. The animals are the most highly cherished possession of the peasant farmers.

The fields were also filled with young Viet children joking around and selling Coca's (Coca-Cola) to the thirsty GI's. The closer we operate to the larger villages the more English the peasants speak due in part to exposure to Americans. For such youngsters, they are remarkably shrewd when it comes to selling whatever it is they are pitching. Most of their items are black market goods so the offering is much the same wherever we go. It is a little unsettling, though, when we are miles from any hamlet or ville and several young kids appear out of nowhere, approach our perimeter and cry out, "GI want Coca?"

No contact. We returned to Tay Ninh.

March 15

Friday – 0530 wake up and then chow, 0730 formation and equipment check and break up cases of frag grenades, smoke and flares, chopper pad by 0805 and all lifts airborne west out of Tay Ninh to recon some old rocket sites and see if we can surprise Charlie. The drop zone was cold and due to dense foliage, we marched away single file in the following order: Delta, Alpha, Bravo. Charlie is off by themselves on a training and rebuilding exercise. Glad to see them getting it back, getting together again but still I somehow feel bad for them. After their devastating loss, the best way to build their numbers back up is to siphon off an equal number of men from the other battalion companies. Nobody is saying it but the reality is that Alpha, Bravo and Delta have used the situation to their advantage by sending what one might be called problem troops to Charlie Company. They – Charlie – will get it back though…they're Manchus. Here's an example. We had a brand new hot shot 2nd Looey named Schwartz who was a little large for his britches, insisted on doing things his way, shunned suggestions from the Old Man and this day finds himself in Charlie Company. Of course, that means our third herd needs a platoon leader but for now a sergeant will fill the slot. Capt. Graves told me privately that he shit canned the Looey. For some reason, perhaps he feels it brings us closer together, Captain Graves likes telling me stuff. Ordinarily Graves said he would not give up an officer.

I'm thinking today is like the Ides of March. I remember somewhere in my cobwebby literature mind about this phenomenon having something to do with a religious observance coinciding with the death of Julius Caesar. How appropriate, the captain just symbolically or, at least, metaphorically assassinated Lt Schwartz. Hey, Schwartzy, beware the Ides of March.

The days operation was again a complete bust if you really dig encountering the enemy and trading tracers with him. We made good time humpin' to the PZ and were back at the company area in time for chow. Stansberry had tubs of soda and beer, Budweiser this time, along with some pretty good Delmonte brand root beer, iced down and sitting in front of the orderly room. Three cheers for Dan the man and Top Clare our First Sergeant. Chow had been set on long tables outside and we were treated to steaks and baked potatoes, creamed corn and cake for dessert. Our mess sergeant, the full-blooded Indian from Muskegon, Michigan, is a first-rate scrounger and as it turns out a pretty good cook as well.

Going in to Tay Ninh most every night or into any hard spot where there is regular chow is getting' me fat. When I was drafted my waist was 35 or 6 and I weighed 205. Coming out of Advanced Training my waist was a 33 and I weighed 185. My waist is now 30 and I weigh a solid 170 lbs.

March 16

Saturday – Up at 0600 and prepared for an Eagle Flight at 0800 but due to heavy ground mist or some weird inversion that drove the cloud layer to ground, we did not become airborne until after 0930 hours.

The fact has not passed unnoticed that not a single element of our battalion has established contact with the enemy for the past three days. While this is welcomed news by us regular grunts, the guys on the tip of the spear, it must be discouraging news to our exalted leader Ltc. Simpson who has vowed to never break contact with the enemy. Forget Simpson's personal feelings here and imagine, if you will, the tremendous case of the ass it gives our division commander, Tropic 6 when we are not kickin' Gook ass all over our area of operation. Again, when we are not engaged with the enemy or wrapped around the axel we always make our trek to various pick up points in plenty of time to return to the perimeter for the night. If this slack period persists we could be ordered to remain in the bush. Landing, called insertion or leaving, called extraction are the most dangerous parts of our operations because the vulnerability means we could easily be ambushed at either time. Most of our troops really like riding on the Huey's but we're actually safer if we have one insertion into an area and then extend our operation for a period of time with limited helicopter utilization.

In a way, today was exactly like that because we must have humped every square inch of Tay Ninh Province. Very hot, dry with blistering sun in a cloudless sky. The most exciting part of the day was when forward observer Jeff Dossett's replacement, a lieutenant named Wilson, called for a marking round of Willy Pete (white phosphorus) to reveal our location. The round whistled close overhead and exploded in a beautiful fluffy white cloud about thirty meters on our left flank. The noise and loud pop startled quite a few newfers who immediately hit the deck and covered their heads. Those of us who have been in the field for months just stood there, took leisurely pulls on our canteens and exchanged knowing glances. God, it seems an eternity since my cherry days when everything scared the shit out of me. It occurred to me that I am about half way into my tour and that means that my R&R and seeing Cindy in Hawaii is coming up pretty soon.

When we finally got to our PZ everyone was really dragging. Captain Graves called for the lead element to pop smoke and only one at the head of each of our two columns for the inbound choppers to establish our exact location. Alpha somehow popped three smokes and their CO got called on the rug. So, what happens with Bravo. Ri-i-i-g-ht, some jokers popped three more. This made it very difficult for the inbound choppers to pin point exactly where they were supposed to set down. More smoke could be seen coming out of the captain's ears than all the smoke grenades combined. We suffered another snafu and finally one of the choppers carrying part of our second platoon had transmission problems and had to autorotate into a field about a thousand meters from Tay Ninh necessitating the troops to hoof it by foot into the perimeter.

After chow, there was a very emotional funeral service for Major Bill Roush. The service had to be held outside the chapel because almost every Manchu in Tay Ninh was there to celebrate the major's life, his service and his dedication to us all. There weren't any dry eyes.

Downed a few cold ones with Stansberry. Did not hit the rack until 2300 hours. You have heard me mention Stansberry many times as well as some of the other personnel to be found in the rear. E 6 platoon sergeants and above are rarely sighted in base camp because they party on their own and seldom mix with the rest of us except on the occasion of a battalion celebration or cook out.

March 17

Sunday – Up at 0400 and mucked around getting ready to ride a convoy down Cu Chi way to deliver an arty battery with guns, ammo and all of their paraphernalia and then pull perimeter security until they get settled in. The Blackhawks will rendezvous with us later in the day and ride us back to base. The ride was long, hot and we looked like bedraggled dust monkeys by the time we hit the end of the line. Need I mention that the farther back in the convoy your vehicle is the more dust you must suffer through. I was perched on top of a load of 105 mm Howitzer ammunition and thought constantly about being blown to smithereens when an enemy RPG would come crashing into the side of the truck. Fuck it, don't mean nuthin' cuz I'm gonna live. Nobody's going to be spending my ten thousand dollars, not my wife, not my next of kin, nobody.

Before the pick-up we got word of an ARVN outpost that was under attack so we moved in that direction until the VC broke off their assault and fled back into the bush. We had several scout dog teams working with us, specially trained German Shepherds, to sniff out enemy positions. The dogs alerted many times but only because there were so many peasants in the area of the rubber plantation we were traversing. The ones we ran to ground to check their papers proved to be laborers from the plantation.

Waiting for the choppers to come in I was reclining on a huge fallen tree and shooting the bull with Captain Graves when Lt. Paris and the Charlie company CO came along. They sat for a while and were, as usual, busting my chops about me bein' a lousy, getting over radio telephone operator. I got the last laugh on 'em this time, though. While sitting there Lt. Paris got a coded message from Manchu 6 and when he pulled out his SOI (signal operating instructions) extract to unshackle the message he discovered that his had expired which meant he could not interpret the message. I knew mine was still current so I handed it over with a huge smile. "Here, LT, why don't you use mine." How fun. These guys love to kid me but I know it is all in fun since we all know that Ltc. Simpson had requested me for his personal RTO and driver.

On the way back in we were hauling ass. The Huey's (I could read the dash) were doing over 105 knots so we were like a bunch of farts in a wind storm, stagger left. The water buffalo in the fields below looked like maggots we were so high.

March 18

Monday – Had to wait at the air strip for an artillery prep of the landing zone (LZ) before we could climb aboard the choppers. Hotter than blazes sitting in loose formation, no shade, no protection. Once airborne we circled for approximately thirty additional minutes before swooping down and into the LZ. We moved into the tree line swiftly and as the Huey's returned to pick up the rest of the company at the air strip they received heavy small-arms fire from the jungle from a location that we had difficulty pin pointing. We laid down a heavy base of fire, moving tactically off the LZ and into the jungle. We then moved in columns toward the source of the firing but made no contact. We finished a hurried sweep and returned to the choppers and they deposited us in a vast, sweeping area of arid land where we rested and cleaned weapons. Headquarters Company was already in the field along with an artillery battery that was, with great efficiency, preparing defensively.

The field was ringed distantly with beautiful coconut and banana palms swaying in a light breeze that reached us across the open fields. We thought about sending a squad to forage for the fruit we felt certain we'd find there but we demurred. And then…do our eyes deceive, or *Oh, my God, are those hundreds and hundreds of young, ripe, basketball sized watermelons waiting to be gobbled?* Well, they were and everyone ate their fill. I mean why not, they're there aren't they.

We had hot chow flown out and even though our bellies were already filled to the puke threshold with watermelon, still we gorged ourselves because we do not get 'hots' all that often. Later in the evening while applying camouflage for our night operation Captain Graves came back from a poop talk at battalion TOC (tactical command center) and he was pissed. The farmer whose melons we consumed came to the battalion command and demanded reimbursement for his crop. According to the captain over five hundred dollars were required to mollify the pissed off farmer. I wondered if we would ever hear the end of that one. There was no denying the crime because the rinds were scattered all over the field.

We were about to embark on an ambush patrol involving the entire battalion, all four companies. I guess I do not need to remind you of what a giant cluster fuck these little soirees always degenerate into. The important element in a night ambush is to be quiet, employ an element of stealth so we can surprise the enemy and kill him. Being quiet while moving during daylight hours on a sweep is important for another reason; If everyone is always chattering, then no one can listen to the jungle and that is so important. Once contact has been made, an ambush is sprung or a fire fight ensues then chattering and shouting and yelling are common.

The intel for our activity tonight was gleaned from a long-range reconnaissance patrol (LRRP) that has been operating in the area for the past week and observed (their function is to observe and not engage) heavy VC traffic along the same trail.

At 0300 hours, three hours late we were finally settling in at the edge of a rubber plantation where we had a long-range view down an incline leading away from the rubber trees. We tried to dig defensive positions with entrenching shovels but the ground was like cement and the resulting noise caused us to give up and just push the foot or so of loose dust outward to form banked circles in which to lay. Stirring the dust and dirt caused us to be swarmed by sand fleas that viciously bit our flesh for the remainder of the night. About 0400 hours we watched through our night vision Starlight Scope as a heavily armed patrol of thirteen VC soldiers, some carrying rocket launchers on their shoulders, came up the slope. Frightening to watch them steadily approach, knowing we'd be engaging them shortly. At the last moment, the Dinks changed direction and disappeared over another small knoll. Anyone who has suffered something like poison ivy without succumbing to the compulsion to scratch the itch knows what we experienced not scratching the sand flea bites for fear of alerting the enemy combatants approaching from our front.

In the morning, we rendezvoused with duce and a half trucks on the road leading back in to Tay Ninh. The road was jammed with motor scooters and small children selling long slender loaves of bread, Coca's and some frozen kind of ice cream that looked like snot on a stick.

March 19

Tuesday – We were back inside base camp around 0900 hours and I have to tell you a really hot shower and a bar of soap never felt so good. The water from the wing tanks mounted above were filled with water heated by the sun and gravity did the rest. A constant flow of luxuriant steamy water covered our bodies. The sand fleas from last night a distant memory.

Chow was a treat this morning with fresh eggs and bacon with cold cereal and milk and toast and jam washed down with ice cold orange juice. Mail call followed and was one of the first in a long time. I received a great letter from Cindy that included a newspaper clip that when I unfolded it and began to read it tears filled my eyes and finally I broke down. The article was from the Tawas City, Michigan, newspaper, and along with a picture of Pfc David K Bruning, were the circumstances about his death and the fact that he had previously been wounded and then returned to action. David was killed by a rocket propelled grenade and was posthumously awarded a second Purple Heart and the Bronze Star. My company was in the same area hunting down the sites that were firing the 120 mm rockets on Tan San Nhut Airbase. Perhaps if we'd found these sites and eliminated the enemy personnel firing them, David would not have been killed. David's wife will at least have the memory of her husband, my friend, as he was the day he left. I have never known such a gregarious, humorous and fun living guy as Dave. He was bright and intelligent yet possessed the innocence of a young child. You could not help but be in love with him.

We were supposed to have the remainder of the day to relax and while this was true we still had to get all of our gear squared away to go out after dark again. Our night action was to set a company sized ambush at the base of the Black Virgin Mountain to try and intercept an attack force headed for Tay Ninh. We observed seven VC through the Starlight but we did not engage. This was a miserable night for me with thinking about Dave and all. I withdrew and crawled inside myself, did not even feel like talking, quietly monitored the radio until first light at which time we hoofed it back to base. No contact.

March 20

Wednesday – Graves told me that he is signing the paperwork for my promotion to Sgt. E-5 tonight and was grinning as he told me this. I asked him what's up and he kept smiling so I pressed him. Finally, he informed me that I'd just have to wait and see. That was it.

We had some down time for the remainder of the day. Our company street is looking outstanding. Platoon hooches have been built and are luxurious compared to the original squad tents on top of square wooden platforms that they replaced. Top Clare as I mentioned is a first-rate scrounger and nobody asks where he got all the new lumber or what he had to trade to get it. The structures are long and have tin roofs and a couple of stairs leading to a screen door and wood floors. There are screens under the overhanging roofs ending at tall sills and these will soon have bamboo matting hanging down that will keep horizontally blowing rain from getting inside.

We are on stand-by and required to respond, be sent out if there is trouble in the field. The opportunity to stand down, be at ease is welcomed by everyone. I read for most of the afternoon and nearly puked from drinking too much Grape Kool-Aid. I probably would not have done this except Stansberry got me a sizeable chunk of ice for our cool can and the ice-cold beverage was so good I could not stop.

Wrote letters home including a sympathy letter to Rita Bruning, Dave's wife. This was the most difficult thing I've ever done. Tears spilled down onto my writing paper and streaked the blue ink from the ball point pen I was using. I hope I do not have to do that again for anyone.

March 21

Thursday – Airmobile west. Upon landing and getting off the LZ we moved effortlessly through a vast thicket populated with a sparse scattering of thin, dark barked, spindly trees that appeared to be a part of the ficus family. The leaf clusters were a dull, dry, dust covered green. We passed through an abandoned VC base camp that I recognized from a long-ago sweep. This was the first enemy base camp that Captain Graves had seen so, naturally, he wanted to cover it with a fine-toothed comb. The only thing we turned up was a single spent cartridge from an AK-47 and a ton of empty peanut butter C-ration tins left by Delta when they went through here the day before yesterday.

Back on the PZ waiting for extraction we experienced another fire caused by a smoke grenade thrown to mark our position for the Blackhawks. The dense purple smoke made it difficult for some of the ships to navigate out and away from the open field. Additionally, two of the choppers being tired and worn or in need of maintenance had trouble lifting their loads and the troops were deposited back on the ground to wait for other extraction ships. Lucky a critical situation did not occur.

I've mentioned how easily your mind can wander. Today's LZ was a sprawling open field surrounded by beautiful deciduous trees. The surface of the ground was festooned with two to three-foot-tall leaves of emerald green grass that shimmered and waived in the heat of the day and reminded me of a lake from my childhood. I was transfixed by the hallucinatory property of my vision.

March 22

Friday – The number of convoys through and around Tay Ninh Province offer opportunities to observe how the people live. The densely-populated portion of Tay Ninh City, relatively speaking, is much like metropolitan cities in any Third World country. Homes are closely situated with brick or mortar fronts and iron grille work to protect them. Most of these dwellings are uniformly close to the street perhaps indicating effective zoning ordinances. There are small court yards with a Vespa motor scooter or two and fences in front with elaborate square wooden posts or entry portals.

As you leave the populated area and approach the rural area you see a business here and there but no signs advertising the nature of commerce. Occasionally we pass the distinctive honey bee looking brick kilns with thousands of red clay bricks stacked precisely on wood pallets. Occasionally one sees a rusted metal sign advertising Dr. Pepper or Coca-Cola or a slate chalk board offering food for sale next to a pile of coconuts used to make drinks. Close to the hub of the city there are petrol stations.

We began our dusty, gritty ride through swirling clouds of ground mist – a sure sign that the monsoon's are approaching. Just before first light we were well past Tay Ninh City.

Papa-san *in front of his Tay Ninh home*

We rendezvoused with our helicopter's around 1000 hours to begin a search and destroy operation on the fringes of the Ho Bo Woods. We again have two scout dog teams and a group from the 65th Engineer battalion with us. I nodded hello to Sergeant Blair. The engineers are carrying several hundred pounds of C-4 plastic explosive to blow any tunnel complex we uncover. The engineers have been engaged in a sustained program to siphon a huge, steady stream of water from the Saigon River, sending it through large fire hoses and into tunnel openings. There never seems to be any progress but we are certain the tunnels are probably never ending and honeycomb the entire woods and jungle under our feet.

Humped for most of the day and again came up empty. When we met the trucks again they had brought with them a camera and sound crew from CBS so naturally everyone had to ham it up for the cameras. This is the first time we have ever had a crew from a major news outlet shadow us for part of a day. The crew, and I have no idea why, wanted to speak with and interview troops from the Dakotas. Don't even know if we have any such soldiers or a better question is how did they know, I mean, what turned the crew onto us?

Stansberry, who I neglected to inform you, is a Specialist 5th Class which is the same as me being an E 5. Dan was instrumental in getting me lined up with the PIO responsibility and the RTO job and now the promotion to the commo chief position. Honestly, though, none of this would have happened without support from the different Bravo commanding officers that I have served under. The last hurdle in the whole process is Sgt. Swenger who is on permanent profile which means an injury that is ongoing and keeps him from returning to combat. Stansberry told me confidentially that the Captain wants to remove Sgt.

Air mobile

Search and desroy into the Habo Woods

Swenger and guess who his replacement is going to be? You got it...yours truly. Am I livin' right or what?

I was catching a cat nap when Sgt. Lykins shook me awake and told me "the Old Man wants to see you." I was a little peeved at having been awakened and had no idea that Captain Graves was going to present me with news that would alter my life considerably. "Day after tomorrow, Sunday," he told me when I walked into the orderly shack, "is your last day in the field. I am moving Sgt. Swenger over and you will be responsible for the radio section and I need you in the rear to do this. There is going to be a surprise CGI -commanding general's inspection – and I need you to begin preparations, build a dust free enclosure for all of our radio equipment." Captain Graves told me that he had not intended to make the switch so soon but changed his mind. He will give me every assist and he expects a bang-up job. "you earned it," he said. I was so excited I could barely contain my enthusiasm.

At 2330 we slowly left base camp and, by truck, moved very slowly less than three thousand meters. Lights off. Before noise could be problematic we dismounted and walked silently to cordon off a ville where it has been reported to us that sixteen Viet Cong have been living while posing as tax collectors. VC living in the ville's or hamlets like this are there to control, intimidate by murder, if necessary and bleed the peasants of their resources. They live in the ville by day and patrol at night to spread their terror.

First Sergeant Clare is with us tonight which is unusual as I may have previously mentioned and it was obvious that he'd spoken to the captain about my situation because he told me gruffly, "Dexter, yer gonna' be like my second skin so get used to it." Top acts tough but he is such a big Teddy bear.

We had completely encircled the small ville by using a series of single flashes from our small strobe lights to make certain our elements closed properly with one another. Settling down we then waited for first light when we would send a patrol inside the hamlet and see how many fish we'd netted.

March 23

Saturday – The silence was broken by chattering wild life as our patrol, accompanied by forty ARVN police, cautiously entered the ville. No gun fire took place and checking ID's and searching suspicious individuals netted seven possibilities that we brought back to Tay Ninh on the trucks for interrogation.

No activity for the remainder of the day.

I feel confident the people back home watching television and consuming TV dinners do not have a clue that we sometimes kill one another here in the Nam, quite by accident for sure but it's true. All they see is footage of fierce firefights mostly from the American perspective which is a myriad of soldiers in grubby fatigues standing and firing their weapons into a dense jungle or across an open rice field. They do not see the exhausted troops of Alpha come in from the field, drop their gear and in so doing one soldier's M-60 machine gun accidentally discharges a burst of six that practically cuts a squad mate in half. They are not in the field with us when Huey gunships work a wood line and accidentally kill a Lieutenant and two other grunts like happened last month. There was one dude in our company it is rumored, shot himself in the foot to avoid more combat and it has been written that almost one third of American casualties are the result of friendly (our own) fire. The reason for explaining this is that we inhabit a very dangerous place, a place where we watch out for each other as much as we do the enemy, but still, shit happens.

March 24

Sunday – This is a little strange. With all of the night ambush patrols and sleep deprivation exercises and the unending sweeps beginning at ungodly hours I still need to be awakened when we are in base camp. Not today though. Got up and over to mess for some scrambled eggs and then got busy filling my canteens and squaring my gear away in preparation for moving out. Word is that we will be engaging in some form of training and refresher courses that will take place in the Michelin Rubber Plantation. Captain Graves did not let me know that I was not going along and when he announced it quite loudly when I fell into formation my good buddies hollered and yelled that I was now officially a Rear Echelon Mother Fucker (REMF). I can take a ribbing as well as the next guy but this got a bit ridiculous, so much so that Top Clare bulled his way out of the Orderly Room to join in the hilarity. I am now officially a garrison troop and as soon as the company made their hat Top came into my hooch with a couple of cold ones to sorta lay out the plan which means that I am going to be his gofer as in go fer this and go fer that. "Understand?" he queried. I did not think a reply was actually necessary but said, "Yup," all the same. "That's yup, First Sergeant," Top smiled.

Spent the day scrounging lumber that I will use to slam together a small shed with shelves to hold all the spare radio's, auxiliary equipment such as antennae and spare batteries. When not in use the radio's will be turned in for maintenance. I plan to have a two-piece Dutch style door for access. Top has informed me that one of my first duties will be to have two galvanized tubs chock full of iced down soda's and beer ready every time the troops get in from the field. "Since you were a boonierat yourself you realize how important beer and soda rations are to troops when they get in," Top said forcefully, "so let's you and me not fuck it up." "You got it First Sergeant," I replied. Of course, my having access to the beer and soda lock up means that Top will have a never-ending supply of liquid refreshment. Well, OK!

Cleaned up at 0300 hours and ate early chow and prepared for bunker guard. As soon as my Buck Sgt. Chevrons are sewn on I will be exempt from bunkers. I was trucked over to the 2nd of the 32nd Artillery with others from the battalion where we had to suffer the 'way they do things' which involved guard mount formation and a drilling on our general orders. I actually recall what I would call two of the most important orders: 1) Take charge of my post and, 2) do not quit my post until properly relieved. These reminded me of basic training.

While on bunker guard and sitting atop the sandbagged structure with two soldiers from the 2nd of the 32nd to catch a little breeze the conversation came around to obeying orders and I mentioned that I could not understand anyone disobeying orders or refusing to fight. My words drew nothing but silence. Crickets! How could I possibly have known that the two guys sharing my spot on top of the bunker were the same ones that came to the field when Baker was CO. You may recall that the two refused to fight and Baker actually grabbed their M-16's and escorted them to a defensive hole out in front of the perimeter that the company had abandoned but not filled in. They were court martialed and got six months at Long Binh jail but Ltc. Henchman granted leniency and reduced their sentences to sixty days of guard duty and eventually

My commo hut

a return to duty with a different unit within the Manchu structure. I was glad that at the time I had not shared any of my exasperations or anger. I had actually modified my feelings after being in the field a little longer. The two told me that when they came in the next morning they were petrified but maintained the strongly held belief that while they could never claim conscientious objector status, still they believed that killing was wrong and could not be part of combat operations. I let them know that I understood and had empathy for their position but I still had to do what I'm doing. The hours passed silently 'til dawn.

Got very little sleep. The 2nd of the 32nd pulls 75% alert all night and the Sergeant of the Guard made regular rounds. Truck picked us up at 0700 hours and we returned to the company without properly being relieved of our post. Go figure.

March 25

Monday – Attended morning chow with Stansberry. This being in the rear is a routine that's going to take some getting used to. Could someone explain to me why I feel a tremendous sense of guilt. I mean, here I am in the rear and charged with the responsibility of straightening out our radio and communication mission and all I can think about is how I should be in the jungle with the company. Oh, well, keep on keepin' on.

Very tired this morning after last night's bunker guard duty and as I labored to build my little communication enclosure I reflected on my conversation with the two soldiers on guard duty last night. I cannot find any reasoning that would eliminate the pair from some mission short of combat like doing what I am doing now but I suppose the duo would split hairs by saying that building a shed to house radios would, nonetheless, be contributing to and therefore be the same as fighting. I'm glad that I am not as conflicted as they are.

Worked like a son of a gun all day, felt the need to keep moving or Top would find something else for me to do. Had a few beers with him after chow. Lt. Paris came around late in the afternoon to keep in touch and see if I would reconsider the battalion radio job. No.

I am about to line the inside of the new commo shack with transparent plastic to keep out the dust. I will then build shelves and will occupy my time with learning as much as I can about all of the equipment. Remember that my MOS (Military Occupational Specialty or job) is eleven Bravo, infantryman, and not a communication and commo guy. Captain Graves did me a huge favor and I owe him.

March 26

Tuesday – Only been relieved of my field duties for several days and I think what's missing is the adrenaline rush. I have never been so stripped bare about how I feel…I love being a soldier and many of the guys would probably say I'm crazy but I even like the feeling I get when we march past a bunch of office poages' (person other than a grunt) or REMF's on the perimeter that are not going out with us. Does this make me feel important, is that it?

In the afternoon, I began putting up shelves inside the commo hut. In reaching into a tight spot at the very back of a shelf, I had to hold a block of wood with one hand and hammer with the other. I massacred a finger, thumb actually, with an errant hammer swing and the pressure that built up under the nail almost made me cry. The color purple, I guess, was somehow a measure of the pain so I walked to the aid station where a medic heated a needle and pushed or melted the needle through the nail, I'd never heard of or seen such a thing. Blood spurted out and the relief was immediate. Back in the company area I used the other hand to hold yet another wood block and bingo, smacked that thumb as well. When I got back to the aid station the medic saw me coming and said, "are you fucking with me, Sergeant, or are you just that stupid? All thumbs was all I could say.

McDermot helped me for the rest of the day because the bandages on both of my thumbs proved too cumbersome. McDermot was a barber back in the World. Imagine the strange partnership we shared with the hammer and saw. My planning really lacked the skills that rudimentary carpentry deserves and every time I wanted to add a new shelf it required yet another support or board.

We were assigned five newfers this evening and while not officially in charge I had a good opportunity to observe the frightened, fearful faces of the new cherries. Wow! Reminded me of myself standing at parade rest in the captain's hooch over six months ago when the crazy dude picked up the hammer on the corner of Baker's desk and lunged at him.

The past few days I have lacked the energy that I had when I was in the field. I believe the reason has much to do with the frenetic pace and while in the jungle there wasn't much time to think about how fatigued I was.

March 27

Wednesday – Completed the shelving today in spite of my thumbs getting in the way. There is some pain today but a few Darvon took care of that. I was able to procure a power saw over at battalion and that effectively cut my time in half though I'm in no hurry to finish.

The company is out near the Phil Ho Plantation again today for classes. I know that you will not believe me but they are actually practicing digging fox holes and defensive positions. I'm certain that, with the possible exception of the cherries, they all remember how the pitiful little entrenching tools would bounce off the cement-like earth sending reverberating shock waves up our arms and into our brain stems. Continuing the futile exercise left fluid filled blisters on our palms and on each finger. In frustration, we would push the top layer of dust aside as we did on that ambush a while back at the edge of the rubber plantation.

When finished at the plantation the troops returned to Tay Ninh for the issuance of the newer version of the M-16. Two improvements were chrome bores and

30-round magazines. The chromed bore could possibly resolve jamming issues while thirty round magazines will definitely increase fire power.

The battalion was placed on a thirty-minute stand by to rally to the aid of a sister battalion that is supposedly in a huge fire fight back up by the Hourglass.

Still no orders cut for my E-5 promotion so no new chevrons on my uniform blouses and I still must report for duty on the bunker line. Much more preferable than being on stand by and having to saddle up. My watch did not form until later and I was pretty drowsy from more Darvon for the pain.

March 28

Thursday – Duce and a half picked us up from our bunker guard position which was close to the Tay Ninh main gate and returned us to the company area. I was about to leave the mess area when Stansberry caught up to me and informed me that Top had been searching all over for me. We were on our way back from taking our chow at Headquarters & Headquarters mess.

"Tell the First Sergeant he can find me in the radio com shop," I said, "and what's up with taking our meals at Head & Head?"

"Some kind of a consolidation effort," Stan replied, "with all companies being deployed it makes sense. One mess hall serving meals rather than a place for each company is more efficient, that's all."

I retired to my little shack and continued preparations to move the equipment in when I heard Top's voice crescendo out my name, "Dexter." "In here, Top!" "Where's my b....?" "Your beer, Top, why it's right here on the shelf waiting for you," I beamed. "Oh, bein' a wise ass so early in the morning," he bellowed. "You know me,

Sarge, just trying to anticipate your every need." "That's First Sergeant Clare or Top to you, rookie," he said with an approving smile. And by the way, where's your weapon?" "Right there on the door jam, Top, and that brings me to sumpthin I've been meaning to ask you."

"Yeah, what's that?"

"Well, um…"

"Spit it out, boy, what's on yer mind?"

"Well, when I first began carrying the radio for Captain Baker he said he'd get me a sidearm cuz that bazooka I was carryin' wouldn't be worth a shit in close."

"Yeah?"

"So, carryin' anything with a long barrel everywhere I go in base camp doesn't make any sense…practically speaking, I mean. How 'bout sumpthin' smaller"

"Get me another cold one."

"Is that a yes?"

"We'll see."

That was pretty much the end of my dream about owning the standard issue military Colt M1911A1 .45. The best part of carrying this sidearm other than its macho appeal is that it can be holstered at the hip or shoulder, no unwieldy barrel like the 16 or, for that matter, the blooper to get in the way. And what are the chances of getting overrun in a large base camp and needing additional fire power anyway?

Late evening basketball game in front of the chapel with Smitty, Jobman, Stansberry and me. Jobman is back in the XO slot. Stansberry and I got our asses handed to us because I didn't care and Stan's fat and out of shape even for a company clerk.

Being in the rear with the gear does have advantages like more beer and you get to violate uniform rules. Back here I can cut my fatigue pants like Top does to resemble Bermuda shorts. Better air circulation. Don't know if I ever told you this but in the bush most guys do not wear under pants, even boxers. Less chance of jungle or crotch rot. Is that where that slang about referring to grunts as swingin' dicks came from?

March 29

Friday – Top's been getting on my case about me being on bunker guard at night because he can never find me in the early morning. I told him it's because I'm not back yet when he comes looking. He said, "E-5's do not pull bunker guard." "They do if their First Sergeant doesn't fix the paper work." "Ok, Ok, I got it. I'll see what I can do to speed up the process."

The commo shack is shaping up well. Did some painting, inventoried some old long range 2-niner-2 antennae's and then cleaned up for chow. The life in the rear is very dull. I have not seen Ehrig from battalion in regards to reporting activities from the field or photo submissions. Also, we have not had movies in the evening since moving from Cu Chi up to Tay Ninh so evenings are pretty much relegated to drinking, reading and eventually sleep. Boring.

Much to Top's chagrin I again reported for bunker guard and this time our duce and a half trucked us over to the 2nd of the 34th. Their bunkers were in horrible shape and contained no sleeping cots. Chiggers and no see'ums attacked us unmercifully for the entire night. The conversation with the other troops pulling guard duty with me was very interesting. These guys had heard about the legendary Lieutenant Colonel Henchman who taunted the enemy on his radio net the day of the Hour Glass battle. Henchman threatened that the Manchus were coming, so you'd better *didi mau* (leave post haste or get lost). I could not resist and filled them in on some of our exploits but they had a few of their own. They are an armored unit and drive M-48 Patton tanks that weigh nearly 50 tons.

There is a legend of their own involving four dozen of their machines breaking through the crust of the jungle and becoming mired to the deck. Their commander challenged that if they could recover all of the tanks and make them operational by night fall they'd get a case of beer for each freed vehicle. Come night fall the Patton tanks were all free. The commander delivered on his promise and since that day the unit nickname and call sign became Dreadnaught because of the way they were able to make the tanks operable in the middle of enemy action. We have worked alongside the Dreadnaughts twice that I recall, once being the day we followed their M-48's into that wood line and my squad leader tripped that booby trap and wounded me and almost killed him.

M48 tank broke through the crust

I can tell by pulling duty in some of the other areas around the base camp perimeter just how good we Manchu's are. Some of these other outfits are truly sloppy and I associate that with poor command. When I returned to the company area I was looking for Top to share a couple of beers, then I started thinking that sloppy work by other units on any section of the perimeter endangers us all.

The company came in this afternoon so the area was filled with late night revelers. Good to see some of the guys. Had a beer with SSG. Otis Boatright, too.

March 30

Saturday – Mail call, well, not actually. Since I am in the base camp someone from the orderly room usually hands me my mail and today I received a letter from Cindy and a picture. The picture was alarming. Part of her hair had been shaved and in the picture, I could see a line of stitches along the side of her forehead. Her Volkswagen slid on a patch of ice, jumped the curb and smashed into the front of a liquor store just as she was leaving East Grand Rapids. Cindy had been spending Sunday afternoon with the family as she does each weekend sharing dinner and football. I really miss these get-togethers because my brother and his wife are always included. Cindy is fine but the car is apparently a total loss.

The company went out again this afternoon to continue the training mission and I actually feel like I am, as the saying goes, shirking my duty if I am not with them. When they saddle up and prepare to move out I make myself scarce even though I know I will not be tagging along. How strange is that in light of my feeling guilt about not being with them? Wouldn't you expect me to be standing by and begging to saddle up and go along?

I was visited by a battalion Specialist 5th Class today to go over my log books which are really a sorry mess and have not been updated forever. He was pretty stern in his admonishment, said I must get this done. Snipes was the last person to do any paper work and that was before Christmas.

Bunker guard with Frank Edwards of weapons platoon and the Rican who shot himself in the ass. We were manning a comfortable bunker in our own sector of the perimeter and were awake all night just shooting the bull. Riverez was jamming me up about being a 'getting' over' lifer. "At least I didn't shoot myself in the ass," I joshed. "That was an accident," he rejoined but I believe I hurt him. The time passed without incident until I had an emergency latrine call, barely found the three holer and got my trousers down before jetting a stream of liquid fire into the barrel below. Pity the fool who gets stuck with shit burning detail tomorrow.

March 31

Sunday – Got back from bunker guard and decided I'd try to avoid Top Clare and sneak in a nap. Didn't work. I've got to tell you that being suddenly awakened by the apparition that is Top Sergeant Clare staring me right in the face is enough to make any grunt immediately forget his worst nightmare. "Get up," he prodded, "we're going to load the jeep and follow the company up to Trang Bang for a coupla days. The Old Man wants us to set up a two-niner-two antennae so we can have a two way there to here, savvy?"

Our convoys, when we moved the battalion from Cu Chi to Tay Ninh, had to pass through Trang Bang which was a scary proposition. Throughout our time in the area the number of combat casualties in that VC controlled city were pretty high. The village consists of a densely-packed population of over one million Vietnamese. The buildings are mostly of yellowish brick with corrugated tin roofs and large, tall doors and small iron-gated court yards. The place had a sinister feel to it made worse by the wide grins the *papa-sans* would give us when we'd pass their gate yards. Also, the enemy would, and often did, pop out from well-hidden places and snipe at us. The outskirts were inhabited by farmers who owned one or two malnourished water boo's and lived in clay dwellings with banana leaf roofs. The small children were friendly but the adults mostly had a fuck you look deep in their eyes. Many of the adult women had blackened, vampire-like teeth that appeared to have been filed to fine points.

In the end, Top told me to "forget it, you're not going," so I messed around the commo shed for the remainder of the afternoon. In the evening, I hooked up with Prince and the two of us thumbed it over to the 587th Signal, one of the few places on post that shows films outdoors at night. We got a couple of beers and watched an absolutely horrible film starring Dean Martin and Ann Margaret titled *Murderers' Row*. The only reason for showing such shit is because the women were scantily dressed in transparent plastic and because of Ann Margaret's popularity in Bob Hope's Christmas shows for the troops that always come to Cu Chi. And that's another fucked up topic I should touch on. Last year when Hope's show was in Cu Chi the only ones who should have been allowed to see the show were the troops, like me, who were stuck in the bush. I'm sure the REMF's enjoyed the show, though.

Joe Lucido leaves for the world tomorrow, lucky stiff. Wenberg left yesterday and Packy leaves in another long (for him) six miserable days. Those that remain are mostly Cherries. I am considered an old timer now. A bunch of us jammed into the enlisted men's bar and hoisted a few on Joe. A good night. If I was still in the bush I might not even be aware that these guys were finally catchin' their American Freedom Bird.

April 1

Monday – Wandered over to battalion with some of my commo records and found a cat name of McMurtrey who I met at the enlisted club over beers. He'd assured me that bringing my book keeping up to speed would be a breeze. Meanwhile, rumors continue to circulate through the ranks about when the big inspection will take place. Just yesterday when I was acting out about the inspection Stansberry brought up the axiomatic bit about what they gonna do, send you to Vietnam? Yeah, right on, hand me another beer. Anyway, the whole thing about an impending inspection continues to eat at me. Seems weird that right in the middle of my war somebody, in this case a group known as the Commanding General's group would trouble everyone from the top down with what amounts to a yearly inventory inspection.

By midafternoon I was really getting into the swing of things, buried in my work as it were, when 2nd Lt. D'Arlando appeared on the other side of my Dutch door demanding to test every piece of equipment I had in the shack. I got a little sideways with the lieutenant when I asked by what authority he was requesting the order. I stated the obvious…most of my equipment is deployed with the company in the field and the remainder of the company's equipment was in various stages of either operating or being repaired for the upcoming inspection and if he wished to check for himself he was welcome to do so. By adding the standard phrase, no disrespect intended, sir, I was able to excuse myself to prepare for chow and bunker guard. And by the way D'Arlando is the dud that retreated off the dike down by Hoc Mon and left his squad isolated and alone when I popped smoke and called in the gunships.

Bunker guard in Manchu section of the perimeter again tonight with Edwards and Anderson. The most popular conversation late at night is, what's the first food you are going to order up when you get home, and I was really amused to find out that most grunts considered pussy to be one of the four major food groups. Another popular subject for discussion was finding the asshole that dissed us back in grade school so we could kick his ass. I think that one's the result of having too much time on our hands. Most guys avoid talking about their wives and girlfriends because secretly they're afraid they might be jinxing themselves or that their women might be steppin' out on 'em. We all remember how in Basic Training the DI's warned us that while we'd be in the Nam "Jody'd get yer girl and be gone!" GI's have anger issues and revenge scenarios as a result of being stuck here ten thousand miles from home with no control over anything.

April 2

Tuesday – Today's main priority is installation of a switchboard in the company area. I had two and in the end neither worked so I carted them over to battalion for service. The project was kind of bat shit anyway. I mean, what are you going to link, the orderly room shack, company armorer and the captain's hooch? A charge of quarters (CQ) runner has always worked with a minimum of effort. What genius came up with this one to begin with, I'd like to know. Hey, wait, check that last statement because I really do not want to know. Anyway, about the only thing I accomplished was to shock the livin' Bejesus outta myself. Let me explain…we have a gigantic generator dug into a ditch and the depth of the ditch keeps the noise at a minimum. The nomenclature for the darned thing is, Generator, Military 10KW and it is a beast. Remember my MOS? It is an indicator of my job in this man's army which is infantry so what I actually know about Mr. Electricity won't even fill a thimble. I know that AMPs can kill and something about the difference between 120 and 240 volts. That's it. So, I thought I'd do everyone in the company area a huge favor and leave the genny running so I wouldn't interrupt anyone's service as I tied the switchboard into our power grid. I was crouched in the ditch when, apparently, and at great risk to my life, I quite by accident crossed two wires. The resulting white light was brilliant. Hell, I believed for a moment that the sun had come to Earth to join me there in that hole. Every hair on my body stood straight up and I was slammed backwards into the wall of the ditch and when I looked down the two wires were black and welded solidly together. I sat stunned, smelling that burnt Ozone smell, wondering if I had cum in my pants. My chest was pounding and trying to catch my breath was reminiscent of huffing too much amyl nitrite after about six beers. *Enough of this shit. I believe I'd rather be in a fire fight.*

Got my paperwork on the road to recovery. Read some more of Atlas Shrugged by Ayn Rand who is the pretty far out author that believes in self-reliance as pretty much the only road to success. She would not last two minutes with the infantry in Bravo Company.

Walked to the PX, the company store that many of my fellow grunts call the Gook Shop. My mission today was to purchase ribbons and awards and new chevrons for my class A uniform that I will be authorized to wear on my R&R to Hawaii when I meet Cindy. Still about eight weeks away but the excitement is beginning to build.

Had beers with Roy Johnson, a soldier who is permanently in the rear, not sure of his job description. Stansberry joined us. I will be moving up to their hooch since technically I am no longer in second platoon. They have it pretty soft with a hooch *mama-san* to polish boots, do their wash and keep things neat. My heart will always reside with second platoon, though.

Not much mail lately and I've been writing less. It goes around, it comes around.

April 3

Wednesday – Uneventful day. Hung around battalion headquarters for a while just killing time. I am recognized now by a lot of the staff and I'm allowed into the communications bunker and can listen to the radio transmissions and listen in on what is happening with the companies in the field. I can listen to the demeanor in the field RTO's voices. Most of them when they are in contact with the enemy sound panicked and the pressure is obvious, they yell. I asked Lt. Paris about this, "did I sound like these guys?" Hell no," he said, "and that is precisely why Ltc. Simpson requested you. Under fire you were, like the ultimate professional, like you'd been doing it forever." "So, I take it that you're going to quit pulling my leg then." "Oh, hell no, that is never going to happen," he chortled. "LT, you make me feel like getting my hair cut, no side walls," I said turning to exit the bunker.

I spent considerable time looking at material samples in a clothing catalog, considered ordering a suit (ridiculously inexpensive prices...stuff originates in China). I'd also heard from several grunts that the stitching was unreliable and when I mentioned that hanging a suit on a shit hanger in your hooch may have something to do with stitches letting go, especially here in the jungle, I was actually laughed at. The guy looked at me with the thousand-yard stare, basically looked right through me. Maybe he'd just bought a suit or two, who knows? Another troop told me that when you receive your new suit of clothes it's mailed to you is a little square box that veritably explodes when you open it. Stand back!

I was preparing for bunker guard when a Lt. Grant called from BN and wanted the serial numbers for all of my radios. I informed the lieutenant that I was readying for bunkers and that I'd run the information over first

Bunker guard

thing in the morning. He got pissed, went around me and called Capt. Graves, who called me on the carpet. Then Top called me to the back of the orderly room where he first locked my heels and then informed me with a wink that he supported me and then he walked over for a talk with BN and informed them that Bravo sergeants do not pull bunker guard. Duh! Maybe this will get settled now.

April 4

Thursday – Returned from bunker guard over at the 2nd of the 32nd and missed chow, mess was closed. Top said "quit yer bellyachin' and suck on these for a while," handing me several wintergreen mints. I think he likes me.

Wandered over to battalion commo shop where one of the guys gave me an assist in filling out some of my Dash 3's which are an integral part of company level paperwork stuff. Read a couple of chapters of Steinbeck's *Winter of Our Discontent*, a story set in 1960's America. The main character Ethan Hawley's father lost a fortune and Hawley's restless wife encourages him to abandon his scruples and accept a bribe. Yawn!

To recover from the depths of the suffocating miasma caused by reading about Ethan Hawley compromising his principles to satisfy his wife's greed, I took Johnson and together in the captain's jeep we rode into Tay Ninh. The back seat of the jeep was piled high with cases of C-rations that we wished to trade for rolls of woven bamboo. The tightly woven matting will hang from the eaves of the hooches to keep out driving rain. Returning we were ten minutes late on our gate pass but managed to slip past the MP's and back onto the base.

Johnson and I nailed the matting in place with Top doing a First Sergeant's social grousing at the foot of our ladders. Later we were invited into Top's accommodations for a cold one and had to hook up some small electric lamps while we were there. Lt. Paris stopped by for a bit later in the afternoon. Top is a fascinating guy and full of tall tales from his days in Korea. His best buddy around here is a sergeant from Charlie Company that survived the ambush. His name is Hettiger and when these two start swapping stories it's mostly Katie bar the door and roll up yer pants legs because the horse pucky gets pretty deep. First Shirts in Nam are a rare breed, part con artist, part crook and fast talking with sufficient parts of charm and bombast. If these guys like you you've got a friend for life otherwise watch the fuck out.

Captain Graves, like most CO's, has little or no idea what the First Sergeant's must go through before they get what we need. The companies are always short of everything so a system of swapping, trading and sometimes stealing is necessary to procure the desired item or items. Here is a rudimentary example of how the system works. Say the thing you need most is lumber but you do not have any. You begin by giving the mess sergeant a case of beer for a large tin of coffee. You trade the coffee to the First Sergeant of another company who needs coffee and has lumber out back. Now you've got your lumber. The routine can be rather complicated but you get the point. Tomorrow Johnson and I are going back to Tay Ninh City for more bamboo. Good thing that C-rations, the universal currency, are plentiful.

Heard tonight on AFVN radio that Martin Luther King Jr. was assassinated outside a motel in Memphis, Tennessee, after delivering some big speech at an evening rally. I am speechless. I believed that he was a great man and had maybe become a threat to especially white people. I do not believe that it's a secret how much J Edgar Hoover hated King. I'll have to think about this for a while.

Sitting atop rolls of the bamboo we traded for rations

Young Viet children at woven goods shop

April 5

Friday – To escape Top I headed for the crapper where I wouldn't be disturbed and could read a few more chapters of Steinbeck. Too bad I bumped into Taylor who was sitting on the middle hole and rolling a bunch of joints. He tried to cover what he was doing. Too late. He asked if I'd join him and thankfully I declined because there was a lieutenant over the partition on the officers' side. Whether or not the LT caught on or not is still in question because we blew out of there when we realized we were not alone. There is no officially stated or written policy about weed only a low-level tolerance about it. Officers reluctantly turn their backs unless they catch someone red-handed or red faced as the case may be.

I returned to the hooch and being barely able to keep my eyes open I decided to lay down and try a snooze. That lasted about five minutes until Top roused me and had me follow him to his hooch where he presented me with six tiny Chinese lanterns that he had purchased from some roadside Gooks. We shared a couple of beers and I wired the lights into the grid after installing outlets. Top must have wondered why I was acting so timid because I had not shared with him my electrifying experience with the 10KW genny.

I heard again from someone at the EM Club that we could qualify for an air medal for all the Eagle Flights that we have participated in. I commented that someone probably would have already done this on a unit basis if the statement was accurate. After several more beers the topic of discussion changed.

April 6

Saturday – A wise old sage, a person of wisdom, I suppose, once said that writers write and I think that's reason enough for me to continue gathering the things I find interesting about the activities of me and my fellow Manchus. Having what I consider the facts put to paper will someday be, in itself, reward enough.

I have had much time to deliberate about my fate, my becoming a conscripted soldier in the Army of the United States of America and I have previously recorded some thoughts about this in my journal, my diary. My greatest pride today, and always will be that I did it, I became a soldier and a good one at that. I worked feverishly and was imbued with the principles of a believer, a Patriot and I will never regret that. However, if I set aside my fever, my pride and my Patriotism long enough to examine my country's ambitions in this war I conclude that there is more to the war than prohibiting dominoes from falling or holding back the inevitable spread of communism. And while bringing democracy to another country could be considered an admirable undertaking it (the bringing of democracy) could also be regarded as a disingenuous way of obscuring the true ambition and that is that war is good for business. I believed the domino thing, the holding back the Red Tide. But now, after being here going on seven months and sensing the futility and seeing no end to it all, it feels an awful lot like my country's convictions and its moral turpitude have tumbled down the deep morass of Alice's rabbit hole. The responsibility that will someday be attributed to this fool's errand, this war will belong solely to the so-called leaders of our country and not my fellow soldier and certainly not me. We served proudly and honorably. The dishonor and the shame belong to the perpetrators of this gigantic ponzi scheme, the free enterprisers squeezing, without conscience, dollars out of a system that they created, that values profit over young American lives. Those who have been fooled into believing that this war is about freedom and democracy have been misled. Spend a little earnest time by yourself in the darkened corner of a room pondering these things, asking yourself questions and you might come to the same conclusion that I have and, when you come out of that corner, we will still wave the flag together because we both believe in God and country. The only difference between me and you is that I put my life on the line and you probably did not.

On a very personal level I believe that combat has been and continues to be for me a test. There are no right or wrong answers, only the opportunity to know myself better and I am learning much that I would not have if I avoided Vietnam altogether. *The Stars and Stripes* and *The Army Times* are filled with the ongoing saga of Khe Sanh replete with descriptions of combat there and similarities to battles of the Second World War. This news piques my curiosity, and in spite of the things I just said there is a part of me that wants to be there, to experience it, to further test myself. What we experience here in the south, on a daily basis, is dangerous and tough but by comparison seems comparatively dull and soft. Am I losing my grip?

Today marks the half way point in my Viet tour

Big time barbecue in the company street. Chicken, hamburgers and hot dogs with all the side stuff one could expect. The street was jammed with everyone including headquarters personnel from battalion as well as guys from Alpha, Charlie and Delta Companies. Simpson made an appearance along with his headquarters entourage. He looks like a dick. Major Bill Roush's replacement, Major Massy was among the spit and polished senior leaders and looks like someone you'd enjoy having a beer with.

Still no relief from bunker guard which I do not mind, really. On the way to guard mount formation I bumped into Captain Graves in the middle of the company street and he did not mention the bunker guard dilemma but he did tell me that the battalion commander was still wanting me for his personal RTO and driver. Graves said he was not going to let me go and I let him know that that is fine with me. I am settled with Bravo and happy.

April 7

Sunday – The company is in the bush so I loafed around for most of the day. Attended church services at the chapel, Dr. (Captain) Crowley presented an outstanding pre-Easter sermon heavy on the dogma, symbolism and the cross. The sermon was non-denominational.

Monitoring the radio in the orderly room we learned that the company was involved in a heavy contact triggered by an enemy ambush. Two Kilos (KIA, killed in action) and fourteen Whiskeys (WIA, wounded in action). Later in the afternoon Top called everyone in the rear together to outline a new plan capable of relieving the pressure on our company in the field when and if, as today, they suffer a large number of casualties. The combined force utilizing every swinging dick available will be known as Fox Force and will be a rapid response reserve element capable of backing up the company in the field. I am included, of course and in the evening, we were trucked along with resupply to the FSB the company is operating from. We will man defensive positions on the perimeter to allow the company to regroup. We learned that one of our WIA's that was alive and lying in the open for over eight hours was recovered. He shared a harrowing story involving three VC women carrying AK's that, believing he was dead, stripped him of his tactical gear and weapon before returning to the bush. The troop said he couldn't breathe for over an hour.

In the morning, the list of wounded and dead circulated. We have had many new cherries added to our numbers since I left the field so the only name I recognized was one of the KIA's, Sgt. Wells.

April 8

Monday – Trucked back to Tay Ninh around 1030 hours and because we did not know if we would be going back out in the evening we left the truck loaded.

Received two letters from Cindy tonight and they were late due to being routed through Bravo Company 2nd of the 14th Golden Dragons rather than Bravo 4/9 Manchu. Don't think I ever recorded the fact that Cindy has a roommate. Ann Johnson, the wife of Wayne who I went through training with at Ft. Knox and Ft. McClellan.

The battalion came in around mid-day, immediately saddled up and headed for Trang Bang to establish a new hard spot, leaving Bravo here to recuperate after yesterday's beating. We will join them in a couple of days. Until then we will act as security for laterite and trash detail outside the base camp.

April 9

Tuesday – Returned to the company area after completing bunker guard and lay down on my cot. Before too long Stansberry sent Lee Levy, who will become Dan's replacement, to inform me that the battalion commo shop called for me to pick up one of my repaired radios.

The team that will be in charge of the Commanding Generals Inspection is reportedly on the post and everyone is nervous. When the inspection will be conducted here in the company's area is anyone's guess.

Stansberry leaves today for his R&R in Hawaii to be with his wife. Levy is filling in and learning the clerking responsibilities.

Tonight, the company is conducting a reinforced platoon sized ambush patrol. This element will be attached to one of the armored units and I am installing yet another radio in the orderly room so we can monitor their activity tonight.

Captain Graves called a formation to hand out CIB's (Combat Infantry Badges) to soldiers who have participated in an active ground combat mission against a hostile enemy force.

We received word that it is raining so hard up around Dau Tieng, one of our forward base areas, that nothing was moving. Johnson and I were hurriedly nailing up some plastic sheeting to keep driving rain from entering the hooches when I smacked the shit out of the first finger on my right hand. I'm getting purple fingers, not Purple Hearts. Ouch! If I hit many more nails (finger type) I won't even be able to button my fly. I doubt that I'll be a satisfactory candidate for rudimentary carpentry lessons at any time in the future.

No bunker guard. I have totally given up about the administrative change being completed that would remove my name from the guard roster. WTF!

April 10

Wednesday – Puttered around the company area, hung out in the orderly room getting acquainted with Levy. I believe he mentioned that he was from the Carolinas somewhere. He is the politest guy I think I have met since being in the Army. Lee never curses and he is so easy going. Unbelievable.

I am a little on edge expecting the inspection team to just stop by unannounced and believe this is probably part of their operating plan...surprise!

The company was called in from the various details they're engaged in and told to prepare immediately for a Chinook move up the road to Trang Bang. Top and I began preparing and assembling everything we will need to move support gear necessary to run the company when we get there. We will drive the Jeep by joining a larger convoy headed that way to resupply Tay Ninh.

Red Cross Doughnut Dollies were in the area offering support, conversation and coffee. I really did not speak with any of them but I must say that I'm curious about where they reside on the base and what exactly is the scope of their mission.

Supposed to leave around noon tomorrow.

April 11

Thursday – As soon as I returned from bunker guard Lt. Jobman asked how long will it take me to get the lead out and prepare to move. Fortunately, Top was one step ahead of the lieutenant and had commandeered a three-quarter ton and completed most of the work. My spirits were exceptionally high because the quick move will get me out of the way of the coming inspection.

Moving out at once is the kind of surprise that causes the air to be filled with expletives such as 'fuck the Army 'or' the Big Green Machine sucks,' when grunts pass one another on convoys going in opposite directions.

After all, it is the grunts prerogative to complain and it seems that there are as many fists raised in Power Salutes by our Negro brothers as there are peace fingers by us white "honkies." Anyway, the surprise of the day is that we are on the convoy which departs for Trang Bang on the hour.

The road to Trang Bang is deeply rutted, long, dusty and somewhat like riding through the world's longest chuck hole. By the time we reached the area the company had staked out alongside the highway on the south of the city I was belching black dirt. We passed the hulk of two rocketed and burnt out personnel carriers that, we were told, had been ambushed by a company of female VC that have been working the area. The armament had been stripped and there were huge gaping holes and burn marks where the incendiary rockets had penetrated the hulls. There were several areas where the metal alloy appeared to have reached temperatures sufficient enough to cause melting.

The new battalion was pretty much dug in when Top, Levy and I pulled in. We immediately raised the hexagonal tent and stowed all of our gear including cots, air mattresses, cooler, portable shower tripod etc. Next, we began to dig our bunker by hand with entrenching tools. Top pretty much said, "fuck this, there's gotta be a better way," and abruptly he disappeared. Well, the rest of us thought that Top's leaving pretty much signaled a beer break so we ditched the shovels, grabbed the Kool Can and popped a few cold ones and when Top returned driving a small caterpillar plow we saw that the First Shirt had a plan. Top scooped a furrow through where we'd begun digging and left a nifty hole in the ground. We set to work and before nightfall had three sandbagged walls completed below ground level. We'll sleep in the hex tent tonight and get busy on the command bunker again in the morning.

The company had a contact in the afternoon before we arrived. One killed and one wounded. The grunt that was killed was a Rican named Ruez. Not sure I knew him. He was killed by an FNG named Collins and I for sure did not know him. Collins apparently went all bat shit section 8 and killed a boonierat brother. We do not know if they knew each other. One living, one dead. Both were dusted off. Stuff like this is pretty tragic no matter the circumstances, no matter whether you've been in the Nam for six days or six months. However, if you were to think of something like this happening back in the World at your school or at a football game you can imagine how hysterical everyone would be. As tragic as it is here it seems almost normal…somebody getting killed I mean.

Convoy to Trang Bang

April 12

Friday – Our new area is very unusual with many of our defensive positions dug in parallel to the main road, the artery that runs from Tay Ninh all the way to Cu Chi and on down to Saigon. There is not a single tree on either side of the road that is arrow straight for as far as the eye can see. The road is alive with traffic both Army and locals, the locals moving to market and going about their daily lives. Seems like we are vulnerable to attack from vehicles zooming past on the paved surface. I know that areas for our new or future base camps are scouted thoroughly by battalion, probably intelligence, and it is not my concern but this place, considering the known amount of enemy activity, frightens me. What we have here is a probable nightmare waiting to happen. I can imagine a pickup truck with a tripod mounted 51 cal. machine gun tearing down the road spraying rounds along the length of the road all the way to the wood line over one hundred meters away. Most people have no idea of the destructive power of a single 51 caliber round. The shell casing and the actual bullet are a combined five and a half inches and can sever a torso or bring down small trees and penetrate most vehicles. A hit and run along our perimeter would take only seconds and wreak havoc.

The company is inside the perimeter and everyone is busy strengthening the fighting holes. Headquarters guys helped us finish the command bunker by laying timbers and metal PSP on top. We also built a crude outdoor shower that must be filled with buckets of water in order to use it. Top also built himself a stand to hold a bowl for shaving and hung a mirror. Levy and I erected the 292 antennae so we can communicate back to Cu Chi.

Late in the afternoon Levy and I passed to the other side of the road where there is a well. We were immediately

Community well near Trang Bang where I met Ly

Ly (in middle) and friends

surrounded by young kids as we bought ice and Cokes that they probably purchased on the black market to sell to us. This stuff is probably stolen from the port facility in Saigon or sold to them on the cheap by GI's. They then mark it up and sell us our own Cokes. Get it? Almost like we scrounge shit. While I was standing by the well looking at the skinniest water buffalo I'd ever looked at I felt a tug on my fatigue pants and when I turned I encountered the sunshine of my life, a diminutive girl child whose smile was as large as the bottle of Coca-Cola she held up to me. "GI buy my Coca," she said while continuing to tug on my tunic. I learned that her name is Ly and later I learned from Sgt. Binh our interpreter that the name Ly means Lion after one of the four mythical beasts in Vietnamese lore.

A dog team joined us tonight and since they weren't going to dig their own hole Captain Graves let the guy and his Fido sleep in our new command bunker while Lee and I took the hex tent. Wouldn't be so bad if the captain gave our hole to a visiting dignitary but what this amounts to is that Levy and I just finished digging a hole for a dog.

I strung land lines supposedly for some kind of radar screens or monitors that I have not seen.

Today was Good Friday for all you Christians out there who are keeping score. Captain Crowley made the rounds of all the company's and preached a sermon. We all sat on ammo crates and sang hymns.

Getting late and I've got to shower and eat and then get inside the tent or the bunker. Every evening just before dark a violent wind circulates through our huge open field and covers everything with an unbelievable amount of dust.

We experienced a cooling shower just before dusk when our ambush patrol and listening posts exited the wire.

April 13

Saturday – Top, 1st Ssg., Clare is driving me outta my ever lovin'. From the first breath I take in the morning 'til the last one at night, in fact every waking moment, Top's billowing voice echoes through the company area as he hollers my name. My nerves are about shot but the nature in which he does this leads me to believe that he actually cares for me.

We re-dug the CP bunker today just to have something to do. The main accomplishment was to actually dig out the floor so we'd be able to stand inside the structure. In the beginning, we were in a hurry to get a place that could protect us from incoming. I'd estimate the dimension of the floor at ten by fifteen feet by about seven feet deep. We also tied a land line into the artillery battery's generator so we have lights at night.

Top, Ssg. Hettiger from Charlie, along with Levy and myself took the three-quarter ton truck and made an ice run into Trang Bang. Specialist Johnson drove. We were heavily armed, prepared for anything as we cruised the streets of the city. Off the main drag there is a crude race track and parade ground and next to that down a side street we found an unmarked business that provides ice to locals. These businesses have electricity but no generating capacity to make ice. The ice which comes in lengthy slabs that are about a foot and a half and three feet long are buried in cement bins and covered with saw dust after being delivered from Saigon. The Vietnamese gentleman who sold us three slabs of his ice was dressed in black pajamas and a yellow silk kimono. He wore old tire tread sandals and a black fez or hat at a jaunty angle. The business was behind metal gates and had huge faded yellow bi-fold doors that stretched from the ground to just beneath the eaves, a distance of approximately fifteen feet.

Sergeant Hettiger had some US currency so the old timer was anxious to sell us the ice.

On the way back through Trang Bang proper we stopped at a Vietnamese shop and went inside for a beer. There were numerous patrons and I admit to being a little skitzo so I joined Johnson who was outside guarding the Jeep. Several small children grabbed my hand and pulled me around in circles. The cutest little girl who was maybe six or seven, but not nearly as pretty as Ly my lovely lioness, opened my hand and placed in my palm what appeared to be a very green leaf that had been carefully folded over itself. I had no idea what I was holding. The little girl encouraged me to open (said in pigeon English). I peeled back the leaf to see a transparent jelly that practically glowed like an emerald inside the leaf. She pantomimed an action that clearly indicated I was supposed to eat her offering. When I bit into the gel I quickly spit it on the ground to the delightful giggles of all of the children. She quickly grabbed the leaf and pulled the rest of the gel off what was clearly some kind of food stuff and pushed it toward my mouth. It was delicious, a kind of candy or child's treat. Just before Top, Hettiger, and Levy came out I thanked her and got in the truck.

Soon after returning to the perimeter Top shouted my name and I came running. He laughed crazily and said that he was testing to make sure I am alert. I had a beer with him and he told me that his home is on the main Island of Hawaii and he was telling me all sorts of cool stuff to do when I meet Cindy in Hawaii for my R&R. He calls me sergeant now so I'd guess my promotion is a done deal.

April 14

Easter Sunday – I did absolutely nothing today and got a very bad case of sun burn while doing it. I sat outside the command bunker with my face tilted so the sun's rays hit me square in the face. I had thought that Top screeching my name would interrupt the process but he never called my name and my badly burnt skin is now testament. My skin was so badly scorched that I could actually smell the damage, smell the burn, whatever. Talk about deja vu! The sensation carried me momentarily back to childhood when my mother would spread lotion all over my back and arms hoping my crying would stop and I'd sleep.

The air is thick with humidity signaling the coming monsoon season. High billowing clouds are stacked above the Earth's surface trading electric greetings in advance of the evening storms which will surely come.

The company had a light contact and claimed an enemy body count and was itself unscathed in the exchange. I still have concerns, let's just say that these concerns do not command as much of my attention as they did when I was in the bush. Five of our platoon members did collapse from heat exhaustion and they were seasoned troops and not newfers so this is an indication of how danged hot it is getting. Reminds me of the Hobo Woods all those months ago. Back then it was not unusual to see a medic holding a paper bag for an overheated grunt to breathe into to keep the troop from hyperventilating. Paper bags were standard issue and included in medical kit bags.

April 15

Monday – Another laid-back day. Policed the area then straightened all of our gear. We are pretty much settled in for now with no word about how long we will be staying in this location. Top has eased up on me and Levy and more importantly, himself. We hardly see the Captain anymore except when the company comes in or when we help with early morning preparation if they are going out. Once the company leaves the perimeter Top naps and so do Levy and I or write letters.

There was one of those accidents this morning that falls into the shit happens category no matter how careful soldiers are. Someone over in third platoon collected all of the heavy cardboard cylinders that hand grenades come packed in and threw them into a fire pit. One of the containers still had a grenade inside and it cooked off slightly injuring squad leader McGuire and a little Viet boy who was standing on the road. This happened before.

Charlie company made contact with a VC patrol this afternoon down by the bridge to the south and we watched as they called for a fire mission and dropped rounds close to the bridge. After dark, we sat on the bunker and watched as gunships raked the area around the bridge with mini-guns and rockets. The tracer rounds make quite a show. Another magnificent sight is to watch Spooky work out. Also known as Puff the Magic Dragon. AC-47's which are similar to the DC-3's that you are probably familiar with are armed with Gatling guns that fire continuous bursts of one hundred percent tracers and can put a round in every foot of an area the size of a football field in less that thirty seconds. Some grunts call it the stairway to heaven because the steady stream of tracers waving up and down give the appearance that you could walk right up them to the airplane.

Levy and I drank several beers and had a frank discussion about racial conditions in the World with the riots and all. This is interesting because Lee is Negro and growing up I have never had the opportunity to share with anyone like Lee. There were three Negroes on the basketball team at Hillsdale College but I did not travel with them, only played ball and talked about ball. Lee feels that as a race Negros have been beaten down badly for a couple of hundred years.

April 16

Tuesday – Colonel Simpson, for some unknown reason, wants all extra vehicles back in Tay Ninh so both of ours have to go back. Battalion sent their own drivers to retrieve them. I had an extra pair of fatigue pants sent to me via recent resupply convoy and I immediately cut them down to shorts to avoid the heat. Top almost lost his mind. As it turns out you can butcher the older and heavier stateside pants but cutting up the new utility pants is verboten. I had no idea. I had performed a monkey see, monkey do type thing because Top is always wearing shorts and, naturally, I assumed it would be ok for me to do likewise. Wrong! I had to ditch the shorts and go back to wearing the hot old nasty pants. Good thing I kept them handy. I guess if a thicket of thorns or the jungle tore the bottom half of your trousers off that'd be ok. WTF!

I received a letter from Cindy at mail call today and discovered that something I had always taken for granted had the power to cause a monstrous boner. Perfume! Cindy's letter was apparently drenched in some exotic fluid perhaps named Forbidden Fruit. Wow! Anyway, she was telling me the good news that brother Jed has sold my 175cc Honda motorcycle. I will probably regret this as soon as I get home because it was such reliable transportation, rode it back and forth to business school before I was drafted. He received $275.00 in the transaction and after keeping a modest twenty-five smackers sent me a money order which I should receive soon and will put toward my new sound equipment. The apartment will rock out with solid cherry wood speaker cabinets that are sand filled.

Rained again this evening after supper and Levy and I had to scramble to patch some of the leaks in the Hex tent to keep our equipment dry. We have been here, what, a week now and no incoming and no probes along the defense line. Unusual considering Trang Bang and surrounds is reportedly in VC control. Lee and I have a few cold ones in reserve and plan to drain them tonight while listening to Phase One, the rock radio from AFVN radio in Saigon.

April 17

Wednesday – After all the beer I've been consuming with Levy and Top I have decided to do some calisthenics and regain some muscle tone. Ripped off two hundred push-ups and a bunch of sit-ups twenty to a set. I will be sore tomorrow and eventually the benefit will be noticeable but nowhere close to the effect of wrestling that PRC 25 radio all over the jungle.

Two sorties into Trang Bang for ice for Bravo and Charlie company. Lt. Taylor grabbed Captain Crowley's jeep and I slid behind the wheel and did the driving. Last time I drove a vehicle we were all in Cu Chi.

An ancient *mama-san*, the proprietor of the shop where we stopped again to purchase the ice, was afflicted, as many elderly Vietnamese women are, with a gum ailment or disorder which is no doubt related to poor health and nutrition. The disease is characterized by severe pain which the *mama-sans* alleviate by chewing beetle nut. The nut is actually more berrylike and has a narcotic property which deadens the pain. The problem is that chewing the beetle nut further deteriorates the condition of the teeth. The spit out residue from the beetle nut is about the consistency and appearance of blood. It is quite a nauseating sight to see these old women with huge gobs of this shit hanging out of their mouths and spitting it everywhere. Maybe the condition results in the pin point teeth I mentioned a while back.

Several days ago, Levy and I stopped by the side of the road between the city and our perimeter to see if we could barter for some bamboo matting to line the floor of our bunker. We were taking pictures of some children who were kneeling and rinsing dishes when Levy whispered to me that he'd spotted blood pools by the cellar door and, "there must be wounded VC hiding here." I took Lee at his word and we split. Once inside the perimeter Levy talked to Top about what we'd seen. Top told Major Massey and together we all returned to the tiny residence and discovered that Levy's blood pools were actually *mama-san's* beetle nut spit, nothing more. We had a good laugh and when we returned to camp, a beer or two. Top later scolded me for not checking but finally dismissed the incident because Levy had never been in a combat situation or he might have been familiar with the practice of chewing and spitting.

April 18

Thursday – Shower day. The company was in and Levy and I volunteered to keep the portable shower filled until the last body had a chance to stand under a stream of cold water. We borrowed Captain Crowley's jeep and made repeated trips across the road to fill five or six jerry cans enough times to keep the huge shower bag filled. (Jerry is, of course, a reference to Germans so, when thousands of the five-gallon metal containers were rounded up after Second World War skirmishes, they were called Jerry Cans). While collecting the water across the road I again encountered Ly and she stayed by my side each time I went near the well.

Later in the afternoon I drove some of the company lieutenants into Trang Bang to get ice and stop for a beer. I believe that repeated visits to this city has lessened the feelings that we may have had about being threatened. In fact, the quaint city has a charm and an inviting feel—at least on the surface—that makes me believe that, except for the obvious language barrier, I could live here. However, if we establish a habitual pattern we could be ambushed.

Levy and I drove the jeep down the road in the opposite direction and Lee wanted to stop and purchase a cold soda from the children. He left the jeep and while sitting and keeping an eye out for suspicious activity I noticed grunts from the battalion going under the bridge with some of the local boom boom girls. Lee returned with his soda and before turning around we sat and, like a couple of voyeurs, watched the sexual exploits of our fellow soldiers. I have to admit that I have not once entertained this idea and the two of us reminisced about the times we had sat in the bleachers at some training session and listened while the cadre warned us about the loose women we would meet in the Nam. "Be careful," they'd say, "the boom boom girls are different cuz their pussies are on the horizontal and they conceal razor blades in there that'll cut your li'l pricks to ribbons." And, they would continue, "if you get past the razor blades, and you contract some rare form of venereal disease, you'll be sent to an island in the South China Sea to be quarantined for the rest of your life cuz there's no cure. Back home Jody will definitely have your girl and be gone." We knew it was all bull shit but, nonetheless, it scared me.

Sat underground in our bunker listening to oldies on AFVN radio and got pretty drunk. McDermott the barber from back in the world gave us all haircuts...it looked like it but really, how many ways can you fuck up a buzz cut?

Top went back in to Tay Ninh for a day or two and left me and Levy in charge of ourselves with the warning there had better not be any slip ups.

April 19

Friday – Company didn't leave the wire until 0100. Just sat around and took it easy listening to Top's war stories from Korea. I did not know this but there was a Death March during the Korean War that rivaled the Bataan Death March from WWII. Captured American POW's were led on a nine-day death march that claimed over one hundred lives and was led by a Korean nicknamed the Tiger. Top was not a part of this but was recalling it for us.

Went over to the artillery battery and watched a fire mission. When the lanyards are pulled to fire the 155 mm Howitzers something interesting happens, the dust all around the guns jumps into the air and shimmers, looks something like a vibration, a perfect circle around the gun emplacement.

No ice runs today but Levy, Johnson and I crossed the road to play with the children and bring water back for the shower bag. Ly was there and playful as always. She has straight, short jet-black hair and pierced ears. Retrieving water from the well proved costly. We lost the bucket and the *mama-san* who believed she controlled the well demanded money. Johnson gave her an American dollar he had tucked away somewhere. Told her we'd bring her a new bucket tomorrow but she still insisted on more dollars. She said, "you no give me dollar you like VC, you number 10. No, you number ten thou." Being number ten is the worst but being number ten thou – as in thousand is the worst you can be according to Vietnamese pidgin, pidgin being a simplified form of their language.

1st. Ssg. Hettiger asked me for a favor today. The favor was to take two of his Charlie Company grunts to town. Later Hettiger came over to the bunker for beers.

Things have been so quiet since we have been here with no incoming and no probes of the perimeter. It's almost as if the enemy cadre had gotten together and intentionally planned to not attack us. Weird!

The company stayed out overnight on ambush. We slept in the bunker with a fan that Top scrounged somewhere blowing cool air over us the entire night.

April 20

Saturday – Woke up at 0700 and made a trip into Trang Bang for, what else, ice. Lt. Veenstra from the weapons platoon and one of his men, Briley, came along for the fire power. Seems like all I do is make ice runs to fill coolers for different squads or fill the shower bag with water so everyone can shower. The repetitious nature of what has become my existence since coming off the line has given me a new perspective…hell, I could train a chimpanzee to do the work I'm doing now, actually match my contribution, and, oh, one other thing. Those troops who are here in Vietnam but never been outside the base camp, never fired their weapon or been in combat, they should trade places with some of the line troops on a rotation schedule, share the load. Those who have been in the boondocks the longest should get a chance to loaf in the rear like the rest of these getting over REMF's and perform some of the support tasks.

The company was supposed to come back in today and stand down but they became involved in a skirmish, traded lead with Charlie but no casualties. They won't be in until late. I walked across the road and sure enough, there was Ly. She kept trying to push me down the road. Finally, she pulled me by my hand. She wanted to take me to her home and her mother met us in the middle of the road. I was not at all sure I felt comfortable but went with them anyway. Their home, a small hut really, with a tin roof sat among three other similar dwellings. There was a rail fence and a small garden and a small court yard that one of the other women was sweeping with a broom. Several chickens scratched at the barren patch. I did not stay long and walking back to the base camp I was thinking that this last stretch here in the Trang Bang area has been very relaxing and very comfortable feeling. I am reminded, however, to use caution.

Ssg. Hettiger came over looking for Top and stayed for a beer. I guess he had forgotten that Top went back to Tay Ninh. Anyway, Hettiiger stayed on and sipped his way through five cans of beer. Came back later and left us a case of Bud from his stash so Top wouldn't be pissed.

April 21

Sunday – I mentioned yesterday that I returned to our base camp because I felt uncomfortable around Ly's family. The reason for my discomfort has its roots in the war itself or to be more succinct, the history of the war in Vietnam. When the French were defeated in 1954 near the end of the First Indo China War, and the Viet Minh or the communist under Ho Chi Minh took control, the DMZ or Demilitarized Zone was established along the Ben Hai River thus cutting Vietnam in half. (What I am relating here is a simplified version but it will explain the discomfort I was talking about earlier). During this period, whoever wished to leave the communist North, and this was mostly Catholics who were loyal to Emperor Bao Dai, the last emperor of Vietnam, were allowed to do so. The table was set: communism in the North and Freedom loving peoples in the south so you'd think that you would be relatively safe wandering about the country side in South Vietnam and, for a while, this was partly true. However, the longer the conflict dragged on the more the south was infiltrated by the North in an attempt to destabilize and overthrow the south. There were also those who resided in the South who were sympathetic to the North's cause and joined the VC. As a result, there were more and more bad guys and because they blended in with the locals it was impossible to distinguish the good people from those who wished to do you harm. Thus, I felt uncomfortable being tugged along by Ly toward her home or driving into Trang Bang because you can never tell who could cause you harm.

Quite unexpectedly we were ordered to break camp to move by convoy to a new FSB. The company left earlier by chopper on an Eagle Flight. Top came breezing in early this morning to break the news and assist with the tear down.

The road was treacherous but when we began traveling across the dry paddy fields things really became miserable. Arrived at what would become our new digs around 0100 and that is exactly what we did…dig. We had a sufficient shelter for the night and will finish in the morning plus dig a new latrine, make another shower and lay commo lines in the new company area.

When the company finally came in Captain Graves told me that Smitty, my replacement RTO's father had died, and he, Smitty, was taking an emergency leave back to the World so I would be needed to carry the radio once again. Top jumped right in and saved my ass, told the old man that he could not do without me. I was prepared to resume duty in the field but was happy to have once again been saved by Top and fell soundly asleep.

April 22

Monday – Again today we labored for almost the entire day to construct yet another command post (CP) bunker. A Captain Reynolds called from battalion to speak with Top who was absent. Battalion had questions regarding logistics and the number of duce and a half or 6x6 trucks would be required to move Bravo Company including all of our equipment and total number of troops. I offered a tentative reply and from the conversation deduced that we would be moving again and relatively soon.

After the Captain came in with the company and after he returned from the evening poop talk over at battalion I learned that I'd been right, and yes, we would be hatting up once again. We will be trucking down past Cu Chi and Hoc Mon to a place called Bau Tri. At this point it is unclear if Top, Levy and I will be at the new forward area or Cu Chi or maybe even Tay Ninh. The new AO or area of operation is said to be similar to Cu Chi, Saigon, Hoc Mon – open, dry paddy and hamlets.

Levy and I were pissed to the max when we considered all of the effort and time spent digging in recently. Top was only somewhat accepting. "Fuck it, don't mean nuthin'," he belched between Budweiser's. Our bad attitude which is pretty much fuck the Army has its roots in the battalion never giving us a heads up on this shit. However, we are also pissed a little with ourselves because we have built some underground hotels for Captain Graves and now he has become accustomed to the high life.

Midafternoon Top ordered me to follow him. We wandered away from the CP and into a sparse stand of trees, could have been macadamia, but not sure. Top had several crates that had previously stored new mortar tubes. Together we hammered two of them together and came up with an end product that resembled a large coffin. Top responded with some pretty dark humor about the darned thing becoming our final resting place. I told him, "then we'd better build another one cuz there's no way I'm gonna be climbin' in that thing with you". He mumbled something about me being a man of little faith and then pulled a huge roll of plastic sheeting from behind one of the trees. "When you've got the plastic inside the 'coffin' and leaks sealed, all you'll have to do is fill my bath with water, and everything will be right with the world." The whole set up worked great but by the time word spread and all the top brass had come over from battalion for a plunge I was too tired to fill the tub for myself. Then, to make things worse, Captain Graves came over to take advantage of Tops ingenuity. I reluctantly filled the tub for the Captain and then, like a poor sport, walked sullenly away.

April 23

Tuesday – Word came down from battalion to get everybody moving – it was 0430. Convoy wasn't due to depart until 0100 but bravo was packed and ready to roll by 0900. Finally, on the move when the lead vehicle hit a mine buried in the road and waiting for a mine sweeping team delayed us further. Bravo and the other companies stayed behind and when we had cleared out the area beside the highway we'd made a perfect pick up zone from which to begin an Eagle Flight/search and destroy.

Once we were under way we learned that our destination is Cu Chi and we will be moving back into our original company areas abandoned back in October. When we entered through the main gate memories of our time at Cu Chi came flooding back, and though we have spent considerably more time elsewhere in our area of operation, this place that I first got my feet on the ground will always be special.

We moved into some weather worn hooches that were left behind including Charlie Company's orderly room and we're supposed to be here for at least five days. Top will chopper out to the company's new laager position tomorrow night and then Levy the following night. This job is supposed to be carried out by an E-5 and Levy is a Specialist 4th Class. Top is training Lee, getting him ready.

The company will change its night defensive position location every other day or two like we did during our time in the Ho Bo Woods. That is the biggest reason to maintain a new rear area and resupply from that area. It would be impossible to carry all of our gear in the field.

We shared several Ballentines ales on the convoy, wish I hadn't. The rough road and all the jostling made me feel as though I wanted to puke. Been a very long time since I stuck my finger down my throat to induce vomiting.

Got two letters from Cindy tonight as mail finally caught up to our frequent moves. Always good to hear from her but sometimes she writes about things that I find a little confusing like the placement of end tables in the apartment. WTF!

Rained like a mother tonight and Top and I had to scramble to plug all the leaks in the roof with ponchos and plastic to keep out the rain.

April 24

Wednesday – Strange being in Cu Chi again. Top let us sleep in which is unusual for him. He is usually pretty intense, hard driving. Busy in the morning preparing excess equipment for a convoy back to Tay Ninh.

Top made a trip over to the PX and when he came back he let me and Levy go. I purchased an AM/FM tuner and sent it home. Considering the time required to fill out all the paper work and get it mailed we were late getting back to the company area and Top had already left for the resupply run to the field. He was, we learned, pissed off.

Hooked up our hooch with electricity.

If the VC hit with force the first of next month as anticipated by intelligence it will herald the beginning of the third main enemy offensive since the first of the year. If that happens, scuttlebutt has it, we would move our rear closer to Tan Son Nhut to better resupply the company.

April 25

Thursday – When Top came in this morning he was obviously under the weather and told us, "I'm too sick to even be pissed with you jokers. You owe me one."

Levy is making the resupply run to the field tonight and I will perform the task tomorrow. I make it sound so simple, the resupply that is. Actually, the preparation and execution is a bit more involved. First, the person in charge like Top, me or Levy must pull everything together from a shopping list received from the field. Mail is a high priority. Getting the mess together if there will be hot chow, including large ash cans loaded down with soda, beer, and ice and a sundry box with smokes, candy, cigarettes and bung wipe. Next the armorer must be brought into the loop for ammunition, grenades and replacement weapons. Overnight squad kits must be collected if applicable and contacting any personnel that may be returning to the field must be notified as to departure time. Next a duce and a half 6x6 must be lined up to carry all of our supplies to the chopper pad. The load master at the pad will have four cargo nets, one for each company spread on the ground. When these are loaded a huge lifting harness is threaded through the mouth of each of the gathered nets and together they are attached by the load master to the belly of the CH-47. Personnel are loaded and the flight departs. When the CH-47 touches down at the night position it is met by a group of grunts from each company. Their job is to carry everything safari style back to their company's command position. Top, me or Levy will always stay out overnight and return with an extraction chopper in the morning.

    Top and I spent some time browsing the large PX concession. He had tags sewn on some of his fatigue blouses. "I'm guessin' it'll be pretty soon that I'll be sewing something on my own shirt, huh, Top," I joked with a wink and a nod. He put his hands on his hips like he does when he's thinkin' up what to say next or watching me work, and answered with a single grunt.

    Decided to visit the old (EM) enlisted men's club for a couple of beers. The old place was pretty much the same, a plank bar over cinder blocks lined with stools and a few tables. The only difference is the establishment has been taken over by the aviation battalion. Maddocks and Ketchum were buying but no big deal, remember beer is ten cents a can. Anyway, the duo are really excited because as a reward for exemplary conduct in the field they are being rewarded with a week-long in country training school. They are going to attend LRRP (sounds like lurp) School in Na Trang. LRRP stands for Long Range Reconnaissance Patrol, a concept that I approach with equal parts of excitement and trepidation. These patrols are sneak and peep operations. The patrol gets dropped off in the middle of nowhere in groups of no more than ten guys to move at night and sleep during the day and report on enemy movement and activity.

Top woke me at around 0100 hours and asked me what the blankety blank happened to our electricity because his fan had stopped blowing air. I traced down my wire to the problem. Someone had severed the wire in three places and ripped the rest of the wires from the poles where I had placed them. Guess they were pissed because I did not ask. What petty bullcrap.

We have another clown from the 2nd of the 14th Golden Dragons that has refused to fight. Now that I think of it he may be one of the two that I shared a bunker with that night. He did spend six months in Long Binh Jail before he was relocated with us, Bravo Company. Listening to these types makes you scratch your head. He wanted to know who would take care of "his people" if he got zapped, whatever that means. And on a totally unrelated topic he mentioned to me, as if it were a big deal, that he had over five hundred dollars' worth of clothes from the Hong Kong tailor in his duffle bag. WTF! I think that more than being worried about "his people" he is just plain chicken.

April 26

Friday – Top took me and Levy with him to observe once again how, as he put it, "everything fits together like a fine symphony orchestra and if it ain't done properly someone gets hurt. I want my friend the load master to see firsthand how Bravo guys are the best." I was to handle the resupply and fly out in the evening and then Top changed his mind. Levy will go. I will fly out in the morning with the extraction sortie, stay the day and jot a list of items that Bravo will need. When evening resupply hits the perimeter, I will return to Cu Chi.

While knocking back a few beers and sitting in the back of the hooch and soaking up the last rays of sun fighting their way through the puckered screen I said to Top, "Top, what's going to happen to me?" "I dunno, son, whatdya mean cuz I have no idea what you're talkin' about." "Well," I offered tentatively, "I do not want you to take it wrong, because I am really grateful for everything you've done for me, I mean, getting me in the rear, and everything. I think that if I was to stay in the Army, make a career out of it, then the things I am learning from you about the Army way will benefit me a lot." "So," he said, "what's the problem?" "No problem really," I offered, "But if I am required to return to the field, to combat, I am afraid that I will have lost my edge. I am losing the instincts that served me so well in the bush and this could be dangerous in a place that isn't so safe. Do you know what I mean?" Top looked at me square on, searched my face before he said, "I do know what you mean and trust me when I tell you that you have just reinforced my own instincts about why I chose you, sergeant. Some of us survive and some of us do not. You sergeant Dexter are a survivor so let's just play this out and see where it takes us, ok?" "Roger that," I said.

Walking past the TOC (tactical Operation Center) which is the heart of the battalion's operational procedures, I heard the most outstanding guitar picking and was drawn to the source, a specialist Miller. Turns out he is in the seventeenth month of his second tour and I'd estimate that to be just about right. He was definitely not a lunatic and I cannot explain this precisely but it just seemed as though specialist Miller has been here in the Nam a little too long.

Watched a movie at the EM Club tonight – first one in a hell of a long time. The title was *Two For The Road* starring Albert Finney and Katherine Hepburn. This really sucked the big one. Whatever happened to the Combat flicks with Vic Morrow that we used to get as a steady diet. The best part of the evening was getting rowdy with other soldiers—the male bonding thing—consuming large quantities of alcohol and gobbling all the popcorn you could handle. Someone brought Jiffy-Pop which was heated over C-ration stoves until the exploding kernels caused several of the rear echelon section eights to dive for cover under the tables to the hoots and hollers of those too drunk to associate popping kernels with small-arms fire. Quite a few crumpled beer cans struck Hepburn and Finney before piling up on the dirt.

April 27

Saturday – Got in a little field duty today vis-à-vis how I outlined these duties being split. When I got off the tail of the CH-47 Levy was getting on and we saluted which seemed a little stupid. He will be back out tonight with the resupply.

I was supposed to inventory our resupply items but when I arrived, the company had already departed and by the time the company came back in Levy had left the resupply and the two of us rode the chopper back to Cu Chi.

Top met me at the pad and took us back to the hooch for several beers. Top got tipsy and rambled on about where I should take my wife in Hawaii. Since he was about to do a pin ball tilt I took advantage and mentioned that I'd been hearing that the old man wanted me at our perimeter during the days and stay out overnight to pull radio maintenance. He said for me to leave the old man to him, he'd take care of it. Top told me that my promotion had been confirmed and, "don't act too surprised when he lays it on you." We played hearts to finish the night.

Rained through the night and we heard the wavering sound of a siren on the other side of the base camp signaling incoming but we didn't budge. The rain continued.

April 28

Sunday – Lt. Jobman, acting XO, came in from the field this morning. Says the captain is a tad pissed because I did not stay. I am hereby ordered to handle resupply tonight and stay. The radios, according to the old man, are all screwed up and need my attention.

Top was supposed to go before the promotion board today but it was cancelled. He is to be promoted to E-9, a pretty big deal, sgt. major.

Went over to the chopper pad around 1400. Muleskinner, the transportation outfit flying resupply sorties, has been really slammed lately and our stuff didn't come up for loading until almost 1800 which is 6 pm Army time. We were later than usual getting to the NDP which did not help the captain's disposition much.

Captain Graves repeated to me what Jobman had said about me staying in the field with the radios. The funny thing is that the radios are in the boonies most of each day and not back in 'til dusk so actually I could do the repairs when I come out with the resupply. Anyway, I should be able to get back to Cu Chi every third day or so and that isn't an altogether bad thing.

In the evening, the captain gave Article 15's to three guys that I didn't know. The punishment is for disobeying orders. I call them traffic tickets because they are erased from your record after a year. Two promotions were also awarded without ceremony and one was my promotion to Sgt. E-5. I showed the appropriate degree of excitement.

I built a shelter big enough for the two people, five layers of sand bags to form a small enclosure with snapped together shelter (poncho) halves for a water proof roof. The addition of several air mattresses made it quite comfortable. Whoever comes out for resupply will have a place to stay. No overhead cover so if we take mortars we'll have to scramble.

Rained very gently throughout the night but we did not get wet. I pulled radio watch for an hour and a half.

April 29

Monday – The captain allowed me to come in this morning on the extraction chopper with the understanding that I get organized and ready to stay in the field so I'll be going back out tonight. I will take a camera with me. The company's encampment is in a horse shoe bend in the Saigon River, a choke point really, where the river narrows. There are several riverine patrol boats, part of what is referred to as the Brown Water Navy, operating close by. My intention is to try and spend an afternoon aboard one of these patrol boats. The troops involved in this form of combat are often in perilous situations. When the boats are not operating independently they tether alongside a larger mother ship and are sitting ducks. The patrol boats themselves have plenty of fire power with 50 cal and M-60 machine guns and flame throwers to mention a few.

I arrived back at the forward area considerably earlier this evening than yesterday and set about unloading Bravo Company's sling. The work is quick but arduous and must be accomplished swiftly to get the chopper out of here before the enemy can set their mortars. My responsibility also includes loading the sling in the morning.

Having a little extra time, I made a trip over to battalion to see if I could get some fuel for our lanterns. I met Shorty on the journey. He is in charge of equipment for the entire battalion and he informed me that we may make a move again relatively soon because Major Massey asked him, Shorty, for a rough estimate of how many sling loads it would require to move the entire battalion.

I will be included in the radio watch rotation. The captain has been acting very cool toward me but I'm ok with that. There is nowhere near the closeness to Graves that I shared with Baker and Weiss. That is not to say the captain is unfair because he is not. He is just more reserved.

Gentle rain throughout the night.

April 30

Tuesday – Back to Cu Chi in the morning. I am beginning to feel like a Chinese Pachinko machine, balls-o-plenty and they're flying everywhere, dropping down. Cripes sake, will you please make up your mind, commander! Do you want me in Cu Chi with the First

Shirt or with you in the field? I can feel comfortable with either, just let me know.

Uneventful day in the rear.

Back at the pad in the evening I learned that the battalion, in fact, did not make a move, still in the same laager. I rode ahead of the resupply Chinook in a huey and carried mail for Bravo. From the first moment the Chinook set down, and I strolled into the company position, I have been harried, set upon, a marked man. It began with the old man. He grabbed the mail bag and shouted, "Christ, Dexter, you've been here for almost five minutes and still I do not have a beer in my hand." He's smiling, I thought, so he must be kidding with me but I couldn't be sure, and kidding or not the little repartee irritated me.

After I got to the little bunker I'd built for me Top and Levy the resupply touched down so back to the pad with a crew to break town and carry our stuff back to the CP. Then I helped Chief, the full-blooded Indian from Muskegon, Michigan, set up the chow line and get the troops moving through. Talked briefly with Mitch. Then it was time to break down the chow line and help the headquarters guys break down the sundry pack and get everything distributed to the platoons. I forgot to tell the captain that I'd brought two replacements with me and the captain immediately developed a huge case of the ass, and while he was ripping into me someone else broke down the beer and sodas. Captain Graves felt that he personally got cheated out of his beers and his share of the ice, started in on me again and threatened to send me out with the ambush patrol. And the whole time I am thinking that Top will laugh his ass about this one, probably have a few words about how I wanted the stripes. Stripes, stripes my butt! Right now, I wish I could tell the Captain what he can do with his stripes. I thought I was the company commo chief and not his personal Cooley and resupply liaison. What a day.

Chief, Bravo Company Cook

May 1

Wednesday – Staying put today. Made my way to the pad and soon the distinctive whop, wop, chop of rotor blades signaled the approach of the chopper and when it landed the first thing I saw was Top's countenance so wide it almost filled the opening in the cargo bay. In his hand, he was carrying the old man's night bag that got lost somewhere in the last days and, did I forget to mention, was also part of the captain's ass chewing last night. Top also had over his shoulder a fresh, new pair of jungle boots that coincidentally enough were Captain Graves size. When I brought Top up to speed on the festivities from last night he grumped that the new boots and overnight bag would help heal the wound. "Welcome to the world of noncommissioned officers," he giggled. "And by the way," he smiled, "here's a new shirt for you. Thought you'd get a kick outta the sergeants stripes." "Thanks a lot, Top," I beamed.

There was a little excitement in Cu Chi yesterday. A Huey gunship accidentally triggered six 2.7 inch rockets. One of the six bounced off the tarmac and shot through the mess hall bringing down a couple of timbers and the roof. Over in Alpha's mess the cook took a broken nose. The company area also received incoming mortar fire but all in all, no casualties. Top said that he thought he should come out to the field where it was safe. Humorous.

As it turned out we had our share of fun out here as well. I had just finished bathing in the shallows of the Saigon at perimeter's edge. The water is dirt brown and very hard and getting the soap rinsed off takes a Herculean effort. I returned to the little bunker and Top and I were writing letters, Top to wife Dorothy in Hawaii and me to Cindy in Michigan when AK fire hosed down the area. Three VC had gotten within one hundred meters of the perimeter and began to fire. Gunships were called up and drove the enemy back toward the river and nailed them.

Rained off and on for most of the day. Beautiful, high, puffy clouds and intermittent showers and heat and humidity so severe it took my breath away. One of the hottest days I have experienced in the seven months I have been here.

May 2

Thursday – I was awakened around 0515 by the soft voice of the captain discussing something with the platoon leaders, what exactly I could not discern. I crawled from my shelter into the misty pre-dawn. The stench of swamp gas permeated my clothes and hung on the mist like a menacing cloud that concealed the ground. The stars shown dimly through the fog like angle hair on the tree of a forgotten Christmas dream.

As I approached the small cluster of blackened silhouettes a voice broke the silence, "Where were you through all the excitement?" It was Top's voice. How had he gotten away from our bunker without me knowing? "Me? I was sleeping, I guess." What in hell was he talking about, what excitement? "God dammit, son, didn't you hear all the rocket and mortar? Must have been fifteen rounds," Top said, registering surprise that I had slept through such concussive racket.

Top and I flew out on the first return sortie back to Cu Chi. The company is moving for sure today and Levy and I will both fly out tonight with the resupply. Actually, Top saved my ass again. The battalion commander wanted one NCO from each company to fly as an advance party to the new perimeter area which can be both tricky and dangerous. Top suggested someone else and the captain bought it. Whew!

Rained like a mother while Levy and I were helping the loadmaster pull all the slings together and hook them to the underbelly of the CH-47 and we were on our way to the new perimeter. We are now much closer to the city limits of Saigon and well inside an overall defense perimeter designed to keep Charlie from any major attacks on the city or its airbases. The area has a comfortable feel to it much the same as the Trang Bang area did but there could be a Cobra in the basket thing going on...you never know. We can see the lights of the city which pretty much blot out the stars so visible when we are deeper in the bush.

We were mortared around supper time just after we had completed getting resupply to the CP. An AP (ambush patrol) from Charlie Company was itself ambushed and had one KIA and two wounded. I don't think we're in Kansas any longer, Dorothy.

I don't know how, but the captain's overnight kit bag got lost again. At the last minute, Kaiser handed the darned thing to me and I got it to Graves without him knowing any different. The bag mysteriously wound up over at Alpha Company and they returned it to Kaiser.

May 3

Friday – After radio watch I decided to grab some Z's in the partially finished fortification that Chief had been working on, rather than returning again to the little shelter I'd built for the resupply guys. I placed a steel helmet on my head, pulled a flak vest over my upper body and wedged my head into the corner of the low, sand bagged wall, feet toward the opening in the roof. My breathing was labored but I fell asleep instantly. I remember thinking, what the hell just happened? I was totally mystified, in the midst of some featherbrained dreamscape, everything out of order, confused, my first conscious recollection was of an unbelievably loud roaring in my ears followed by a flying sensation like tumbling through air and then I was awake and lying on my back outside the shelter. Where the fuck's Chief I wondered? It felt like someone had swung a baseball bat and smashed it into both of my legs, once against my right calf and then again on my left calf but up high, almost at the hip joint. I was stone-deaf and there was a tremendous ringing in my ears. I could not move my legs but finally, by pulling at the ground with my hands and flexing one shoulder, I was able to turn myself over. I tried to stand but immediately collapsed back to the ground. Every nerve, every part of my lower body tingled as though I had been electrocuted. After a very short time the smell of cordite filled my sinuses and finally, my hearing slowly began to return. Wooshing sounds followed by loud explosions were taking place all around me.

Finally, it became apparent that we were under a ground attack. The perimeter had been breached somewhere and, in the ink black darkness of the moonless night, I observed silhouetted Viet Cong soldiers streaming silently past me. I lay motionless without a weapon, fearful of being shot through the head or stabbed while marveling at an enemy that was bold enough to lob mortars into our positions and then run in before they exploded.

The 105 battery near me was firing salvo after salvo, adding to the chaos. I knew I must seek cover and began to pull myself along with my arms, dragging my useless legs behind me. I crawled slowly past small shelters abandoned when my buddies sought cover underground. At last I came up against a paddy dike and crawled through a garbage sump that was overflowing with discarded chicken carcasses from the evening meal. I was next to a bunker but not being able to locate the entrance, and afraid to move because mortar rounds were still falling, I began to tear at the sand bags with my bare hands and yell until I heard voices from within. Soon there was a hole sufficient enough for the grunts to pull me inside. Edwards, Usarsky and Berger, weapons platoon guys, tore at my pants legs and I heard one of them say, "holy shit, Dexter." At that moment I was not at all sure of what I had left down there, were my legs gone? The pain was the most excruciating feeling I'd ever experienced. Flashlights bounced their beams crazily about the inside of the bunker, interrupting the blackness. A medic from the artillery battery was soon at my side with words more calming and reassuring than those I'd received from any of the weapons grunts. The medic administered morphine by jamming a syrette somewhere into my lower extremities and the relief was almost instantaneous, some of the ache was replaced by numbness. Westcovitch, Jackson and Berger, along with Usarsky, carried me to a triage area near the battalion command post where the wounded were tagged, numbered and lined up in order for evacuation. A strobe light was placed in the field bordering the CP and anxious moments passed waiting for the dust-off ships to arrive. I was panicky knowing that the enemy might re-bracket our position and begin a new mortar barrage.

There were seventeen of us wounded severely enough to require immediate medical evacuation, many of them worse than me. Priorities went first, then non-life threatened, followed by ambulatories and so forth. Loading commenced with the first Red Cross Huey that was able to get in. I did not go out until the third lift. Captain Crowley and Major Massey were there beside me for a time. The major read my tag which indicated my condition and that I'd been drugged. He lifted my head and spilled some Ballentines ale into my mouth mumbling something about it'd be OK since I didn't have a sucking chest wound. I was cold and began to shiver uncontrollably. Top came by and said he'd be checking on me.

The guys were all there but everything was so deranged. I was in a fog and the numbness morphed into excruciating pain and I could not concentrate on anything except wanting the pain to go away, to cease, give me more dope! My stretcher was hoisted and dropped on the first try as the medics were loading me onto the flight deck of the Huey. "Sorry, Sarge, "they spoke in unison. The ship lifted out of the clearing and up into cooler air, and executed a banking turn. Even with the slap of the rotors I could hear moaning all around me and I slipped into a drug induced rapture, travelled back to a long-ago childhood Christmas and viewed myself sitting alone in the living room of my family home next to the family tree. The twinkling lights of Saigon, blurred by my tears were transformed into the lights on my Christmas tree and as we headed away from the battlefield I called out across the miles, mom, dad, I am still here.

May 4

Saturday, 3 a.m. The attack on our perimeter, like those on many other installations throughout South Vietnam, was part of a coordinated three-pronged assault on and around the city of Saigon that had begun with the Tet offensive back on the first of the year. The enemy action was carefully planned to keep constant pressure on us and all of our allied friends.

The Red Cross ship carrying me touched down on a huge painted red cross, and looking farther, I could see dozens more dust-off choppers in a line that stretched down the tarmac as far as my vision would allow, all of them were full of wounded troops like myself.

The orderlies from the 12th Evac facility jarred me hard as they removed my litter from the chopper and transferred me to a wheeled gurney. This was the first of many painful maneuvers that I would endure this first night in being admitted and treated at the MASH.

When the medics rolled my gurney into the triage area there was no place to deposit me except on the floor in front of a water cooler which belched a never-ending stream of condensation on me. I shivered convulsively, goose bumps all over, until an orderly mercifully covered me with a blanket. My clothes were stripped off and my watch and rings and the gold cross and chain that Cindy had given me were removed.

A nurse in operating room greens took my blood pressure and with the assistance of a technician I was lifted onto a huge glass x-ray table that was freezing cold. I continued to tremble while being instructed to perform a series of inhumane contortions so that my limbs would be flat on the table to allow the desired images to be taken. This was the first opportunity I had to view my lower extremities. I did not cry but I was very upset and on the verge of tears the entire time. Blown up! That is the only way to describe what I was looking at. Blood everywhere and I could see almost all the way through my right calf. The muscle tone was gone already. The left leg had fragmentation holes everywhere from one on the top of my ankle to a badly destroyed calf and a huge hole in the hip above the waist. The nurse called me by name, from viewing my dog tags I'm certain. "Everything is going to be OK, Dexter, we are going to take very good care of you." The two of them, the nurse and the technician, touched me and helped me to reposition myself on the table. Nothing in my life has ever hurt me that much and now I did begin to weep.

Next, I was carried to the operating theater and placed on one of the tables. Several doctors moved efficiently about the table, examining my wounds and another, a nurse wearing captain's bars, slid my arm under hers – and being in such close proximity I surreptitiously let my hand caress the mound of her breast. I gazed into her eyes but nothing. No connection. First time I'd copped a feel since high school.

The nurse began shaving the hair from my body and I watched as tiny blood trails flowed away from the razor as she pulled it down my legs. The light above the table was a bright searing white, so bright in fact, that I knew I'd be able to touch the very edge where it joined the blackness beyond the table but I was drug paralyzed and could not reach my hand up from the table. We were, all of us, eminently alone and shrouded in a cone of brilliant light. Just before a transparent rubber cup was placed gently over my nose I said to the nurse, "make sure they don't take my legs." She again reassured me that everything was going to be fine and to breathe. My pain was so intense that I breathed as deeply as I could. And then I was gone.

May 5

Sunday – When I awoke it was mid-day. Top, Levy and my old bunker guard buddy, Edwards, were all standing at the foot of my bed. I peered at them dully. "Howdy, boys," I said, "glad you could make it. I take it that I'm at the 12th Med Evac in Cu Chi cuz I know Graves wouldn't give you time off to visit me in Saigon." Top said, "Correct, you are in the Michigan suite along with your other poages from Michigan." I wasn't to be humored by these guys but at least they were trying their damnedest. I was beginning to regain full consciousness and the fog in my brain was dissipating like mist over an Alpine meadow, sunlight was streaming through the windows above the beds as the guys said their goodbyes. Looking down I viewed my feet and knew that my legs had been saved. I was completely wrapped in white gauze bandages from my waist down and for the first time in seven months I was in a real bed with real sheets, a pillow and a white linen pillow case. I was miserable. The traumatic pain that

I'd suffered in the attack had morphed into something new – a dull, all body, pulse pounding pain and if it weren't for that I would have preferred sleeping on the floor. Much of the rest of the day was devoted to cleaning my upper torso which was still messy from the field.

Between conversation with guys from the company that continued to come by in the afternoon, I began to reach out to those around me. The soldier on my left had stepped on a land mine, lost a leg. He was from Adrian, Michigan, a small liberal arts college close to Hillsdale and in the same sports league I'd been a part of while at Hillsdale. The guy on my right is the brigade mess sergeant who broke both legs when he was attempting to hook a loading swivel to the bottom of a Chinook helicopter and was blown back onto the tar mac. And I know you're not going to believe me but the troop directly across the aisle, a Negro, had the end of his peter blown off in a friendly fire incident in his squad hooch inside the wire. I wanted to ask him how'd they manage to wrap bandages on a messed up johnson but passed.

The facility is overcrowded and many of us will soon be evacuated to Japan. There was a rocket attack tonight. When the hospital began to receive incoming, orderlies scrambled back and forth between the beds placing us on the floor and covering us with the mattresses we'd just been on. I was petrified, prayed for Jesus to save me. Rounds penetrated the corrugated ceiling on the end of the structure away from me but the really painful part of the ordeal happened when one of the staff personnel tripped over my leg as he ran for cover. Being lifted back onto my bed was very painful.

I slept poorly and this is just the first night. The nature of my injuries is such that I must sleep on my back and I have been a stomach sleeper all of my life. Beside that I have been in and out of consciousness probably due to the drugs. Nurses ask me, "how's the pain," seemingly every five minutes and I always say very bad to improve the odds that I will be administered more drugs. To my knowledge, I have been administered some morphine that is injected into the saline drip bag hanging above my bed, other times I am given Darvon 2 in a small paper cup. The nurse on the ward watches to make certain that I swallow the drug but occasionally, when there is confusion, I am able to retrieve the capsule from my mouth and hide it in my hand. The soldier in the next bed, the grunt from Adrian, told me to break the Darvon capsule and separate the little Codeine B-B from the powder and hide the B.B.'s in the corner of my pillow case. And, then, "Swallow them all at once, it'll get you through the night," he said with a wink. And then Robert, that's his name, told me to always tell them your pain is horrible, even if it is not, because it may land you some extra drugs.

Hope I get to see Top one last time before I am moved but I'm beginning to have doubts. I know he is busy. He leaves for R&R on the 9th and is also going before the promotion board for sergeant E-9. I hope he gets his promotion because he has earned it.

May 6

Monday – The most helpless feeling in the world, that I can imagine, is the one I'm in the middle of right now: lying flat on my back, staring up at the underside of the corrugated ceiling above and fixating on the realization that at any moment another mortar could explode through the ceiling and blow me away.

A lieutenant Wells came by this morning accompanied by several of her orderlies and together they removed the gauze bandages from my legs. Blood and fluids had seeped from most of the wounds and stuck to the bandages, making removal slow and painful, even though the doctor was doing her best to be gentle. I was biting down on a terrycloth towel while this was going on. I really wanted to avert my eyes because I have always been repulsed by unsightly scars or cuts. Guess I'll have to revisit that attitude, won't I? Even stronger than wanting to look away was an almost compulsive curiosity to view what was going on and when I looked I was horrified. I could see almost all the way through my right leg because the flesh drooped down so much. The left one was almost as bad but with many more smaller cuts and abrasions. All muscle tone is gone and the legs are limp and I cannot, at this point, wiggle my toes. The legs will not be stitched for a while due to fear of infection which is a concern in tropical environs.

Frank Edwards came by mid-way through the procedure and watched without displaying any emotion whatsoever. Maybe he felt that I'd be stronger if he wasn't going ape shit. He'd probably have felt different had they been his legs. No matter how I look at what has happened I must consider myself lucky. Things could have been much worse. I am feeling quite weird about all of the uncertainty. I have known Frank and Top and Levy for what seems an eternity and now I will be ripped away from them. I said goodbye to Edwards as best I could but wondered, where am I going? Home? Will I be back? So many thoughts and questions and the nurses through necessity cannot tell me anything meaningful about my condition. Will I walk again, be an invalid, disabled, crippled or lame? Right now, I do not know and even though this is advice easily given to others, for the time being I must take things one day at a time.

News! I will be part of a group being sent tomorrow by air to a place called Camp Zama in Japan. The journey began in the afternoon when we were bussed from the 12th Med Evac to the Cu Chi air strip where between fifty and seventy-five of us were loaded through the lowered ramp to the interior of a C-123. The inside of the plane was outfitted with row upon row of pipe racks that were five high and configured to hold the stretchers that all of us were resting on. There were three troops below me and one above. We will spend the night at a staging hospital near Tan Son Nhut Air Base then on to Japan in the morning.

Determining where I am is difficult. I can only tell you that we are a short ride by another bus to a building or hospital like area that has no windows. There are medical personnel getting us settled, fed and medicated. I have got the same pillow so my little private stash of Codeine B.B.'s is safe. An Army Specialist stopped by my bed and changed my MPC or military currency back into US dollars. I'm not sure how he pulled it off but he returned my wallet, pictures and dog tags along with my gold cross and chain.

It just occurred to me that I needn't worry about R&R and meeting Cindy in Hawaii. I do not know if my family and wife have been notified or if they have been given any contact information for me. Come to think of it they could not be aware that I am on my way to Japan.

May 7

Tuesday – A sustained mortar and rocket attack began to hit the runways at Tan Son Nhut at 0330 hours and continued until sunrise. This time we were placed on stretchers and again placed under the beds with mattresses on top of us. The nurses were occupied with so many of their patients that confusion ensued and in all of that I was able to appeal to several different nurses for more Darvon and was successful. By the time we were placed on top of our bed, still on the stretcher, I had received six Darvon and ingested them all at once. At first, I believed I would vomit but after that everything was glorious and I was grooving all the way to Japan.

When the mortars ceased and the all clear was sounded seventy-two of us were rolled single file out on the tarmac runway and, one at a time, carried up the tail ramp and loaded onto pipe rack receptacles for the stretchers that reached to the ceiling. We were on a humongous, silver, Air Force, Lockheed, C-141 that had no paint except for three tremendous, black, block letters... MAC standing for Military Airlift Command, painted on the tail. All of the pipe rack contraptions were arranged around a center aisle beginning in the rear of the hold and running forward. I was on the bottom with my head toward the ramp at the rear of the plane, so I could not see what was transpiring but as the ramp was being ratcheted closed more mortars fell on the runway behind us. I began to worry that we would not make it out.

The fuselage vibrated as the four large Pratt & Whitney turbofan engines revved, spooled up and we finally taxied down the runway and were airborne. First there were mortars exploding through the hospital roof and now mortars following the plane down the runway with me strapped to my stretcher. Is it any wonder that I experienced a complete meltdown with an accompanying anxiety attack? I began to cry uncontrollably, and I swear this much is true, a nurse wearing a white cap bearing a Red cross hugged me and said, "God bless you, son," as she pressed a small New Testament bible into my hand. I struggled until pain be damned I was able to turn on my stomach, and surrounded by the droning, never-ending white noise inside the cargo bay, I fell into a void of white dreamless sleep. The flight to Japan took over five hours.

At the time, I did not believe there is another feeling in the world as powerful as the one you experience if you're fortunate enough to leave a combat zone.

After landing at a huge air base outside of Yokohama we were bussed to the 20th Evacuation Staging Area. [this is where we are now]. Tomorrow we will be flown by Huey's to the hospital known as Camp Zama, a handful at a time. At present, we are experiencing a huge rain storm with lightning and thunder and there is a deafening roar as sleet pelts the half round metal roofs of this already dismal place. We are, however, receiving good food, plenty of attention from the nurse attendants and, of course, pain meds. My pain is still substantial and only bearable because of its consistent and unrelenting nature. I pray for a break in the weather so we do not get hung up here.

On the way from the air base I was situated on the uppermost row right where the roof of the bus curved down to a bank of windows so I have no idea what Japan's countryside looks like. I am among soldiers with all sorts of wounds. Many are missing a hand, thumb or leg. Guess I'm pretty lucky so far.

May 8

Wednesday – Weather report, gloomy. Disposition of the men, cheerless. Rain continued throughout the morning as we were loaded on the bus for the short journey to Camp Zama. The report that we would be flown by helicopter was either false or the deteriorating weather prohibited the use of the helicopters. Doesn't really matter though does it as long as we at least keep moving toward our next destination. Each move away from that muddy, dirty, leech and mosquito infested environment, where I was wounded for a second time, and spent the last seven and a half months of my life, has been accompanied by profound changes or improvements. Once I had a bunker to sleep in or the ground for a pillow and now I have a real bed. Once it was a poncho or a shelter half and now I have clean sheets. I once had to defecate in a square ammo box or cat hole in the ground that I dug. Now at least I have a bed pan but soon, I hope, I will be able to sit on a real commode. If you add relatively good, nutritious food to that I feel rather fortunate.

Arriving at Camp Zama, and being wheeled inside with the large manila envelope of x-rays at my feet, I noticed, as I did at each previous facility, overcrowded conditions caused by the recent VC offensive in the jungles I have just left. The ward to which I have been assigned has one hundred and thirty beds and there are another ninety new patients expected later today. Before being assigned to a bed on the ward I was set in a corridor on my stretcher and fed some pretty good chow.

Soon after being transferred from the gurney to a fresh bed in the ward I was again placed on a gurney – keep in mind I have not sat upright since the night I was wounded – and taken by elevator to the first floor where I was rolled into the office of the head of osteopathic surgery. He was stuffy, did not address me by name or did he introduce himself. He reached to the front of his desk and retrieved a pipe with a straight stem, placed it in his mouth, and sucked on it ceremoniously as though the useless activity would bring some life to it. He wore a white hospital coat and I could not see a name anywhere although the rank of major could be viewed near the edge of the white coat. His office was absent and décor except for the chain of command. I recognized Johnson and the secretary of the Army Stanley Resor.

My gurney was situated parallel to the front of the major's desk. He pushed back his chair and walked around to retrieve the envelope containing all of my x-rays and returned to sit behind the desk. The pipe made a clacking noise as he reinserted it into the front of his mouth. He pulled slowly and dogmatically on the unlit Kaywoody and I began to nod and reasoned a cat nap, although inappropriate, would probably not impede the process any. My father had said to me once, and probably inaccurately, that pipe smokers were slow on the uptake, to put it charitably, and needed slow pulls on their pipes in order to figure what to say next. I may have nodded, maybe not and what the major said next cut through the fog if there had been any. Your wounds are not all that bad. I almost exploded. "How could you possibly make that judgement from just a fleeting glance at my x-ray? My legs are still enclosed in gauze and there's a blanket covering my torso."

The Major reminded me coolly that I should remember my rank or more precisely, that I should respect his rank and that we'd be doing things his way. "After the operation," he informed me authoritatively, "which is scheduled for tomorrow morning, you will be rehabilitated here at the hospital and utilized as a ward orderly emptying bed pans or however else you can be useful." Knowing this should have provided me with at least some consolation, but it did not. I asked the major if at any point, I would be given an R&R and he said no, I don't think so. I was pissed. In my mind, I was half way home already and I could not wrap my mind around not moving in that direction. I yelled incoherently and made a fuss and when I looked over at the Major sitting beneath the chain of command photos, he maintained a stoic posture, clacking away at his pipe. I told him that he'd better fix me up and either send me home or return me to my company unit but there was no way that I was going to do bed pans. The Major summoned an orderly and I was returned to the ward.

May 9

Thursday - Early in the morning the ward nurse administered a pre-op sedative while the troops around me silently consumed their morning rations. Waving back over my head to everybody, I was rolled to the elevators and down to the first floor and the operating theatre. At that point, my mind was more about rainbows and unicorns than it was about a scrambled egg breakfast on the ward. I have been pricked and prodded, my blood has been drawn and tested and an IV port has been attached to the back of my hand. The major, to his credit, paid me a friendly and professional visit on the ward to inform me of the order of march, an IV drip was started and I was administered two units of whole blood because my count was low. Time passed, I do not know how much, before I was wheeled into the most sterile, white room that I have ever been in – the operating theatre.

I cannot recall going under the anesthetic and the first thing I remember is coming around in a brightly lit room tiled in white. Male nurse's, each holding onto one of my legs, were applying the finishing touches to plaster casts by dipping long strips into a bowl of concocted liquid plaster and smoothing them to the contour of my calves. My legs were then suspended in a kind of stirrup contraption until they dried. They worked silently but one did say welcome back or something that sounded like that. The cast on my left leg was above the knee at about mid-thigh and the cast on the right leg began just below the knee.

The major materialized next to my bed as though he'd just stepped through a magician's smoke bomb and without lowering his face close to mine as nurses seem to do before shouting, "and how are we doing today, Sgt. Dexter," he acknowledged my return from the nether world. He was very level, displaying the amount of concern required of him by protocol when he asked, "how are you feeling son?" While explaining how groggy I felt the major moved to the foot of the bed and pulling a slender metal probe from his breast pocket he poked at the toes of first my left foot and then the right. "Feel that," he queried. "yes," I answered. "See if you can wiggle your toes." I could. He then informed me that my injuries were more severe than he had at first anticipated, took over two hundred sutures to close the various wounds. "You will, no doubt, be happy to hear that you are going to be sent stateside as soon as possible. Your name has been added to that list sergeant." I thanked him sincerely but could speak no further because tears had begun to cascade down my cheeks and I was sobbing. I was rolled back to the ward and I never saw that major again.

I closed my eyes and slept for most of the day. Around supper time I rejoined the living. The clatter and noise of mess trays being distributed on the ward intruded on my lethargy. There was a colored staff sergeant named Leonard in the bunk next to mine and he asked, "how ya doin', sarge? "I reckon I dunno exactly," I said slowly. When I looked down at my new casts I really could not see them because they were obscured by blankets. They were covered by ice filled clear plastic bags and the unbearable stinging sensation added to the dull throb and was so terrible I could not bear it another moment and moved my legs back and forth until the bags tumbled to the floor. A nurse was there immediately to replace the ice bags. She explained without much emotion, and there was little room to misunderstand her authority, hell, I could have been a bird colonel and it wouldn't of made a lick of difference to her. "The purpose of the bags is to keep the swelling down in your legs, sergeant, which have been subjected to even more trauma during the operational procedure than when they were first hurt." I can assure you," she told me, "that if you do not allow the bags to do their job, your legs will swell until they push against the casts and the pain will be worse than anything you have experienced to this point." "Well, then, can you give me something for the pain?" I asked. She moved away and when she returned she smiled down at me as though nothing had happened and then she gave me an injection. She recorded the event on the chart hanging on the end of my bed. For a minute or two, before the pain killer worked its magic, I luxuriated in the fact that I am sleeping on a mattress. It occurred to me that sleep is the only thing that is really under my control and I wanted to hide in it for as long as possible. I finally lost the battle of the ice bags, and after finding the codeine B.B.'s I'd stashed in my pillow, I spiraled down into a nightmarish slumber.

May 10

Friday – Feeling much improved this morning but the pain is still intense. Leonard from two beds over was able to get to the hospital PX and he brought me a crossword puzzle book. I haven't worked on one of those for years and will but first things first. I have not shaved in a week and I am feeling grubby so I am trying to flag down a nurse or orderly to bring me a bowl of water so I can clean myself a little.

No one has bothered to tell me that morphine and other drugs cause terrible constipation. I had to figure this one out on my own. I had a tremendous urge to evacuate my bowls and talked to one of the nurses who brought me a bed ban and then placed a privacy screen around my bed. I had a very difficult time sliding the pan under my butt and when I was finally able to mount the darned contraption I was so exhausted I had trouble. I did not have enough energy left to push but did manage by applying herculean pressure downward to cause perspiration to pop out all over my forehead. That is when the nurse informed me that the busiest area in the hospital is the enema ward. I cannot believe that I have not been administered any laxatives. This is something that I should not have to ask for? What's up?

Lights were on in the ward until well after midnight due to all the new arrivals. Some are coming by bus; the weather has cleared and the heliport right outside my wing of the hospital is busy day and night, medical evacuation helicopters coming and going.

Time to try contacting Cindy. I hadn't a clue what time it would be in Michigan and my brain was too addled for me to accomplish the simple arithmetic. I knew that the difference was approximately twelve hours…early morning back home. A nurse placed an old fashioned black Bakelite telephone next to me on the bed; the curved ear and mouth piece sat across the top. There was no rotary dial or any obvious method to assist me in placing a call. I became frustrated and pushed the phone from the bed. The nurse retrieved the device and explained that if I would simply pick it up an operator would assist me. I could not understand the Japanese operator but finally got her to understand the number and place the call. When I heard Cindy's voice for the first time in almost eight months I could not speak a word. I drew my breaths slowly, breath escaping slowly over my teeth, and was eventually able to speak. Since the call was placed on a collect basis Cindy knew it was me. "Oh, Dear God," she said emotionally. "Todd, is it really you? Are you all right." "Fine," I said trying to be strong and hide the sobbing. "Where are you?" "Camp Zama just outside of Yokohama," and then I unfolded as much as I could about what had happened since the initial wounding back on the third. We spoke for a few more minutes. It was early morning in Michigan, and Cindy was on the way to her teaching job. We exchanged 'I love you's' and I hung up without tossing the phone to the floor this time. My tank was empty. I was spent, wiped out, and immediately dozed off and slept through supper. A very kind nurse brought me a plate and sat at my bed for a while, injected me with more pain killer to help me get back to sleep.

May 11

Saturday – Having the time or the leisure to sleep soundly and for as long as one desires is the most profoundly marvelous thing you can imagine; sleep has been very elusive, has to be stolen or snatched in between bouts of episodic pain which words cannot describe. Infrequently the pain subsides or ebbs but only so slightly and makes me think that maybe it is over. But then it (the pain) returns with a vengeance. It was during one such period that the nurse brought me the telephone and said, "you have a long-distance call," and I thought, what the fuck other kind of call is there for me. I mean, who even knows where I am or that I am alive. "Hello," I questioned. "It's me, mother," the words crackled through the wire. "How did you know where I am?" I wanted to know. "Well, your father, after speaking with Cindy and learning that you were in Japan, called the offices of Congressman Jerry Ford, and he, Jerry, that is, made some inquires and here we are. Are you OK?" "Yes, mother, I am doing OK. My doctor, a major, says I will be shipped to the United States in a matter of days."? "Do you know where you will be going," mother wanted to know. "I am not sure at this point. Nobody says very much." "What can you tell me about your injuries?" "Not much. I was wounded in the legs, both of them, and I have casts on both legs for the time being but long term I cannot tell you very much." We talked for a little longer and mother said that dad sends his love and I signed off.

 I lay for a time staring at the ceiling contemplating my situation. Silently, tears ran from the corners of my eyes and, stinging, drizzled down into my hospital gown. My eyes are hot and I am exhausted and the longer I live the faster everything seems to be moving. Whatever happened to the warm fuzzy days of my well spent childhood with summers that stretched on forever. Compared to those long-ago days the last eight months have been a never-ending montage of rapidly paced dreams, that somehow seem to have been slowed only by my wounding. I feel as though I'm running in motor oil, a fly suspended in amber. In the end I have, perhaps, been my own worst enemy. Because of the curiosity that I nurtured about soldiering, I set the fate driven wheels in motion, wound up in Vietnam and now lie here staring at ceiling tiles and fluorescent light fixtures wondering if it was all worth it just to prove to myself that I had sand. Well, I found out that I have the balls, that I measured up but at what cost? Now, I'm afraid I'm in a bit of a pickle.

 I have observed a Sergeant 1st Class stopping by the beds of many soldiers in the ward to pause and look at the charts to determine that he will be speaking with the proper troop. Today the sergeant checked my chart and stopped to address me. His job is to schedule the hospital to which we will be sent. When he asked me if I knew the nearest facility to me back home I mentioned the Great Lakes Naval Training Facility. He appreciated that but said that I am Army and would probably be assigned to Walter Reed Army Medical Center just outside Washington, D.C. He said that Reed is the nation's most outstanding facility for treating orthopedic conditions meaning my leg wounds. I presume that in the end I will be sent to the facility that will care for me the best. The soldier two beds down is from Detroit and he is being sent to Valley Forge Pennsylvania. Not everyone can be near his home and I have heard that as soon as I am deemed stable I may be granted a convalescent leave to travel home.

The ward I am currently in has many different injuries. One guy was shot through the foot and has already been told that he is being returned to his unit. Another was shot through the leg by an AK-47 and his disposition was not clear. Some around me are barely conscious and moan through the night while others are missing a limb. Talking with many of these guys reminds me of how lucky, at least initially, I am. And I still cannot believe that I am going home.

I have been bothered by the sensation that I must feel guilty or like I am deserting my comrades by going home. While I was still in the field and heard that so and so received a million-dollar wound and was going home I felt no animosity. In fact, I was very happy for those guys and would hope that those I've left behind would feel the same for me. I did all I could. I served well and will continue to honor my uniform and my country.

My pain is definitely abating. The acute ache has been replaced by a relentless dull throb. I can wiggle my toes and I am still receiving pain meds and I am horribly constipated. I have kept this pretty much to myself but things are becoming pretty critical. Friends would say what they have always known...Dexter is full of shit!

May 12

Sunday – Today marks day number five here at Camp Zama and I have yet to see a single doctor or group of doctors with interns making rounds on the wards. Reasoning behind this could be that everything that can be accomplished for us medically has been tended to and now we are in the capable nurse's hands. There are charts at the foot of each bed that contain vital information for the nurses. There is also a unit patch to identify us so passersby can stop and chat if they are from my unit. A guy named Fred stopped this morning. He was in my company and was wounded in the same mortar attack as me. He identified himself as Pineapple, a nickname he picked up, or so he said, because he was from Guam. He has not heard when he is leaving either. I am getting anxious to reach my final destination hospital to finally learn the extent of my wounds and what that means relative to my recovery.

New arrivals filling the wards are balanced by an equal number of soldiers departing for the United States. Each night the public-address system in the hospital calls us to attention and this is the only time during the day that absolute silence prevails. Names of the individual soldiers are called followed by the name of the state side hospital they will be sent to. This represents progress and no matter how grievous the soldier's wounds most are happy to be moving on.

Being here has become boring as there is nothing to do but sleep. The casts on my legs make an attempt at walking impossible. I could get into a wheel chair but no one has mentioned or discussed this with me. I am guessing that I will be departing in a day or so and then probably stay at the 21st staging area one night as I did in the way in.

May 13

Monday – The ward was awakened this morning at 0530 hours when the PA system crackled to life and an Orwellian voice announced that, "water will be supplied and you will clean yourselves up." Translation: you will receive a bowl, said bowl will have a measured amount of water, there will be washcloths, and on and on…you can figure the rest. We used a small kit that the Red Cross had supplied us when we entered the hospital. Absolutely no idea of when I will be able to stand up and take a shower or sit down and take a crap as the constipation continues. I am about to follow the old one liner that I am certain you've heard, the one about the constipated mathematician who worked it out with a pencil. Oh, boy, I crack me up!

After preening like a cat I slept for most of the day. Feeling is, in a very general sense, returning to my legs and I am referencing the pain that has been constant since leaving that field near Hoc Mon. A doctor finally made a small sweep of the ward, stopping by my bed to tickle, probe and prick my toes. I could feel more this time than the last. A good sign, I should think. However, if I had not been looking directly at the toes I would not have been able to tell the doctor exactly where the sensation was centered. And, I'll never forget the first look at my legs when the bandages were removed—they were so mutilated that I was frightened.

I listened to one of the soldiers speaking to his parents about the loss of his leg. He seemed awfully accepting as he attempted to explain how the prosthetic leg would join what was left of his own leg. I cannot imagine how I would respond under similar circumstances.

Just before lights out on Ward 2, my ward, the loudspeaker rattled faintly then came alive with the evenings announcements. The placement of the loud speaker is just around the corner near the nurse's station making hearing difficult. I have listened every night with great anticipation. Learning the next phase of my journey back to the World is all there really is to contemplate. And then it happened, wow, my name was called and the sergeant first class from several days back was correct. I will be going to Walter Reed Army Hospital near Washington, D.C. Because I will be at such a prestigious place, the weirdest thought was the first thing that popped into my mind when learning of my destination. As a sergeant do I salute an officer doctor from my bed? Then I had a few more rational or appropriate thoughts: 1) I will be receiving the best care available, 2) I will be allowed a leave(s) as soon as rehabilitation reaches a certain level, 3) Is being sent to such a prestigious facility in any way an indication of the seriousness of my wounds and 4) by being in our nation's capital I may see some sights. This is all very exciting as well as good news.

May 14

Tuesday – At precisely 08:00 hours a bunch of corpsmen wheeled those of us who are leaving today out to the chopper pad in the courtyard of the hospital. Very soon a slick (it seems strange to see a UH-1 helicopter without armament) swooped in and plucked us off the small pad. The signature wop wop of the blades and the sudden downward rush of air, the hum of the turbine engines and the smell of aviation fuel are things that will remain with me for the rest of my life. How many times did these same choppers arrive just in time to whisk us safely away. How many times had the enemy been closing in on us, just missed the opportunity to engage and kill us?

The helicopter landed in Yokohama and we were again bussed, this time to the 21st Staging facility. As before I was on the top rack just under the curvature of the roof and could not see any of the area we were travelling through. My view from the chopper was, however, very different from absolutely no view on the top shelf in the bus. Everything is lush and green from the early Spring. The major difference is the number of beautiful Pagodas, many of them configured with multi-tiered square roofs that slope upwards at the edges and have colorful tile patterns. I could also see many very tall cylindrical pines or maybe they are arborvitae. Other trees are shorter and stout and have that intentionally trimmed Bonsai look. A most beautiful country from what I was able to observe.

When the corpsman moved me into the 21st I saw many of the same guys that were at Camp Zama so apparently, we are bottle necking or being collected here to make sufficient numbers to make up a full plane load. Once settled in and fed a nurse, a major, came by and informed me that we would be leaving tonight. Good!

I had such an urge to go to the bathroom that I summoned a nurse who came to my bedside with a wheelchair and in a stern way said to me, "'bout time you got up and started to move around on your own. Your rehabilitation begins now, sergeant." She set the brake and stood by like a gymnastics spotter while, for the first time, I placed my feet on the floor. I was overcome by such dizziness that I flopped back on the bed with my feet still on the floor. The nurse grabbed ahold of my hands and gently coaxed me back to a sitting position and watched as I struggled to seat myself in the wheelchair. I was able to find the bathrooms and finally get the chair on onto inside of a stall with the door shut. I dragged myself onto the seat. The effort represented quite a milestone as I'd previously sat unsuccessfully on a number of bed pans; and unlike the square ammo boxes of the field through which shit would fall into a hole, I was on a smooth, white plastic toilet seat. I still could not move my bowels but I was seated properly. The aforementioned constipated mathematician with a pencil (in the form of my index finger) was summoned and I finally worked it out. Once begun it went on and on, smelled like a regiment of VC had died and been buried in there but this was a landmark day.

After that experience, I got myself back into my rack and fell asleep immediately, had to be shaken awake for dinner. At 0930 hours, we once again loaded on the bus and forty-five minutes later we entered Yokoda Air Base where we were greeted by a handful of grinning Red Cross girls, the same ones we'd met on the way in. Without delay we were loaded through the tail ramp of another Air Force C-141 Star Lifter and in minutes we were airborne – no mortars as the door was cranked shut – we were now on our way back across the Pacific Ocean, past the International Dateline and on into Elmendorf Air Base Alaska. The stop is principally for refueling but there is a base hospital at Elmendorf so it is possible that some of our numbers will remain there.

May 15

Wednesday - Will the day that we land in the USA be the same day it was when we left Yokoda? I give! The flight was miserable. I am unable to bend my legs because of the casts and because I am always on my back I do not sleep well. All the way to the states I stared at the bottom of the stretcher on the rack above me and the only thing I had to look forward to was the next feeding which seemed to occur about every thirty minutes. The food we are receiving is delicious but my appetite is very small.

When we finally landed in Alaska no one cheered, but at least we were back in the USA. When the tail ramp was lowered, it was fifteen minutes to one in the afternoon. Chilled Spring air rushed into the hold of the Star Lifter. The air was delicious. We learned of a technical difficulty with one of the four engines and were told that there would be a delay while we were all off-loaded and put on another plane. Two things. Number 1) I feel like a piece of damned luggage that has been shipped all over the world, each time to the wrong destination and 2) I feel as though I am being pursued by a doppelganger or some evil spirit who is intent on destroying me or making certain that I never reach home. I mean, really? I have survived my wounds, mortar rounds crashing through the hospital roof, being dropped by orderlies, and then more mortar rounds that followed our plane down the runway as we made our escape to Japan. And on top of all that a bad engine forcing a plane change.

The final leg of the flight put us down at Edwards Air Force Base around 6:00 PM local time. We were told that Walter Reed was full and could accept no patients so we were shuttled to another staging area and that is where we are now. The Red Cross arranged one free telephone call and trying but not being able to reach Cindy I called mom and dad. We talked for a short time, told them I was OK and that I'd call when I finally reached Walter Reed Hospital.

Tomorrow we will arrive at Walter Reed. For now, I am happy to be resting quietly between fragrant, white sheets and knowing that I am safe. No more mortars, no rockets or long exhausting sweeps with funky water, mosquitoes and little food. No more Eagle Flights, ambush patrols, killing for a questionable cause or lazy afternoons in a stinking fox hole with wet feet and rotting sox. No more blown up bodies or blood dripping flesh, screams of terror or muffled cries where nobody gives a shit whether or not you die. Fuck it, don't mean nuthin'… I am home!

May 16

Thursday – I am inside Walter Reed Army Medical Hospital somewhere. I am completely disoriented just as I have been in all of the previous facilities in which I have been warehoused. I am still on the stretcher that I was on when I departed Japan. I am resting single file with numerous other soldiers, up against the wall in a brightly lighted corridor. The foot traffic is considerable. I have been fed and my meds have been updated. The osteopathic ward is full and I am not sure where I will be placed.

May 17

Friday – I was moved early this morning into a ward that appears to be another warehousing situation but this time I am surrounded by much older retired Army officers. I noticed when being transferred to a bed that the soldier next to me is a two star, major general and in my estimation, he is not going to be leaving here under his own power. He has a phlegmy, syphilitic cough that has no beginning or ending just goes on to the point of exhaustion, his and mine. He may have been unconscious for he never spoke or moved his head.

In the afternoon, a pretty nurse chatted me up when she observed me making notations in my diary. I shared some of my story with her and the journey that brought me here to her ward. She said that she'd very much like to read what I had written. I hesitated, she begged, I hesitated more but in the end, I relented and handed her my red, leather bound diary which she promised to return to me tomorrow. Later in the day I panicked thinking about what I'd done. All the effort, what if something happened to my work or worse, what if she was transferred or never came back. I barely slept at all even with a sedative administered by another nurse.

In the morning, the nurse came back and I could tell by the way she carried herself, the look in her eyes, that something had happened. She handed my diary back to me, pages were torn and she apologized. "My dog," she offered timidly chewed your diary while I was in the shower." "Don't fret", I said, trying to be reassuring, "let's take a look, I'll bet we can fix it." And with Scotch Tape we did just that. When done I said, "Now my diary looks as though it has been through a war, just like me. She smiled.

The next day I was transferred to the Osteopathic ward.

May 18

Saturday – There are over three hundred beds in my new home. I am on a wing that has the appearance of a very old sun porch on the North side of the building. There is plenty of indirect sunlight. A nurse rolled me in a wheelchair right up to the first bed in a long line just around the corner from the rest of the ward. She took a neatly folded stack of sheets and a pillow case which had been resting on my lap, pitched the bundle onto the bed and said, "Make your bed and then get into it." I did as I was told. Making the rack was a chore and when I finally locked the chair and got into the bed my attention was drawn to the guy in the next bed and those for several beds down. I guessed that their curiosity was piqued so I asked, "Do the nurses here give great blow jobs like they did in Japan?" All three of them looked vapidly at me and, in unison, exclaimed, "Huh?" I charged right in, "So, maybe that was kind of rash. My name is Todd," I offered to shake and in return the guy offers me his left hand. I noticed his right hand had a black metal harness that surrounded his wrist, each of his fingers hung suspended below in a trapeze. There was a flap of skin on the back of his hand that I was guessing, allowed doctors to look inside. He grasped my fingers in return and said, "My name's Cecil, welcome. And by the way, we're not getting' any head but occasionally a pint of whiskey'll find its way onto the ward."

 A nurse whisked by the foot of my bed and I flagged her down to find out about chow. She said, "in the mess hall, you'll find it, sooner or later." Cecil's eyebrows shot up and he says, "They're tough but you'll get used to it."

 Later in the day I took to the hallways in my new transportation. The feeling of moving, going anywhere, the freedom after so long in my immobilized state was exhilarating. To be using my arms to propel me down the corridors was amazing. Turning a corner, I saw a Negro walking toward me and decided I'd ask him if he knew the way to the cafeteria. One of his eyes was obscured by a sizeable bandage and at first, I did not recognize the soldier. As we were about to pass it registered. "Snipes," I cried out. "Man, how the hell are you doing?" "Dex, long time, no see!" This was like a minor miracle. Last time I saw Snipes was when he was heading out on convoy and promised to find my little reel to reel tape machine. I couldn't believe it. We travelled together to the mess hall and whether it was visiting with an old friend or something else, the food was superb and the comradeship even better. He was to be discharged in another day and I'd not see him again but, oh, what a magical moment.

May 19

Sunday – Unbelievable, there were actual rounds being performed by doctors and staff. I was excited, anticipated that I would learn something about my condition. One doctor seemed to be in charge and the rest were in attendance, following him through the ward and stopping at each bed. He came down the row and after speaking with Cecil, the doctor whose name was Eberhardt stopped, examined my chart and spoke to one of the nurses. He addressed me professionally and said matter of factually, "Why don't we have a go of it, see what's under these casts, OK?" I was game after having never spoken to a single doctor and I said, "Why, of course, sure." I felt like an idiot.

One of the nurses produced a tool that she plugged into a wall mounted socket. The contraption looked somewhat like a wheel used for cutting a pizza into equal slices, had serrated teeth and a guide to allow a cut to a preset depth. She began on one side of the cast on my left leg and proving the depth setting wrong, buzzed through the plaster of Paris, snagging on the metal sutures once or twice before getting both casts removed. She apologized sincerely. My legs, when fully exposed, were terribly emaciated and appeared weak. Doctor Eberhardt examined my appendages but said little. Later in the afternoon the nurse who had removed both casts returned with a tray on which sat a hypodermic needle, a stainless bowl containing sudsy water and several scalpels. She informed me that the areas around my sutures had become infected and she was immediately beginning a regimen of penicillin shots to be administered every six hours around the clock until things improved. Then she began to do something that I can only describe as being close to orgasmic. She soaked my feet in the warm soapy water and rubbed them for some time. Then she scraped and trimmed all the callouses from the bottoms of my feet. The activity was so pleasurable that I could have cried. Before leaving the nurse informed us that there was a big surprise tomorrow. I looked at Cecil, gave him the old wink and said, "Ya think?" He laughed heartily.

Five of us had an informal wheel chair race to the mess hall and later, we careened through the corridors and up an incline to the floor above, and I could not believe it, we were at a beautiful movie theatre that was rapidly filling. We lined our wheel chairs along the back wall and waited for the movie to begin. The play bill coming into the theatre advertised the weirdest movie I have ever seen that featured a gorgeous, tall woman in a gossamer dress that exposed her legs nicely. In her hand, she carried a coiled bullwhip. The plot was so cheesy that we laughed through the whole movie. The evil woman's goal was to eliminate all men from the world and replace them with her beautiful and evil courtiers. The title was *The Million Eyes Of Su Maru*. Really horrible. We rolled back onto the ward and fell into a fitful, horny sleep. Of course, I was awakened at midnight to be stabbed in the butt with still another injection of penicillin.

May 20

Monday – This was an amazing day. I awoke to commotion that seemed to be emanating around the wall behind me and the first manifestation of that commotion was a male photographer who stepped down into our ward. He was holding a camera that had a flash attachment which was suspended away from the camera itself. A neutral colored card to deflect light in the desired direction was very near the flash bulb. What the f**k, I thought, am I still asleep. No, not really, because a huge entourage of persons followed the photographer onto the ward and stopped right at the foot of my bed. I'll be damned, I said out loud as Johnny Carson, late night TV mega-star, and Doc Severinson, stopped at the foot of my bed. Johnny lit a cigarette, glanced down at the name on my bunk to make certain he had the name right and then said, "how ya doin' Dexter?" "Amazingly well now that you're here," I said., "I'm a huge fan and my mother is especially fond of you as well. News at eleven and then you, wow!" "Are you looking forward to returning to duty?" Johnny asked. 'Yes, I am." Mr. Carson began to move down the aisle backlighted by the indirect sunlight coming through the bank of windows. As he moved on I said, trying to be cute, "You know, Johnny, I think you should invite me to be on your show." He turned slightly, flicking cigarette ash on the floor and said, "Really, why is that?" "Because I might have an interesting slant on things regarding Vietnam that your audience would like to hear." Interesting was all he said but as he moved away to talk with Cecil and the rest of the ward one of Mr. Carson's troupe wrote down my name. Later Cecil laughed big time and says, "Dexter, you've got a huge set of balls." "Nothing will come of it," I reiterated, "but I took a shot, eh."

    My bandages were changed again in the afternoon, the pain seems to be abating day by day. One of the nurses told me that tomorrow I will begin two a day physical therapy. "Time to ditch the crutches," she said, "Uncle Sam wants you back again." I find it interesting that my pain was so intense at one point that I could do the silent crying thing, be very morose and feel really sorry for myself.

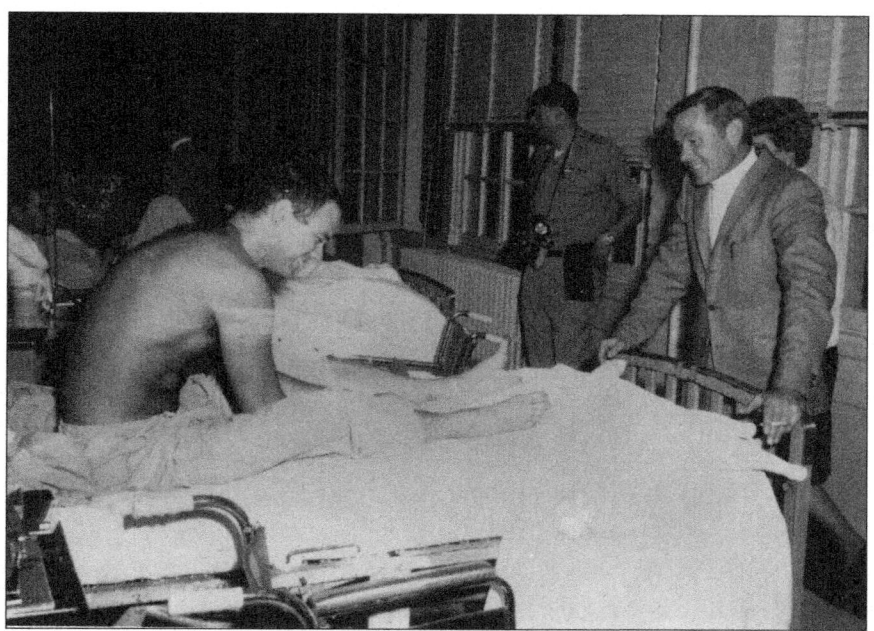
Me with Johnny Carson, Walter Reed Army Hospital

Now that I am mending, sort of coming back together, I can actually feel the pain lessening its grip, it's intensity and the difference even if slight, makes me feel so good that, again, I can easily cry.

Getting to sleep, though, continues to be problematic. The injections to cure the infection interrupt what little sleep I get and often I am bedeviled by nightmarish visitations where I am back in the jungles. Duty nurses roam the wards at night and some of these dedicated practitioners would give Florence Nightingale a bad name. Last night a nurse placed her body across my upper torso as I lay in bed and, wordlessly, comforted me. I could not think about what happened as illicit behavior and I would ask you to consider the context. I don't believe I have ever been lonelier in my entire life. More context: I have spoken to my wife and my parents and they did not even ask me if I would like them to visit me here in the hospital...they all said that I'd be home soon enough and they were not coming to see me. Well, I guess I feel like a worthless piece of excrement. I mean, what the fuck, it couldn't be more than a ten-hour drive or a miserable little pissant flight in a puddle-jumper from their local airport.

May 21

Tuesday – Bright and early a nurse rolled a wheel chair next to my bed and instructed me to swing my legs over the side and," climb aboard," she said. "After you've been down for some chow," she continued, "get yourself over to the first-floor rehabilitation center. They will be expecting you. Just follow the blue line on the floor when you exit the mess." I did as I was instructed.

The rehab center was completely outfitted with the newest exercise equipment and items necessary to help vets to recover from their injuries. There are racks with dumb bells in rows ranking from lightest to heaviest. Rowing and leg exercising machines as well as parallel bars to practice and learn to walk again. Mats, like those from my old school for wrestling, were arranged in a geometric pattern and were about ten or twelve feet square and raised two feet above the floor so therapists could easily work with their patients. There was a movable track attached to the ceiling that moved about the room and held a harness into which patients could be strapped or suspended to assist their learning to walk once again. Different sized medicine balls were scattered randomly about. Corner tables were to be found in several places and there were rows of round dowel pegs attached in wood frames that reached from floor to ceiling that I thought might be for stretching or pulling one's body upright.

I checked in at the desk and was assigned to a physical therapist who pushed me over to a set of parallel bars, set the brake on my chair and began an examination of my legs to determine the range of motion. His name was Miller and the first thing he said to me was, "Well, sergeant did they have you make your own bed, find the mess hall, the crapper?" "Yeah," I smiled, "They did." "They're tough as nails but with purpose. We are going to get you out of the chair and walking very soon." "Now, let's get you up with one of these rails under each arm, then I am going to ask you to raise up on your arms, I will assist you, and we will see how much weight you can put on your legs, if any." Dragging my lifeless legs, I struggled to an almost standing position. When I lowered myself so some weight was on my feet, I did not see how I'd ever be able to walk again. My legs were emaciated, the calf of my right leg approximately twice the size of the left one. The scars, while they appeared to be mending, were virulent, scary looking.

The therapist guided me the length of the parallel bars, sweat popping out on my forehead, and got me turned around and headed back. Finally, I collapsed, exhausted in my chair. The therapist encouraged me, "Not bad," he said. "Now I want you to wheel yourself over to that mat yonder and sprawl on it. I will be there shortly to show you some things you can do with rubber bands to strengthen your legs." When I got to the mat I lay flat on my back. "How you doing," I heard someone say and I did a half roll and was looking at a huge smiling face. "My name's Max, what's yours?" "Todd, and I 'll feel better when I get the drill, get the hang of it all." I answered. I did not catch his last name and Max did not inquire 'bout mine. Maybe next time. "That's the spirit," he said. How could anybody that appeared as he did be happy but he really was. He was missing both legs just around the knee and his right arm at about the elbow. He was catching a sizeable medicine ball, balancing it gingerly with just his left arm, and pitching it back to his therapist.

Miler came over and worked with me for a while, massaged my legs and manipulated my toes and said he'd see me later on in the afternoon. My sessions went on for several weeks and were grueling but my strength returned slowly. I saw Max every day and drew courage from him and inspiration to continue on, to get better. The injections for the infection continued and I was wakened every night but I was sleeping better.

May 22

Wednesday – Rehab first thing in the morning. Rather the same as my first session yesterday. Max was again on the mat and I recognized several others as well. Those that I observe are laboring intensely and with great purpose, driven by the mantra of the therapists, if you do not use it you will lose it. The driving force for me is that I will be sent on a convalescent leave as soon as I can navigate on my own, walk without crutches. About my third time through the parallel bars Miller asked me to hold up which I did. "Lift your left foot, replace it on the ground then lift the right foot." I complied. "Notice how your foot or feet, I should say, have a tendency to droop, keep pointing toward the deck?" "I guess," I offered lamely. "It's called drop foot and we must dedicate ourselves to strengthening your feet at once. I am going to send you to Prosthetics." "Why's that?" I inquired, "I'm not missing any limbs." "True enough sergeant Dexter. The prosthetic department does lots of good stuff though. For you I am going to order leg braces that will be attached to your shoes and be loaded with substantial springs so your feet will be lifted for each step. In the process, you will be able to push back against the springs to strengthen your ankles."

In the afternoon, I began to use the crutches that someone had placed on my rack. However, I kept the wheelchair close at hand for the evening wheelchair races to the movie theatre. The prosthetics department measured my calves, gave me a brand-new pair of bright black uniform shoes that the braces will be fitted to and sent me on my way.

I walked, if walking is what one would call my ambulatory excursions, back and forth in the ward between the windows and the ends of everyone's rack. I did not encounter anyone from the Twenty Fifth Division but I did introduce myself along the row, stopping occasionally to chat. Then I maneuvered my chair up the ramp and travelled through several other wards. I observed that the wounded have been segregated in separate wards according to the type of injury. The first ward I visited was for head injury and trauma. I saw soldiers that in spite of huge bandages were missing a part of their head. Moving farther into the ward which was dimly lit I encountered a troop who was sitting cross legged on the top of his bed. His forehead was caved in and his sightless eyes were aimed straight down where his nasal cavity once resided. I almost lost it and then in a very thin voice I heard, "Is someone there?" "Yes," I responded, "I am here." "Come closer," he said, "Don't be alarmed. What is your name?" "Todd," I offered, rolling my chair into the space between his bed and the one next to it. "My buddies used to call me Gunner 'cuz I carried the Pig, you know, the 60." I was curious and asked, "What happened?" "Got hit on patrol, I stopped an RPG that didn't detonate. What about you?" "Mortar exploded very close to my legs, messed 'em up pretty bad." "Lucky you," was all Gunner could say. A long pause ensued and, finally, Gunner said, "would you hold my hand, I'm so alone...and frightened." I held onto his hand forever. When I left, he pleaded with me to come back again. I am having a difficult time...being surrounded by hardened veteran soldiers who have seen so much and been through more and still, at the very heart of it all, are insecure, alone and worried about the simplest thing like going home to their families.

After being awakened by my midnight injection I tossed and turned until the first light of dawn crept through the windows and into the ward. So much death, so many destroyed lives and families not to mention the division in our country. And all for what. My thinking has changed so much. For instance, I now believe that Communism and the Domino theory, the doctrines that allowed me to favor the war in the first place, have become the scapegoats proffered by elitist Americans and politicians to mask their imperialist agenda.

Can we just be perfectly honest for just one damned minute? The end game is, and will continue to be, the extraction of as many dollars from America's resources and economy that capitalists can get away with. The question is will the country's citizens ever wise up and raise hell? In the meantime, my legs could have been sawn off and discarded into a throw away bucket, and the fate of every soldier laying in a hospital someplace in this country is in question because we bought into the myth that this illegal war, this police action is about Patriotism and Democracy. It is not! The war has been about opportunistic men and corporations of questionable morals who are amassing great personal wealth from the sale of bullets, flak jackets and tanks to the Department of Defense. We who serve so faithfully and so unquestionably are the grease or the detritus, if you will, that turn the wheels of such a foul enterprise. I believe that now I am a conscientious objector but don't you dare judge me or the love that I have for my country, my patriotism.

May 23

Thursday – A ward nurse came to my bunk this morning and informed me that I had a visitor. I, of course, thought that it might be my wife paying me a surprise visit so I prayed the disappointment didn't show on my face when the nurse brought an old friend and not my wife to my bedside. "Buzzy," I said, "what brings you to this neck of the woods." "Well, the generals gave me some time off from keeping their Pentagon running on schedule." "Great," I responded, "but how'd you know I was here?" "The rumor mill works exceedingly well no matter where one happens to be-- your mother told my folks about your hospitalization and here I am."

Buzzy Dahlberg's parents and mine had been especially fond of one another because of their common denominator, old demon rum; they were great cocktailers on the summer-resort party circuit. My mother and Buzz's got very loud after consuming the explosive contents of huge glass pickle jars brought to our beach in Dahlbergs' Wagemaker, moulded, wooden power boat. Each of their inane jokes was accompanied by uncontrollable laughter and huge, throaty snorts. My father meanwhile was disrespectful of everyone and everything and referred to Dr. Dahlberg, a gynecologist, as the pussy plumber and indicated that he also thought little of my abilities by saying once that if he'd cut my head open pussy'd fly out, but enough of that.

Buzzard and I took a leisurely walk outside the hospital and found a live oak to sit under, lean our backs on. Buzz pulled out a brown bottle in a paper sack and then set two telescoping, yellow, plastic cups on the ground and filled them equally with Jim Beam. "Welcome home," he said. I teared up. We spoke quietly about his assignment at the Pentagon and our long ago summers in Northern Michigan. When Buzz left me at my bed I was slightly drunk and thankful for his visit.

It wasn't too late so I rolled over to see Gunner. "It's me, Todd" I said, seeing if he was awake. He was. "You know sumpthin', Gunner, I been thinking about you. Who were you with in the Nam?" "The Americal Division," he replied, "and I still am, even now." Long pause. "You know, Todd, we were in many a tight spot and that always meant action and in a firefight everything happens too fast for fear to paralyze your mind. Shit happens. I mean, I can accept what has happened to me but what I am having trouble with is that the last vision I will ever have in my life, my last sight, is of dead Gooks spread out in a ditch and not my smiling wife and two children." I risked Gunner's rejection. "Can your face be rebuilt? "They're talking about it. The occipital lobe which is in the back of the brain, is undamaged and can technically still transmit stuff dealing with my sight but the eyes are gone." "I had to ask." "I know," Gunner said just before falling asleep. I sat by him for a while before returning to my ward.

I joined the wheel chair derby with Cecil and we rolled up to the theatre to see *Kill a Dragon* with Jack Palance and Fernando Lamas. Son of a bitch! Would it be too much to for once show a decent movie to a bunch of beat up soldiers that put it all on the line for their country?

May 24

Friday – A specialist 4th class stopped by the ward to inform me that my foot locker had caught up to me from Vietnam. This surprised me because there wasn't a thing of value in it. I had occasionally used the darned thing to store my tiny reel-to-reel Sony tape recorder while I was in the jungles. I followed the specialist's directions and reported to an office in the bowels of the hospital where an employee used bolt cutters to remove the lock on the olive green, oblong box. It was filled with uniform remnants and other junk that I did not recognize. No tape recorder. However, all of my black and white photographs were there so I removed them from the foot locker. I cannot recall if there were missing items so I wasn't disappointed about that. If there were any valuables they had been removed back in Nam by whoever prepared the locker for shipping. I signed off and told the clerk to burn everything.

I went to the rehab center and worked on the parallel bars and rolled around on one of the mats for a while, said hello to Max, learned that he was from Atlanta. "Never been there," I said. "You'd love it, especially the Spring when the trees along Peachtree bloom," Max said.

Miller told me that my braces would be available later in the day. I look forward to the rehab sessions with anticipation because I can feel myself becoming stronger each day. Miller says that I am progressing nicely and that the pace of the actual recovery will move faster and soon I will be able to attempt walking unassisted.

On the way back to the ward I stopped by the prosthetics department where a young soldier who was also a physical therapist slipped on my new shoes, adjusted the buckled leathers around my calf's and instructed me to stand and take several steps. What a weird feeling. When I lifted first my left leg and then the right, the springs performed remarkably well and lifted my toes off the ground.

Returning to the ward I parked my wheel chair, grabbed the crutches and headed off for the mess hall. For my first solo things went very well. I pounded down four dishes of lime Jell-O with mostly happy soldiers like myself who are recovering from a myriad of injuries. Names rarely get exchanged and everyone wears the same light blue jammies with matching robe. When I sat down I was privy to a most remarkable discussion. I observed, listened and watched but did not offer an opinion because, honestly, I had not devoted any thinking to the topic. These guy's all agreed that if they could, they would go back to Vietnam on the next available airplane. Had they abandoned their buddies and their units, were they feeling guilty about being home even though they had to have been wounded and banged up to have this status? Or did they just love combat or the Army that much?

As I sat and listened I began to wonder if there is something wrong with me. I could not discuss how I honestly felt. All of the detonating mortars that seemed intent on killing me before I could escape the country had really petrified me. I swiped imaginary sweat droplets from my brow and then in an equally imaginary and very theatrical way pantomimed snapping my wrist to expel the sweat. Silently I said, praise God I made it! Personally, I have never been prouder than I am of myself for having performed up to expectations, everyone's as well as my own. I have stood in the middle of fire fights exposing myself to enemy fire to both return fire and take photographs and along with my buddies I have moved forward and through enemy ambushes. In short, we measured up! But as much as I love my buddies back in Tay Ninh, I feel that I've done my part. I may feel guilty about those I've left behind but I have a family and I have been spared and now, by God, it is time to go home.

May 25

Saturday – There is a courtyard concert on the hospital grounds. Karen and Richard Carpenter, the recording phenoms are performing for everyone, and as I record these thoughts, I can hear the mellifluous sweetness of *Ticket To Ride*, their own rendition of a tune made very popular by the Beatles back in 1964 or 1965. I am not exactly a fan and would have attended. In fact, Cecil asked that I go along, but I have physical therapy a little later.

I walked on my crutches to the phone bank by the movie theatre and called Cindy. What a strange call. I do not know if others are experiencing similar difficulties when calling loved ones, I can barely explain it myself, but something is wrong. I am not talking about the anger or angst I may be experiencing about my family not coming to visit me in the hospital here in D.C. It's more like I barely know what to say to my wife. I have not seen her in over eight months and I guess I'm having as much difficulty talking about what is going on in my life as she does in hers. I want to believe that being together even if just for one weekend would rectify some of the ambiguity that I am feeling.

Miller takes my crutches from me as soon as I appear at the door to the rehab facility. He will not allow me to use the parallel bars for support either. I am beginning to walk through the various wards on my floor but now standing here with no assistance makes me feel extremely awkward. Miller smiles and I get an occasional thumbs up. I have tried a flight of stairs nearby and have discovered new pain. I believe that I will walk normally and completely without help very soon. My weight is coming along nicely. When I arrived at Walter Reed I barely weighed one hundred and forty pounds and my waist measurement was less than thirty-two inches.

Already my waist is thirty-three and a half inches and I weigh almost one fifty.

May 26

Sunday – A day for rest. No rehab. I slept in and then walked the grounds of the hospital leaving my crutches on the front stoop. When I returned, I met the nurse from my first night in the old Generals ward, the nurse whose dog attacked my diary. She was holding my crutches and said, "Well, look at you, I never would believe you'd be recovering so rapidly." I know," I returned, "before you know it I'll be flying." She walked along beside me and we entered the hospital and found our way to the mess hall and had a bite before I returned to the ward.

May 27

Monday – Dr. Eberhardt made rounds with other staff in tow this morning. He said that my wounds while still colorful are healed enough and that he had spoken with my nurses and rehab personnel and did not see why I could not be sent on a one-week convalescent leave. He said to discuss being fitted for new Class A uniforms and receive travel pay as soon as possible. When my leave is up I will move to a huge, old Victorian looking manor which is on the hospital grounds called The Glen. There is more freedom there as I will make the transition to another leave before being assigned to my final duty station.

I obtained directions to the uniform shop and when I entered the ground floor room across the hospital grounds that is part of the commissary complex, an older gentleman, ex-service I assumed, said that he could take my measurements at once. The uniform would be ready by June second, and when I learn the outfit to which I will be assigned, I can return to have the appropriate shoulder patch sewn on the sleeve. I suggested that the clerk make the final measurements a bit loose but not too lose as I will be gaining weight. I also purchased some khaki pants and a plaid shirt to be worn when I leave the reservation. I also stopped by the paymaster's office and submitted paperwork for back as well as travel pay. The combined amount will be enough to get me home on leave plus a little extra. My current base pay is $260.20 plus an additional $16.00 overseas pay and $65.00 combat pay for a grand total of $307.20 a month. Please do not get me revved up about how little I get paid for putting my life at risk to kill Gooks as opposed to, oh, say, the president of any large manufacturing company suckling on the teats of commerce and receiving dirty money for supplying the war effort. Remember, war is good for business and good business is good for our country. All of us are called upon to sacrifice something, it's just that some like me are called to sacrifice more.

    I made the entire trip around the complex without my crutches or the wheel chair. I am totally free from pain meds but still experience some leg pain due mostly to the restraint caused by the leg braces. Good chow tonight and a movie. I told Cecil and others on my row that I might not be around that much longer. They seemed genuinely happy that I'd be moving on even if they weren't, not just yet.

May 28

    Tuesday – Early in the morning I took a shower and dressed in my new khaki's and plaid shirt then walked to the front of the hospital where there is a cab stand. I slipped excitedly into the back seat of the Yellow Taxi and pulled the crutches after me. Destination, I shared with the driver, Dulles International Airport. I sat back and relaxed as the cab passed through a bucolic area and along a parkway running beneath worn overpasses. The airport is approximately twenty-six miles from Walter Reed and once coming to a stop on the long circular drive in front of the Delta terminal I crutched my way inside and found a counter that looked promising. I purchased a round trip ticket leaving Dulles on June 2, the day after my birthday, and returning June 8. On the return trip to Walter Reed, I was able to get limited views of the D.C area. This was the first time I'd been in the nation's capital and I made a mental note about checking out the Mall and maybe the Smithsonian Institute as well as other attractions.

In the evening, I called Cindy and related the good news about my visit home. She wanted to know how long I'd be staying and let me know that the whole family would be there to meet me at the airport. She also wanted to know if I had heard anything about my next assignment. I could only tell her that I'd probably know by the time I arrived home for the leave. I shied away from discussing my assignment because I was expecting her to accompany me though I knew she would resist. There was bound to be unhappiness due to the dedication Cindy has for her teaching job and her securing the necessary year-long leave of absence she'd need in order to go with me. When we hung up I wondered if there was something the matter with me. Nothing had been larger in my mind for all those nights I'd spent in the jungles than thinking of the glorious day when I would return and be embraced by my family. This was not proceeding well.

May 29

Wednesday – I hailed a cab outside the hospital and instructed the driver to take me to the Washington Monument. The day had arrived for my first big test and, yes, I realize that I could easily have taken the elevator to the highest point but I was going to will myself up each of the stairs in that damned tower. Most fortunate that I did not ask the taxi driver to wait because the journey was long and arduous—almost two hours, but I made every last one of the 879 stairs mentioned on the plaque at the first level. Many of the limestone blocks on the inside wall of the monument are filled with carvings that were presented as gifts from states, societies and organizations at the time construction began in 1848. When I reached the top of the obelisk I had to wait on line for what turned out to be an unspectacular and narrow view of our capital city through the thick concrete. The window openings, covered in thick Plexiglas, one each for North, South, East and West are approximately a foot and a half high by two feet wide. Coming down was less difficult but painful, nonetheless. On the way back to the hospital I fell asleep in the cab and the driver had to revive me. He said, when I asked the amount of the fare, "It's on me, buddy, thanks for your service." Wow, that was unusual. Back on the ward and exhausted I fell immediately into a deep and dreamless sleep.

When finally, I awoke, Cecil asked me if I'd like a slice of pizza. Of course, I said yes. It seemed possible to get anything one desired on the ward with the exception of a blow job, but the pizza got me thinking about change. Less than a month ago I was caught out in the open in a mortar attack while slogging my way through a garbage sump trying to get rescued. Now everything was clean and neat and moving rapidly toward normalcy. Food is great, clean white sheets and no hostile enemy fire. Soon I will be home and able to touch, feel and caress those who, to this point, have been nothing but an ethereal dream, a figment of my imagination impossible to reach except through reminiscences under a full moon while sitting on the edge of a fox hole.

May 30

Thursday – I spent the day preparing for and thinking about my leave. The ward nurses delivered my orders authorizing me to be away from the hospital and to be travelling. I picked up and tried on my uniform, called mom and dad and gave them my flight information, Delta from Dulles to Chicago and a connecting flight that would get me into Grand Rapids International around 0840 hours on the evening of June 2.

In the afternoon, I paid a visit to the rehab facility and talked briefly with Miller and also visited with Dr. Eberhardt who will issue my final release from the hospital in about another month. Everything he had to share with me was encouraging. He said my rehabilitation would be as close to perfect as possible but I must be patient and I must continue to work, "most importantly," he said. "Many of the capillaries and very tiny veins in my lower extremities were impossible to repair or reattach and general numbness in your legs could persist for many years."

One of the guys on the ward had gotten a fifth of liquor and after lights out on the ward we stayed up like delinquents and passed the bottle up and down the row of beds. I received the last penicillin shot two days ago and other antibiotics have been suspended as well and I feel ready to leave Walter Reed behind.

May 31

Friday – Slightly hung over this morning. Walked to the mess hall with Cecil and consumed huge quantities of orange juice, bacon, eggs and, of course, coffee. Later in the morning I stopped by the head injury trauma ward to see Gunner. I was surprised to find his rack occupied by another young soldier who was wearing a halo traction device to keep him immobile while his neck and spine healed. He said he had no idea what had happened to Gunner so I asked at the nurse's station. Gunner's family moved him to a private facility closer to his home where he would receive more personalized attention.

I read for most of the afternoon and participated in a wheel chair race using a borrowed chair that I no longer needed. Cecil liked the movie that while still a big loser was a notch above the crap the hospital has been showing us. The flick was from last year and was titled *In like Flint* starring James Cobrun, Lee J Cobb and a hottie named Jean Hale. It was supposed to be a James Bond knock off but other than having a few 'eye candy' scenes the film failed to get off the ground. The plot was similar to the *Million Eyes* debacle we watched a while back where a gaggle of beautiful women were trying to rule the world. Please, stop already.

Tossed and turned for most of the night thinking about my leave the day after tomorrow. I will go to the commissary tomorrow and purchase something to carry my shaving stuff and all of my black and white pictures.

I really have nothing else to take. I have plenty of civilian clothes at mom and dad's and also at Cindy's and my apartment.

June 1

Saturday – Happy Birthday. No cake or other bull crap but I did get a card from Cindy that the whole family had signed.

Mid-morning, I walked to the uniform shop and tried on my new, green class A duds. They fit well and the pants were sized perfectly to hide the leg braces. I grabbed one of the shuttles that move from place to place around the hospital campus and decided to visit the Glen because I will no doubt be assigned there when I return.

The facility has, as I mentioned, a certain medieval look to it and is situated beneath beautiful stately trees. I casually walked, as well as a guy with spring loaded braces could, into the front entrance and was impressed by the immense size of the place, the openness. I walked straight ahead, drawn by laughter and the sound of billiard balls clacking against one another. This was going to be all right I thought. There was more than one table in the room and the green felt on the surface of the tables was bathed by lights hanging above. Usarsky, the mortarman who had pulled me into the bunker the night I was wounded near Hoc Mon pitched his cue stick on the table and came up and circled his arms around me. "I'll be a sumbitch," he proclaimed joyfully. "What the fuck ya doin' here, Dex?" "Recovering just the same as you apparently," I said.

We sat and had coffee in the lunch room and got caught up. Usarsky had seen Snipes but no one else from the unit. He told me that several weeks after I was evacuated he was grazed by a bullet that made a crease beginning right at his eye socket and running back along his face and across his ear. "Just a fraction of an inch more," he said, "and my skull would have exploded." The battalion was still in the Hoc Mon area when he was evacuated to Japan. I told him that I was busy getting ready to go on convalescent leave and I would be returning in about a week and would be billeted at the Glenn. "Good," he said, "I'll see you when you get back."

June 2

Sunday – The Delta flight from Dulles to Chicago was claustrophobically full, and the tightness of the rounded hull so confining that I wanted to get up and run until the braces exploded from my legs. After a short lay over in Chicago I boarded a smaller DC-9, one of the twin engine, center aisle air frames that I had built back in 1965 when I was employed by Douglas Aircraft on Lakewood Boulevard in Long Beach, California. How ironic, I thought. Before the letter arrived that began the process of drafting me into the military, I could have enrolled at Long Beach State College just across the street from the aircraft plant, but I did not. The predictable result was Vietnam.

Now I was returning home, two hundred and forty-one days, a handful of hours and a few minutes after leaving for Ft. Lewis, Washington for the Republic of South Vietnam. The cabin was almost empty and very dark. The stewardesses had retreated to their seats against the forward bulkhead. I was jammed in a row up against another bulkhead that separated first class from coach. Isolated and unattended I stared at the dark inky void of Lake Michigan. My legs ached fiercely but I lacked the energy to change to a different, more comfortable seat. I could see the lights of St. Joseph, Michigan, as the plane crossed over the shoreline and began its descent into

Grand Rapids. The Captain announced that we would be landing shortly and please buckle your seat belts. The uncertain air buffeted the small plane as I stared down at the yellow orange lights along 28th Street, the bustling center of activity where as a youngster I had my first pizza date and a stop at Michigan's first McDonalds where hamburgers were only 15 cents. We were heading straight for Kent County International Airport and a rendezvous with family. I could scarcely gather my thoughts. After so many months away what was this going to be like? What am I going to say? What will my wife say, my mother and father? I had, in my life, been separated from girl friends and family for short periods of time but nothing like this. This was going to be such a joyous moment but I was, nonetheless, feeling confused, visited by the vagaries or should I say the remnants of at least two periods in my life where I realized now, I had been gripped by clinical depression. Was it happening again? Tears built up on my eye lids and cascaded down my cheeks.

The plane touched down and taxied to the terminal. Once stopped, the gangway was rolled into place, and I walked on wobbly legs through the portable tunnel and into the terminal and amidst the gaggle of curious onlookers staring at my uniform, I picked out a single voice and stopped dead in my tracks. The voice of my wife Cindy struck a memory chord and the vast reservoir of tears I'd been harboring for almost nine months burst and I was overcome with emotion. And then, there they were…Cindy, my brother Jed and his wife Linda and my mother and father and everyone was crying and hugging, embracing and kissing. I imagined homecoming scenes similar to ours happening all across the country every day and wondered if other returning soldiers felt any discomfort as I was feeling now. I could not stop the splinter like thought that passed through my mind for less than a nanosecond as I jumped up and down in the embrace of my family. I was somehow feeling strange the same way I had as a young child on my birthday, feeling guilty opening gifts and being treated so well on my special day when for the other three hundred and sixty-four days of the year I was a dick. I somehow did not feel comfortable with my own homecoming after looking forward to it for the past eight and one-half months.

Cindy grasped my hands, and at arm's length looked at me as we slowly turned in a circle both of us leaning slightly back, tears in our eyes. She looked lovely and I pulled her in and kissed her perfect lips. Saying I missed you or I love you seemed unfitting so I just clung to her. I could not believe I was home.

The six of us piled into dad's 1967 blue, Chevrolet Impala, and headed for my parents' home in East Grand Rapids. At the corner of 28th Street and the East Beltline we passed an enormous construction project. "Woodland Mall," my father offered, "be completed next year." Everybody had something to add about the new shopping center to fill the dead spaces in our uncomfortable conversation. "Progress," my brother harrumphed, "there's going to be six lanes from all four directions." Arriving at the home our passage into the garage was blocked by a huge cardboard sign perched on an easel that proclaimed, "Welcome Home Toddy Bumpits!" How embarrassing to see my mother's pet name for me mounted in huge letters for the entire neighborhood to see. In a perverse way, it reminded me of the time as a teenager I had, in a drunken stupor, pucked and wet my bed and mother leaned the stained mattress against the mailbox to humiliate me. Jesus, why would that creep into my mind now? Anyway, the endearment, Toddy Bumpits that is, was an unsolved mystery in my life, I'd never asked the origin of the nickname and mother never

Cindy meeting me at Kent County Airport

Happy to be home

shared it with me. "Bill and Mary Wilson's handy work, no doubt," mother said.

Dad cut the engine and we navigated the tight circular walk to the front door. The beautiful birch that mother had used as a back drop to photograph me and Cindy the day I left was dying and wilted, a carpet of dead, wrinkly leaves covered the ground. Foreshadowing, I wondered silently as mother unlocked the front door and we all entered. The faint odor of stale cigarette smoke enveloped me reminding me of how the home smelled each fall when we returned from the cottage to resume our studies. Drinks were poured and, as was my family's customary behavior, one was never enough. We laughed uproariously avoiding the elephant in the room, Vietnam, as we continued to swap reminiscences and share drinks.

My brother and Linda hung for a while and had to split because Jed had work the next day. After their departure dad got down to business. "How we doin' over there?" he asked. "I could use another drink," I offered coyly, being intentionally provocative, "how 'bout you, Cindy?" "I meant Vietnam," dad said with irritation. "I know," I shot back. "As soldiers, we performed every task ever requested of us and never lost an engagement but, still, it is not enough." "Are we winning?" He asked. "No," I said, "We are losing and more lives and more time will not change the outcome." Mother sensing the tension, interrupted with, "I'm just so happy to have my baby back, aren't you?" she interjected while looking at Cindy. "Yes, I am." "Dad," I jumped back in, "the question you asked me was purely political. I would have preferred that you ask me how am I doing. But I will say this. Since I have been back in the States I have been able to follow the news that as soldiers in the war zone we did not get. The information that the press is given for dissemination says that we are winning, but remember that men like Lyndon

Me posing beside the Welcome Home sign by neighbors showing my mother's never-explained nickname for me

Banes Johnson (whose only concern was not being the first US president to lose a war) and super Hawks like Robert S Mc Namara are the ones telling you, dad, that we are winning. The conversation stalled and Cindy and I left for our tiny apartment near downtown Grand Rapids. My parents did not ask me how I was doing or what was next for me, or tell me they were proud of me for serving.

    We drove home in silence, Cindy sitting close to me. I felt comfortable being with her. In our apartment, we undressed and lay on top of the bed covers and, without saying a word, Cindy massaged my scars, and then before making love to me she caressed my wounds. Words were unnecessary, there would be time later. In the morning, we dressed and I drove her to her job. Summer recess for Cindy's students was only two days away. I kissed her at the curb saying that I'd see her soon and pulled away and drove over to see mother, dad was at work. Over coffee on the porch my mother asked, "Son, how are you doing, really? It felt strange being home I told her and then, "I don't believe dad likes me at all." "What on Earth would lead you to say such a thing" she said, "your father loves you very much." "Well, he failed to ask about me personally and veered in to politics. He blames me for getting drafted and I think he is short sighted and believes the military ruined me and my life. He has never expressed pride in anything I do in spite of the fact that I spent the first fifteen or sixteen years of my life trying to please him." Mom tried to reassure me, "Do not give up on your father, ever," she said, and the rest of the day passed pleasantly until it was time to go for Cindy. She invited us for dinner tomorrow. "Be here around four," she concluded and kissed me goodbye. "I love you," she said as I drifted out the door.

That night as Cindy and I sat on the front porch drinking wine and watching the traffic on Lafayette Street we talked about my next assignment and she mentioned her apprehension about taking a leave of absence from her teaching job to go with me. At just that moment Jed and Linda pulled up in front and joined us on the porch. They had several bottles of wine which we consumed while enjoying each other's company well into the early hours.

June 3

Monday – Cindy had a slight hangover when I dropped her off at school. I had a nagging sensation when I viewed her in the rearview mirror, a gut feeling actually, that I was not doing very well with being around my family, interacting with them. I was thinking about being back in the hospital or better still, back in Vietnam where I knew the drill and what to expect or do next. I stopped for a little fast food and watched television until it was time to pick Cindy up at her job. We came home, messed around for a while and finally Cindy said, "time to go to your parents for dinner." "Yeah, oh, OK, I forgot, let's go."

When we drove down Bonnell, my parent's street, we could not find a place to park. I had never seen so many cars. What's going on I asked?" "I haven't a clue," Cindy said with a broad smile on her face. We parked and walked the sidewalk toward the house. I heard loud Do Wop music ahead and as we walked up the drive somebody thrust a large cup of beer into my outstretched hand. I was surrounded by well-wishers, old friends shouting welcome home while reaching out to touch and embrace me. I was totally uncomfortable. My brother was there and my sister Terri from Detroit, high school buddies, basketball team mates from college and neighbors from up and down the street and around the neighborhood. My old buddy Bob Raemer was there along with Bruce Rourke who had served in the Nam the same months I had and had been put in for the Congressional Medal of Honor. (In Nam we called the medal the CMH – Casket with Metal Handles – because a high percentage of recipients are dead meaning they're awarded the medal posthumously). We stepped out into the back yard and passed a joint then sat on the grass. Small groups of friends were everywhere.

Later in the evening when things had calmed down I had an epiphany, a major discovery about myself. Friends repeatedly asked, 'what was it like? or tell us how you were wounded.' and what I discovered was that I could share these incidents OK with military buddies but when it came to family, and now at home with my friends, I could not relate circumstances about what had happened to me in Vietnam without losing control of my emotions or crying. I spoke with mother and father. Dad at one point hugged me and told me that he loved me and was glad that I had made it home safely. I believed that it was a put-up job from mother. The party and the drinking went on 'til early morning. I barely recall driving home.

June 4

Tuesday – Drove Cindy to her teaching job in Grandville. We were both feeling like dog shit. After I dropped her I drove down 28th Street and hit the drive through at Ole Taco, ordered two green meat chili burritos and two cartons of white milk. I then stopped by a prominent second-hand store to see if I could find some music. I unwrapped one of the burritos and went down on it about half way. Holy shit, I never expected a commercial Mexican burrito to have the kick I received. I couldn't open the first milk carton fast enough. I chugged half the contents to combat the fire in my throat when the rancid cottage cheese texture of what was supposed to be milk registered in my hung-over mind. I hastily rolled down the window and blew lunch all over 28th Street. I chased the mess by polishing off the remainder of the burritos just to rid myself of the shitty residue taste the rancid milk had left in my mouth.

I detoured off 28th Street one block to 29th which was a community of row upon row of warehouse's and freight forwarders. I found the one that matched the address on the slip of paper I had in my pocket and stopped to retrieve the five boxes I'd ordered from the PX in Tay Ninh the day I was with Top Clare. I loaded them all in Cindy's Chevrolet Impala which was, I guess, now equally mine and headed for the apartment. Unwrapping the containers was amazing. The speakers I had ordered were unbelievably heavy because the cabinets were filled with sand to dampen vibration. I also unwrapped an

Akai reel to reel tape recorder, a Pioneer stereo AM FM receiver and a Marantz 6300 turntable. For a first try and a guy that really was not an audiophile, one who knew what he was doing, I felt that I had scored big time. I got all this stuff at a fraction of what I'd pay here in the States. Cindy was unimpressed probably because music was not as important to her as it was me.

In the evening, we stopped by the Trading Post and visited with Ray in the back room. I mentioned quite some time ago that Ray was an old-time friend and my book maker as well. I'd made and lost lots of money betting on college and professional football games. I seized the opportunity and once again thanked Ray for the bottles of champagne that he had given us as a going away present. "I never doubted you'd return, Todd. The guys stopped in frequently to ask if I'd heard anything from you." Cindy and I purchased several bottles and refused Ray's attempt to gift us.

We visited with mom and dad for a while and then drove leisurely through and around East Grand Rapids. I had difficulty getting to sleep and was troubled by the notion fogging my mind that my return actually seemed insignificant. Wasn't the homecoming supposed to be huge, large, magnificent? It seems to me that everything returned to a state of normalcy as though I'd never been gone.

June 6

Thursday – I rolled over and sat on the edge of the bed. Early morning sun streamed in past the old-fashioned Venetian blinds that I'd forgotten to shut. I reached out sleepily and snapped on the television set and was greeted by a huge informal banner proclaiming *BREAKING NEWS* followed by the image of Bobby Kennedy thanking the crowd for his California primary win and then proclaiming "now it's on to Chicago and let's win there." Minutes later he was dead. My world was rocked but perhaps not in the way you'd imagine. My mind tripped back to a talk with my father and me telling him that our country's leaders had a special agenda, a reason for repeating over and over again that we are winning in Vietnam. You'll recall that the message to my father was that special interest [money] people only say that we are winning while soldiers who have first-hand information say that we are losing. Keep in mind that Bobby Kennedy vehemently opposed the war in Vietnam and vowed that he would end it. And he (Bobby Kennedy) had won every primary that he'd entered and was clearly going to be the man to beat. I'm thinking the assassination has darker more sinister implications tied to special interests that would prolong the war. Of course, we will never know and if I said such a thing my father would dismiss me as usual with a wave of the hand and the comment that I am paranoid. Yeah, right, dad.

Cindy and I were united in our grief and spent most of the day in bed. What a tumultuous year this has been and not just for me but our whole country. Martin Luther King Jr. and now another Kennedy. It feels like someone grabbed the loose thread of the Country's sweater and we, as a nation like the sweater, are seriously unraveling.

Tomorrow I return to Walter Reed to finish my rehabilitation and receive my orders for my next and last duty station.

June 7

Friday – We arrived at the airport with plenty of time to spare, parked in short term parking and Cindy accompanied me to the gate where we sat and talked until my flight was called. I was dressed in civilian clothes and carried my uniform in a travel bag. I already had the back end of my round trip ticket so I would not be asked for copies of my orders.

Cindy wanted to know if I had any idea about where I would be reassigned for the last nine months. I said no but probably to a post that was concerned with the training mission. Rather than ask her what her specific plans were to either accompany me or not I stressed the importance of being together. This seemed to satisfy Cindy and I kissed her goodbye and boarded my flight saying I would call her when I was safely back at the hospital.

I had some time on the airplane to think about the leave and what I would call the shock of being reintegrated into my family. The social whirl left little room for Cindy and me to be intimate. In fact, I was beginning to wonder if I even understood the meaning of that word. To this point all of my relationships with women were limited to dating, alcohol and fumbling in the back seat of an automobile. And, then, all at once, I was married and immediately left for the war. Now, it seems, I am expected to know the ins and outs of husbanding. I need experience and I need practice but what am I to practice. I do know that Cindy acts ambivalent about coming with me to finish my service. I did not have the courage nor did I want to insert myself into the firestorm that would ensue if I told her that I would not return to her if she did not support me in this. I'll have to wait and see.

Back on the main ward I made my bed and then walked down to the mess hall. The nurses on the ward informed me that specialist Miller wanted to see me in rehab so I immediately stopped in to the first-floor facility. It had been several weeks since I had been in and looking around, I did not recognize a single person. I thought about asking after the triple amputee, Max but did not. Miller had me go over to one of the mats and taking a position on his knees beside me he began to manipulate my legs to, I guess, determine or check the range of motion as well as my flexibility. The therapist examined the scars and also the bottoms of my feet, and after noting that they could use a good scraping, he referred me to my ward nurse. "I am going to suggest to Dr. Eberhardt that you could be released for duty after another home leave." I thanked him and returned to the ward.

June 8

Saturday – After I had requested help with my calloused feet a nurse showed up with a basin of warm, soapy water and massaged both of my feet while using a scalpel to trim off the excess dead skin. I cannot remember if I shared with you something I learned about callouses. Callouses occur where there is injury or trauma or as in my case, exceptionally high arches that cause the feet to work harder to support my body. Callouses form when excess cells develop and then die leaving behind hardened and thickened skin. Other callouses are formed when repetitive tasks like yard work or raking cause a thickening of the skin. Anyway, the nurse said that as my flexibility improves and I am able to easily move my legs I can do some things on my own to remove the callouses and care for my skin.

The nursing staff informed me that on Monday morning I am going to be officially transferred to the Glen for the remainder of my hospital stay. She informed me that she placed a request for someone from administration to visit me at the Glen to discuss my reassignment and any questions I might have.

Cecil and I walked to the theatre and watched *The Blue Max*. Cecil's hand is healing nicely and the metal trapeze that helped hold his fingers suspended has been removed. He had a pint of whiskey and we passed it back and forth while watching the movie about WWI German flyboys. The movie was best by far of any movie we have seen and by far the best part of the feature was the presence of stunner Ursula Andress.

June 9

Sunday – Read for most of the morning and then took a cab to the National Mall and visited the Lincoln Memorial and then made the considerable trek over to the Jefferson Memorial before coming back to walk along the reflecting pool. The entire basin is covered with apple trees that bloom and make a beautiful showing in April each year. Someday I will revisit this beautiful city, maybe with Cindy and our family.

Upon returning to the hospital I was exhausted and fell asleep early. Tomorrow I move to the Glen.

June 10

Monday – I was told that I'd been discharged from the osteopathic ward and to report to the Glen which I did after saying goodbye to the guys who occupied the row of beds facing the windows and courtyard. I grabbed a bus out front and after a few intermediary stops was let off at the Glen. There is not a description I can think of that describes the place; maybe early Gothic, Frankenstein-like, cold, foreboding, scary. In fact, I had had a friend in high school whose parents home always gave me the creeps and fit the description of the place I was about to enter. There was a jagged water leak hole in the ceiling replete with hanging drywall tape and a combat boot dangling precariously in the opening as though someone's foot had broken through from the floor above.

I carried my uniform bag and a few possessions in through the foyer to the front desk and reported to the CQ/Officer of The Day who welcomed me and assigned me a bunk on the second floor. Arriving at the room I discovered three beds, all made so militarily tight that the proverbial quarter would bounce off the blanket when dropped from a height of three feet. Nobody ever entered the room except for myself. I went back to the first floor, checked at the desk and was informed that the other two inhabitants were always away on leave. I told the clerk that I was not sure how long I would be at the Glen until my final discharge and I needed to be put in touch with the proper personnel that could talk to me about my final duty post. My separation date from the military will be 10 May 1969. The clerk told me that he would take care of it. "Probably take a while," he said, "things move pretty slow around here."

I found my way to the day room, grabbed a coffee and finding one of the pool tables unattended I set a rack, chalked a cue and began shooting around a little. Usarsky came in around one p.m. "Lookin' good," I said, "I see the doc removed your bandages while I was gone." A very prominent, pink scar was visible beginning at the corner of his eye and trailing off toward his ear. "Grab a cue and let's check to see if your vision has been impaired." Thus, began the only activity we could engage in at the Glen to kill the weeks of boredom that would follow. We did leave the campus-like atmosphere of the Glen some nights to check out local drinking establishments.

June 11

Tuesday – I've never shared much about my reason for keeping this diary. I have always been a journalist of sorts recording my thoughts here and there, on scraps of paper or book jackets as well as having an interest in writing letters. In college, I audited a journalism class taught by an elderly professor named Applegate. I loved him as well as the course material but regarded writing fictitious make-believe articles simply to meet Applegate's deadlines as hokey. At the time, I could not see the broader picture…now I wish I had pursued that endeavor. Since that time, I have been lazy about my writing and the truth is that the informal format of journaling gives me a pass from actually being required to practice the skill of real writing. So, when I began this diary back in Cam Ranh Bay I devoted zero thought to who might actually read my thoughts someday or who exactly was I writing for. My family would, I suppose, be the logical audience. But here's the kicker. While I was home on convalescent leave last week, I discovered that my nuclear family had zero interest in what I'd been through in Vietnam nor did they ask a single question about what the experience was like. Most hurtful of all was the absence of my father and my wife expressing even a single word about my survival or my accomplishment with my accelerated promotion through the ranks, of serving my country in uniform. The only remembrance I have is my father's hollow bluster about me 'going over there and killing those commie bastards and not coming home until you've killed 'em all,' or some such shit. I attempted to show some of my photographs (of both combat and beautiful bucolic scenes) to my family but they declined and quickly changed the subject. By the way, my buddies were very curious and wanted to look at the photos as well as hear the stories behind them.

I am telling you this because right now I am having to face the question of what it means that not a single member of my family has come to see me while I have been here at Walter Reed. I am trying to understand the imposition I may be placing on my family for them to plan and execute a trip to see me but words fail me. A handful of concerned words wouldn't put them out too much but let me tell you, it's putting me out plenty. So much so, in fact, that the thought has crossed my mind to just reenlist, get the fuck outta here and rejoin my unit in Vietnam.

The next couple of weeks are a blur. I am in a grand funk and leave the hospital most nights to sit on a bar stool somewhere. My conversations with 'home,' Cindy, mom and dad and my brother are meaningless and as soon as I hear their voices I try to think of some escape mechanism that will allow me to hang up.

July 1

Monday – I was up early and answered a knock on the door and opened it to see a Specialist 5th Class. Finally… he wanted to discuss my next and last duty assignment, where I would be assigned. When I asked my options, he let me know that combat veterans can pretty much choose where they would like to be placed and if the Fort or Post was part of the Army's training mission my chances were almost 100% that he could find me a billet. I said that I'd heard good things about Ft. Ord near Monterey, California. He said as he left that he would take care of it and get back to me.

I checked with personnel in charge of the Glen and requested a leave to travel home for the 4th of July long weekend and was denied because I'd recently had a convalescent leave. This information which I believed was unfair coupled with the fact that the facility is being run in a very unstructured fashion pissed me off. Because I had never seen my supposed roommates or even heard of a formation being called or required, I weighed the consequences of taking off, being AWOL or absent without leave and decided my need to be with my family to determine what on Earth was going on outweighed any punishment I might receive.

July 2

Tuesday – I arose early and put on my uniform, made my bunk and just for the hell of it bounced a few quarters off the blanket to determine if I'd pass muster. Then I tucked my slippers under the bed, placed my folded robe and PJ's on the pillow and left through a side door and grabbed a taxi for Dulles Airport.

I approached the Delta counter and asked the attendant for a one-way fare to Grand Rapids, Michigan. She said I would be happy to assist you Sergeant, may I see a copy of your orders?" Holy shit! I had not thought about this very clearly and I was sure as hell not going to admit to being AWOL so I reached inside my uniform jacket pretending to search like crazy for my orders. With a perplexed look on my face I said lamely, "Gosh, I must have left them at the hospital." She frowned disinterestedly. "I am sorry, Sergeant," she said looking at my name plaque, "Dexter, but without your orders I will be unable to assist you," I asked her the amount of the fare for the ticket, thanked her and left.

What was I to do? I hadn't dressed and then ducked the scene at the hospital just to turn back now. I was going to go home. I was standing in the middle of the concourse when someone tapped me on the shoulder. I turned and standing before me was another soldier, a uniformed PFC who was approximately my size, a good looking younger kid really who asked, "Hey, Sarge, I'm wondering if you can help a fellow soldier?" "Will if I can," I responded. "Well," he continued, his name was Pederson, "I'm trying to get home on leave and I'm fifty bucks short. I'm wondering if you…" I stopped him short, interrupted him mid-sentence and in a New York minute outlined how we could help each other and be on our separate ways. I explained that I'd left my orders at the hospital and if he would step in line and with my money and purchase a one-way ticket on his orders I would give him the fifty dollars he needed. The transaction was completed and I was able to board for home.

    Cindy was totally caught by surprise when I pulled up to the apartment in a cab. We had a marvelous weekend including a celebration with fireworks display over the Grand Rapids river on the evening of the fourth. We packed a cooler with sandwiches and took some beer. Sitting together on a tiny blanket I broached the subject that had been so much on my mind. I explained, "You know, hon (I was not given to using such endearments)," I spent the last nine months fighting for my life in that far away Hell hole and now I expect you to fight as well… for our marriage. Together we can begin our life but I need you with me." Cindy kissed me and said, "I know we can do it." We had a great week end together that included dinner with my brother and his wife over at my parents' home before I returned to the hospital on Sunday, the situation about my father's feelings regarding my service still a question.

July 7

Sunday – I arrived back at the Glen in the late evening, cicadas vibrating at fever pitch among the oaks that dotted the property, street lights blinking through the foliage. I checked my room which appeared to be undisturbed and set out to find Usarsky in the day room. "Miss anything?" I asked. "not a thing, brother," he came back. "pretty sure nobody missed you but there was an award ceremony in the theatre and your name was called so you could be presented the certificate for your second Purple Heart. You may want to figure a way to check with administration. As far as they're concerned you were here but failed to get the word and, therefore, not AWOL, if you know what I mean." "Yeah," I smiled, grabbing a pool cue, "I get the drift."

July 8

Monday – I remained at the Glen and Walter Reed for several more weeks. My status of not knowing exactly when I'd be leaving, was a mixed blessing. Each day that I remained at the facility was another day closer to the date that I would be permanently separated from the military and that was fine with me. However, the uncertainty of not knowing where I was going, what I'd be participating in, would Cindy be with me, etc. all created anxiety.

Two events that resolved my concern occurred during the first week in August. First, I received word from administration that my assignment to Fort Ord, California, had been approved. I would be joining the Second Advanced Infantry Training Brigade at the post that was an integral part of the Sixth Army Command. I was instructed to report by September 7. This would allow me an almost thirty-day leave. The second event of importance was my final interview with Doctor Eberhard. I was administered a physical examination and evaluation. Doctor Eberhard talked at length about how smaller arteries and capillaries were to small to have been reattached during my leg surgery. They may one day, in effect, reattach or grow together, a self-mending process. For the remainder of my service I would be on what the doctor called a permanent profile meaning I could re-enlist and remain in the service but no forced marching, lifting or extreme forms of exertion.

July 10

Wednesday – I concluded my stay at Walter Reed with a final visit to the uniform shop to have patches for the Sixth Army sewn onto various uniform pieces. I made flight reservations and phoned my family to let them know my flight information.

September 1, 1968

Cindy and I packed the powder blue Chevrolet Chevelle she had purchased to replace the VW Bug she'd destroyed when accidentally running it through a liquor store window, and we drove across country to Fort Ord which is situated on the eastern shore of Monterey Bay. We occupied a modest tract home overlooking Monterrey Bay and were comfortable among other non-commissioned officers who also worked on the base. Cindy and I had adequate time off to travel to places like Santa Cruz, Cannery Row, San Jose and San Francisco. I was a Primary Instructor on The Survival Escape and Evasion or SEE

Committee, training replacements heading for Vietnam. I received commendations for my teaching skills, gave lectures on closed circuit TV and was promoted to SSG. E 6 before Cindy and I returned to Grand Rapids to enter the private sector after my separation on 10 May 1969.

Cindy's and my marriage lasted twenty-four years. We have two sons who are remarkable, no drugs, alcohol or tobacco and absolutely zero challenges that seem so prevalent with some families. Our boys now have families of their own. The astonishing thing is that we all survived me. Back in the years immediately following Vietnam there was very little accepted or understood wisdom or knowledge regarding Post Traumatic Stress Disorder and this allowed me and my anger to fly below the radar masked somehow as just a quirky personality disorder. I finally sought help and today I am in a better place but that is a story for another time.

Afterword 2017

In 1995 while living on Lake Michigan with my second wife Jan, I received a letter from Larry Mitchell, my old friend from Second Platoon and together we began locating some of those with whom we had served in Vietnam. Late that year a small group of us met in Chicago and every year since there has been a reunion in September. The numbers of attendees swelled at first and then, as age, philosophical differences, economics and other factors took a toll, the numbers began to dwindle.

Initially I believed that nothing could disrupt the bond that, as infantrymen, we held in common. I believed that we would always be together at least spiritually if not physically. I believed that even as we grew old and the light left our eyes, we would, like old cavalry war horses slobbering into the bottoms of our oat bags, sing military dirges and bury one another with dignity and honor. Time, distance and age have revealed a greater reality, and that reality is that these days, we barely occupy the furthest reaches of each other's individual consciousness. The hard truth is that for the majority of men who I served with in that war, Vietnam was the defining experience in their lives. As one reunion member said to me as tears filled his eyes, "I don't need no help with PTSD cuz these reunions are my psychiatric couch." I drifted away because the most important moment of each reunion centered around pulling out old terrain maps and retelling the shopworn tales of battles long past and who did what to whom with what. In the beginning, I was very interested to learn what my fellow confederates' lives had become since Vietnam. Apparently not much.

For me the most poignant remembrances that I have about the men from Vietnam would not have been possible were it not for that letter I received from Larry

"Mitch" Mitchell. That letter was the well spring, the genesis that began a wonderful communication between comrades. The only regret is that the communication has been reduced over the years to several Christmas cards that lacked the initiative to even include a personal hello. There were also one or two emails so detached, so impersonal as to render them about as useful as Native American smoke signals.

I received two such emails just this week. The first was a one-line question from our venerated company clerk...Were you aware that Watty passed away Friday? I was. The second transmission was from Mitch and was a bare bones recitation about Hector Colon's (our First Platoon's heroic leader who survived the Hour Glass) wife having to place Hector in an adult day care center because she could no longer cope with Hector's worsening Alzheimer's disease and dementia. Hector no longer recognized anybody.

The impersonal nature of these two contacts, besides offering a wonderful opportunity for old war buddies to speak to one another on the phone, rankled me for another reason. Both emails revealed a lack of knowledge about the extremely close relationship both my wife and I shared with Hector and his wife Margaret and also with Watty Smith and his wife Helen.

When the phone rang yesterday I monitored the screen and saw that it was Helen. I wanted to talk to her but when I was ready and decided to listen to the news that her message contained. Helen was in so much pain that I cried. She was surrounded by all of her children and twenty-two grandchildren and several of the great grandchildren but still she was having trouble keeping everything together. I retrieved the phone from the cradle and struggled through the details with her. I knew Watty had recently suffered with pneumonia. He never recovered, had lost forty-five pounds and could no longer breathe because of more complications with COPD. He had gotten up on Friday morning, dressed himself and sat in his favorite recliner to watch golf. Helen said that Watty would not open his eyes and his breathing was extremely shallow. A helicopter was called and landed in the field across from their home and took Watty to the emergency room and intensive care. He was placed on a respirator but he did not make it.

When Jan and I owned our Blue Ridge Mountain home near Dalton, Georgia, and would drive there from our Florida Keys place we would get together once a month for dinner with Watty and Helen either at their home in Etowah, Tennessee, or a restaurant close by. One year we spent the entire Thanksgiving weekend with the Smith family. Watty was one of the warmest and most generous gentleman soldiers I have known. He was a Green Beret warrior who served with the 10th Special Forces Group and also with my company in the 25th Division in Vietnam. He was a company commander who served two terms in Vietnam before my time but not one of the three CO's that I served. When Major Watty passed away last week he was 80. He received a full military burial and one of Tennessee's Senators gave the eulogy. Watty had over twenty awards and metals including the Bronze Star with V, the Purple Heart, Meritorious Service Medal, Combat Infantry Badge and Vietnam Cross of Gallantry with Palm.

Hector Colon: retired from the Army as a first Lieutenant. He and his wife Margaret visited Jan and me at our Georgia home for a week in the year 2008. I knew Hector very well while we were with Bravo Company in 1967 and 1968. Hector was an extremely humorous and fun loving patriot. During our visit, we went for walks and shared great dinners but he preferred to isolate himself and read a book about Vietnam that I was working on at the time. Hector never really came all the way back and more importantly, how could you after being surrounded by an estimated five hundred hard core NVA soldiers and fought hand to hand with the enemy.

Me with LTC. John Henchman, Las Vegas

John Marshall Henchman, 1928–December 6, 2016: John was, in many ways, my soul. He represented the father I always wished I had. He once said to me, "the men would not understand the mutual love that you and I share and express for each other." I spoke with John the day before he died and I told him that I loved him. He said, "I love you, Todd, and I will speak with you soon." He had very real challenges and was using a walker for support. John told me that from the neck up he was perfect but everything else was falling apart. After a reunion in

Portland not too many years ago Jan and I drove with John and his wife Betty to their home in Bend, Oregon, for a four-day weekend. We shared a picnic and he and Betty showed us the sights. John entered the Army in 1951 as a second lieutenant and distinguished himself in combat operations at Heartbreak Ridge, Korea. I have a cherished photograph of John standing atop The Ridge. In Vietnam in 1967, John was Manchu 6, our battalion commander. He served in the military for 28 years. He also served as Chief of Staff of First Logistics Command. He was awarded the Silver Star, Vietnamese Cross of Gallantry, the Legion of Merit (3 Oak Leaf Clusters), the Air Medal (with Valor Distinction), the Combat Infantry Badge and numerous other decorations and service medals. In Vietnam John was our heart and soul.

I think about John every day, and his leadership during those difficult times. I miss him.

Alfred W. Baker, the greatest soldier I have ever known. To me he was THE Captain, the commander for whom I carried the battalion "push" radio. Al died in a Harrisburg, PA hospital in 2010. He was 69 years old and a retired Colonel who served three tours in Vietnam. His last assignment in the Army was closing down the Berlin Brigade in Germany. In 1969 Al was blown up by a Viet Cong satchel charge that ripped off half his face and broke most of the bones in his body, including his back. It took fifteen operations to put him back together again. He has been referred to as an American Legend. He was segregated in the triage area reserved for those who had been passed over as being critical, not going to make it. A priest was administering last rights when AL cleared the teeth from his mouth and told the priest, "I'm not Catholic and I am not going to die today. Al and I were the same age when in Vietnam, he a twenty-five-year-old captain and me a twenty-five-year-old specialist 4th class. Al delighted in telling the story of how he chased me all about the perimeter with an entrenching tool one night because I'd responded to his question about how old I thought he was (we all called him the old man) and I said, "about forty, I'd guess." I had dinner with Captain Baker at a reunion banquet in Vegas in 2009 and hugged him before dinner was served and I told Al that I loved him. He also visited my home near Key West in the Florida Keys. If any of us ever complained, Captain Baker would tell us to "put some mud on it and keep moving." At one time, Al was the most highly decorated veteran of the Vietnam War era. He was the recipient of four Purple Hearts, a Silver Star, two Bronze Stars, three Legions of Merit, the Combat Infantry Badge and many other honors.

Captain Alfred W. Baker

I caught up with Sergeant First Class (SFC) Oatis Boatright while I was serving at Fort Ord, California in 1968. He and his wife Betty lived on post not too far from me and my first wife Cindy's home. Oatis was into home brew and when Cindy and I would visit on Sunday afternoons to watch football, Oatis would un-cap the long neck bottles and after the yeast had foamed off we sipped the white lightning that remained in the bottom of the bottles. Oatis wanted to retire back East somewhere, Carolina's, I think, and purchase a car wash. I have tried for many years to locate him but no luck.

Around 2004, another Bravo grunt, George Paparelli, located me while I was residing in the Florida Keys. George had located Top Clare, our First Sergeant from Nam. Top Clare was living right under our noses with his wife Dorothy in a high rise that sat on a huge expanse of lush grass bordering the harbor entrance to Ft. Lauderdale. We all visited several times and drank a few beers. Top had a compressor that he'd retrieved from an auto salvage yard. When we'd visit he would fire up the compressor which had a double chromed air horn from an eighteen-wheeler rig attached to it. When the cruise ships would head from the harbor for the high seas Top would deafen everyone in the high rise with repeated blasts of that horn. We all roared as we pounded beers. Top was fading fast, however. He had Alzheimer's and dementia. He could remember guys from Korea but not us. Very sad. One night as we sat on a bench outside an Outback Steakhouse waiting for our table to be called, I grasped Top's hand and thanked him for saving my life in Vietnam when he kept me in the rear with him. A tear rolled down his cheek and the only thing he said was, "I don't remember." Not too long after that Dorothy had to place Top in an assisted living facility where the staff placed a tracking device on his ankle because he would wander away from the facility. One day he was gone for over twelve hours. Dorothy called, frantic. Then we heard. Top had somehow gotten out into the middle of the I-95 that ran through the city and was hit by a truck. He died instantly. There were law suits. The funeral was a mess with television news crews and cameras everywhere, all around the Synagogue. Top was buried with full military honors. I knelt on a small knee bench beside his casket. Top Clare had been laid to rest in his class A dress uniform. I touched his white, cottoned, gloved hands and said, barely a whisper, "goodbye" to a great soldier and an even better friend.

The triple amputee to whom I spoke at our rehabilitation sessions at Walter Reed was Max Cleland who became a US Senator. He lives in Atlanta. I sent Max the copy of his book *Heart Of A Patriot* that I had read. He autographed my copy and sent it back. I still receive a Christmas card from Max. We have spoken and I believe he was just being politically correct when he said that he remembered me.

My *Afterword* could not be complete without a word about several others who were important to me and my experience.

During the time I knew Darrell Jobman in Vietnam he was no ordinary soldier. No, he was a Titan, a utility infielder, a Jack of All Trades and the go to man in every situation. Darrell was one of our first lieutenants. He served as the Executive Officer of Bravo Company as well as a platoon leader in the jungle and filled the slot of company commander on several occasions. Darrell returned to civilian life and a successful career in the publishing business near, I think, Chicago. Darrell and his wife Linda are still regular attendees at almost every reunion.

Denny Wagoner, Gunner, was wounded, shot through both forearms on the same day that our battalions operations officer Major Bill Roush was killed. Denny, who was in the banking business in the great Northwest was, in my estimation, one of the most well-adjusted members of our group. He and his wife spent a week in the mud at Woodstock which was apropos for a Nam Vet but had absolutely nothing to do with his being a well-adjusted ex-grunt.

Larry Mitchell lives near Cleveland and owns and runs a small electric company.

I could go on forever...but, well...I had an acquaintance once say to me when seeing a jacket patch of mine for the Military Order of The Purple Heart, "do you have a purple Heart?" I said yes and the person said, "you're a hero." I said, "yeah, right."

About the Author

Todd Dexter studied English at Hillsdale College, Michigan, before serving as a combat infantryman in Vietnam in 1967 and 1968. While with Henchman's Light Rangers he was a grenadier, a rifleman, a radio telephone operator (RTO) as well as a company level Public Information Officer. He retired to Sedona, Arizona, in 2015 where he lives with his wife Jan and their Australian Kelpie Ella. This is his first published work. He is currently working on his second book. You can reach the author at jantodd3@yahoo.com.

Todd P. Dexter

Printed in Great Britain
by Amazon